Finding a Common Interest

THE STORY OF DICK DUSSELDORP AND LEND LEASE

This important book demonstrates how businesses can operate both profitably and ethically—by finding a common interest between all those involved in their operations. It does so through the example of Dick Dusseldorp, founder of Lend Lease, one of Australia's most admired blue-chip corporations. Arriving in postwar Australia with only one construction contract and a handful of workers on his company's books, Dusseldorp built Lend Lease into a billion-dollar property development and financial services concern. Widely respected for his business success, Dusseldorp was equally well known for his commitment to sharing the fruits of that success with the workers, shareholders, and clients of Lend Lease, and the communities where the company conducted its business.

Not only does *Finding a Common Interest* tell the story of Lend Lease and its founder — it demonstrates how business can be done both profitably and inclusively, and so provides a workable model for corporate governance.

Finding a Common Interest is a must-read for business leaders, management students, shareholder, union and policy activists, indeed for anyone interested in a better way of doing business.

Lindie Clark spent many hours interviewing Dick Dusseldorp before he passed away in April 2000. She had extensive access to internal company documents in researching this book. She has been heavily involved in public policy and management as both a student and practitioner, and was the recipient of a Harkness Fellowship to Harvard University's Kennedy School of Government in 1997.

Finding a Common Interest

The Story of Dick Dusseldorp and Lend Lease

LINDIE CLARK

CAMBRIDGE UNIVERSITY PRESS

PUBLISHED BY THE PRESS SYNDICATE OF THE UNIVERSITY OF CAMBRIDGE
The Pitt Building, Trumpington Street, Cambridge, United Kingdom

CAMBRIDGE UNIVERSITY PRESS
The Edinburgh Building, Cambridge CB2 2RU, UK
40 West 20th Street, New York, NY 10011–4211, USA
477 Williamstown Road, Port Melbourne, VIC 3207, Australia
Ruiz de Alarcón 13, 28014 Madrid, Spain
Dock House, The Waterfront, Cape Town 8001, South Africa

http://www.cambridge.org

First published 2002

Printed in Australia by Brown Prior Anderson

Typeface Times New Roman (Adobe) 10/14 pt.   System QuarkXPress®   [PH]

A catalogue record for this book is available from the British Library

National Library of Australia Cataloguing in Publication data
Clark, Lindie, 1962– .
Finding a common interest: the story of Dick Dusseldorp
and Land Lease.
Bibliography.
Includes index.
ISBN 0 521 82531 8.
I. Dusseldorp, Dick. 2. Lend Lease Group of Companies –
History. 3 Directors of corporations – Australia –
Biography. I. Title.
338.7690092

ISBN 0 521 82531 8 hardback

Contents

Illustrations

13 Academy of Science, Canberra. (Photograph by Douglass Baglin, by permission of Lend Lease.)

14 Hobart Place, Lend Lease's first office block development in Canberra. (Photograph by Capital J. Plan Printing and Photographic Company, by permission of Lend Lease.)

15 Plans for Monaro Mall, Lend Lease's first shopping centre development in Canberra. (Photograph by Norman L. Danvers, by permission of Lend Lease.)

16 Dusseldorp and Prime Minister William McMahon at the opening of Canberra's Woden Plaza, September 1972. (By permission of Lend Lease.)

17 G. J. (Dick) Dusseldorp in his Australia Square office, c.1968. (By permission of Lend Lease.)

18 Shaping the Sydney skyline: Blues Point Tower, Australia Square, and the MLC Centre. (Photograph by Max Dupain, by permission of Harry Seidler.)

19 Shaping the Sydney streetscape: Australia Square's public plaza, c.1967. (Photograph by Max Dupain, by permission of Harry Seidler.)

20 Dusseldorp addresses the 1984 annual general meeting of General Property Trust. (Photograph by Frank Lindner, by permission of Lend Lease.)

21 Dusseldorp signs in for a site visit of Lend Lease Petroleum's Bass Strait oil rig. (Photograph by Rob Walls, by permission of Lend Lease.)

22 Dusseldorp and Ron Brierley at the board table for the 1984 annual general meeting of MLC. (Photograph by Frank Lindner, by permission of Lend Lease.)

23 Appletree Hill Estate. (Photograph © Wolfgang Sievers, 1966/Licensed by VISCOPY, Sydney 2002, by permission of the National Library of Australia.)

24 Dusseldorp and Federal Treasurer Harold Holt at the opening of the Coach House Inn, Thredbo, 1963. (Photograph by Douglass Baglin, by permission of Lend Lease.)

25 Notice of Auction for Sydney's Theatre Royal, September 1969.

26 MLC Centre tower, plaza and sculpture, c.1976. (Photograph by Max Dupain, by permission of Harry Seidler.)

27 Apprentices competing in the Sydney regional WorkSkill Australia competition, 1984. (Photograph by Frank Lindner, by permission of Lend Lease.)

28 Tjerk Dusseldorp at the Sydney regional WorkSkill Australia competition, 1984. (Photograph by Frank Lindner, by permission of Lend Lease.)

Preface

Persistence usually pays off. Tjerk Dusseldorp found that to be the case when in 1999, after years of persuasion, his 80-year-old father finally gave in and agreed to the production of this book. The argument that convinced Dick was this. Over the years, the Dutch-born founder of Lend Lease, one of Australia's most respected blue-chip corporations, had forged a smarter way than most of doing business. While his goal—the building of a profitable enterprise—was one commonly aspired to by his peers in industry, the way he had gone about achieving it was not. For what had marked Dick Dusseldorp out from the pack was his unshakeable commitment, not just to making the profits, but to sharing them as well. In an environment characterised by frequent industrial and political conflict, Dusseldorp had built Lend Lease around the value of finding or creating a community of interest between its key stakeholders. By bringing labour and capital together to work towards a mutually beneficial goal—and to share the resulting rewards—he had demonstrated a highly profitable, and sustainable, way of doing business. But while the product of that creative approach—Lend Lease Corporation—was well known, the thinking behind it had hardly been universally embraced. Now that the 'old guy' was nearing the end of his working life, his son suggested, wouldn't it be worthwhile if some of his ideas were captured for the benefit of those who were just starting out on theirs? Tjerk had a point, his father had to agree, and the idea of this book was conceived.

The Dusseldorp Skills Forum—which you'll read more about in Chapter 8 —commissioned this book with management students in mind, but we think it will be of interest to anyone searching for, or thinking about, a better way of doing business. In one sense it is a classic rags-to-riches tale. Dick Dusseldorp arrived in Australia in 1951 with $20,000, a handful of Dutch workers, and a contract to build 200 houses for the Snowy Mountains Authority at Cooma. When he retired from Lend Lease in 1988, the market capitalisation of the company he had founded thirty years earlier stood at $1.4 billion, its employees numbered 6000, and it was widely regarded as one of Australia's most successful construction, real estate, and financial services organisations. Today Lend Lease operates in forty different countries, employs over 10,000 people globally, and its shareholder funds exceed $5 billion. But the thing that is perhaps most remarkable about the company's success is the way in which it has been achieved. The creative thinking behind the Lend Lease Corporation bears the indelible mark of its founder: and *that* is what this book is all about.

The list of people who made this project possible is a long one. At the top are the trustees and staff of the Dusseldorp Skills Forum, in particular the Forum's Chairman Tjerk Dusseldorp, who imagined, initiated, funded, encouraged, and contributed to it from the word go. Kerrie Stevens, Ern Mac Donald, Kaye Schofield, Meredith Edwards and Eric Sidoti, all of whom are associated with the Forum, also deserve special mention for their input. The active engagement and support of Lend Lease is likewise very gratefully acknowledged: particularly that provided by Stuart Hornery, Eric Goodwin, and Amanda Wyllie, the latter of whom proved a great research assistant. (Thanks, too, to Sharon Goldie and Pauline Steele for their assistance and patience with those archive boxes!) Mary Murphy, author of *Challenges of Change: The Lend Lease Story*, was similarly most generous in sharing with me her insights.

The recollections and reflections of all those people who agreed to be interviewed for this book were, quite frankly, invaluable. Those people are, in alphabetical order (and sans honorifics): Milton Allen, Gerald Boegman, Peter Ciacciarelli, Alan Cull, Frank Cuzzocrea, Anne Dusseldorp, G. J. (Dick) Dusseldorp, Tjerk Dusseldorp, Kerrie Fahy, Keith Fleming, Sharon Goldie, Eric Goodwin, Diana Grafton, Richard Hammond, Bob Hawke, Stuart Hornery, Karin Jacobson, Jack Klompe, Richard Longes, Frank Lowy, Ern Mac Donald, Merle Marks, Ken McGrath, Geoff McWilliam, Colin Moore, Dick Morath, John Morschel, Jack Mundey, John Overall, Karl Pahl, Joe Purcell, Lenneke Quinlan, Albert Ricci, Roy Robinson, John Rothery, Harry Seidler, Stan Sharkey, Ray ('Mac') Steele, Alan Stretton, David Thorne, Sandra Triulzi, Albert Van der Lee, and Bill Webster. Thanks also to Kahron Allen in her various capacities; to Suzanne Culph for, amongst other things, sniffing out the

Media, Entertainment and Arts Alliance's newspaper clippings on the Theatre Royal dispute; and to Rita Doran of the Reporting Services Branch of the NSW Attorney-General's Department, who so quickly tracked down the transcript of the court case resulting from the Bankstown bribery scandal. The photographs used in this book appear courtesy of Lend Lease, Harry Seidler, Ern McQuillan, the National Library of Australia, News Ltd and the Fairfax Photo Library; the granting of permission to use these images is acknowledged with thanks.

A number of people read various drafts of the manuscript, and I would particularly like to thank them for their helpful comments. Some have already been mentioned above in other contexts; in addition I would like to thank the members of the Dusseldorp family, Lurline Harrison, Brian Norris, Jacqueline Gillespie, MaryAnn McLaughlin, Kerry Schott, and Janet Mackenzie. A very special thankyou to John Buchanan who provided constructive advice at numerous points during the course of this project. As for Peter Debus, Academic Publishing Manager at Cambridge University Press, he demonstrated the substantial value an editor can add. The usual disclaimer applies.

Dusseldorp senior never got to read the product of his son's persistent and, as it transpired, very timely entreaties, for Dick died at his home in Tahiti in April of the year 2000. Memorial services in his honour were held in Sydney and London, and tributes to the man poured in from around the world. Albert Ricci, a builders' labourer for Lend Lease's construction company for the best part of thirty years, put it as well as any in the course of an interview I conducted with him not long after Dick's death (at Concord, 21 July 2000). 'I sometimes wonder what would have happened', Ricci said to me, 'if, at the time that Dusseldorp came out to Australia in the 1950s … if we had had a hundred men like him in the key jobs in the country—in government, in business, etcetera. Imagine what Australia would be like today—how much in front of the rest of the world would we be! I know this can't be, but I would like to say it anyway: people like him should never die, because on this planet they're very, very badly needed.' I, for one, can't argue with that.

Abbreviations

ACTU	Australian Council of Trade Unions
AMP	Australian Mutual Provident Society
ASTF	Australian Student Traineeship Foundation
BLF	Builders Labourers' Federation
BWIU	Building Workers' Industrial Union
GPT	General Property Trust
IEL	Industrial Equity Ltd
MBA	Master Builders' Association
MLC	Mutual Life & Citizens' Assurance Company Ltd
NCDC	National Capital Development Commission
PCG	Project Control Group
TAFE	Technical and Further Education
TRAC	Training for Retail and Commerce

Unless otherwise specified, all sums of money are in Australian dollars.

Right from day one we were convinced that a worthwhile and profitable contribution to society could only be *satisfactorily* achieved by developing a true partnership between investors and employees. The profit growth per share over thirty years attests to the economic validity of this proposition.

G. J. (Dick) Dusseldorp

Introduction

For all the cranes that dotted Sydney's skyline in the first half of the 1980s, the number of major building projects completed in those years seemed strangely small. Construction hoardings adorned the downtown streets, but a glimpse behind their facades—littered as they invariably were with gradually accreting posters—all too often revealed little more than another large, lifeless hole in the ground. One such gaping hole, itself a stark reminder of various building projects that had failed to materialise the decade before, was the site of the Sydney Police Centre in the inner suburb of Surry Hills. Plans for a modernistic seven-storey building for the site had been approved in October 1979, bulk excavation started in the New Year of 1980, and the first signs of construction were observed that September. The city's new lock-up would be finished by 1983, the government works department boldly proclaimed as the initial sod was turned, but almost as these words were uttered, the first (of many) strikes on the site started. Work had barely recommenced before another stoush erupted, and from then on, over the six-year period of construction, the stop-start pattern of work remained the same. In all, more than 600 days were lost on the project due to industrial action, and when the new centre was finally completed in 1986, its cost had blown out by 80 per cent to some $63 million.[1]

If Sydney's new Police Centre was the site of more industrial disputes than most in those years, it was by no means atypical. The early 1980s was a time of severe disputation in the city's construction industry—much as it had been the decade before. When plans for a 51-storey tower to serve Qantas as its new city headquarters were drawn up in 1970, few thought the airline's executives would have to wait till 1982 to occupy it. Nor did the Flying Kangaroo anticipate having to find more than twice the amount originally estimated for the privilege of doing so.[2] Many other Sydney building projects fared as badly as these.

1

'Continuous progress', remarked *Rydge's* business journal in 1981, 'is more an aberration than the norm in construction projects nowadays'.[3] And so too, as a result, were cost over-runs. When Sydney's new Entertainment Centre was completed in 1983, its final cost was double that initially estimated;[4] while the city's new Greater Union cinema complex, begun that same year, took five times as long—and cost nearly three times as much—as its owners first thought it would.[5] It was a sad tale and, regrettably, all too familiar.[6]

Irrespective of who was to blame for all the trouble—and neither 'bloody-minded bosses' nor the industry's 'mighty tough unions'[7] could claim the high moral ground—one thing was certain: *both* parties suffered its consequences. Construction firms saw profits squeezed and the number of forward contracts dwindle as escalating costs forced potential clients to reconsider their building plans.[8] With fewer viable projects on the contractors' books, building workers (and their counterparts in up- and down-stream industries) had fewer jobs to vie for, and longer bouts of unemployment between them. Whether the extra money they had won in their pay packets made up for that outcome was doubtful—more so as the broader economy started to dip into recession. The damage, of course, was not confined to the protagonists in the disputes. For those clients who decided to press ahead with their building projects regardless of the industrial strife, the massive time and cost over-runs left them seeing red. Meanwhile, the wider Sydney community, and the city's coffers, were also suffering the consequences. Those barricaded, dormant holes in the ground were not just unsightly and inconvenient for the public: they were a stark reminder that the city's economy was running at a good deal less than full-steam.

A few kilometres across town from the site of the Sydney Police Centre, and a couple of doors down from that of the Qantas building, the city's residents were being treated to a very different scene. On the site of another major city building project—construction of the $50 million Regent Hotel at harbourside Circular Quay—the jackhammers were working overtime and the cranes and concrete trucks were in constant motion. What many had expected to be another strike-prone project—especially given its high visibility—was actually proceeding six months *ahead* of schedule. Floor by floor the Regent's high-rise tower was ascending and, with work virtually uninterrupted by industrial action, its construction costs were being kept well in check. The scenario was unusual enough to attract national media attention, and the press was by and large 'astounded' by the 'fairy-tale progress' on the high-rise hotel.[9] Those involved with the project, while delighted, were not altogether surprised by its speed. For the Regent was being built by Civil & Civic, the construction arm of property developer Lend Lease, and with the firm's long-standing reputation for completing buildings on time and within budget, the Regent was proving another demonstration of how and why it had earned those stripes.

What was the secret of the construction firm's success? How was it that, while its counterparts were suffering such significant industrial trouble, Lend Lease's construction subsidiary was leading an apparently charmed life? These questions puzzled some in the Australian investment community in the early 1980s, as Bill Webster, then Investment Director of international finance house J. P. Morgan, remembers. 'There was no doubt that Lend Lease was quite different,' Webster says, recalling his first impressions of the company.

> It had an energy, it had a method of doing things that was different … I think the expression bandied about sometimes was that the company was 'slightly pink'—and that was because of the relationship it had with its workers, and with the unions. In Lend Lease parlance, that was all being part of the same team. But it was in an era when employers and employees or unions typically saw each other as the enemy— one was always trying to have a go at the other and get some sort of advantage. Yet the strike rate on Lend Lease projects seemed to be very low and they seemed to be coming up with solutions based on working together to achieve things. And they *did* seem to achieve things pretty well, so that raised some questions as to *how* they actually did it … There was clearly something going on there, but we in the investment community didn't quite know what it was.[10]

Whatever was going on, it was certainly delivering results, as Frank Cuzzocrea, a scaffold rigger who notched up his twenty-fifth year of employ-ment with Civil & Civic on the Regent Hotel project, explains. 'If we had followed the example of the Police Centre at Surry Hills,' he says, laughing as he thinks back on the period, 'we would be broke by this time! You know, they started that job before us, and by the time they had finished that seven-storey police station, we had finished the 36-storey Regent.' (With excavations start-ing in April 1980, construction of the new high-rise hotel was complete by the end of 1982). 'Then, when we finished the Regent, we went on to build the 36-floor Connaught apartment building on Liverpool Street. Then we moved to the [40-floor] State Bank project at Martin Place. We finished that too, and they *still* hadn't finished the seven-storey Police Station!'[11] With its capacity to deliver on time and in budget on display, Civil & Civic was inundated with forward orders from both new and repeat clients. The firm won almost two-thirds of the new building business contracted in Sydney's central business district in 1983,[12] enabling it to declare a record profit that year and keep its substantial workforce steadily employed. The financial results brought a smile to the faces of the shareholders of its parent firm, Lend Lease. With its 3000-plus employees collectively owning some 15 per cent of the latter company, and all participating in its innovative profit-sharing scheme, the workers had a number of reasons to join in the celebrations as well.

What was the secret of the company's success? There they were, operating in what *The Australian* described as a 'cut-throat concrete jungle'—an industry 'where time is big money but shortcuts can kill'—and yet Lend Lease was managing to deliver the goods, profitably, with an evidently well-satisfied work-force. Two main factors gave the company its edge, according to observers quizzed by the newspaper in 1981. One was its 'pioneering' method of project organisation (of which more later); the other, its distinctive approach to labour management. Not only did the company provide 'security, safety, and steady work' to its employees—all rare on the construction scene—but it also provided them, through profit-sharing and share ownership schemes, with 'a vested interest in how well their company does'. 'I don't know if the [workers'] smiles are any bigger on a Civil & Civic site,' the head of the 'hardline' Builders Labourers' Federation told the newspaper, 'but with the extra benefits they've got to be more contented with things.'[13] And with employees more contented, less time was lost through strikes. 'The result,' another union boss pointed out, '[is] that Civil & Civic [are] able to tell their clients the finishing date of a building and stick to it, which in the building industry is a very big advantage.'[14] It all added up to a unique industrial partnership, *The Australian* reported, and it was one that was proving profitable for everyone concerned. It was not, however, some newfangled idea, for 'the Lend Lease brand of indus-trial relations has been a cornerstone of the company's business philosophy from its start'. Both it, and the company's advanced project management methods, bore the unmistakeable hallmarks of the corporation's founder and (then) current Chairman: an 'astute and idealistic Dutchman'[15] by the name of Dick Dusseldorp.

Although the United States enjoys the reputation of being one of the world's great immigrant nations, on a head-for-head basis Australia could stake just as sound a claim to the title. Since its establishment as a British penal colony in the late eighteenth century, the indigenous inhabitants of the world's largest island have seen successive waves of migrants reach their shores. One of the largest of these mass arrivals occurred not long after the end of World War II, as boat- and plane-loads of European refugees and immigrants, keen to make a fresh start, decided to try their luck on the other side of the globe. Carpenters and doctors, managers and farm workers, teachers and labourers—they came seeking a new life in a country promising them space and opportunity, freedom and prosperity: a chance to leave behind the horrors and hardships of war, a place to start again. Amongst their number were a young Dutch engineer, his wife and five children who left their hometown of Utrecht bound for Sydney in early 1951. Wisely sceptical of the hyperbole—for not all would find Australia the land of milk and honey its boosters claimed—the Dusseldorp family planned to give the place a try for five years, then see where life took them from there.

At thirty-two years of age, Gerardus Jozef ('Dick') Dusseldorp arrived in Sydney as the Construction Manager of a large Dutch building firm (Bredero's Building Company), his instructions being to win contracts for his employer and its joint-venture partner (a major Dutch civil engineering concern) in Australia's expanding postwar reconstruction market. A small construction company, Civil & Civic, was established for this purpose, of which Dusseldorp became Managing Director in 1953. Within five years the Dutchman had not only fulfilled his initial mandate—having lifted Civil & Civic's annual revenues substantially—but, sensing that there was more money to be made further up the value-chain, he had also floated one of Australia's first postwar property development ventures, a company called Lend Lease. Lend Lease soon acquired its sponsor, Civil & Civic, through a share swap with the latter's Dutch parent; and by the time the remaining corporate links with the Netherlands were severed in the early 1970s, Australians were proudly claiming Lend Lease— and its founder—as their own.

They had good reason for wanting to do so. Unlike many of its erstwhile competitors, the corporation had survived the dramatic vicissitudes of the postwar property cycle, boasting, by 1974, a ten-year record of annual profit increases. It had built some of the country's most outstanding buildings, including Sydney's first concrete-framed skyscraper (Caltex House), its first integrated commercial/plaza development to give valuable open space back to the public (Australia Square), Stage 1 of the Sydney Opera House, and Canberra's innovative Academy of Sciences. It had invested heavily in Australia's fledgling national capital, a move which went against the trend—for most other developers found Canberra's central planning system inimical—but which had proved both profitable for the firm and of benefit to the community. (Lend Lease's investment in Canberra, a future Australian Prime Minister would note, made an 'enormous' contribution to the city's further development.)[16] By the early 1970s Lend Lease had also sponsored Australia's first listed property trust, the General Property Trust, and was expanding its operations overseas.

From there, the corporation went on from strength to strength. By the time Dusseldorp retired as its Chairman in 1988, Lend Lease, with a market capitalisation of some $1.4 billion, was one of the country's most respected blue-chip stocks. Still firmly grounded in the property and construction industry, it had also branched out, through acquisition of one of Australia's largest life insurers, to become a major player in the burgeoning financial services sector. Its founder and Chairman was himself regarded as one of the nation's most eminent—and enigmatic—businessmen, a reputation deriving as much from the distinctive way in which he led the Lend Lease Corporation as from the scale of its success. For, as everyone who knew, or knew of, him agreed, there was something quite different about Dick Dusseldorp.

Over the years many would try to encapsulate what it was about Dusseldorp that made him unique. Journalists variously described him as 'the prince of property', 'a powerful and steel-reinforced tycoon', 'probably the shrewdest operator the Australian property market has ever seen', 'a true Australian entrepreneur'.[17] All these phrases sit oddly with another set of labels he attracted in equal measure: the 'Dutch socialist', 'a revolutionary', a 'radical ... very much on the side of the under-dog', 'a boss who really cares'.[18] Long-standing Lend Lease executive David Thorne sums him up in a slightly different way. 'I call Dusseldorp a great capitalist when making the profits, and a great socialist when distributing them', Thorne says. 'Because he always had this plan of giving the profits to the stakeholders—the shareholders, the employees who produced it, and the customers who provided the jobs.'[19]

In today's parlance, Dusseldorp would probably be branded an early pioneer of 'social capitalism', for he built Lend Lease around the value of finding or creating a community of interest between its key stakeholders—getting them to transcend their traditional conflicts and divisions and work together towards a *mutually beneficial* goal. While employees and shareholders of Lend Lease were at its centre, this web of common interest also embraced the corporation's clients, its professional associates and suppliers, and the broader community in which it operated. It was a philosophy that manifested itself in every aspect of Dusseldorp's approach to business—from the project and labour management strategies he employed to enable buildings like Sydney's Regent Hotel to rise in double-quick time, to his engagement with community and public sector planning interests on urban development projects such as Canberra. Such an approach, in his view, was not only the most sustainable way of doing business, it was the most profitable as well. As companies today look for ways to meld precisely these two goals, the way Dusseldorp went about achieving them becomes of much more than historical interest. His working life offers a very practical demonstration of *how* it can be done.

If the Gordon Gecko mantra 'greed is good' was the anthem of the corporate world of the 1980s, it is a somewhat different beat to which a small but increasing number of companies are beginning to dance today. Whether it be motivated by a genuine recognition that business needs to be more accountable to the wider community on whose human, physical, and social resources it depends, or by a more utilitarian desire to protect brand reputation and boost flagging sales, some firms now openly acknowledge that the pursuit of profit at any cost may well be exacting too high a price. Concepts like the triple bottom line—the notion that companies should look to enhance not just economic but also environmental and social value in their operations (or at least seek to minimise harm in each dimension)[20]—are enjoying wider currency, in manage-ment-speak if not always in management-practice. While the concept might go by different names—North America's interest in 'social capitalism' mirrors a concern with 'corporate social responsibility' in Europe and Australasia; 'sustainable business practice' is another widely used term—the underlying principle is essentially the same. That is, it is in the long-term best interests of companies (and their shareholders) to conduct themselves ethically, to behave responsibly, to do the right thing by the communities and environments in which they operate. *Not* because they will gain kudos by doing so, but because their own corporate future ultimately, and increasingly, depends upon it.

Exactly what does sustainable business practice involve? The most comprehensive definition encompasses all aspects of a corporation's behaviour—the way it engages with entities both inside and outside the firm. It includes such things as the way it treats its *shareholders*: the dividends and capital growth it generates for them, the degree to which it stands accountable to them, as well as the extent to which it encourages their involvement in corporate governance. It also includes the way the company recruits, rewards, develops, and respects its *employees*; the quality, safety, and security of the working environment it provides for them, and the extent and methods by which it encourages their participation in the firm. Firms acting sustainably also recognise obligations to external parties—to *clients, partners, and suppliers* they owe a duty of fair treatment, the best distillation of which, Dusseldorp believed, was to do unto others as you would have them do unto you.

Finally, socially responsible businesses recognise that they have obligations to the *local community, wider society,* and *natural environment* in which they operate. These are not simply (or even) obligations that can be met by doling out donations to worthy causes. Tobacco firms that dish out dollars to cancer research, or sweat-shop manufacturers that sponsor 'family-friendly days', do not convince an increasingly well-informed and globally linked public that they are doing their bit for the greater good. The issues at stake here run much deeper than expressions of philanthropy—they go to the fundamentals of business activity. As a prominent adviser on corporate social responsibility puts it, 'The test is whether companies see as important the issue of *how they make their money.* If irresponsibly, in social or environmental terms, then no amount of good-cause giving will tilt their overall contribution to society back from the negative to the positive.'[21] Why, some might ask, does that even matter? It matters because running a sustainable, socially responsible business is *not* a matter of altruism. Consumers, investors, employees and regulators are the people who make up that amorphous group, 'society', and if *they* demand safe products made in an ethical way, then it is in both the long-term *and* short-term interests of business to satisfy those desires.

Such a comprehensive notion of sustainable business practice might sound good in theory, but can any corporation really be expected to do it all in practice? Although it is unlikely that *any* company could boast a pristine record on every one of the above-mentioned dimensions, some consistently do much better than others on most. Ever since the first surveys of corporate reputation were conducted in Australia in the early 1980s, Lend Lease has been consistently ranked—by its peers, expert observers, and stakeholder groups—as one of the nation's best.[22] It is not a status that has been achieved overnight. Rather, it reflects a set of values, beliefs and repeated practices—in sum, an entire corporate culture—that has been embedded in the company from the start. That culture, described by one senior Lend Lease manager as 'combining the best of the performance characteristics and orientation of the US with the socially responsible characteristics of Europe',[23] begins with its founder Dick Dusseldorp.

The imprint that Dusseldorp stamped on his business ventures—primarily Lend Lease, but also those which came before and after it—and the ways in which he made that mark, form the subject of this book. Focusing on his working life, it is not a full-blown biography; nor is it a corporate history—the first twenty-five years of the Lend Lease story have already been well told in Mary Murphy's *Challenges of Change*.[24] Rather, by looking at the ways in which Dusseldorp translated his 'community of interest' philosophy into every aspect of his business practice—from organising production to managing labour, from developing new markets to negotiating with interest groups, from influencing public policy to governing the firm—it seeks to distil the key aspects of his distinctive, and distinctly successful, approach. It does so in the belief that Dusseldorp's experience holds valuable lessons for contemporary managers, policymakers, educators, and students—indeed, for anyone looking for a better way of doing business. And these lessons are all the more powerful because they show what has actually worked.[25]

The book is structured into eight thematic chapters—essentially self-contained, and for the most part sequenced chronologically—through which runs the central thread of Dusseldorp's 'community of interest' philosophy. Taken together, Chapters 1 to 4 describe the key aspects of the new business model that Dusseldorp established in the years following his arrival in Australia in the early 1950s. Despite its critical importance to the nation's reconstruction efforts, the building and construction industry that the Dutchman encountered in his new homeland was in a parlous state. Shortages of materials and skilled labour, anachronistic work and management practices, inefficient organisation of the product market, and antagonistic and fragmented relationships between different industry players all left their mark in the form of low productivity and spiralling costs. Dusseldorp set about tackling these problems head-on—in the process managing to completely redefine the boundaries of the traditional building firm, introduce a whole new mode of organising the (design and) construction process, and revolutionise industry relationships by building new bridges between employees, managers, investors, and clients.

One of Dusseldorp's first targets was the tender-based system of construction that formed the dominant—and, in his analysis, grossly inefficient—mode of organisation of the Australian building industry. The story of the challenge he mounted to it is told in Chapter 1, 'Production Management'. Under the tender-based system, a client wishing to initiate a construction project would do so by hiring an architect to draw up the building plans and put them out to tender; competing contractors would then lodge fixed-price estimates of the construction costs of the project, the lowest of which would usually be selected as the winning tender. Dusseldorp believed there were two basic problems inherent in this hierarchical mode of project organisation. First, its counterproductive separation of design from construction denied clients the benefit of practical construction advice in the design planning phase (which, if incorporated then, could potentially reap significant cost savings without compromising the building's aesthetics), and it was also one of the main reasons for the on-site communication breakdowns between the various specialists that plagued most building projects. (Construction of the first stage of the Sydney Opera House—the story of which is told in Chapter 1—proved ample demonstration of that.) The second major drawback of the tender-based system was its flawed incentive structure, which, Dusseldorp argued, both encouraged architects to design edifices and prompted contractors to cut costs in any way they could—neither of which necessarily served the best interests of the client. Convinced that there must be a better way of organising a building project—one that yielded superior outcomes for *all* the parties involved—Dusseldorp set about finding it and introducing it to the Australian marketplace. The swift and smooth completion of another landmark Sydney project, Australia Square—the story of which brings Chapter 1 to a close—proved a concrete demonstration of the benefits of that 'better way'.

A further cause of the low productivity characteristic of building and construction in postwar Australia was the antagonistic nature of the industry's labour relations. Dusseldorp's approach to tackling this problem is discussed in Chapter 2, 'Labour Management'. Accustomed as he was to the cooperative relations between employers, employees, and unions that prevailed in Northern Europe, the Dutchman was taken aback by the bitterness which he soon found characterised industrial relations in Australia. The number and severity of disputes in the construction industry, already high, was on the rise, and, as a result, cost and time over-runs on building projects—particularly the new multi-storey jobs in the capital cities—were fast becoming the norm. To Dusseldorp, the path to a solution was clear. Why not sit down with the building workers and their union representatives and find out from them, directly, exactly what was causing all the grief? When Dusseldorp did just that on the site of his company's first high-rise construction job in Sydney in 1956, it was an event that proved pivotal to his firm. For that meeting laid the foundations of a ground-breaking productivity agreement between Civil & Civic and the trade unions that represented its workforce (the first ever that the latter had been willing to sign). As well as providing a framework to address the poor pay and conditions, escalating injury rates, and the intermittent nature of employment that the workers told Dusseldorp were their chief gripes with the building industry generally, the agreement jointly committed workers and management both to lift productivity on the company's sites, and to share the resulting rewards. As this cooperative approach began to bear fruit, there were plenty of the latter to share.

In Chapter 3, the spotlight is turned on Dusseldorp's approach to 'Business Development', highlighting the key features of his strategic approach to wealth creation that put his company on the map. Although construction contracting had given him an entrée to the Australian market, Dusseldorp was soon convinced that it was *not* the business to be in—the margins were too slim, for one thing; the factors outside his direct control (yet influencing project outcomes) were too numerous, for another. And so the Dutchman set to work on enhancing both control and profits by ratcheting his firm up the value chain. Providing clients with an improved building service—by managing a project's design and construction in an integrated way—took Civil & Civic the first step up that ladder. Moving it up the next rung, however—to sponsoring its own development projects—required access to capital on a scale that was exceedingly difficult to obtain in Australia's then rather primitive financial markets. Dusseldorp's innovative solution to the problem was to go public—and in 1958 he floated, in Lend Lease, one of Australia's first listed property development ventures. (Some thirteen years later he again chose this path, creating Australia's first listed property trust, the General Property Trust.) The story of how Dusseldorp steered his new corporate ship through the dramatic upheavals of the postwar property cycle is told in the remainder of Chapter 3. It is one where his disciplined adherence to a set of core principles—combined with an entrepreneurial capacity to detect and create new business opportunties—proved critical to the enterprise's success.

The four chapters dealing with the new business model that Dusseldorp forged in the Australian postwar construction industry conclude with Chapter 4. This chapter examines Dusseldorp's approach to business ethics and corporate governance, in neither of which the construction industry—with its dubious tendering practices, graft and corruption, episodes of blackmail and instances of violence—enjoyed a (positive) reputation. Operating in such an environment, Dusseldorp was determined to make his company's repudiation of such practices perfectly clear. So when, in the early 1960s, a bribe was sought from the company to guarantee regulatory approval for a major development project it was planning, Dusseldorp used the opportunity to make a public stand. The story of the Bankstown Square bribery scandal begins, in Chapter 4, a discussion of ethical business practice—a comprehensive definition of which goes well beyond compliance with minimum standards of behaviour dictated by law, to issues at the heart of how, and to what ends, a corporation is governed. For some, such questions boil down to one thing—the maximisation of shareholder value. Dusseldorp had a different view. 'Right from day one,' he told Lend Lease's annual general meeting in 1988, the year he retired as Chairman, 'we were convinced that a worthwhile and profitable contribution to society could only be *satisfactorily* achieved by developing a true partnership between investors and employees.'[26] Some of the key ways in which Dusseldorp expressed this philosophy are discussed in this chapter, as are the means by which he encouraged employees and investors to join with him in embracing it.

By the early 1980s Dusseldorp's Lend Lease was firmly established as 'Australia's most successful property developer'.[27] With its operations encompassing all aspects of the property sector, its geographic reach extending beyond Australia to South-East Asia, the Pacific and the United States, with employees numbering in the thousands and annual revenues exceeding $400 million, the corporation was, in many respects, at the very top of the tree. In 1981 Dusseldorp received news that threatened to challenge all that. A well-known corporate raider was buying up the shares of the corporation's long-term client and largest shareholder: the major Australian life insurer, the Mutual Life & Citizens' Assurance Company Ltd or MLC. If the raider gained control of the MLC, Dusseldorp feared, it would be in a good position in turn to mount a hostile takeover of Lend Lease. Hatching a plan to ensure both organisations' mutual defence, when Lend Lease acquired a strategic stake in the nigh-on century-old insurer, the market knew that the MLC had found itself a white knight. But what began as a defensive move Dusseldorp soon came to see as an incredible opportunity. With assets of around $2 billion, Australia's fourth-largest life office had strong reserves, but it had been losing market share for years. Its product range was out-of-date, it wasn't selling enough new business, its bureaucratic structures were stifling innovation, and its sales force was dictating how the business would be run. The MLC was an organisation ripe for change—and as Lend Lease increased its shareholding in the insurer to take full control of it by 1985, Dusseldorp and his team were the ones ready and willing to change it. The story of how they did so is told in Chapter 5 'Organisational Overhaul'.

In the last three chapters of the book, the focus turns to the various ways Dusseldorp's business ventures engaged with the broader community. Running a business simply for its own sake was, for him, insufficient: it was necessary that it also make a 'worthwhile and profitable contribution to society'.[28] This objective could not be fulfilled, however, by means of hand-outs or donations —the conventional expressions of corporate philanthropy. Dusseldorp's business ventures had to demonstrate regard for the community in their *every-day* commercial operations: from the way employees conducted themselves in dealings with the public, to the type and integrity of products and services they supplied. This ethic was not based on some warm and fuzzy sense of altruism, but on Dusseldorp's firm belief that pursuing it served the *best* interests of both parties. Not only would society be made better off by business' contribution, he was convinced, but business would be (literally) enriched by it too. (Here is the 'community of interest' theme again.)

Chapter 6, 'Creative Negotiation' takes up this theme by examining how Dusseldorp deployed his common interest philosophy in the resolution of three multi-faceted and seemingly intractable problems, each of which involved issues of significant community concern. Two of the cases discussed in this chapter directly gave rise to public policy reforms that had a major impact on subsequent urban development: leading, respectively, to the requirement for developers to contribute to infrastructure provision in Australia, and to the enactment of the country's first strata title law. The other case involves a somewhat different set of circumstances. In the early 1970s Lend Lease was planning a major city redevelopment project, a key aspect of which involved demolition of a theatre that had occupied part of the site for more than one hundred years. These plans brought the company into conflict with various community-based cultural and heritage groups—a coalition whose bargaining power was dramatically increased when Jack Mundey's Builders Labourers' Federation joined the cause. With the union voting to impose a Green Ban on the project to prevent the theatre's destruction, it seemed that Lend Lease's plans were doomed to fail. But while many other city projects were tied up for years as a result of such bans— and some never saw the light of day—the Green Ban on Sydney's Theatre Royal lasted all of two weeks. How Dusseldorp, Mundey, and the coalition of activists were able to resolve the conflict—by reaching what the union leader describes as 'a principled compromise',[29] and what Dusseldorp calls a 'common interest solution'—is also described in Chapter 6.

In Chapter 7, 'Building Communities', the focus turns to another way in which Dusseldorp's desire to make a 'worthwhile and profitable contribution to society' found concrete expression. This chapter discusses a number of large-scale projects undertaken by Lend Lease over the past four decades, all of which were conceived as long-term, integrated, comprehensive, area-based developments—characteristics which distinguished them from the pack and which, in typical Dusseldorp fashion, were designed to pay off all-round. While this integrated development approach was pioneered in suburban Melbourne and Sydney in the early 1960s, it also found expression in the company's development of Australia's first year-round alpine resort at Thredbo in the Snowy Mountains. Dusseldorp found it was still at work when, some ten years after his retirement as Lend Lease Chairman, he visited the company's latest areal development project—the new suburb of Newington, which would begin life as the Athletes' Village for the Sydney 2000 Olympic Games.

Mention of his retirement brings us to Chapter 8, 'Building for the Future', which discusses Dusseldorp's post-Lend Lease ventures in Australia, the United States, and the United Kingdom. When, in 1988, Dusseldorp took leave of the blue-chip corporation he had founded some thirty years earlier, the occasion was marked by the employees and shareholders of Lend Lease in a unique and significant way. Both groups banded together to present him with a gift that would both reflect and continue his contribution to working life.[30] That gift was the Dusseldorp Skills Forum, a non-profit association with a brief to stimulate and promote continuing investment in Australia's workforce, with a particular focus on developing the skills and personal effectiveness of young people.[31] Following his departure from Lend Lease, Dusseldorp maintained an active working life for the next twelve years, not only as inaugural Chairman, then Patron, of the Dusseldorp Skills Forum, but also as Chairman of his own group of property management and investment companies in the United States and the United Kingdom.[32] As Chapter 8 demonstrates, Dusseldorp was often able to combine both post-retirement roles, using his business ventures as fields in which initiatives inspired by the Skills Forum were planted, tested, and spread. His self-described 'last project', however, was one that addressed a problem facing people at the other end of their life cycle: working to create a financial vehicle to release cash out of residential property for the asset-rich but cash-poor elderly. Centred in his long-held belief that property equity *should* be able to be securitised, the scheme was designed, characteristically, to yield benefits for all its participants. Sadly he would not see it through to fruition, for Dick Dusseldorp died at his home in Tahiti in April 2000, before the remaining obstacles to the scheme's implementation could be cleared.

But the philosophy that underpinned both his last project, and his whole working life, did not die with him. The various enterprises that Dusseldorp led over the years survive him, and they continue to bear the distinctive imprint of their founder. His impact, however, need not end there. Although the global business environment is continually changing shape, the premise of this book is that Dusseldorp's working life offers lessons of enduring significance to businesspeople today. (Some of the key ones are drawn out in the concluding section of Chapter 8.) Questions such as how to create and manage a profitable and sustainable business, how to foster a culture of innovation, how to engage clients, shareholders and employees in the pursuit of common goals, and of how to do *all* that in a socially responsible way, will always be with us. And while the answers that Dusseldorp's long-term, stakeholder-driven approach to business suggest may not always be in fashion, it is worth bearing in mind that they were hardly conventional wisdom when he was making his mark. Having the courage to adopt a different approach did not stop Dusseldorp from building one of Australia's most successful corporations from scratch—and it need not stop others from doing likewise today.

Dusseldorp's Early Life and His Arrival in Australia

Bill Hudson stood at the window, peering out across the row of factories extending from his Alexandria office, a stone's throw from Sydney's international airport. Hands in pockets, gently puffing on his pipe, the man in charge of constructing Australia's Snowy Mountains Hydro-Electric Scheme pondered the arrival of his next appointment: a Mr Gerardus J. Dusseldorp of Bredero's Building Company of Utrecht. The year was 1950 and Hudson was looking forward to meeting the young Dutchman, as the latter's company might be able to help tackle part of the massive project he had in front of him. The Snowy Mountains Hydro-Electric Power Act, passed the previous year, had empowered Hudson, as Inaugural Commissioner, to 'construct, maintain, operate, protect, manage and control' the world's largest hydroelectric power and irrigation scheme.[33] The dimensions of his brief were mind-boggling, and the domestic resources of postwar Australia were, on their own, totally insufficient to the task. Hudson was looking to Europe and North America for much of the expertise, labour, plant, and materials he needed to fulfil his charter—and Dusseldorp's firm, he hoped, might be able to supply a small but important part of that.

Word of Australia's plans for the Snowy Mountains Scheme had first reached Bredero's—one of the Netherlands' largest residential construction companies—via an Australian Trade Mission visiting Europe in the late 1940s. With the Snowy said to be but one (albeit the largest) of a raft of national development schemes envisaged by Australia's postwar Labor government, the Managing Director of Bredero's decided that the opportunities on offer on the other side of the world merited an on-the-ground assessment. The Royal Dutch Harbour Works Company of Amsterdam—a large civil engineering concern with expertise in dam construction—shared this view, and the two firms decided to join forces for the investigation. The head of Bredero's construction department, a young engineer called Dusseldorp, was assigned the task of visiting Australia on a three month fact-finding mission in the spring of 1950. Thirty-one years of age at the time, married to Anne, and with five children whom he did not relish raising in war-ravaged Europe, Dusseldorp embarked on the task in an optimistic frame of mind. He arrived in Australia with a number of appointments on his books, one of the most important of which, as it transpired, would be with Bill (later Sir William) Hudson, Commissioner of the new Snowy Mountains Authority.

The problem occupying Hudson's mind when he first met Dusseldorp was Australia's acute shortage of skilled labour. The Commissioner desperately needed workers for the construction of his hydro-electric and irrigation scheme, but how could he attract people to the sparsely settled Snowy Mountains when he had nowhere to house them? And how could he house them when building materials were almost unobtainable in Australia? What's more, given the antiquated and oligopolistic state of building materials manufacturing in the country, the price of those few materials which were available was sky-rocketing.[34] Could the Dutch firms help him out, Hudson wanted to know? Could they deliver, at a fixed price, in a highly inflationary environment, 200 cottages to the mountain village of Cooma, starting in March the following year? It would not be a straightforward task, Hudson warned Dusseldorp, for Australian government policy at the time required all labour and materials for the project to be imported.[35] Was that going to be a problem, he asked the Dutchman, or did he think the firms could do it?

Dusseldorp's mind was racing as Hudson presented him with the challenge. The Netherlands itself was hardly flush with building materials after the war—they too were largely reliant on imports in their efforts to reconstruct a badly damaged economy[36]—but surely, the Dutchman figured, he could find a way around that obstacle. If prefabricated housing frames could be shipped in from Finland, and plumbing acquired from England, and if Belgium could supply the roof coverings … he began to see that it just *might* be possible. If all of these materials could be delivered to Australia, unloaded at the docks and transported to Cooma, then tradesmen and labourers could be flown in from the Netherlands to put the houses together. It would be a major logistical project to arrange, Dusseldorp realised, but if he could do it, the rewards were potentially large. Not only the monetary value of the contact itself—around the million-dollar mark—but the job would also give the Harbour Works Company an opportunity to familiarise themselves with the Snowy Scheme well before they had to lodge a tender for construction of the dams. All these things considered, Dusseldorp's answer to Hudson was yes.

Dusseldorp lodged a formal tender for the Cooma housing project on behalf of the Dutch joint-venture partners in November 1950, and it was quickly confirmed as the winning bid. With that job in the bag, and a couple of other possibilities on the boil, it was an enthusiastic young Dutchman who returned to the Netherlands to make his favourable report on the potential of the Australian market. His report was well received, and soon Dusseldorp was making travel plans again—this time for a longer stay in Australia, and this time with his whole family in tow—for the joint-venture partners had decided to try their luck in the new country, at least for a five-year trial period, and Dusseldorp was one of those selected to go.

The Dusseldorp family touched down at Sydney airport in March 1951 and made their way to their new home—a house which would also serve as the initial head office of the newly established construction firm Civil & Civic. The man who had won Civil & Civic its first Australian job was initially appointed the firm's Construction Manager. It was a role Dusseldorp would perform for two years, much of which time would be spent in the Snowy Mountains where he oversaw the Cooma housing job and tendered for work both locally and in not-far-distant Canberra. When, in 1953, the then Managing Director of Civil & Civic took his leave, the company's board saw Dusseldorp as the logical choice for promotion. He quickly expanded the firm's activities beyond straight tendering into design and construction and property development, and Civil & Civic's fortunes began an upward climb. When decision time rolled around in 1956 neither the board of the Dutch-owned firm, nor the Dusseldorps themselves, had much difficulty making the choice: they were in Australia to stay. But they had been through a lot to get there.

Gerardus Jozef Dusseldorp was born into a large and wealthy Catholic family in the central Dutch city of Utrecht in December 1918. The second-oldest of seven children, he was also raised with five stepbrothers and sisters from his father's first marriage. Occupying a four-storey house on the canal circling the inner quarter of the historic city, the Dusseldorp family at first enjoyed a rather grand lifestyle. A chauffeur drove the children to school—they were the first family in the neighbourhood to own a car—and a governess helped look after them at home. There were sleighs for transport in winter, and a house at the resort of Katwijk on the North Sea where they spent their summer holidays. Perhaps reflecting all this bounty, the somewhat stout young Gerardus was fondly known in the family as Dik—a shortening of the Dutch word for 'chubby' (*dikya*). The nickname cannot have caused him too much pain, however, for in Australia the by-then slim Dutchman would anglicise its spelling to Dick, the name he was most often known by in business circles. Many of his Lend Lease colleagues, however, preferred to call him Duss.

Dick's father Carolus was a wheat merchant whose international grain-trading business—which he had built up from scratch—was the basis for the family's fortunes. He also owned two livestock farms and a grain mill used by local farmers to crush wheat into flour. It all made for a rich empire in the buoyant economic times of the 1920s, but Carolus' good fortune would soon come to an end. When commodity prices tumbled in the crash of 1929 his grain-trading business was completely wiped out. Having often told his children that if you took risks, it was your responsibility to pay your debts—regardless of the consequences—Carolus refused on principle to declare bankruptcy. The consequences of the crash were grim indeed, however, for he was forced to sell all his holdings, including the family home, to meet the mountainous debts. 'They sold everything,' Dick recalls, 'even our personal clothing.'[37] Carolus, his wife Martina, and their children packed up what little remained of their possessions and moved out to what Dick refers to as the 'boondocks' of Utrecht. There they set up house and shop in a corner store and garage works, where Carolus tried to rebuild his grain-trading business, supplementing this income by selling and delivering petroleum to the local farmers.

Carolus' experience would have an enduring impact on his son—influencing, as we will see in Chapter 3, his own approach to risk management and business strategy—but it was not to this side of the family that Dick credits his 'entrepreneurial genes'. His maternal grandfather and namesake, Gerardus Kuijten, another self-made businessman, was, Dick claimed, the source of these. Orphaned at ten years of age, Gerardus Kuijten was brought up by his uncle on a farm some twenty kilometres from Utrecht. There was a stream running through the property, and it was there that the young Gerardus would indulge his love of fishing. The hours spent thus, however, were by no means idled away. The peak demand for fish at the *vismarkt* in the Catholic quarter of Utrecht occurred on a Friday. Gerardus would fish all day Thursday and on into the night, placing his catch in an ice-packed box which he lined with peat for insulation. Borrowing a wheelbarrow from his uncle, at first light he would trundle his catch into Utrecht, sell it at the best possible price, then return home to the farm with the proceeds.

From this small start, Gerardus Kuijten went on to build a huge seafood marketing empire stretching right across Europe. He and his wife raised twelve children, nine of them girls, all but one of whom were posted by their father to key spots around the continent. Dick's mother Martina was the daughter who stayed at home to look after her mother. Her sisters acted as agents buying fish for the vast Kuijten trading enterprise, which Gerardus would then on-sell to various domestic and international markets. The sons also had a role to play in the business. When Gerardus developed a fish and eel farm on a large tract of land in the south of France, he used railroad cars converted into huge, water-filled and oxygenated rolling fish tanks (his own invention) to transport the live catch to port. Gerardus' three sons were designated engineers on these 'fish trains', a job which, according to Dick, involved having to manually operate the pistons if they broke down. Dick, who would visit his grandfather once a month as a boy, is convinced it was 'this guy who gave me my entrepreneurial genes'.[38]

Back in the boondocks of Utrecht, however, things were not proceeding quite as smoothly. The neighbourhood into which the once wealthy Dusseldorp family had moved was a rough one, and it was not long before the boys, and Dick in particular, were getting into fights. Each day the brothers would make the one and a half hour trek back to their old school—on foot now, instead of being chauffeured—and Dick, it seems, brought his newly acquired fighting skills with him. When, at age fourteen, he struck a teacher who was hauling him out of the classroom by the ear, he was immediately expelled from the school. Dick initially saw his expulsion as an opportunity rather than a set-back. He had developed a passion for sailing over the long summer vacations at Katwijk, and ever since had set his heart on joining the merchant marine. Now, it seemed, he had all the time in the world on his hands—so why not fill it by going to sea? Quite tall and strapping by then, having outgrown his boyhood chubbiness, Dick upped his age to sixteen and got a job as a deckhand on an oil tanker travelling the Atlantic. For the next eighteen months that ship would be his home.

Returning to Utrecht in 1934, Dick sat the formal exams for admission to the merchant marine. Although he passed the written tests, the compulsory medical assessment revealed he was colour-blind; to his great dismay, Dick was told that condition precluded his admission to the corps. The news distressed him deeply, as his older brother recalls. 'Dick was very upset,' Hank Dusseldorp says, 'and it was some time before he could get a grip on what to do next.'[39] Hearing of Dick's dilemma, a priest at his old school decided to take the young lad in hand. If he wanted to get anywhere, the priest told him, he needed to complete his secondary education. But with his old school unwilling to re-enrol him, the only way he could study for his Intermediate Certificate was by means of personal tutoring. With the priest agreeing to provide just that, Dick was able to sit his final exams in 1935. To his great relief his grades were sufficient to allow him to enrol in a five-year civil engineering course at Utrecht's Middelbaar Technische School, where he specialised in hydraulic engineering. That course set him on a new career track that would take him to the other side of the world; but Dick would never forget what he owed to the priest's intervention and support.

Cycling to technical college in Utrecht one day with a friend, Dick tipped his hat to a striking young woman riding her bicycle to work in the opposite direction. 'At that time all the young men on their bikes would wear hats,' Anne Dusseldorp remembers, 'but to tip it was unheard of ... He was very quiet, he didn't say much in those days, but he had a certain flair.'[40] Although Dick Dusseldorp and Anne van der Kroon had grown up in the same neighbourhood, they had lost touch when Dick's family moved away. Their acquaintance, renewed while cycling that day, took two or three more years to become serious romance. By then it was 1939 and, despite its declared neutrality, war was about to engulf the Netherlands. In May 1940, as Germany prosecuted its blitzkrieg campaign against France, many Dutch cities also came under fire. Fifth Column land-based forces backed up the aerial attack, quickly overwhelming the Dutch army. Within five days the country had surrendered and the Nazi Occupation of the Netherlands had begun.

Having completed the final exams for his engineering diploma in July 1940, Dick married Anne in August. In September he found work as an engineer at a military airfield not far from Utrecht in Soesterberg. It was a well-paid job but it lasted only three months, Dick being sacked when he refused to join the Nazi Party as a condition of his continuing employment. A job with a trucking company followed, but he took his leave when that business was incorporated into the logistical machinery of Occupation. By then all Dutchmen of working age were being rounded up and deported to Germany for forced labour, and it was not long before Dick too met this fate. Leaving behind Anne and baby daughter Lenneke in Utrecht, the young Dutchman was removed to Berlin. 'I did not hear of him for quite some time,' Anne remembers, 'but then one morning he arrived on the doorstep at my parents' house where we were staying. He had escaped from Germany, walked across the border, and made his way back to Utrecht.'[41] It had been a treacherous journey, and it would not be the last time he would make it.

Things started to look up somewhat when Dick got a job with a Danish firm that was constructing a railway line from Copenhagen to Hamburg.[42] The family moved to a small village on the route of the proposed railroad—just outside Lübeck in the Prussian province of Schleswig-Holstein—where they stayed for the next two and a half years. Dick's brother Hank and his wife Miep joined them, their first child being born there in October 1942. By late 1943, however, with the war starting to go very badly for the Germans, the railroad project was scrapped and all available resources were redirected to the front line. Dick, Hank and their young families were transported to Krakow, where for nine months the brothers worked as forced labour for the Siemens organisation.[43] There, through the owner of the apartment block in which both families lived, the Dusseldorps made contact with the underground movement. In August 1944, as the Red Army crossed into Poland on its march to Berlin, these contacts supplied the families with false papers and the Dusseldorps prepared to escape. Fleeing Poland and crossing Germany, they were able to reach the Dutch border—but there, to their horror, Dick was detained by the German police. He spent two weeks in German custody before he managed to escape once again, secretly crossing into the Netherlands with the help of his aunt who lived on the border. Safely home in Utrecht, the young family's travails were by no means at an end, for, as Anne recalls, 'then we went into the Hunger Winter'.[44]

As the contours of Nazi oppression had taken shape in the early years of the Occupation, the Dutch resistance movement had employed tactics of both passive and active resistance. People would boo or walk out of cinemas when German newsreels were played, illegally tune into Radio Oranje broadcasts from the Dutch government-in-exile, and wear orange carnations on national commemorative days. Many spoke out against the Nazis, while others published underground newspapers. Clergy preached resistance from the pulpit, while students in their thousands refused to sign an oath of loyalty to the occupying forces.[45] These protests reached their pinnacle as the Nazis began to tighten the screws on the Jewish population, requiring them to be registered, removing them from certain towns, outlawing their employment in the civil service, and making plans for their deportation to concentration camps.[46] Organised underground groups and individual Dutch families responded by helping those persecuted go into hiding, while many other Netherlanders joined spontaneous collective protests against the Nazis' oppressive measures.

In mid-September 1944, as the Allied Forces entered the southern provinces of the Netherlands, pushing the Germans back across the Rhine, another collective action was about to take place. With the twin aims of supporting the Allied offensive and hampering German defences, the Dutch government-in-exile called on railroad workers to walk off the job. They did so in their thousands, and rail traffic ground to a halt across the country.[47] In response, the German Occupation forces placed an embargo on *all* forms of transport, cutting off the food supply lines on which the Netherlands depended. The embargo was partially lifted in early November, but by then the country was in the grip of an early and harsh winter—the canals were frozen over and food simply could not be transported into the western region of the country. With provisions already in short supply, the consequences were devastating.[48] For the next six months, until Liberation in mid-May 1945, the western provinces of the Netherlands, home to half the Dutch population, were gripped by severe famine. The city-dwellers of Utrecht, along with those of Amsterdam, Rotterdam, Haarlem, The Hague, Leiden, and Delft, bore the brunt of the Hunger Winter.

Anne Dusseldorp, by this time pregnant with their second child, Tjerk, remembers that time vividly. 'We could do nothing,' she says. 'Starting in September [1944] we had no transport whatsoever, because all the Dutch transport workers had gone underground, and then it became the Hunger Winter and there was no food transportation at all ... We had nothing to eat, nothing to keep warm, for the next nine months.'[49] The family managed to eke out an existence by using peat for fuel and finding food wherever they could. Meagre rations were still available in exchange for food coupons—'you could get a bit of black bread made of tulips and things like that,' Anne remembers, 'and sometimes a little bit of oil'[50]—and twice the Red Cross managed to deliver a loaf of white bread for each adult and some butter. But for the most part the Dusseldorp family relied on whatever food Dick, accompanied by two of his sisters, could find in the surrounding countryside. Cycling around the farms to the north of Utrecht, 'they took what blankets and woollen underwear that we still had left,' Anne remembers, 'and they would exchange these for food. So you would get a little milk, or a bit of bread ... and that is how we survived.'[51] They were desperate measures for desperate times, however, for if a prime-aged male like Dick had been caught, he would undoubtedly have been arrested and deported to labour camp.[52] It was not until the Allied Forces liberated the rest of the Netherlands in May 1945 that the terrible hardship came to an end.

Not long after the end of the war, Dick's younger sister Riet was employed as a secretary by a large residential construction company: Bredero's Building Company of Utrecht. Founded in the 1870s as a small private carpentry and joinery concern, by the time Bredero's became a joint-stock company in 1921 the firm had expanded its operations to all facets of home building, and by 1940 it had opened offices right across the Netherlands.[53] With the war bringing residential construction to a halt, Bredero's used the downtime to research and develop new construction methods. Making use of prefabricated concrete panels, combined with standardised building components (bricks, windows, and the like), this ushered in 'a more industrialised method of building' that would be put to good use after the war.[54] 'A great deal of time, study and funds went into this research programme', according to the company's Managing Director, Dr Jan de Vries. And the investment paid off. 'They were very good at what they did,' Anne Dusseldorp remembers. 'They could put together houses just like Meccano sets.'[55]

With the Nazi defeat in 1945, the massive and urgent job of Dutch recon-struction could begin. The physical devastation of the Netherlands rivalled that of Germany, according to economic historian Jan van Zanden, with recon-struction efforts starting 'from a lower level than in Belgium or the Scandinavian countries'.[56] There were dikes and canals to rebuild—many had been blown up by the retreating Germans and the advancing Allies, inundating the surrounding land with water[57]—bombed buildings to restore, and, most urgent of all, a severe housing shortage to meet.[58] Wartime destruction and the cessation of residential building during the Occupation had resulted in a post-war deficit of some 300,000 homes.[59] It was the latter task in which Bredero's was principally engaged, although the firm also began to specialise in public and industrial buildings in the early 1950s.[60] With the volume of work on its books, Bredero's needed some bright young engineers to work in its Construction Division. Riet Dusseldorp knew two young men who fitted the bill: her brothers Hank and Dick joined Bredero's in 1945.

Although Dick had fallen into the residential construction industry almost by accident—with a young family to support and with jobs hard to come by, he really had no option[61]—the social value of the work, and the magnitude of the task at hand, nonetheless attracted him. 'We were young and we felt that we wanted to change the world,' says his wife Anne, 'and the need [for housing] was so very urgent after the Second World War. So that was very important to him, and to me as his support.'[62] Hardworking, ambitious, and good at his job, within a year of joining Bredero's Dick was acting as the firm's Construction Manager; by 1947 he had been promoted to that position on a permanent basis. In that capacity, at the ripe old age of twenty-nine, Dusseldorp was in charge of the firm's entire standardised cottage building program, which by then extended right across the country and employed almost three thousand people.[63]

> The company was doing *very* well, [Anne says] and it was around then that the Australian government was making overtures to European firms ... to see if they would be interested in investing money in Australia. My husband was sent out [there] in 1950 for about three months—he visited the Snowy Mountains Scheme, which, being a hydraulic engineer, was very interesting to him—and then he came back to Utrecht and he brought in his report. And that was when Bredero's decided to start a company in Australia with the Royal Dutch Harbour Works Company, and to put in for the contract to build 200 houses in Cooma.[64]

And *that* was the beginning of a whole new phase—both in the lives of the Dusseldorp family, and in the building and construction industry of Australia.

CHAPTER 1

Production Management: From Tendering to Design & Construction

Not far from Elsinore, site of the Danish castle immortalised in Shakespeare's *Hamlet*, a beautiful, flat-roofed house made of brick and glass sits amongst the seclusion of a grove of beech trees. Under the skylight, in a large open-plan room, the designer of that home—a tall, good-looking architect in his late thirties—stands locked in thought. On the long drawing table in front of him are three slightly different sketches of the same sweeping curve of road. After assessing them thoroughly, he finally picks up two of these (labelled '20' and '21'), draws a red line through them, and puts them aside. He looks again at the third sketch ('22'), and to this he adds the header 'Vehicle concourse: Working draft'. Picking up this sketch, he files it in a stack of vertical shelves, finding a space amongst the hundreds of other drawings for different aspects of the same project. The architect is Jørn Utzon and the job he is working on is another beautiful house—but this one is a long way from that in the Danish forest, and it is not a residential project. When it is eventually finished, it will be acclaimed as one of the world's architectural marvels: for the working sketches on Utzon's drawing table are for the Sydney Opera House.

'Utzon was a man who couldn't give a damn about cost,' according to Dick Dusseldorp, whose company would build the first stage of that famous Opera House.

When I visited him at his home in Denmark he had these twenty-two designs for the curve of the vehicle concourse that brings you to the steps leading up to the main halls. He would get up each morning, look at the sketches, and eliminate one or two … He was something of a professional competition-entrant. The Sydney Opera House was about the thirty-first such international competition that he had decided to enter. He had won a few, but this was the daddy of them all.[1]

The 'daddy of them all' had its genesis in the vision of Eugene Goossens, resident conductor of the Sydney Symphony Orchestra in the late 1940s. Sick of plying his trade in the city's small and acoustically less-than-perfect Town Hall, Goossens dreamed of his orchestra playing in a specially designed Concert Hall in a purpose-built performance space: ideally a monumental building befitting the world-class city that postwar Sydney was set to become. Goossens began touting his dream in the press, and before long the Labor Premier of New South Wales, J. J. (Joe) Cahill, was as enthusiastic about the idea as he. With the Premier on board, and a spectacularly situated headland on Sydney Harbour selected as the site, an international competition for the design of a 'National Opera House' was announced. The instructions for the competition entrants were clear. Their design should accord highest priority to acoustic and visual excellence; and, while they were told to 'bear in mind the necessity for sound judgement as to the financial implications', no actual limit was imposed on the building's cost.[2]

When the competition closed in late 1956, the panel of four judges, all of them distinguished architects, had over two hundred entries from right across the globe to consider.[3] It was the vision of the young Dane that captured their collective imagination. Utzon's sail-like concrete shells soaring majestically from the shoreline would, the judges felt, give Sydney 'an Opera House which is capable of being one of the great buildings of the world'. While the winning drawings were 'simple to the point of being diagrammatic', and no one was sure if the shells were technically feasible to construct, there was no doubt in the judges' minds. 'Because of its very originality,' they declared, 'it is clearly a controversial design. We are, however, absolutely convinced.'[4]

But while there was certainty about the aesthetic merit of Utzon's plans, there were considerable doubts about the building's price tag. Even as the enthusiastic Premier Cahill started publicly touting a figure of $7 million—well before tenders for construction had been called—worry creases began to appear on the brows of the bean-counters in the state Treasury. There were good grounds for their concerns: the Sydney Opera House would take some fourteen years to build (instead of the four years bravely predicted by the government in 1958),[5] and its construction costs would top the $100 million mark, almost *fifteen times* the initial estimate. The blowouts on the project would not be confined to the bottom line. Those fourteen years of construction would be marked by such acrimonious relationships between the project's architect(s), engineers, builders, and client, that very few of the originals would be still left standing—let alone talking to each other—when the resulting masterpiece was officially opened in 1973.[6] But in the late 1950s, all that palaver was some way down the track …

In the offices of Civil & Civic Contractors in January 1959, a project team was putting the finishing touches on its tender. Civil & Civic was one of six building firms asked by the state government to submit a bid, and its Dutch-born Managing Director knew that winning the contract to construct the Sydney Opera House would earn his young company a reputation well beyond Australian shores. Just eight years before, 32-year-old Dick Dusseldorp had arrived in the country with a handful of tradesmen and but one job on the company's books: a contract to build 200 houses for workers on the massive Snowy Mountains Scheme. Other small building jobs in the mountains and in nearby Canberra had followed for Civil & Civic, but it was not until the mid-1950s, when Dusseldorp turned his eyes to Sydney, that the firm had taken off. And here he was, a couple of years later, being asked to bid for the country's most prestigious construction job.

With a number of high-rise apartment blocks, some industrial and commercial premises, and a residential estate on Sydney's harbour foreshores to his credit, it was the construction of one of the city's first skyscrapers that had earned Dusseldorp and his company a name. Completing the 21-storey Caltex House building—on budget and three months ahead of schedule[7]—was a newsworthy achievement in the strife-torn building and construction industry of the 1950s. While most other construction companies were slugging it out with the militant building unions, both on-site and in the courts, Caltex House had risen in relative industrial peace at the then unheard-of rate of one floor every twelve days.[8] The man who was giving Sydney's skyline a 'striking face-lift', *The Bulletin* magazine opined, also seemed to have developed 'a mystical *rapport* with that pillar of pre-stressed independence, the Australian worker'.[9]

Besides what *The Bulletin* described as his 'mastery of labour relations, unparalleled anywhere else in the industry',[10] other features of the Dutchman's approach were attracting attention. For one, he seemed intent on turning traditional roles and relationships in the Australian construction industry on their head. In the 1950s, a client wanting to build new commercial or industrial premises would usually initiate that process by hiring an architect. The architect in turn would engage specialist design consultants and together the design team would come up with plans for the building. The architect would then call tenders, assess the competing bids, and finally hire the building contractor on the client's behalf. Once the client had arranged finance, the construction process could begin. In short, the architect, reporting directly to the client, was the boss of the process; design planning was the exclusive prerogative of the design team; and the building contractor, his workforce and subcontractors were at the end of the line and the bottom of the pile.

A major problem with this traditional tender-based process, in Dusseldorp's analysis, was that the incentive structure was wrong. As he reminded potential clients reading *Rydge's* in May 1958, it gave 'almost uncontrolled power to the designers whose remuneration, let us not forget, is fixed by way of percentage of the total cost!'[11] And while the architect was rewarded for designing edifices, Dusseldorp argued, the contractor—who was usually engaged on a fixed-price basis—was left to cut costs in whatever way was possible. Not all of those ways—such as building to a lower quality—would be in the client's interests. In sum, the financial microscope was being applied at the wrong end of the process: 'one goes to a lot of trouble analysing tenders to obtain "best value" for a pre-determined design,' Dusseldorp argued; 'whether the design itself is "best value" is, however, taken for granted.'[12] If the design team *consulted* the contractor in the design planning process, he suggested, simple adjustments could be made—say in the siting, dimensions, or building materials used—that would reap significant cost savings for clients without compromising the building's aesthetics.

There were other advantages of bringing the design and construction experts together early in the course of a building project, for another major disadvantage of the traditional way of organising construction in Australia was that it fostered a set of hierarchical—and usually antagonistic—relationships between the key players.[13] Architects, engineers, estimators, carpenters, plumbers, tilers, electricians, scaffolders, and riggers, to name but a few, all need to work in concert if a building is to be completed successfully. But all too often the first time the many different specialists involved in the design and construction of a building would come together was on the actual site. 'And then', Dusseldorp observed, 'the coming together would most often be a crash, as it was realised that the plans of the architect were unrealistic, or that what the builders had built was in the wrong place and needed to be broken up and the whole thing started again.'[14] The resulting level of antagonism and mistrust between the different specialists was, as Dusseldorp put it, 'the recipe for a huge amount of unproductive waste and unnecessary cost'.[15] Wouldn't it be better, he asked, if the key players could come together in a 'building team', to collaborate on the project from the very beginning? Wouldn't that result in a more economical use of both 'materials and manpower'?[16]

Implying a fundamental change in the relationships between client, architect, and contractor, Dusseldorp's advocacy of an alternative approach to the organisation of construction projects ruffled a few feathers in the industry. A 'comparative newcomer in building circles', Sydney's *Daily Telegraph* reported in early 1959, '[Civil & Civic] has surprised the building industry because of its unconventional ideas and the way it has carried off many major contracts … Many of the company's revolutionary ideas have resulted in reduced building costs, higher quality buildings, and higher pay for building workers. The question being asked by others in the industry is "How do they do it?"'[17] Another, less polite, question being asked in some parts of the industry was 'How can we *stop* them doing it?' For Dusseldorp's 'unconventional ideas' were meeting stiff resistance from a number of quarters, chief amongst them the architectural profession. Decidedly wary of his teamwork approach, traditional architects were disinclined to invite this 'untoward novelty' to submit tenders on their projects; meanwhile the 'non-conforming bids' that Dusseldorp would sometimes lodge nonetheless would rarely make it through the architectural gatekeeper to the client.[18]

Characteristically unfazed by such resistance, Dusseldorp simply sought a way around it. To break the stranglehold of the conventional tender system, he knew he needed to get to potential clients—better still, get them to come to him—*before* they engaged an architect to initiate and control the building process. Amongst other things, that meant raising his firm's profile in the market. Caltex House had been a boon in that regard, its swift completion attracting many plaudits in the press. Likewise, construction of the much-publicised, copper-domed Academy of Science building then under way in Canberra was earning the company considerable kudos. On the latter job, Dusseldorp had put aside his distaste for the tender process to lodge a bid, gambling that the business flow-on from completing such a prestigious job would outweigh the headaches involved.[19] The irony of having to work within the system in order to break its monopoly grip was not lost on Dusseldorp. But his instincts were being proved right in Canberra, and now an even bigger opportunity was coming his way: an invitation to tender for a project that would undoubtedly receive attention on the international stage.

His design for the Sydney Opera House having been chosen, in mid-1957 Utzon and London-based structural engineering firm, Ove Arup & Partners, set to work on the detailed specifications for the building. While this design work was going on in Europe, back in Sydney Premier Cahill was anxious to get construction under way as soon as possible. As the judges had predicted, Utzon's scheme had sparked some controversy—amongst the public, the architectural profession, and even the Premier's own political party—and the opposition Liberals, amongst others, were asking curly questions about how such a 'desirable but lavish venture'[20] could be financed. As journalist John Yeomans put it: 'Old Joe [Premier Cahill], knew that the only way to get the Opera House up was to build it first and argue about it later.'[21] 'Knowing that if ever this iron grew cold it would fall right off the anvil',[22] the Premier pressed for an immediate start to the building 'whether the architect or engineers were ready or not'.[23]

Because the architect and engineers plainly were not ready—the problem of how to construct the roof shells would take many more years to solve—the contract for constructing the Opera House was split into three stages. In early November 1958 six building firms were invited to tender for Stage 1: construction of the massive, granite-clad podium and its attendant staircases, concourse, and 'boardwalk', stage wells, offices, and workshops, cloakrooms, reception halls, and experimental theatre—basically everything under the 'sails'. At some $400,000 under the second-lowest bid, and some $1.6 million under the most expensive, the $2.8 million tender from Civil & Civic Contractors Pty Ltd was accepted by the state government in February 1959, and the first work started in May that year.[24]

If building the Academy of Science was causing some minor headaches for Civil & Civic, the difficulties of the Sydney Opera House job could only be compared to a migraine. As the author of one of the (many) books about the (many) problems involved in the design and construction of the Sydney Opera House remarked of Stage 1: 'There is not a great deal to be said about the construction of the podium except that it ran over time, ran fantastically over estimate, caused great ill-feeling and was a misery for everybody concerned.'[25]

The problems began with the foundations. Despite uncertainty about how much weight they would eventually have to bear, the building's concrete footings were to be set on 'good Sydney bedrock sandstone, at whatever depth that was found'.[26] Plumbing those depths proved unexpectedly difficult, slow, and expensive. Richard Hammond, one of Civil & Civic's site engineers on the Opera House, remembers it all too well. 'The ground that we were digging out was not the same as that depicted in the contract tender documents', Hammond says. 'It was *quite* different. It was all reclaimed land and it just wasn't supposed to be like that.'[27] In the end some 550 concrete piers had to be sunk through the reclaimed rubble of Bennelong Point—some to a depth of 25 metres below the lowest floor of the podium[28]—a slow and laborious process involving a specialised pile-driving rig, which had not been allowed for in the company's tender.[29] When water started leaking into some of these holes, divers had to pump it out before the concrete could be poured, and special cofferdams (watertight enclosures) installed to prevent any future seepage.[30] Regrettably, the difficulties of the project did not end there.

Anxious to start work on the next stage of the podium's construction, Civil & Civic were stymied by the long wait to receive working drawings from the structural engineers. With construction forced to start well before *anything like* final architectural plans were ready—on a project where the 'difficult geometry and the scale of the job' were without precedent[31]—such delays were almost inevitable. Perhaps less inevitable—and even more frustrating—were the subsequent revisions to these drawings well after they had been handed to the builder.[32] Various changes of tack by the architect and the client during the course of construction resulted in an 'endless stream'[33] of variations and amendments to Civil & Civic's riding instructions. These delays and changes were costly: not only in financial terms, but also in the 'immense confusion and ill-feeling [generated] on the site'.[34] 'We have had to plan and replan again and again', Dusseldorp complained to Ove Arups in early 1960.

We have had to construct, pull down, and reconstruct. In many instances we have been forced to construct without any planning at all in order to avoid greater calamities as a result of not doing so. It is my firm belief that any other contractor would have thrown in the towel under these circumstances. We would have done so ourselves if it had been any other job than the Opera House.[35]

As the job (and the months) rolled on, the difficulties and frustrations of the construction process escalated. Parts of the design of the podium involved construction of features that had never before been attempted: building these would '[push] known technology to the limits'.[36] Dusseldorp has vivid memories of one such feature in particular. 'The beams that go across the vehicle concourse'—the curve that Utzon had rejected twenty-one earlier sketches of—'these are all pre-stressed concrete. And such a long stretch'—spanning some 49 metres—'had never been done before. It gave me the willies! These beams were freestanding—no columns—the longest bloody things that had ever been built.'[37] It was not only the length and freestanding nature of these beams that would test the skills (and patience) of the construction contractor. Adamant that the exposed concrete surface of the beams be of an exceptionally high quality, Utzon set exacting standards for the formwork used in their construction. Dusseldorp remembers:

He [Utzon] insisted on the formwork being lined with plywood so it was perfectly smooth. And then he wanted to have the nails ... just tucked into the surface of the plywood so that when [the formwork was stripped], there would just be a tiny little mark [in the concrete] to show honestly where they had been.

Because numerous trials and errors were involved in achieving such exacting standards, Dusseldorp says, 'that alone cost us a fortune'.[38]

As is often the case on a tender job, if the contractor finds that the work it is required to do is significantly more demanding than that originally envisaged in the tender documents, it will request a variation to the contract to get reimbursement for the extra costs involved. If the client or its principal agent agrees that these cost increases are legitimate, they are generally paid. Many such 'extras' were requested by Civil & Civic—and authorised by Ove Arup & Partners—over the course of construction of the Opera House podium.[39] While most claims were settled 'in the normal way'[40]—that is, by agreement—the contractor's claim for recompense for the standard of formwork finish required on various sections of the job proved a sticking point. Civil & Civic said that more top quality work was required than specified in the contract; Ove Arup refuted this and 'countered with claims of poor craftsmanship'.[41] Unable to reach agreement, the disputants went to independent arbitration. Two subsequent Governors-General of Australia would press the opposing parties' claims before the arbitrator—William Deane for Civil & Civic and John Kerr for Ove Arup—and a negotiated settlement, in the contractor's favour, was eventually reached out of court. 'In the end, we just broke even on the job,' Dusseldorp says. 'That in itself was quite a major achievement, because for a while there it just looked like a sink-hole.'[42]

Civil & Civic completed the construction of Stage 1 of the Opera House in February 1963. It had taken almost three years longer than anticipated, cost almost twice as much as the original tender price,[43] and worn the nerves of those involved red-raw. (The cost blowouts, delays, and acrimony did not end with Stage 1, although Civil & Civic's involvement with the Opera House project did; but that, as they say, is another story.)[44] And although the job was not without its compensations for the company—Dusseldorp found that holding the first construction contract for one of the world's most talked-about buildings opened many of 'the right doors'[45] when he sought finance overseas for major development projects—he was by no means sorry to see the end of it.

There is no doubt that some of the problems experienced during the construction of the Sydney Opera House derived from circumstances unique to that particular job: the push to start construction before the question of how to build the roof had been solved was the most glaring of these. But almost every other aspect of the project confirmed for Dusseldorp the more general drawbacks of the traditional, tender-based mode of building organisation: the flawed incentive structure, the antagonistic relationships between the design and construction specialists, the communication breakdowns, and the resulting cost and wastefulness. There had to be a better way.

———

Industry revolutionaries take the entire business concept, rather than a product or service, as the starting point for innovation ... [They] don't tinker at the margins; they blow up old business models and create new ones.[46]

For Dusseldorp, that 'better way' meant one thing: finding a more profitable means of doing business that clients would embrace—along with other key stakeholders—because it made them better off too. The key would be to stem the 'gushing stream of unproductive waste'[47] bound up with the tender system, for then the resulting savings could be shared amongst all concerned. Clients (and the broader community) would get high-quality buildings constructed on time and at the lowest possible cost, while the design and construction specialists (himself included!) would benefit through sharing in the time and cost savings of improved coordination, and through increased market demand for their services. Dusseldorp would act towards this mutually beneficial goal on a number of fronts and in a number of stages over the years. But he was not one for 'tinkering at the margins'. Displaying a striking ability to view all kinds of organisational (and other) boundaries as permeable, he came up with answers that would challenge traditional definitions of how the construction market operated, what the tradeable product was, what the typical building firm looked like, and how that entity related to 'outside others'. A key plank in his thinking would be laid in a place where, at least in the 1950s, few construction contractors had ventured before.

In 1957, Dusseldorp enrolled in a six-week Advanced Management Program run by the Harvard Business School at the University of Hawaii. By this time in charge of a rapidly expanding enterprise employing some 500 people, the trained engineer was feeling the lack of any formal management education. 'I felt I didn't know enough,' he says. 'I hadn't studied as a manager: I was doing it all by the seat of my pants.'[48] Joining the 60-strong student body drawn from the US military and large industrial and commercial enterprises across the Pacific, Dusseldorp, one of some fifteen Australians on the course, was the first person from the construction industry ever to attend.[49] The pedagogical approach of the Harvard professors—then as now—relies on case studies. Students form small groups and together work through a large number of cases documenting real-life business or management dilemmas which organisations and individuals have confronted. One particular case study in the course that year would exert a substantial influence on Dusseldorp's thinking; so much so that, some forty years later, he could still vividly recall its details. The case concerned the US shoe manufacturing industry.

'The average business life expectancy of shoe manufacturers in the United States was seven years,' he remembers. Barriers to entry were low and a large number of people were attracted to the field. What these budding entrepreneurs failed to take into account, however, and it was the primary reason for the high rate of bankruptcy in the industry, was that there was no controlled relationship between manufacturing costs and the wholesale price of shoes.

> The main raw materials of shoe manufacture—animal hides—were bought by the pound weight. Highly skilled artisans would carve these hides up. But because the hides were inherently of uneven quality, these guys making up the shoes would put a piece from this hide here, and a piece from that hide there … And what that means is that you had absolutely no hope of accurately relating the prime cost of the raw material to the end product.

With accurate cost information non-existent, manufacturers would set prices by doing a quick market survey of retail shoe prices in their local town, then taking a slice off that to make their product competitive. Of course, this price did not bear any rational relationship to real costs, and so 'the more shoes the manufacturer sold, the more money he lost, and the faster he went bust'.[50]

'That case reminded me of the Australian building industry', Dusseldorp recalls, 'because it also works on that basis. There is just no way in the world that you can accurately predict the cost of construction of a building just on the basis of architectural specifications. Yet you have to put in a tender, and so do others who are equally uninformed.'[51] One way for builders to get a rational grip on the cost–price relationship in the construction market was to collude. Dusseldorp describes how this would often work:

> The tender documents would come out, and then everyone would do their own rough working out [of the building costs]. Then they would all get together in the back room of a pub somewhere and open up what they had. Some retired guy, who wouldn't be biased one way or the other, would pick the one [tender] that had the *highest* price. And then collectively they would all add more to this bid for submission, and then the difference [between the proposed tender price and the 'winning' one] would be allocated amongst the other participants. Then they would all up their original bids, to make sure [the 'winning' tender] looked competitive in the eyes of the architect.[52]

Such collusion, although illegal, was rife, as the subsequent Royal Commission into the New South Wales Building Industry would find.[53] Dusseldorp refused to be involved in such practices—'I never participated in that', he says 'because I didn't like it'—but he could nonetheless see its economic rationality. A builder locked into the traditional tender system had few options: 'they think that [collusion's] wrong, but it was the only way to survive'.[54]

The shoe industry case inspired Dusseldorp to think about another way in which builders could get greater control over the cost–price relationship in the construction process. It would, however, mean a fundamental challenge to the way the industry worked, completely circumventing the existing tendering system. 'If I learnt anything there [on the Harvard course],' Dusseldorp reflects, 'it was that the building industry was not on its own. The shoe industry was like that too, and that was no way of spending your life … And that is where I decided that I had to get control of my destiny: that I would no longer be a servant to the architects'.[55] The first step in his bid to get control was based on a concept that was just starting to make inroads in urban property markets in the United States and the United Kingdom.[56] It was an integrated building product called 'Design & Construct'.

In his history of the Australian building industry, written in 1992, Oscar Gimesy observed that 'the dichotomy between design and construction practices is so pronounced in traditional construction practices that recent trends to integrate the two, which is taken for granted in other arenas of economic production, is considered a radical leap'.[57] 'Design & Construct', as the name suggests, means treating the whole building process, from initiation of design through to the building's completion, as an integrated project: one that is managed as a totality. In essence, the Design & Construct 'product' is a project management service: clients wishing to commission a building could, instead of hiring an architect and going down the traditional tender route, engage Dusseldorp's firm to manage the entire building project. The integrated approach could also be employed on building projects which Dusseldorp's firm 'self-sponsored' through its new finance and development arm, Lend Lease (see Chapter 3). If the concept caught on, Dusseldorp realised, it would enable him to bypass the tender system and its attendant wastefulness.

If Design & Construct was considered a 'radical leap' by Gimesy in the 1990s, how much more so some four decades earlier when Civil & Civic was amongst the first building companies to offer it to the Australian market.[58] 'The whole concept of Design *and* Construct was novel to the builders and architects in Sydney', recalls a close observer of the industry at the time, 'and there was *strong* opposition [to it], violent opposition.'[59] The concept was initially fought tooth-and-nail by the old guard in the architectural profession, who saw it as a direct assault on their power base.[60] Clients, too, were wary at the start. But, convinced that both groups would come round to the idea in the long run—or at least enough rebels within them would do so—Dusseldorp persevered. His determination would pay off. By the mid-1960s Design & Construct 'package deals' were accounting for well over half of Civil & Civic's revenue, the great bulk of which was repeat business, and by the 1970s this type of work was generating 70 per cent of Civil & Civic's total turnover.[61]

As Dusseldorp saw it, the key to the system of Design & Construct was the idea of the 'building team'. 'The complexity of modern construction projects is increasing very rapidly', he told an audience of potential clients in the early 1960s, 'for which there is only one answer. *Teamwork.* ... Nothing short of organised teamwork—from the decision to build to the handing over of the completed project—will solve the problem.'[62] Dusseldorp's ideal 'building team' would comprise a 'Senior Executive of the Client's organisation', along with representatives from 'each major specialist field involved in the project, including the contractor', with all of the specialists accorded 'equal status' on the team.[63] These building teams, or Project Control Groups (PCGs) as they were later called, became *de rigueur* on all Civil & Civic Design & Construct projects. They also became the 'fundamental management unit'[64] of the growing company, for Dusseldorp saw PCGs as the ideal way to guard against bureaucracy—which he abhorred—and to achieve a flat, flexible, fluid and team-based organisation structure in its place.[65] 'The idea of the Project Control Group ... was quite novel to the building industry', recalls Milton Allen, the former head of life insurer MLC, who, as a major client of Civil & Civic's services, would participate in a number of such teams. 'And it proved a *very* efficient way to go about the whole process.'[66]

Coordinating the work of the team was the Project Engineer: the person on Dusseldorp's staff personally responsible for managing each building project 'from the first stage of working out [its] commercial justification', through its design phase, and on into the construction period.[67] Richard Hammond was working as the company's Site Engineer on the Sydney Opera House when Dusseldorp asked him to become one of Civil & Civic's first such Project Engineers:

Up till then, construction jobs had been controlled by architects and [Dusseldorp] was quick to realise that architects weren't necessarily good managers. He decided he wasn't going to put up with this any more—it was causing too much trouble— so he set up the first of the project managers—Project Engineers they were going to call them. Duss … had us all in the Board Room—all the people that were selected—and he gave us his thoughts on the matter. He said 'I don't really care what the people are who I have employed doing this—they can be butchers, they can be architects, they can be engineers, or whatever—if they are good at management, well, they are the people I'm going to put in charge of the projects. And the architects will report as part of the team to the manager.' So that was the start-up of that.[68]

Dusseldorp made equally clear his expectations of how these teams would work. Irrespective of the branch, department, or profession to which they form-ally 'belonged', the specialists on the team were expected to look 'not to the sectional interest of the individual, whatever his speciality might be, but [instead] be oriented towards the end product of all their collective endeav-ours'.[69] The construction specialists on the team were always drawn from Civil & Civic's ranks, but the architectural or engineering designers need not be. Although external design consultants were generally used, Dusseldorp had deliberately increased his own firm's capacity in this area by setting up a Design Services Group in the late 1950s.[70] This not only enabled Civil & Civic to do some of its own project design work, but even more importantly, as a subse-quent Managing Director of the company remarks, provided it with sufficient expertise to 'keep the external designers honest, by setting the brief up correctly and then monitoring their performance'.[71]

Dusseldorp used to liken the advantages of this project management approach to the workings of a well-oiled gearbox, as long-term Lend Lease executive Eric Goodwin explains:

In a gearbox you've got the gears that are enmeshed: and they represent the various specialists that you have on a [project]. But unless you add a catalyst, those gears don't work and those specialists would just produce what they've been trained to produce. The project manager and the project management system … was akin to the oil that goes into the gearbox. Without the oil the gears come to a grinding halt very quickly because they overheat and they don't work. And that was the analogy that [Dusseldorp] would use to represent project management: in that it was the art of getting—and it was an art, and still is an art—the art of getting people to think beyond their traditional boundaries to come up with a solution, collectively, that was better than any one of them individually could come up with.[72]

The need for such collaboration was accentuated by some peculiar characteristics of the building and construction industry that lessened the scope for cost-saving measures used elsewhere in the economy. Construction was and is a labour-intensive process, geared to the production of a relatively customised product. The extent to which new technologies could be deployed had always been regarded as small compared, for example, to the scope for mass production techniques in manufacturing.[73] As a result, the cost of building had, over the years, risen significantly in comparative terms. Whereas forty years ago a motor car cost three times the value of an ordinary suburban home, Dusseldorp told the *Daily Telegraph* in March 1959, 'now a suburban home costs three times as much as a motor car. That shows the progress that industrialisation has brought to the production of automobiles. In the building trade, on the other hand, there has been very little industrial progress since Noah built the ark.'[74]

With limited scope for industrialisation, the design planning phase offered perhaps the most potential for reducing costs: 'that's where the savings [are] made', Dusseldorp would say: 'in the mind and on the drawing board'.[75] The first job of the project team, therefore, was to consider 'alternative ways in which the various problems encountered in the design of a building can be overcome.'[76] These alternatives would be mulled over, costed and compared, in conjunction with an assessment of alternative methods of construction, 'to enable the correct solution to be obtained'.[77] The 'correct solution' was the best *value* solution for the client. Reconfiguring the building on its site, standardising its dimensions, ensuring that the building materials and methods required by the design were available at a reasonable, not prohibitive, cost: small adjustments such as these could save thousands in total project costs. With the client actively participating in the project team during the initial design planning, they were in a position to reach an *informed* decision as to which alternatives generated the most value for them.

Meanwhile, behind the scenes, an intensive research and development effort was directed at expanding the range of design and construction alternatives for these project teams to consider. In 1959 Dusseldorp created an R&D department with a straightforward charter: 'to identify better things to do and better ways of doing things', so as to keep the company 'at least one jump ahead of the competition'.[78] A totally new concept for the Australian building and construction industry at the time, the R&D group—initially comprising research architects, engineers, and a training officer[79]—searched for these 'better things and better ways' by scanning practices and technologies worldwide, investigating ideas suggested by workers on the company's sites, and doing original research. While some of the resulting innovations were fizzers—a concerted campaign to get architects, builders, and materials manufacturers to adopt standardised (modular) dimensioning, for example, failed to catch on—others proved successful. The invention of a safer and more efficient formwork hoist, a range of new concrete formwork systems, and the 'Progressive Strength' system of high-rise concrete construction,[80] for example, all 'simultaneously improved the rate of construction and worker safety, were adopted throughout the industry, and remained the standard for many years'.[81]

In the early 1960s, the first fruits of this research effort—and the bona fides of Dusseldorp's integrated Design & Construct philosophy more generally— were about to be tested on a project whose scale would rival that of any other building project then under way in Sydney's central business district (including the one slowly taking shape down at Bennelong Point). Touted in the press as the city's $40 million answer to New York's Rockefeller Center,[82] that project was Australia Square.

———

When Dusseldorp and his firm had completed the 21-storey Caltex House in 1957, it had been one of the first few Manhattan-style high-rise office buildings to appear on the Sydney skyline.[83] Such was the novelty of these new buildings that most included viewing platforms from which the public could gain the nearest thing to a bird's-eye view of the central city and its surrounds. For many years prior to that, the city's 'low-scale urban fabric'[84] was best observed from atop the southern pylons of Sydney's famous Harbour Bridge.[85] Looking towards the city from there, along the narrow roads inherited from an era of horse-drawn traffic, the immediate vista was dominated by four- to five-storey brick and stone warehouses, bond stores and government departments,[86] interrupted only by the occasional turret, smokestack, or radio tower. Beyond that, the commercial heart of the city comprised, alongside vestiges of its colonial and Victorian past, a collection of more modern buildings, few of them rising more than a dozen floors high. Most of the latter had gone up in the 1920s, the last time the city had experienced a building boom. Recession and war, combined with regulatory restrictions on building height,[87] had kept Sydney's skyline relatively low-rise during the 1930s and 1940s. All that, however, was about to change, for Caltex House and its contemporaries signalled the beginning of a new trend.

What started as a trickle in the late 1950s became a torrent in the ensuing decades as large corporations wishing to trumpet their presence clambered after the multi-storey office blocks being haphazardly erected in the city's centre. The public sector was equally keen to jump on the high-rise bandwagon. Reflecting an influx of property investment capital from the insurance industry, booming conditions in the economy, advances in construction methods, and more than a little one-upmanship, the upward reach of these buildings was ever increasing. The removal of the regulatory restrictions on building height in 1957 provided a further impetus to this trend.[88] The dawning of the new decade saw many high-rise office buildings under construction: amongst the majors were the AMP Society's new $10 million head office at Circular Quay, the Reserve Bank's $8 million development at Martin Place, and the $6 million Commonwealth Offices in Chifley Square. (Meanwhile, work was continuing on the Sydney Opera House at Bennelong Point, with total costs then estimated at $9.5 million:[89] one-tenth the *actual* final cost!) In addition to the Opera House, and a number of residential and industrial projects besides, in early 1961 Dusseldorp's firm alone had five commercial high-rises under construction in Sydney and its southern sister city Melbourne. But they all paled in comparison with 'the big one': the development of Australia Square.

———

'Well, what do you all think?' asked Dusseldorp. 'How are we going to build this thing?' Sitting around the table at corporate headquarters in mid-1961, the members of the Australia Square project team stared at the model in front of them. On a large rectangular board, two buildings faced each other across a sea of open space. The first building was, at least at first glance, conventional: a

13-storey office block, rectangular in shape, with a frontage onto busy Pitt Street. The building's distinction, however, was apparent at ground level, where it rested on huge 'trestle-like' clusters of 'double V-shaped columns',[90] opening up the space under the building proper and providing a 'portico'[91] into the large plaza beyond. During the day, the idea was, office workers and shoppers would pour into this plaza, lunching in the sun beside the fountain and under the trees, enjoying a break from the bustle of the traffic in the city's first privately created open public space. At night the building's columns would be floodlit from their base, creating 'mysterious patterns of darkness and light' for the 'lovers of Sydney' to enjoy.[92] This first building, to be known as Australia Square Plaza, would provide 'a termination and foil' for its partner.[93] For it was the second building, the Tower, which caught your eye, and it was to this that Dusseldorp's latter question related.

For a start it was huge. Rising some fifty floors, the Tower, when built, would be by far the tallest building in Sydney, indeed in the whole of the country. And although it would occupy only 25 per cent of the two-thirds of a hectare site, its total floor space would be twelve times that area.[94] But even more than the dimensions, it was the *shape* of the building that demanded your attention. For Australia Square Tower was to be a circle. This apparent paradox would puzzle Sydneysiders for years, and Dusseldorp probably lost count of the number of times he was asked to resolve it. 'Was it some kind of Dutch joke?' one journalist inquired. 'The Dutch don't have a sense of humour,' Dusseldorp replied, smiling wryly as he belied his own remark. 'It is the open plaza, the civic square, that gives the development its name.'[95] Why, then, a circle for this Square?

'[The circular Tower] is … like a tree trunk,' the architect explained. 'It throws the least shadow on the surrounding areas and offers least wind resistance.'[96] Aesthetically handsome—some thirty years after its completion it was still being described as 'one of the world's most elegantly resolved skyscrapers'[97]—the circular design of the Tower had more tangible benefits as well. For one, it would yield the maximum floor area, given regulatory constraints on the width, setback, and floor space ratios of city buildings at the time.[98] This advantage had been critical in convincing the scheme's overseas financial backers of the viability of the circular design, despite the hesitation of their real estate advisers, who initially thought the concept a marketing disaster. And it also had the blessing of the construction specialists on the project team, who viewed it as the 'ideal structural form' for such a tall building.[99] With no interior columns, external concrete fins and the central service core would support the tower: a configuration lending itself ideally to 'speedy, repetitive and mechanised component construction'.[100] A masterly blend of aesthetics and economy, the plan was to build the bulk of the Tower out of lightweight concrete: a high-strength material just starting to replace denser concrete on high-rise projects overseas, but which had never been used on such a scale before. All of which prompted Dusseldorp's question about how 'this thing' might be built.

That question had, of course, already been addressed in general terms by the project team, for considerations such as speed and economy of construction had formed a central part of their initial design brief. Answering it in detail, however, would involve more than two years of further research and planning, in the process bringing together some of the best design and construction brains in Australia, and drawing on expertise from across the world. The innovative design of the circular Tower and the desire to dedicate a large portion of the site to public use would throw up a variety of hurdles along the way—economic, architectural, engineering, and logistic (not to mention those of a financial, legal, and bureaucratic nature)—but the great bulk of these would be scaled 'on the drawing board', as it were. And while the weekly meetings of the project team would sometimes be stormy, the pay-off from these intensive and inte-grated deliberations would soon be apparent to the denizens of Sydney as the city's biggest commercial development took shape in record time. In doing so it would, according to a leading professor of architecture at the time, 'convince even the most sceptical'—read the bulk of his own profession—of the 'impressive fruit' yielded by 'the single-minded and concentrated application of modern technological and management techniques'.[101] For Australia Square would provide, amongst other things, a concrete demonstration of the benefits of Dusseldorp's Design & Construct approach.

In the early 1960s there was at least one architect willing to give that new approach a try, and that was Harry Seidler. Still a youthful thirty-something when he designed Australia Square, Seidler—who would later be recognised as 'one of Australia's and the World's leading architects'[102]—had already demonstrated that he was neither a captive of orthodoxy nor afraid of controversy. A student of Gropius, Breuer, and Niemeyer, Seidler before he met Dusseldorp had worked mostly in the private residential field. There, amidst Sydney's postwar 'sea of suburban roofs', Seidler's 'Modernistic' suspended concrete structures had managed to incense conservative local councils, draw crowds of curious onlookers, and ignite much debate about the future of modern architecture in the city.[103] Also unorthodox was his attitude to the integrated approach to design and construction being pioneered by Dusseldorp and his firm, the demonstrated results of which had brought the two men together in the first place.

'I was a young architect who'd really been building mostly smallish things at the time', Seidler recalls of his first encounter with the Dutchman.

> It was 1957 and all of Sydney was aware of the fact that suddenly there was a tall building going up—it was Caltex House—and it was simply unbelievable. Every other week there was another floor on this thing. Nobody had ever seen anything like it. It was one of the first office buildings being built, and it was being built *fast*.[104]

At the time, Seidler had in his portfolio designs for an apartment block to be built on a piece of land, owned by his brother, in Sydney's harbourside suburb of Elizabeth Bay. Looking for someone to sponsor the building's construction, and 'impressed with the way this man was building things', the Seidler brothers decided to approach Dusseldorp and his firm. 'And the answer came back,' Seidler recalls, ' "Mr Dusseldorp doesn't think much of your scheme because [the apartments] look like monk's cells: they're too narrow and too small! But, he *would* be interested to build something on that site if you could adjust your proposal to what the local real estate people feel is marketable." '[105] Seidler did his market research and quickly produced a revised plan on the basis of the new brief. Dusseldorp was impressed—'Harry had interpreted properly what I wanted: this time the designs were absolutely fabulous'[106]—and the project, Ithaca Gardens, went ahead. Netting Seidler the 1959–60 *Journal of Architecture and Arts* for the best building of the year,[107] Ithaca Gardens also marked the beginning of a partnership between the two men that would span some thirty years and well over a dozen projects, including, most famously, Australia Square.

'He was like the ideal client,' Seidler says of Dusseldorp. 'He spelt out what was needed, but never interfered with aesthetic decisions.'[108] 'Against other advisers' opinions he was supportive of Australia Square's planned public plaza, which he saw as a place "for the people of Sydney". But he was firm on timing and how to build.'[109] From the start, Dusseldorp had made perfectly clear to Seidler and the rest of the Australia Square project team the parameters within which they were to work. Number One was 'timing': the buildings had to go up *fast*, because otherwise the interest rate on the borrowed funds would be 'a dead loss'.[110] Delays in construction were always costly—'it feels like riding in a taxi and watching the meter', Dusseldorp once observed of the property development process as a whole[111]—but on a project of this scale, they were potentially fatal. Indeed, the scale of the Australia Square project and the nature of the financial risks involved demanded a staged approach to its construction: the Plaza building would be built first (1962–63), followed by the Tower (1965–67), with the latter itself sequenced in three stages. Parameter Number Two ('how to build') was also clearly spelt out: the Tower was to be constructed 'without internal columns or external scaffolding'.[112] Internal columns were 'out' as they reduced rentable floor space; and external scaffolding would be rendered redundant if the facade of the Tower could be built slightly ahead of the main structure, thus providing a safety barrier for the workers and saving money to boot.

Within these parameters, the project team could invest as many resources as necessary (within reason!) in up-front research, coordination and planning. If they needed to, they could travel far and wide to find the *best* advice available for the design and construction of what Dusseldorp wanted to be a world-class development. For, although he was violently opposed to wastefulness in the traditional design process—the bulk of which, as we have seen, he attributed to lack of collaboration between design and construction professionals in the initial planning stages—Dusseldorp was no skinflint. He recognised the value of spending money in the short term to save it in the future: he spurned waste and extravagance, but he would gladly invest in things that would generate sustainable value in the longer term. It was an attribute that impressed the architect.

'When he presented me with [the initial] brief,' Seidler remembers, 'he said to me "You really want to get some advice from people who understand urban renewal", as it was called then. And I recommended I. M. Pei in America ... a classmate of mine from way back, and he sent me there to talk to him about this project.'[113] Later, when the architect wanted to engage, as the structural consultant on the Tower, 'the *best* man in reinforced concrete construction',[114] Italian architectural engineer Pier Luigi Nervi, the idea raised some hackles on the project team, but Dusseldorp backed his call: 'Harry goes to Rome.'[115] A third overseas trip would see Seidler (accompanied by his wife Penelope and Dusseldorp's lieutenant, Jack Klompe) search the world for 'a public sculpture of international standard'[116] to grace the Tower's George Street frontage. This resulted in the commissioning of a 12-metre high stabile, entitled 'Crossed Blades', from internationally acclaimed sculptor Alexander Calder; tapestries by Le Corbusier and Vasarely would later be chosen for the lobby. 'When I came back with a $US55,000 price-tag [on the Calder sculpture],' Seidler recalls, '[Dusseldorp] didn't really quibble with that. He was realistic. He had a much broader vision than most people. Most people look at what's immediately here, but he looked much further ahead. He could see the broader picture. And that was so amazing about him.'[117]

A rainy day in December 1962 saw Sydney's Lord Mayor, Alderman Harry Jensen, mark the start of the first stage of construction of Australia Square by burying a copper time-capsule in the Plaza building's foundations. (Amongst the items inside that capsule was a letter from Jensen, addressed to the Lord Mayor of Sydney in 2062, and a marketing brochure from Dusseldorp's firm: as many of his colleagues have remarked of 'Duss', he was always thinking ahead!) Some ten months later the Plaza building was structurally complete; by mid-1964, not long after its official opening, it would be fully leased and 'revenue producing'.[118] But by this time, the focus of the project team had shifted to Stage 2 of the development: the landmark circular Tower.

In July 1962, the Australia Square project team had begun a rigorous program of research, investigation, preliminary and detailed design and planning, aimed at identifying and solving 'all design and construction items and problems that could be associated with the Tower building'.[119] Week in and week out for the next two years they would meet, argue, query, suggest, criticise, and plan. They investigated, disaggregated, estimated, and synthesised. Alternative approaches to problems were proposed, questioned, reworked, and tried again, in an effort to come up with the best solution. As Roy Robinson, Civil & Civic's then Managing Director, says:

> The project control system that we operated on Australia Square—and every other project—was outstandingly successful … It provided a system whereby you could question people's ideas without abruptly confronting them. You've got half a dozen people there, all in a position … to be critical. [Someone would present a proposal and] you'd say, 'OK, that's quite good, but why did you do it that way? What's the reason? Is there a better way?' And it forced people to think, to defend their proposal and have reasons for it. The project control group was a mighty tool for that sort of thing.[120]

If those questions could not be answered in Australia, the team would look further afield. Team members were despatched to comb the United States for the latest developments in lightweight concrete, air conditioning systems, elevator bank design, fire protection systems, and lighting. Others went to Italy with Seidler to work with Nervi on the design of the thin, high-strength, gracefully patterned ceilings of the Tower's vestibule, and its tapered external concrete ribs. Another went to the Soviet Union, then world leaders in precast concrete and prefabrication, to see what could be learnt there.[121] Back at home they built a scale model of the Tower and tested its resistance to hurricane-strength winds. The methods engineer used the critical path method and multi-activity charts to put together an ingenious construction plan that would enable each floor to be completed in a five-day cycle.[122]

Such was the innovation of the design of the Tower that the project team quickly realised that many of the building materials required for its construction would not be readily available on the Australian market. Dusseldorp had bumped up against this obstacle before, and in the late 1950s he had embarked on an acquisition program that netted his firm, in sequence, 'a lift manufacturing company, a timber company, metal window frame makers, … and a firm of electrical engineers, a lightweight aggregate concrete [plant], and a brick concern'.[123] Representatives of all these firms were roped into the Australia Square planning process at an early stage. Often drawing on external expertise to design and produce the more innovative of the required materials and components, they worked to ensure that there would no bottlenecks in the supply chain when it came time for construction to begin.

That day arrived in 1965. When excavation of the site was complete by the middle of the year, everyone was ready to roll. The end result of the project team's integrated efforts was, as the architect describes, a building that could be erected with amazing speed. 'Australia Square [Tower] was one of the most immediate, quick to build kind of structures—it only has one beam, it only has one column, and all the floor elements are the same—so it was a real mass production job. That made it possible to build very quickly.'[124] Alan Cull, the methods engineer on the job, says of the Tower's construction:

it was 'tool-intensive': we really got sophisticated with the tools! There was a multi-activity chart—we were using that on all our jobs by then—but it was different in that it spiralled up. And we had three self-climbing formwork hoists [another Cull invention] operating on it. We had that many innovations on the Australia Square job: it was highly mechanised and highly systematic. It was great … it was a beautiful thing to watch, it was a machine.[125]

The construction of the Tower was also observed by the then Professor of Architecture at University of New South Wales, John Freeland, who describes it thus:

On a cramped and restricted site a central core of in-situ concrete served as an ever-growing platform from which pre-cast and pre-finished concrete units were positioned to form the columns, spandrels and beams. The units were shells with the reinforcement already positioned. They served as both formwork and finish to the concrete cores which were poured in-situ. By working from the inside out the circular tower rose, free of the usual entangling cobweb of steel scaffolding, swiftly and cleanly at the rate of three floors each four weeks. As it did it convinced even the most sceptical that the single-minded and concentrated application of modern technological and management techniques yielded impressive fruit and that in this regard the Australia Square Tower was the most important building in Australia since the [1956] MLC building.[126]

On 5 May 1967 Sydney's *Daily Telegraph* announced that Australia Square was structurally complete. Declaring its Tower 'undoubtedly one of the most impressive buildings in the world', the newspaper described the '50-storey colossus' as 'a tribute to Australian workmanship'.[127] 'Such was the planning and organisation that the two buildings were completed ahead of schedule and within the projected budget—a rarity in large-scale building works in Australia.'[128] In a roof-top ceremony to mark the Tower's completion—a European ritual he had introduced to pay special tribute to the contribution of his workforce to the building project, a contribution rarely recognised in the official ceremonies that marked the beginning and end of other Australian projects—Dusseldorp himself would describe 5 May 1967 as 'the day of the worker'.

> The tallest job they have ever built, [Australia Square] ... has had the highest output per man-hour in terms of any jobs that we know of. It has a roof now, without a death having been incurred and, putting aside the ... [odd] incident, ... we have had no industrial strife at all ... I would like to pay a very sincere tribute to all the men who have constructed this job ... I am exceedingly proud of you, and you can be proud of your job.[129]

The construction workers were not the only ones receiving praise for their contribution to Australia Square. His design of the project won architect Harry Seidler the 1967 Sulman Medal—the highest architectural honour in the state[130]—along with that year's Civic Design Award from the Royal Australian Institute of Architects. And while the Tower has, in its own right, been acclaimed as 'Australia's finest tall building ... a perfect resolution of rational geometry, structural ingenuity and heroic form',[131] the 'epoch-making'[132] nature of the Australia Square concept as a whole has drawn equal praise. It was probably the country's first privately sponsored urban renewal project to return such a large portion of open space to the public.[133] The gift was appreciated. 'Few later city developments have equalled its success,' writes one architectural commentator, 'which can be gauged by the crowds thronging it, especially at lunchtime during the week.'[134]

Some six years later, another magnificent building opened its doors to Sydney, this one on the city's quayside peninsula called Bennelong Point. Few would deny the Opera House masterpiece status, particularly as some thirty years have gone by since its completion, and the memories of the angst, controversy, delays, expenditure overruns, and monumental bust-ups that marked its design and construction are starting to fade. For some, however, the smell of acrimony lingers: tragically, architect Jørn Utzon has never returned to Australian shores to see his wonderful creation and to receive the adulation that the city, belatedly, would love to bestow on him. In the year 2000, the Sydney Opera House joined Australia Square amongst the seven Australian buildings nominated by the Royal Australian Institute of Architects as warranting recognition on the World Register of Significant Twentieth Century Architecture.[135] While they share this accolade, in terms of process Australia Square and the Sydney Opera House stand at opposite extremes. As someone with the most intimate experience of both, Dusseldorp knew he had found his 'better way'.

CHAPTER 2

Labour Management: Redefining Work, Employment and Industrial Relations

'There's a stop-work meeting on this morning': word went round the Sydney building site where, in late 1956, construction of Caltex House—the country's first concrete-framed high-rise office building—was in full swing. Such meetings were not infrequent on the Sydney building scene in the late 1950s, especially on the well-unionised multi-storey projects that were just starting to pepper the city's skyline. Poor working conditions, escalating injury rates, and the intermittent nature of employment in the industry gave workers good grounds for complaint, while the postwar boom in construction and an acute shortage of skilled labour gave them industrial muscle to flex. With the dominant trade union in the industry committed to a militant strategy to press its members' claims, and the main employers' organisation equally determined to fight them, the scene was set for some major stoushes.

Indeed, the number, severity, and bitterness of industrial disputes had risen steadily over the past few years,[1] and as they did, cost and time over-runs on building projects became the norm while productivity levels plumbed new depths. 'Get tough' tactics on both sides of the industrial fence, lamented the *Sydney Morning Herald*, were landing an industry already 'grievously sick with industrial trouble' in an even more 'doleful plight'.[2] News of yet another stop-work meeting in the city's building trade, therefore, would barely raise an eyebrow under normal circumstances, but the one being held at Civil & Civic's Caltex House site that day would be different. For the Managing Director of the firm, Dick Dusseldorp, was planning to attend in person.

Dusseldorp had been warned about the parlous state of industrial relations in the building and construction industry when he first stepped onto Australian shores in 1950, and the warning had come from someone in a position to know. On a three-month study tour to assess investment prospects for the two Dutch building and engineering companies he represented, Dusseldorp had made a point of calling on Albert Monk, president of the national labour confederation, the Australian Council of Trade Unions (ACTU).[3] Also holding the state presidencies of both the Australian Labor Party and Trades Hall in Victoria,[4] Monk was a key player in the industrial and political wings of the Australian labour movement.[5] In one or other capacity he was involved in every major industrial dispute in the country; and with a general upsurge in activism over wages and conditions after the war, there were enough such disputes to keep him busy. Some industries, however, consumed more of Monk's time than others, and, unbeknownst to his Dutch visitor, the strife-torn construction industry fell well within this camp. When Dusseldorp told Monk of the Dutch companies' interest in setting up shop in the building trade, the response was candid, if somewhat unexpected: 'You must want to have your head read,' Monk had said. 'The building industry is *terrible!*'[6]

There were good grounds for Monk's bleak assessment, for even then industrial relations in the construction industry displayed all the characteristics of trench warfare (and this was before things *really* deteriorated!) The federal branch of the dominant tradesmen's union—the communist-led Building Workers' Industrial Union (BWIU)—had been expelled from the national arbitration system two years earlier, the Industrial Court judges having been persuaded by building industry employers that the militant union's continued operation posed a serious threat to postwar construction activity.[7] But this move in itself had done little to calm the industrial waters. A number of state branches of the BWIU continued to operate in their own geographical spheres—despite applications by the employers to deregister them,[8] and attempts by rival unions to poach their members[9]—and the union's commitment to militancy, if tactically 'refined', was nonetheless steeled by the various assaults upon it.[10]

While the BWIU was the biggest and probably the most bolshie of the thirty or so unions in the construction industry, members of the Builders Labourers' Federation (BLF), the next biggest in size, were no less willing to make their industrial mark. Jack Mundey, who was later elected state secretary of the BLF in New South Wales, describes the prevailing mood he encountered when he joined the industry in Sydney in the early 1950s:

> The worker on a building site was more transient; he (only he in those days)
> seemed more left wing, more ready to take industrial action, but also more

undisciplined than his counterpart in the factories where I had worked. The factory worker stays on the same bench year after year and he has more time to pursue his objectives. He has a different type of thinking. The worker on the building site has to pursue his objectives very quickly because the site doesn't last. On building sites, it is often dog-eat-dog, catch-as-catch-can ... On a new site, the struggle has to start all over again.[11]

And indeed it was a struggle—for even the most basic of conditions—because in the opposite corner of the ring, and also spoiling for a fight, were the building industry bosses. 'Tough nuts' populated the management ranks of many of the large construction companies at the time, and it was their 'hard-nosed',[12] confrontationist view that prevailed in the then dominant employers' organisation in the industry, the Master Builders' Association (MBA).[13] 'They had foremen who had been foremen in the building industry during the Depression', an apprentice bricklayer—who would go on to lead his union— says of a typical company from that era.

> And that was their mentality ... The Deputy General Foreman on the job used to get [to the site] early in the morning to cut up the *Sydney Morning Herald* of the day before [for the workers to use] as toilet paper. He'd put a string through it, and go and hang it on the hooks. That was the mentality of them. And so to 'waste time' on things like safety, sick pay, and [paid] public holidays, was just something that they couldn't get their brain around.[14]

In the view of these companies, and the employers' organisation that represented them, unions seeking to improve pay and conditions were to be fought at all costs, and if that meant beating them around the head in the courts, so be it.

Accustomed to the more cooperative relations between employers, employees, and unions that prevailed in Northern Europe, Dusseldorp was taken aback by Monk's grim prognosis. 'It was an eye-opener for me,' Dusseldorp says, 'because nobody had told me that before. So then I explained to him how we handled such things in Holland.'[15]

For many years the Netherlands had enjoyed relative industrial peace—with the occasional blip[16]—thanks in large part to the social compact that had developed within and between unions, employers, and the government. As a respected observer of Dutch industrial relations describes it, by the late 1920s 'the three parties seemed to have reached an understanding that bipartite and tripartite cooperation was preferable to industrial conflict, that it best served the national interest, and that it should preferably be implemented through a hierarchical structure of consultative boards and councils at every level of the economy'.[17] This willingness to cooperate 'for the mutual furtherance of public and private interests'[18] was proving central to the country's successful fight to rebuild its economy after the tremendous devastation wrought upon it by World War II. Industry by industry, employers and unions were moderating wage and price increases to keep inflation in check; meanwhile the government was doing its bit by liberalising trade and improving the social wage (funding universal health care, old-age pensions, unemployment benefits, and the like).[19] Echoing a long history of the Dutch banding together to fight common enemies[20]—invading Vikings, inundating oceans, occupying Nazis, or now the threat of postwar recession—the cooperative pact was already proving its worth.

After listening intently to Dusseldorp's characterisation of Dutch-style industrial cooperation, Monk gave a wan smile. 'Well you'd never get that here, in this country,' he said.[21] It was not that the idea didn't appeal to him—indeed, Monk had been advocating such a consensual approach to industrial relations and economic management for some time—but his experience to date had left him deeply sceptical. It seemed there simply was not sufficient trust or goodwill on either side of the industrial divide to make such cooperation viable: *especially* not in the construction industry. But Dusseldorp begged to differ. 'People are the same all over the world,' he maintained. '[They] react the same if you try to put one over them; if you do the right thing, they react the same also.'[22] Militant unions are usually that way for good reason—'unhappy experiences have taught them to be wary of management'—but if he could convince them he was 'fair dinkum', surely they would 'respond to a fair go'?[23] Monk remained unconvinced. 'And that was really the challenge', Dusseldorp remembers.[24] The Dutchman determined then and there to prove Monk wrong.

━━◂

If anything since the war has changed in character more than the population of Australia, it is the sky-line of the cities. And it seems appropriate that our newly cosmopolitan communities are receiving their most striking face-lift from a New

Australian with steam-shovel and concrete-mixer, a Dutchman named
G. J. Dusseldorp. At present directing [$30 million]-worth of construction, ranging
from the tallest residential block in Australia to the most remarkable opera house
in the world, this newcomer to the local scene has not only revolutionised our
current approach to the techniques and financing of building, but has managed,
somehow, to create an almost mystical *rapport* with that pillar of pre-stressed
independence, the Australian worker.[25]

Some five years before receiving this enthusiastic rap in a 1961 edition of
The Bulletin, that 'New Australian with steam-shovel and concrete-mixer' had
been making his way to a stop-work meeting on the site of his company's first
commercial high-rise, Caltex House. Crossing the Harbour Bridge from Civil
& Civic's headquarters in North Sydney, Dusseldorp was thinking about how
much the Caltex House project meant to him. Far and away the biggest job that
Civil & Civic had undertaken to date, it would be a test for the company on a
whole range of dimensions. For one, it would break new technological ground.
Unlike its contemporaries, which were made of structural steel, Caltex House
would be Australia's first concrete-framed office building;[26] it would also be the
first building in the country to make such extensive use of the new flat plate
method of construction.[27] And as the country's tallest building, and one of
Sydney's first skyscrapers, its construction was bound to attract the media
spotlight: which could be both blessing and curse for the new kid on the block.

Then there was the unique method of financing the project to consider. For
this was no conventional tender job, commissioned by a client and financed by
its retained profits or bank loans. Instead, Dusseldorp had been called in to
rescue the project when the Melbourne businessman who had initiated it as a
speculative venture ran out of funds between the design and construction
phases. Dusseldorp was interested in getting involved, but not as a mere
participant: he insisted that Civil & Civic become 'the sole entrepreneur', and
have 'total control' of the land, the plans, and the building.[28] And so the deal
had been done. Having managed to inveigle from his sceptical Dutch parent
company enough money to buy the land and start site preparations, Dusseldorp
had then managed to convince Australia's largest life office, the Australian
Mutual Provident Society (AMP), to make one of its first investments in non-
owner-occupied property[29] by buying the then-unbranded building off-the-plan.
The AMP was nervous, and had only agreed to come into the project on one

proviso: that Dusseldorp find a Triple A-rated tenant to let the building on a 40-year head lease, with a guaranteed return of 6.25 per cent per annum![30] This he had managed to do—again, not without some drama—in the shape of the multinational petroleum company, Caltex Oil, which was looking for new Sydney headquarters for its Australian operations. It was a brilliantly stitched-together deal; but if any party faltered, the whole thing could unravel, and with it Dusseldorp's and Civil & Civic's reputation.

The one most likely to falter was Caltex, and the reason for it was industrial relations. From the start the top men at Caltex in New York had been nervous about the likelihood of their new Sydney building being completed on time and within budget, having had terrible industrial trouble of their own while constructing oil-refining facilities on the city's Kurnell peninsula. As Dusseldorp remembers:

> They had just completed the Kurnell Refinery and they had been given hell by the unions ... [they'd had] tremendous cost over-runs and delays ... And I had to fight for this Caltex [House] deal over in New York where they were fully aware of the situation, and very worried that this would affect the building ... In the end we got them to commit ... but it was then that the main agitator from the Kurnell Refinery was transplanted onto the new Caltex [House] job, and they thought they were going to do the same thing there.[31]

Dusseldorp knew he had to act swiftly and decisively to allay Caltex's fears if he was to keep them in the deal. But what should he do and how should he do it? For in fact Caltex House represented yet another first for Civil & Civic. Since Dusseldorp had met with Albert Monk some six years earlier, all the company's construction jobs had been located in either country New South Wales, suburban Sydney, or the nascent national capital in Canberra. While it had had contact with the building unions in all of these places, Caltex House would be the first time the company had engaged with them on their home turf and traditional stronghold in central Sydney. If the *Sydney Morning Herald*'s assessment of the 'doleful plight' of the city's construction industry was any guide, it promised to be a whole new ball game. With so much at stake on every front—technical, marketing, financial, and industrial—Dusseldorp was deter-mined to ensure Caltex House got off to a good start. If the workers or their unions had gripes, then he wanted to hear about them: up-front, in full, and *before* they went on strike. Which is why, that day in late 1956, Dusseldorp was on his way to the site.

———

Also on his way to Caltex House that day was the recently elected Secretary of the Building Workers' Industrial Union (NSW Branch): Pat Clancy. Having joined the union while working as a bricklayer in the Port Kembla steelworks during the war, Clancy had been elected its South Coast District Secretary in 1943, 'the same year he'd joined the then illegal Communist Party'.[32] His subsequent rise through union ranks, culminating in election as State Secretary of the BWIU in 1954, had been duly noted by Australia's main internal spy agency, the Australian Security Intelligence Organisation (ASIO). In the heyday of Cold War paranoia, ASIO kept a close watch on Clancy and his Communist ilk, convinced they were 'subversive militants' who posed a threat to Australia's national security.[33] With his active involvement in the party, his recent trip to China, and his swift trajectory through the ranks of the militant BWIU, this 'young and energetic'[34] union official looked like trouble to the spies.

If nothing else, ASIO was right about Clancy's energy levels. According to a close union colleague, Clancy was no armchair official: he liked to '[get] out among the blokes, to deal with disputes and discuss union policy and questions'.[35] So it was not surprising to see him making his way to the construction site at Caltex House that day. What *was* surprising was that he was going there at the invitation of the boss. A few days earlier, Dusseldorp had been on the phone to introduce himself to the labour leader. With the Dutch accent coming down the line, Clancy at first must have thought that he had heard wrong. 'Pat, we're going to be in this business a bit, perhaps forever,' Dusseldorp had said. 'What about coming and having a talk about the relationship we should have between the union and ourselves in the future?' 'Yeah, all right,' came the reply from union headquarters at Trades Hall. 'My office or your office?' 'No,' said Dusseldorp. 'Come to the site and we'll talk in front of the men.'[36]

When the two big guns arrived at Caltex House that day, the entire workforce—some hundred or so men—had already assembled to meet them. Word had gone out early that morning: a big union stop-work was on, Clancy was on his way, and the boss was going to be there too. 'Which boss?' some of the workers asked. 'Dusseldorp himself' came the reply. This caused a bit of stir—most building industry executives wouldn't be seen dead on the same platform as the unions,[37] as Albert Ricci, a builders labourer working on Caltex House at the time, recalls. ' "What's the boss doing coming to address the union meeting?" we all wondered', he laughs as he remembers their surprise. 'Anyway, we decided that we had *all* better go along to the meeting that day to find out!'[38] By the time Dusseldorp and Clancy arrived, there was an air of expectation amongst the gathered crowd. Necks were craning from the back rows to confirm that the boss himself had really turned up on site. Yes, it was true: there was no chance of mistaking the 'tall, ruggedly handsome' Dutchman[39] or the equally recognisable Clancy. The two men sat down and the talks began. They would last for most of the day.

'The big issue for the men at the time was job security,' Ern Mac Donald, later Chairman of Civil & Civic, recalls, 'because conditions in the building industry at the time and on that front were pretty rough.'[40] Most labour hire in the private construction sector was on an hourly basis, giving employers the power to sack a worker virtually on the spot.[41] Dusseldorp was appalled when he heard the workers at Caltex House talk about their own experiences at the receiving end of this management 'right'.

> It was [there] that I learned that an employer could sack a man with an hour's notice: *one lousy hour's notice*. And in practice, they [management] would be cowards ... They didn't give the notice [in person], they'd just add an hour to the pay of the man at the end of the day. 'Don't bother coming back tomorrow', the worker would be told as he got his pay ... Well, I just thought that was the absolute bloody pits.[42]

Even for those who avoided this particular indignity, a job in the on-site construction industry in the 1950s meant very little security of tenure. It is still the case today that building workers (and particularly labourers) have shorter jobs, and more frequent job changes, than do workers in other industries.[43] Building projects are one-offs: when the building is finished, the on-site worker's job also comes to an end. Especially in times of recession, the time between the end of one project and the start of the next can be long, straining the financial and emotional resources of building workers and their families. In theory, workers were compensated for periods of unemployment between jobs through a loading in their hourly rate of pay,[44] but whether this was sufficient to cover the financial (let alone psychological) costs is a moot point. Meanwhile, there was no compensation at all for some of the other side-effects of the discontinuous nature of their employment. 'At that time there was no payment for public holidays, no sick pay, certainly very few building workers—maybe 0.01 per cent—ever achieved the possibilities of accruing long-service leave,' Stan Sharkey of the BWIU remembers. 'And of course, if anyone at that time had have suggested that building workers should get superannuation they'd be deemed to be mental.'[45]

Little wonder, then, that when Dusseldorp asked the men at Caltex House what their greatest concerns were, these issues were at the top of the list. 'Their greatest concern was job security,' Jack Klompe, Dusseldorp's second-in-command, remembers.

> 'We are engaged on a particular construction job,' they said, 'but as soon as that job is finished, we get the sack.' And then they'd have to look again for another job—and that might take one week or it may take five weeks. The second big thing was wages—in those days the rates of pay were very low relative to the cost of living—and the third was safety.[46]

Building and construction work had never been safe—'deaths were frequent, serious injury relatively common and other occupational hazards such as noise, dust, and constant exposure to the elements ever present'[47]—but the advent of high-rise construction was making this situation worse. As the multi-storey office blocks scaled new heights, the construction industry soon overtook metals manufacturing as the most dangerous one in which to work in New South Wales, with the number of compensated injuries almost doubling over the 1950s.[48]

From that moment on, Klompe says, the issues raised by the Caltex House workers would also top the list of Dusseldorp's greatest concerns.[49] Monk had warned him about the industry's terrible labour relations all those years ago, and now, he figured, he had found the root cause of the problem. 'I submit that each industry has the labour relations it deserves,' Dusseldorp would tell an audience at the Australian Institute of Management not long after those talks at Caltex House.

> The construction industry is no exception. What does it offer its workers? Extreme job insecurity. ... Only the wharf-labourers are worse off in this respect. It offers hazardous and dirty occupations; exposure to all weather conditions; award rates interpreted as the maximum rates payable unless the law of supply and demand forces over-award payments.

Meanwhile management—'in the full view of all workers'—was busy generating 'substantial waste' on most construction sites by making frequent, unplanned structural alterations to buildings mid-stream. 'Often these things happen just when the workers are asking some amenity or wage adjustment. The men are told that the industry can't afford the concession they ask—but they see many times its value squandered on alterations which would never have been necessary with proper planning.'[50] It was little wonder workers and their unions were discontented, and little wonder that productivity was ebbing towards an all-time low. Changes were needed in the way the industry worked, and Dusseldorp was determined to be the one to make them.

The talks that began that day between Dusseldorp, Clancy, and the Caltex House workforce marked the start of a new relationship—one that would continue for decades after that particular project was complete. 'When we heard him [Dusseldorp] talking at the meeting,' Albert Ricci remembers, 'you could see that this was not an ordinary man. This is somebody more than that: he was thirty or forty or fifty years ahead of his time ... And from that time on, *even the union* started to realise that there was a lot in what he said, that it made sense.'[51] Indeed, when Caltex House was completed in October 1957—three months ahead of schedule[52]—the State Secretary of Ricci's union, writing in the *Builders Labourers' Journal*, would declare it a real 'step forward' for his members and the industry as a whole. Not only did the job give workers experience in 'the modern trend of construction', 'Banjo' Patterson wrote:

It also shows that the building workers' productivity is of a higher level where there is harmony between the employer and employee, such as was the case on this project. Strange as it may seem, it gives the men a feeling of pleasure that they have been able to play their part in bringing to completion such a fine example of modern construction as Caltex House, and for once in the history of the Building Unions in this State, they have the knowledge that their value has been recognised. We had a few industrial disputes in the early stages of erection, but as the job settled down these differences cleaned themselves up. Our Federation takes this opportunity to state through our delegate on the job, that at all times the management was prepared to meet him and discuss the day-to-day problems which occurred. The federation is looking forward to other projects that the firm of Civil & Civic will undertake, knowing that this firm's approach to the relationship between Unions and Management will lead to better understanding in the building industry.[53]

The Australian Manager, too, was full of praise for the goings-on at Caltex House. By completing a building ahead of schedule in the strife-torn construction industry Dusseldorp's firm had 'achieved ... the almost impossible'.[54]

Others, however, were less enthusiastic about the Dutchman's approach. To his competitors in the construction industry, Dusseldorp was a spoiler: while the Master Builders' Association was busy fighting the unions in the courts, he had broken employer ranks by dealing with them direct, no doubt making many 'concessions' to their claims. 'Of course it is possible to buy industrial peace,' unnamed 'rival master builders' told the *Sydney Morning Herald*, 'and that is what Civil & Civic does.'[55] This comment, oft-repeated over the years, reflected, amongst other things, the stark difference between Dusseldorp's attitude to wages and labour, and that of many of his peers. 'We follow the principle of paying our people as much as we can afford,' he would say, 'rather than as little as we can get away with.'[56] But Civil & Civic would get their comeuppance in the end, the company's rivals were sure, if past experience was any guide. 'We have had experienced foreign firms coming here before this, completing their jobs, and then tiring of Australia and fading away. They stay long enough to upset the labour market.'[57] No doubt this impudent newcomer would go the way of his predecessors: increasing labour costs would price his firm out of business.

As usual, Dusseldorp begged to differ. 'The trouble in the Australian construction industry', he argued, 'is that management regards wages simply as another building cost, like materials. [But] to the men, wages are income. The two points of view are opposites, but they must be reconciled.'[58] And there *was* a way of reconciling them, he maintained. By sharing the benefits of increased productivity, employees could get higher incomes, and employers lower unit costs; clients too would benefit, by getting their buildings completed on time.[59] The key was to strike an agreement between the parties as to how this could be achieved. With unions in the industry vehemently opposed to any kind of 'productivity incentive pact', the master builders were adamant that such a thing 'could not be done'.[60] Little did they know that Dusseldorp had, in fact, been laying the groundwork for just such an agreement since he had first arrived in the country. It had not been easy, but the goodwill and trust established at Caltex House convinced him that it might just be possible. As it transpired, he was proved right within the year.

Bredero's Building Company of Utrecht, the large construction company that Dusseldorp had joined after the war, enjoyed, like many of its Dutch counterparts, a good relationship with its employees and their unions.[61] 'In the building industry as elsewhere', its Managing Director declared, 'one can hardly devote too much attention to the human factor.'[62] According with his own beliefs, Dusseldorp had brought this philosophy with him when, in 1951, he set up the Dutch company's Australian subsidiary, Civil & Civic Contractors Pty Ltd, having won the firm its first contract building workers' houses on the Snowy Mountains Hydro-Electric Scheme. With Australia experiencing a severe post-war shortage of skilled labour and materials, the company had been required to import everything it might need for this particular construction task: not only the pre-cut timber, the bricks, the pipes, and the wires, but also the carpenters, the bricklayers, the plumbers and the electricians to assemble them![63] And with rapid completion of construction contracts high on the agenda of Bill Hudson, the man responsible for the Snowy Scheme as a whole, Dusseldorp had wasted little time in importing another Dutch practice: a system of individual incentive payments aimed at boosting labour productivity.

Back in Holland, Bredero's had operated a similar scheme, 'in close co-operation with the unions', to which the company's employees were 'favourably disposed' because it 'brought them wages above the average'.[64] Dusseldorp himself had been pivotal in bringing that scheme about, as he later recounted to Australian industrial relations expert Patricia Huntley.

Before coming to Australia from Holland [he told her], I was in charge of several thousand workers on some 20 different building sites … At that time (just after the war), it was a criminal offence if any employer paid more than the prescribed wage. Rather than just acceping this situation … I sought a way to demonstrate to the Government that they would get better productivity from workers if they paid more … After a lot of argument, the Government finally agreed to give me a six-month trial. They hired a team of management consultants with stop watches to stand around the sites and watch and time the workforce. The unions really hated these stop watches. So did I. But it was a means to an end and, as I explained to the unions, we had a common enemy—the Government. But to defeat them, we needed the scientific people to provide us with the data to break down these stupid laws. We succeeded and productivity bargaining became an industry norm.[65]

The new scheme had proved itself a classic win-win arrangement at Bredero's: not only did employees get higher incomes, but the company's unit labour costs could actually be lowered through increases in productivity.[66] But Dusseldorp soon found it was another story in Australia. Although his predominantly Dutch workforce were keen to introduce the incentive scheme to their new country, the officials of the Australian unions of which they were members quickly made known their opposition. With his workforce onside, Dusseldorp initially pressed ahead with the arrangement. But as more local workers were hired by Civil & Civic, and as the company's operations spread to Canberra—where the union officials held more sway—Dusseldorp found that 'trade union criticism of the payment by results scheme began to have more influence on the workers' attitudes'.[67]

His first instinct was to try and talk the Canberra unions round to his point of view: to 'persuade them that the [incentive payments] scheme held no "traps" or "catches"'.[68] Many joint management–union conferences were held to this end, but during the talks, an interesting thing began to happen. Dusseldorp and his management team, he says, 'became increasingly conscious of the fact that [we] had no satisfactory answer to several questions which the unions persistently put to [us]'.[69] 'What happens to the older man, who may have more family responsibilities?' the unions asked.[70] And 'what is to become of the apprentice?'[71] 'What of the partly incapacitated man? If every firm introduced such a scheme, and employed only the fittest and most productive workers, what would happen to the rest?'[72] Half the working population, the unions feared, could well end up 'on the scrap heap'.[73] Other companies might have countered that such problems were not *their* responsibility, but that was not Dusseldorp's way. Not only had the unions raised 'vital questions' to which he had no answer, but, through a process of observation and research, he had come to the view that individual incentive payments might not be the best way to encourage productivity anyway. 'A new approach was necessary', he realised, but exactly what form should it take?[74]

Dusseldorp would later liken his approach to this problem to the decision process leading to the purchase of an expensive new machine. 'Any capital investment takes considerable study and planning,' he would say. 'Errors in judgement cannot be easily rectified [and so] the installation requires care.'[75] He let the issue lie for a while following the talks with the unions in Canberra, to give both parties time to reflect. But once Caltex House was complete—its success in no small part due to the cooperative relationship that had been established with the unions on the job—Dusseldorp decided it was time to revive discussions on the productivity incentive issue. Besides, he had a new proposal to put to them, one that he believed could, amongst other things, answer the vital equity questions raised by their Canberra counterparts. The proposal was this: management and unions would get together and agree how *both* parties could increase productivity on the company's projects. The resulting savings would then be shared between them—one-third to the company, two-thirds to the workers—with the latter receiving their share as a flat-rate amount on top of their normal wages. Instead of differentiating between workers on the basis of their individual output, 'everyone [would] share [the productivity] benefits equally'.[76] In this *collective* approach to productivity and incentives, it soon became apparent, Dusseldorp had found the winning formula.

━━━━

'Building unions in incentive pact with big company' reported the *Sydney Morning Herald*.[77] 'New agreement makes history in building' proclaimed the *Management News*.[78] After many months of discussion and negotiation, in October 1958 Civil & Civic and the nine unions forming the Building Trades Group of the New South Wales Labour Council signed a remarkable document. (The latter's counterparts in Canberra would sign a similar one before the year was out.) The nine-page productivity agreement—the first ever that these unions had been willing to put their names to[79]—committed both parties 'to make every effort to bring about [an] increase in productivity' on Civil & Civic's sites, detailed their respective responsibilities, and spelt out how the resulting benefits would be shared between the workers and the company.[80] 'It was light years ahead of the rest of the industry,' says Civil & Civic's Ern Mac Donald.[81] Stan Sharkey, Pat Clancy's successor at the BWIU, agrees.

> That first Civil & Civic agreement was a real groundbreaker. It gave the building workers ... benefits which were unheard of—unknown—in the building industry generally... It didn't win Dusseldorp many friends amongst the Master Builders' Association—and that in itself says a lot for the man, in my opinion—he was thirty years in front of his time.[82]

Even today, more than four decades later, the agreement still looks revolutionary. The first thing it sets out is what the *company* will do to improve productivity at work: a stark contrast with traditional analyses that concentrate (often exclusively) on how *workers* should lift their game. For its part, Civil & Civic would 'continually strive to improve the planning and organisation of work', introduce and maintain the best available plant, introduce better methods of construction, and 'improve the ability of managers and foremen by careful selection of new appointees [and] by training of existing staff'.[83] Safety committees would be set up on each project, the company would make every effort to remove hazards from sites and to reduce the number of accidents, and it would provide 24-hour sickness and accident insurance for all employees. The company would also 'endeavour to maintain steady employment' for its employees (all of whom would be union members) and, except for those specifically engaged as casuals, each new worker would be guaranteed a minimum of three months' continuous employment.[84]

Meanwhile, the unions agreed to 'use every means available to them' to encourage their members to increase productivity.[85] Workers would be expected to take a positive approach to their work, increase their output, adopt better methods of work and standards of workmanship, reduce absenteeism, eliminate avoidable material waste, and take better care of equipment and finished work. Every effort would be made to keep the company's sites dispute-free, with the unions promising to discuss any problems with the company before resorting to strikes or bans; a disputes procedure was also put in place to handle those issues that could not be resolved in the normal way. Communication channels between management, unions, and the employees' elected representatives would always be kept open, and weekly site meetings held where any party could put forward proposals for discussion.

With everyone sticking to their side of the bargain, the resulting 'productivity savings' would be shared, with workers receiving their two-thirds' worth through payment of a flat-rate weekly allowance on top of their normal wages. At 90 cents a day (at a time when the base daily rate for a builders labourer was $6.25),[86] the allowance was far from chickenfeed. 'In fact a lot of other builders said we'd go broke paying it,' Ern Mac Donald remembers. 'And we *did* pay it—even if [the workers] hadn't strictly earned it on the theoretical way you were supposed to work it out—because we got so much out of it in terms of goodwill.'[87] The extra money in the pay packet was certainly appreciated by the workers, as Peter Ciacciarelli, who started with the company as a rigger the year the productivity allowance was introduced, remembers.

A lot of us were migrants, and we were all short of money: trying to settle and get married and buy property. When they started making a profit, [Dusseldorp] gave us the productivity allowance, and he started to share profits. We never asked for that: that was his own doing, to offer that to us. No one would have thought of asking for it at that time. But he said: 'If you boys are loyal to me, I'll be loyal to all of you'. And that always impressed us.[88]

Our expectations from the Agreement are of a long-term nature. We want to develop our Company on a sound, lasting basis rather than on opportunity business of the 'hit and run' type. This can only be done by recognition of staff and workers as human beings rather than production tools. Apart from making our short stay on this earth more significant, it also pays—both ways.[89]

Dusseldorp regarded the 1958 productivity agreement as a long-term invest-ment: having researched it, planned it, and carefully installed it, there was no point in scrapping it if at first it did not run smoothly or yield an immediate return. Maintenance was 'all important', he reminded an audience at the

Industrial Relations Society who had gathered to hear about the historic agree-ment, and 'all operators [would] have to be trained in using the new machine'. 'Many will oppose it,' he predicted (rightly: there were representatives of a few rival building firms in that audience, and one in particular thought that the agreement set a very dangerous precedent), 'but if in time the machine proves itself, many will install one of their own.'[90] (Just for the record, they did not, at least not in the construction industry. Most other building firms were happy to stick with 'the old-style', belligerent approach to industrial relations. 'They were totally opposite to us,' says Civil & Civic's Ern Mac Donald. 'They were knock-down, drag-out, fight-cat-and-dog types ... and they were always in the [Arbitration] Commission, whereas we ... just had a different ethic ... a different way of doing things.)[91]

Despite Dusseldorp's longer-term view of the benefits to be had from the productivity agreement, it soon yielded short-term results as well. Within the year he would be able to report that 'the atmosphere on all our jobs has been free of irritation and petty disputes', and that 'this response by the workers has given us the courage to embark on a larger volume of business than would otherwise have been advisable'.[92] Pat Clancy, who signed the agreement on behalf of the NSW Branch of the BWIU, agreed. Although the unions were initially sceptical, he said, before long the advantages of the agreement for all 'sides' were clear: 'employer–employee relations developed, ... disputes were able to be overcome by consultation, and the job conditions were changed. The result was that Civil & Civic were able to tell their clients the finishing date of a building and stick to it, which in the building industry is a very big advantage.'[93] Banjo Patterson from the BLF (who worked as a scaffolder on many Civil & Civic projects) was just as impressed. Not only did the agreement give employee–employer relations a 'shot in the arm', but it also provided workers with 'a really genuine incentive to give of their best and to work for further improvement in the joint benefit of themselves and the Company'.[94] And in the national capital, where the agreement's antecedent had an initially rocky reception, the President of the local Trades and Labour Council described it as 'one of the biggest steps forward ever undertaken in Canberra'. He, for one, hoped that 'other firms would adopt the practice'.[95]

It was no surprise, then, that when the initial productivity agreement had run its one-year course, the company, the workers, and their unions were all keen for it to be renewed. For the next thirteen years, aside from updating the allowances, modifying some of the clauses, and including a few new matters, the productivity agreement between Civil & Civic and the building trades unions emerged from each annual renegotiation with its basic format intact and its underlying spirit unchanged. As a result, while the construction industry as a whole sank further into industrial relations malaise—the early 1960s in particular were a period of '*intense* disputation'[96]—Civil & Civic enjoyed a level of industrial harmony unmatched by its peers. Although there was an occasional 'blue' on the company's jobs, the matters in dispute were usually sorted out quickly. 'That was the key to their success,' Stan Sharkey recalls.

> They set out to avoid unnecessary industrial action, and they did. They solved any
> problems by negotiation, and by recognition—that was the big difference between
> them and the mainstream builders and developers—there was a *recognition* that
> labour provided a most important ingredient to profit-making. And a recognition
> that workers have a pride in their productive labour and in the skill they carry
> forward.[97]

This same spirit was expressed through the range of employee programs that Dusseldorp pioneered in Civil & Civic in this era. In 1963, more than twenty years before the rest of the industry, superannuation was introduced for the company's on-site workforce: 'as a *right*, not a *ploy* to retain employees'.[98] Other companies may have had retirement income plans in place for their managers, and some for their staff (Civil & Civic had had a policy covering both groups since 1956), but, as we have seen, one union official graphically stated that, at the time anyone who suggested that on-site building workers should get such benefits would have 'been deemed to be mental'! Later, Dusseldorp would use the superannuation scheme as the vehicle for yet another industry first, when he issued shares in Civil & Civic's publicly listed parent company, Lend Lease,[99] to his blue-collar workforce (of which more below).

The company also introduced a range of measures to improve working conditions on site—'they pioneered things like high safety standards and good amenities that mean so much to the man on the job'[100]—sorely needed in an industry where the work was dirty, dangerous, and hard. 'When I first started in major construction in the 1950s,' remembers Joe Purcell, who joined Civil &

Civic in 1958 and worked there for the next thirty years, 'there were no toilet facilities, there were no wash facilities, never a tap on the site. You used to have to put a nail on the wall to hang your clothes up, and go to the nearest hotel to go to the toilet.'[101] Such conditions (or lack thereof) were grist to the unions' mill, as Stan Sharkey of the BWIU recalls.

> I worked as a CBD organiser in the 1960s and, as an old Marxist, I used to think, when I walked onto a job, … if there were no amenities, no toilets, etcetera—and that was regular, by the way – … I used to think, 'Beaut. This will be an easy job to organise', because the employer is treating people in such a way—without dignity, without feeling—that it was much easier to get a delegate elected, and to get a militant approach on the job. When I went onto a job like that, I thought, 'Well, *my* job is halved'. But you'd go on to a Civil & Civic site and everything would be there: a first aid station, a proper tea room, a separate change room to the eating room, and all that. It was so different, it was great.[102]

Safety was another personal priority for Dusseldorp, given the industry's high and rising fatality and injury rates, especially with the advent of multi-storey construction:

> It was terrible, the industry's record was horrible. And I couldn't handle that—wouldn't have it—the thought of widows coming and crying on my shoulder [he shudders as he contemplates the prospect]. I knew the problem had to be tackled at source, it had to come from the men in charge. So at Caltex House we got the foremen together and really read the riot act at them. Rather than run a 'safety campaign', as people seemed dulled by that, we were going to have a 'danger campaign'. They were going to *frighten* people into working safely! And that was quite effective.[103]

Later, as part of the 1958 productivity agreement, bi-partite safety committees were set up on each Civil & Civic project; roving safety officers were also appointed to identify potential hazards on each site and report any remotely dangerous incidents directly to senior management.[104] 'The idea was to make everyone—and especially the foremen—more safety conscious.'[105]

Skills formation was another big priority for the firm. From the beginning, Dusseldorp made a major investment in providing skills development opportunities for the company's employees, both at entry level and throughout their careers. 'They [Civil & Civic] were clearly, for many years, the leader in the Sydney metropolitan area in terms of employment of apprentices,' Stan Sharkey remembers.[106] 'And they put the apprentices right through,' says Joe Purcell. 'They really thought that if they trained the kids they'd have their managers, even their directors.'[107] It was a similar story with the professions. Eric Goodwin, today Lend Lease's Group Executive, tells how he started with Civil & Civic in 1963 as a cadet civil engineer.

> I started what in those days we called a 'traineeship': they took me on as an undergraduate and put me through university part-time. The economy was in a recession then, and there was a dramatic downsizing of our staff within probably six months of me starting, but they kept me on. That was fairly common with the way the company operated. Duss was always one to try to ensure that you've got the resources for the future as opposed to just making cuts to satisfy the short-term bottom line.[108]

The learning didn't stop once you were in. The commitment to staff development was such, according to Graham Taylor—who was 'brought up' in Civil & Civic and now runs another building firm—that the company was 'regarded as the university of the construction industry'.[109] Employees at all levels were encouraged to acquire 'new knowledge relevant to [their] current or future position' based on their own assessment of their needs.[110] Such self-initiated skills development was complemented by in-house training programs designed either to provide specific skills or to 'broaden knowledge'[111] in line with the company's assessment of requirements. These custom-designed programs bolstered a whole-of-company approach to skills development in areas such as Professional Management and Marketing. '*Everybody* in the company eventually went through those two particular programs,' Project Engineer-cum-Marketing Director David Thorne remembers, 'be they in management, on-site, or in the office, because everyone in the company had a part to play.'[112]

The skills learned on the marketing program, for example, were put to good use. 'When potential clients were shown over a project under construction'—Australia Square was a popular choice—'it wasn't only the so-called marketing people involved,' says Thorne. 'It was the foremen and engineers and all of the technical people, finance people ... all involved in telling them [potential clients] why what was going on at the site was better than anything else in town.'[113] And coming as it did from the troops, Thorne adds, the spiel had much greater force than a sales pitch delivered by a conventional marketing manager. Beyond their direct functionality, such training programs seem to have acted as a kind of corporate cultural glue. Speaking of the Professional Management Program, first run in the early 1960s, methods engineer Alan Cull says: '[It] was what really *integrated* the company, because it gave us a common under-standing of the management process, and a common language ... The culture started with Duss, but this [management training] really cemented it, developed it, and gave a language basis for it.'[114]

Early on, Dusseldorp started another tradition that is still part of Lend Lease culture today: providing twice-yearly briefing sessions for all employees about the state of the company's health. Styled 'State of the Nation' addresses, these began in the 1950s, according to Dusseldorp's successor Stuart Hornery, 'just in a single room, with Dick and a small number of employees'.[115] 'It was a great idea', says Ern Mac Donald. 'At the close of business on the day that the company's financial results were due to be lodged with the Stock Exchange, Duss would get up on the chair and tell the people what those results were.'[116] He would also outline what he saw as priorities for the company in the months ahead, and encourage employees to ask questions. With the advent of new communications technology, the reach and sophistication of these 'State of the Nation' sessions improved—from 'tenuous land-line' connections to some of the states in the 1960s, to national satellite link-ups by the 1980s[117]—but the invitation list remained the same. *Everyone* in the company was asked to come to the briefings—be they 'staff from 45th level administration in Australia Square Tower [or] excavation workers from the newest construction site'[118]— and the great majority (upwards of 75 per cent)[119] would attend.

'Communication was always Duss' long suit', Ern Mac Donald says.[120] As well as the 'State of the Nation' sessions, an internal company newsletter called the *Link* was started in the late 1950s, to keep people in touch as the firm's geographic reach extended. Dusseldorp would also personally visit the construction sites as often as he could. 'He'd go round to all the sites and talk to the men', says Mac Donald. 'He was very popular. All the old-timers knew him. I remember one Christmas Banjo Patterson—a big, strong, rough bloke, ex-soldier, ex-Secretary of the BLF in NSW—jumped up on the table and led the blokes in "three cheers for Dickey Dusseldorp!"'[121] A reporter from *The*

Bulletin who accompanied Dusseldorp on a round of site visits in the early 1960s—and witnessed one of Patterson's toasts to the boss—would be struck by 'the almost mystical *rapport*' that the Dutchman seemed to have with his workforce.[122] On these site visits, Dusseldorp would make a special point of catching up with workers who had joined the company in the early days. Frank Cuzzocrea, who started with Civil & Civic as a scaffold rigger on Caltex House, remembers one such occasion. He was working on construction of Sydney's Regent Hotel in the early 1980s when Dusseldorp turned up and invited all the old hands from Caltex House to dinner on the top floor of Australia Square. 'That dinner,' says Cuzzocrea, 'that was a really extra bonus for *anyone* at that time. Because by that stage he was so busy, you hardly could see him. To invite us for dinner, we never expected that, that was a really big deal!'[123]

Loyalty to the firm was something that Dusseldorp always valued and encouraged, and it cut both ways. 'I still meet people that I know from Caltex House days,' says Jack Klompe, who himself came out to Australia with Dusseldorp in 1951 and retired from Lend Lease in 1990. 'They've retired now, of course, but they'd worked with Civil & Civic until the day they retired. And because we were loyal to them, they were very loyal in turn ... and they would do a good job for us.'[124] Such bonds were quite unusual in the building industry, where the insecurity of tenure, especially amongst on-site labourers, meant workers 'had few loyalties to their employer.'[125] According to the authors of a major work on the Builders Labourers' Federation, building workers 'were far more likely to be devoted to their unions precisely *because* of job insecurity: while their employers changed continually, they always belonged to the same union.'[126]

Unlike their industry counterparts, who made much greater use of sub-contractors on their sites, for many years Civil & Civic retained a relatively large number of permanent employees on its payroll, many of whom stayed with the company for most of their working lives. It was a way of working that fitted the company's desire to 'push the envelope' in construction methods, as Eric Goodwin explains.

With a really innovative job like Australia Square—where we were learning as we went—most of the work was done by our own labour. We couldn't get someone else in to do the job because there wasn't the skill amongst the subcontractors in

those days; that, and they couldn't price it—it was all too new. So we had to put
our money where our mouth was and say, 'Okay, we believe *we* can do it', and
then work through the innovations ourselves. And you could only do that with your
own workforce.[127]

Even when the company started to make greater use of sub-contractors from the
mid-1970s onwards, it still kept on board a core of essential tradespeople and
labourers to deploy on key aspects of construction. As well as developing a
network of preferred sub-contractors and suppliers to ensure project quality did
not suffer as a result of the out-sourcing, Civil & Civic also put in place
measures to ensure sub-contractors met certain standard conditions of employment and to counteract the potentially deleterious impact of sub-contracting on
apprenticeships (see Chapter 4).

The sort of relationship that Dusseldorp established with his workforce was,
characteristically, one that suited both the firm and its employees well. His
treatment of workers with dignity, his refusal to get bogged down in continual
argument about 'elementary workers' rights',[128] and his commitment to
'management by faith, not fear',[129] lifted the company's work, industrial, and
employment relations to a higher plane. 'And that was a big part of how the
company really got going', says Karl Pahl, who joined Civil & Civic as a
carpenter in the early 1960s and went on to become one of its general foremen.

> Civil & Civic as a builder, we had very few bad strikes. Our men just wouldn't do
> it, because they had everything: they had hot and cold showers, dining rooms,
> change sheds. The company looked after their people in every respect. The
> working conditions were very good … And people who were loyal to the company,
> and worked for them, well, they didn't do badly at all when they retired.'[130]

By the end of the 1960s, the predictions of Dusseldorp's rivals that he and his
firm would soon 'tire of Australia and fade away' were looking, as Mark Twain
had earlier described rumours of his death, greatly exaggerated. Civil & Civic
had introduced a range of employee programs and improved pay and conditions
to a level previously unheard of in the Australian construction industry, and yet
the increased labour cost burden still had not driven them under. In fact, with

annual revenues topping $50 million, and profits on a steady upward climb, the company was looking alarmingly healthy! 'Naturally our costs [had] increased,' says Dusseldorp, 'but, despite predictions to the contrary, so [had] our profits.' This phenomenon, he reflected, 'revealed the notion that "caring—*of itself desirable*—also pays" '.[131] But he would soon be forced to ask himself whether such 'caring' was enough. As the 1960s drew to a close, a young man would prick the Dutchman's conscience, asking him a question that would cause Dusseldorp to reflect in much the same way the Canberra unions had some twenty years prior.

Dusseldorp later recounted the experience:

A young graduate ... had studied our latest annual report, [and he] had calculated the income and the profit per employee and figured that the *profit* per employee was in excess of the average income per employee for that year. His question was, 'Did I think that was right?' The question stung! Firstly, because I had never figured profits that way. Secondly, if his figures were correct I could not give an opinion on whether such a division was equitable—never having thought about it.[132]

But think about it he then did. And in doing so, Dusseldorp turned to the reflections of social historian Richard Tawney, in his introduction to a reprint of Max Weber's *The Protestant Ethic and the Spirit of Capitalism*.[133] Writing a couple of years earlier, Tawney had observed that contemporary capitalism was 'cloaked in an aura of inevitability and respectability', yet in its youth it had been 'a pretender', 'for it involved a system of relations that were sharply at variance with venerable conventions'. 'So questionable an innovation [as capitalism]', continued Tawney 'demanded of the pioneer who first experimented with it as much originality, self-confidence and tenacity of purpose as is required today of those who would break from the net that it has woven.'[134]

'The young man's question and this quotation merged in my mind into other questions', remembers Dusseldorp. 'What *is* the something in the net that capitalism has woven that causes so much turmoil in the workplace today, despite its unquestioned contribution to rising standards of living wherever it is practised? Was the profit versus income question putting the spotlight on that *something*?' The more he thought about it, the more convinced Dusseldorp became that lack of employee involvement in the running and rewards of the enterprise was at the heart of that invidious 'something'. It was not *just* a question of caring, he now saw, it was also a question of participation and fairness. History had shown the value of political democracy as the minimum requirement for individual well-being, he believed. 'Could it be that *corporate* democracy [was] a minimum requirement for *economic* well-being as well? Should we be sharing more equitably in addition to caring?' he asked himself. 'I concluded the answer to that question had to be yes.'[135]

'From that time', Dusseldorp says, 'dates the concept of benefit sharing in our group in addition to the caring practised since inception.'[136] In 1972 Dusseldorp struck a new national industrial agreement with Bob Hawke, Albert Monk's successor as President of the ACTU, which issued in a whole new dimension in equitable benefit sharing in Civil & Civic and the Lend Lease group as a whole. With both parties committed to 'foster improved productivity in general', and to stick to their agreed dispute procedures in particular, any distinctions between the social security benefits paid to the company's salaried and waged employees would be eliminated.[137] In addition, a set proportion of the company's pre-tax profits would be placed in a pool, and this would be shared out as a flat dollar amount to all employees: be they chief executive or rigger, secretary or steel fixer, architect or accountant.[138]

The following year, Lend Lease shares were issued to all employees in the corporation, via their superannuation fund, as 'a tangible recognition of the common interests of staff and shareholders in the success of the Company'. Further share issues followed in succeeding years, so that by 1978 employees collectively became the corporation's largest single shareholder.[139] Uniting *all* employees' and the company's interests in this way—decades before most other corporates even twigged to the idea—was a strategy that soon began to (literally) pay dividends. 'Employees … *responded* in a million ways that [were] reflected on the bottom line', says Dusseldorp.[140] At the same time that many other property developers were biting the dust in the spectacular property crash of 1974 (of which more in Chapter 3), the upward track of Lend Lease Corporation's profits hardly missed a beat. 'In retrospect,' he would tell shareholders in his retirement address, 'I believe that the surge in Lend Lease profitability is closely related to the employees awakening to what was going on, and acting on it.'[141]

Coming as it did at a time of industrial relations pandemonium in the rest of the construction industry, the 1972 agreement with the unions was the last straw for Dusseldorp's colleagues in the Master Builders' Association. If Albert Monk had thought industrial relations in the building industry 'terrible' in the 1950s, by the time his 35-year reign at the ACTU came to an end in 1969, they were approaching their nadir. As one journalist put it: 'Industrial relations in the Australian construction industry had traditionally been rough, but in the early 1970s they descended into guerrilla warfare.'[142] When Dusseldorp once again bucked the industry trend, the NSW Master Builders' Association issued him with a notice to 'please explain'. Not only had he rejected the Association's confrontationist *modus operandi*, but he had yet again established a new benchmark in pay and conditions that his competitors were totally unwilling to meet.[143] Rather than 'explain' what Dusseldorp believed to be self-evident common sense, he responded by resigning his company's membership of the association.[144]

But the 1972 agreement—which set the framework for the relationship between the company, its employees, and their unions for many years to come —was better received in other quarters. 'It was ground-breaking', says Bob Hawke, Dusseldorp's co-signatory to the agreement, who would become Prime Minister in the 1980s.[145] To Hawke, the agreement was a typical expression of Dusseldorp's 'enlightened approach' to employee and industrial relations.[146]

> He *genuinely* regarded workers as a unique component of business, compared to some other entrepreneurs who just regard labour as another input along with materials and capital ... And he reflected that, not only in being at the forefront in terms of the formal wages and conditions of employees, but he was imaginative in terms of encouraging training, and encouraging participation from the workforce, and that, to me, was the outstanding characteristic ... [of] the man. He had a broad vision: he wasn't *just* a moneymaker—although he was very good at that too. He created a magnificent enterprise; ... [and] one of the reasons he created such a magnificent enterprise was this broader vision that he had ... He thought that [workers] really were, in a sense, fundamental elements in the creation of wealth, and they were entitled to participate in it.[147]

When, in 1988, Dusseldorp retired as Chairman of Lend Lease, he used his last address to shareholders and employees at the corporation's annual general meeting to outline his vision of the 'dream corporation of the future'. Gazing into his crystal ball, he did not ponder what this creature might look like in terms of future technologies, nor did he try to predict where it might be active in terms of emerging markets. There was no mention in that speech of what he thought might become the next big fad in business strategy, or the most pressing issues to address in future corporate relations. Instead, using the prism of his own experience, Dusseldorp outlined his 'vision of the ultimate corporate democracy that might hopefully evolve sometime in the next century.[148]

Although he considered the material benefits to all stakeholders of the 'caring and sharing' formula that he had pioneered in Lend Lease to be 'the maximum achievable at this point in time', he believed there was still a long way to go:

> My blueprint for a truly democratic corporation of the future would be based on but a few basic principles. I see the future corporation as a joint venture between capital and labour. Management would constitute a third group independent of the others ... the appointment and dismissal of the management [would] be by democratic vote of *all* the participants in the enterprise as [this is] the only realistic way to ensure that attention is paid equally to those parties. Shareholders to have, as now, one vote. Employees to have one vote per person ... The key issue to be voted on would be the election of the members of the Board comprising independent and executive directors, i.e. the Management. A further basic principle would be the equitable sharing of the surplus of the enterprise, enabling employees to experience ownership and the benefits and motivation that comes with it ...[149]

Dusseldorp saw the potential benefits flowing from such an arrangement as enormous, for *all* participants in the enterprise. 'Where is the shareholders' compensation to come from ... you may ask? As in the case of Lend Lease, through reduction in waste from lost time and generally improved productivity through ownership motivation.'[150] But the benefits would also extend beyond the individual enterprise. The fact that 'the prevailing relations between share-holders and employees are heavily loaded against the employees', Dusseldorp argued, '[is] the root cause for the poor performance of Australia as an eco-nomic entity, despite the riches with which it is endowed by nature'. His vision for corporate democracy, he believed, could fix the problem by addressing it at source. His alternative scheme 'would remove the conflict component in the relationship between capital and labour that now prevents their respective contributions to blossom to their fullest potential for the benefit of all.'[151] Albert Monk, if a little sceptical of the chances of its implementation, would no doubt have risen with Lend Lease employees and shareholders to give the retiring Chairman a standing ovation.

CHAPTER 3

Business Development:
A New Approach to
Wealth Creation

That Australia was a long way away from the Northern Hemisphere centres of business and finance was a fact international travellers had much time to contemplate during the four-day plane trip from Sydney to London in the 1950s. Even the relatively direct flight across the Pacific from Australia's east coast to Hawaii took the best part of two days in the pre-jet age. Having completed this leg but a few months earlier, returning to Sydney from Honolulu after attending the Harvard Advanced Management Program, in early 1958 Dusseldorp was once again packing his bags and getting his passport in order. This time he was off to Europe, where a range of business appointments beckoned. But along with the papers and proposals, the suits and the ties, the business shirts and cufflinks, Dusseldorp also tossed a pair of swimming trunks into his travelling bag; for the Dutchman was breaking the long-haul flight with a short stopover in Tahiti, where he planned to visit what many regard as the most beautiful island in the world.

With its turquoise lagoon ringed by a necklace of coral, and lush green volcanic mountains rising up to form the island's backbone, Bora Bora can certainly lay claim to the accolade. Enchanted with its beauty, Dusseldorp would return to the island many times—often sailing there from the home he built in Tahiti in the 1970s—but on this particular trip, as it happened, he had little time to enjoy its pleasures. 'On the way in to Bora Bora,' Dusseldorp remembers, 'I saw this little island that I thought I'd like to take a closer look at.'[1] Tracking down a member of the local aero club, the owner of one of Bora Bora's two single-engine planes, Dusseldorp persuaded the pilot to fly him there. He would stay on the islet for the night, and the plane would return the next day to take him to Papeete, where he could make his connections for Europe. At least that was the plan.

In those days, long before optic fibres connected the countries of the globe, the more populated islands of the Tahitian archipelago were linked by radio telephone: each island was allocated half an hour on the airwaves during which the most urgent of despatches could be conveyed. Having spent the night in his newly discovered paradise, the next day Dusseldorp switched on his radio to listen to the local news. As he recalls,

> So it comes Bora Bora's half hour, and lo and behold [there is a] 'Message for Mr Dusseldorp'. It's from the pilot. 'Sorry', he says. 'Bad weather on Bora Bora. Fog coming soon. Can't come to pick you up as it's too dangerous'. Well, at first I thought, *'Oh no!* I have all these arrangements—plane tickets, airline connections, business meetings to attend—what will I do?'

But as the first grip of anxiety loosened, his frown turned into a smile. Here he was: literally stranded on a tropical island. All he *could* do was swim in the balmy waters, lie on the beach, imbibe the relaxing atmosphere, and engage in a bit of navel-gazing. As it transpired, the unexpected down-time would be spent pro-ductively. For 'it was there', he says, 'that I came up with the idea of Lend Lease'.[2]

'Lend Lease', the name Dusseldorp would bestow on the property financing, development, and investment vehicle that was the fruit of his Tahitian musings, would grow to proportions its founder could hardly have conceived of that day in early 1958. By the time he retired as its Chairman, some thirty years later, Lend Lease Corporation would be a property and financial services giant, with a market capitalisation of $1.4 billion and a virtually uninterrupted record of annual profit growth. (Its 17-year-old sister organisation, the General Property Trust, would also boast a similar market capitalisation and unbroken profit run.) Unlike all but the most steadfast of its competitors, Lend Lease successfully rode out the booms and busts of numerous economic cycles, and earned a reputation as one of the best-managed, prudentially geared, and innovatively financed outfits in the country. And it all had its genesis in a question that the then Managing Director of construction firm Civil & Civic was contemplating as he splashed around in the Pacific that day in 1958. How could he get greater control of his destiny?

It was a question Dusseldorp had been pondering for some time now, and he had already taken the first steps toward answering it. While attending the Harvard management course in Hawaii the previous year, he had become convinced that participation in the traditional tender-based system of construction —with its inbuilt wastefulness, adversarial relationships, protracted delays, and cost over-runs—was 'no way of spending your life'.[3] He resolved then and there to free himself of the tender system's shackles by instead going to clients direct and offering them an *integrated* 'Design & Construct' building service. The benefits to be had from his alternative approach—with its up-front coordination and planning led by a team of design and construction professionals, and its efficient execution by a well-paid and productive workforce—were already on display in the very concrete form of Caltex House. One of Sydney's first skyscrapers, that building had been completed on-budget and three months *ahead* of schedule, a virtually unprecedented achievement on the city's construction scene.

> That project [Dusseldorp reflected as he lay under the Tahitian sun] had lifted us one leg up above the masses. With Design & Construct, the decision node from the architect to the client had been [broken] ... which was the first step towards [property] development, but I wanted to go one step higher. At Caltex House, I still didn't have *control*: I was still dependent on the financier, I had to go begging for the money.[4]

While Dusseldorp had been firmly in charge of the *building* process at Caltex House—he hired the architect and the other design consultants himself (thus turning traditional contractual relationships on their head), and he oversaw construction with his firm's own engineers—someone else was still controlling the purse-strings. Even though he had personally played a crucial role in arranging its financial backing—by bringing together a cash-rich financial institution (Australian life insurer AMP) dipping a tentative toe into the property investment waters, and a blue-chip tenant (multinational petroleum company Caltex Oil) looking for new corporate headquarters—it was the former, the keeper of the money-bags, which not only had the final say on the development, but had also grabbed the lion's share of its profits.[5]

'If I wanted to control my destiny from A to Z,' Dusseldorp realised, 'I knew I needed to get control of the money.'[6] With sufficient capital at its disposal, his

1 Dick, Anne and the five Dusseldorp children arrive in Sydney in March 1951 after a five-day plane trip from Amsterdam.

2 Dusseldorp and Bill Hudson (left), head of the Snowy Mountains Scheme, who gave the Dutchman's firm its first Australian contract.

3 With severe shortages of skilled labour in postwar Australia, the first employees of Dusseldorp's Civil & Civic were all flown in from the Netherlands. Dusseldorp is seventh from the right.

4 The press capture the Premier of New South Wales, J. J. Cahill, signing the contract with Civil & Civic for construction of the first stage of the Sydney Opera House, as Dusseldorp (second from right) looks on.

5 Construction of the first stage of the Sydney Opera House involved building everything under the roof shells. It was a tender job, and although it earned Civil & Civic considerable kudos, the length, cost and frustrations of the project firmed Dusseldorp's resolve to find a better way of managing the building process. Here, work begins on the cleared site (bottom right) in 1959.

6, 7, 8 Australia Square, finished in 1967—ahead of schedule and within budget—demonstrated the cost and time advantages of Dusseldorp's integrated approach to Design & Construction. When the circular Tower was complete (*next page*), a pine tree was hoisted onto the roof as part of a 'topping off' ceremony (*above*), which Dusseldorp held to pay special tribute to the efforts of the workers on the job. Meanwhile, the Opera House, still under construction (*below*), would not be finished for another six years.

company could sponsor its *own* property development projects: the resulting buildings could then either be sold and leased back on completion, or retained as long-term capital investments for the firm. That way, he would get greater control over the development process, and greater control of its profits. A sufficient capital base would also enable him to offer short-term debt finance to potential clients of his company's Design & Construct package deal, which would surely stimulate demand for the service. After all, that sort of thing was already happening in the automotive industry: the hire-purchase finance being offered by car companies to customers to 'help them buy' was in turn 'helping the producer to produce'.[7] Getting control of the money, he realised, would help free him from the remaining decision nodes in the property development process: Design & Construct had been the first step, this would be the next.

It was while swimming around in the Pacific that the idea of *how* he might do this dawned on him. He would create his *own* finance and investment company—a company that would *lend* money in order to build and *lease* property in order to make money[8]—a vehicle to act as the financial arm (Lend Lease[9]) to his production arm (Civil & Civic). With Australia's capital markets then relatively undeveloped, there was only one way to get his hands on sufficient funds for the type and scale of operation he had in mind. 'The only way', he realised, 'was to go public: to tap the savings of people in Australia by way of a public company.'[10] He would still have to raise debt from the banks and life offices for individual development projects, but an injection of funds from the public would supplement these more traditional sources of capital, giving him greater leverage, flexibility, and control.[11] It was a brilliant idea, but would it work? Never afraid of taking on a challenge, Dusseldorp knew there was only one way to find out.

In early 1958, a rested and invigorated Dusseldorp returned to the Australian property development industry, which might fairly be described as embryonic. Apart from the occasional one-off speculator—it would be stretching it to call them developers—owner-occupiers and investors then constituted the two main groups responsible for 'creating new real estate'[12] in the commercial property field, and even the latter of these was a relatively new recruit. For the most part, the new factories, department stores, and high-rise offices that were starting to appear on the skylines of the country's capitals had been funded by the postwar profits of the corporations that occupied them. Buildings like Caltex House, construction of which had been financed by an institutional investor, were rare in 1950s Australia. The handful of companies that *could* properly be classed as developers all operated primarily in the residential property field; and they were, like Civil & Civic, mainly reliant on the banks and life offices to finance their activities.[13]

The 'next step' concept that Dusseldorp had come up with in Tahiti represented a real innovation to building finance procedures in Australia.[14] Its novelty initially caused doubts among his fellow directors of Civil & Civic—Dutch Chairman Jan de Vries[15] and two Australians, lawyer John Rothery, and accountant Keith Fleming. 'When the corporation was formed,' Keith Fleming remembers, 'I really thought Dick was a bit ahead of his time.'[16] Fleming was not the only one. Amongst the financial institutions, Dusseldorp remembers, the idea of floating a property finance and investment corporation went down 'like a lead balloon'.[17] When the Dutchman ran the idea past Milton Allen, then 'sixth in line' at life insurer MLC,[18] Allen himself could see the merits of the concept, but his employer was far from keen. 'At that time Dick wanted both me and Keith Steel from the AMP to join his [new] board,' Allen remembers. 'But neither of *our* boards would permit it.'[19] In Allen's case, this call would be reversed the following year. When, in 1959, the MLC became the first financial institution to take a significant stake in Lend Lease, he became one of the latter's directors—a position he would hold for some twenty-two years, including six years as Deputy Chairman.[20]

Despite the initial scepticism, Dusseldorp pressed ahead. The newly established broking firm of Charles A. Ord & Minnett was persuaded to underwrite the float. (While this brokerage would later become one of Australia's most successful,[21] in 1958 Charlie Ord, having just started it, was, according to Dusseldorp, 'about as nothing in his field as I was in mine!')[22] A board for the new venture was assembled, comprising three directors of Civil & Civic and three independents;[23] to give the new venture market credibility, the latter were carefully drawn from the 'more conservative elements in business'.[24] Bankers were engaged (the Bank of New South Wales, Australia's first and oldest bank);[25] John Rothery's firm, Freehill, Hollingdale & Page, was appointed the company's lawyers; and Keith Fleming, from accounting firm Offner, Hadley & Co., resigned as a director of Civil & Civic to become auditor of the new concern. On 12 March 1958, a name for the new venture having (at the last minute) been chosen, Lend Lease Corporation Ltd was incorporated in the state of New South Wales.[26] The finishing touches were applied to the prospectus, and the advertisements announcing the company's debut placed in the press. Now it was over to the market: how would they—and the investing public—react?

They'd never seen anything like it. 'Hire purchase for buildings', the press proclaimed.[27] 'Plan for factories on terms.'[28] What on earth was the Dutchman up to, the business journalists wondered? Lend Lease Corporation would certainly rank as 'one of the greatest enigmas of the Australian stock markets',[29] but could it possibly succeed? It looked like a good idea on paper to the *Australian Financial Review*, but were Australian investors really ready for such a 'genuine innovation to business procedure'[30] as this? The market was similarly nonplussed, as foundation director John Rothery recalls. Lend Lease was regarded as 'a strange new creature' by its fellow corporates: one certainly worth watching closely, if only to see when it would go bust, as assuredly, they predicted, it must.[31]

The investing public, however, had quite a different view. With the company's prospectus envisaging a 5 per cent dividend in its first full year of operation, and thereafter not less than 8 per cent,[32] Lend Lease looked like a good bet to the mums and dads of Australia. Their level of enthusiasm was such that the float was over-subscribed within two days[33]—the bulk of it taken by individual investors[34]—and when Lend Lease listed on the Sydney Stock Exchange in mid-May 1958 its shares came on at a 20 per cent premium, reflecting, the *Australian Financial Review* somewhat grudgingly observed, general public optimism about the potential of the stock.[35]

By 1962 it seemed that the public had got it right. In the space of four years, Lend Lease Corporation had grown to become a fully fledged property developer, financier, investor, and manager: and a very successful one at that. By means of a series of acquisitions back up the supply chain, including the purchase of Civil & Civic from its Dutch parent Bredero's, Lend Lease had also added design and construction, and manufacture of critical building materials and components, to its list of revenue-generating activities. The group's building and development projects spanned the commercial, industrial, residential, civic, and community fields, and its geographic reach extended to every state in Australia and the country's Capital Territory. Shareholders' funds had increased 20-fold, revenues were up 30-fold, and profits after tax had grown 25-fold.[36] And despite the 'quick massing of equity', the dividend rate had also risen— from 8 to 10 per cent per annum—so the original shareholders had good reason to smile.[37] With such a 'superlative' growth record, 'steady earnings' and 'spectacular' profits, the *Financial Standard* opined, Lend Lease could well be considered 'one of the top grade growth stocks on the market today'.[38]

As further indication of the viability of Dusseldorp's Tahitian concept, others quickly followed his lead. By 1960 a number of companies were touting their wares as property developers on Australia's stock exchanges. But a few years later, many of those names had disappeared from the listing boards. For what was perhaps most remarkable about the early, spectacular success of Lend Lease Corporation was that achieving it had been far from plain sailing. Within two years of the corporation's 1958 debut, Dusseldorp and his competitors had found themselves in the middle of a crisis as the favourable economic climate into which they had been launched suddenly turned sour. It would take some skilful steering to ride out the ensuing economic storm and the journey would be far from pleasant. But for the few who, like Dusseldorp, survived the voyage, the experience would prove formative. For one thing is certain when you join the property development industry: you're in for a bumpy ride.

───▶

By all the odds, Dick Dusseldorp should have gone broke along with so many of the other entrepreneurs who were his contemporaries in the 1960s (and the 1970s and 1980s). But he survived and, better still, instilled in his successors firm rules that are enshrined in his company's strategic bible.[39]

When Lend Lease Corporation was launched in the first half of 1958, the prospects for the future had looked rosy. The Australian economy had been growing at a slick but seemingly sustainable rate of 4 per cent per annum over the 1950s, with the construction industry both contributing to and benefiting from this robust growth. With strong demand for housing fuelled by postwar immigration and the beginning of the baby boom, and with demand for new industrial and commercial premises also high, building firms were on a roll.

They were not the only ones. Everywhere you looked, there were signs of an economy riding high: the value of manufacturing production was increasing dramatically (albeit from a low base), retail sales were burgeoning, and income from Australia's predominantly rural exports was going through the roof. 'Spend, spend, spend' was the motto of the country's mushrooming hire-purchase industry, and the citizens of Australia were taking that advice to heart.

Reflecting these buoyant conditions, by the third quarter of 1960 both Lend Lease Corporation and construction firm Civil & Civic were up to their ears in work. The development arm of the corporation alone had around $30 million of projects 'in hand or in an advanced state of planning',[40] including two large office buildings, two blocks of professional suites, five blocks of high-rise home units, and five residential estate subdivisions. On top of this, two large commercial sites in Canberra had just been obtained at auction; and in 'the biggest city land deal in Australia's history',[41] Lend Lease had just paid a deposit on the site in central Sydney where it planned to develop the $40 million Australia Square project. Design and construction services for all these development projects were being provided by Civil & Civic, which also had millions of dollars worth of projects for external clients on its books—including the first stage of the Sydney Opera House, construction of which was proving somewhat more difficult and costly than first anticipated (see Chapter 1). At the same time the corporation was undergoing major expansion and restructure, busily acquiring a range of companies in the building materials, real estate, leisure, and retail industries and, in a number of cases, giving the less-than-profitable of these new subsidiaries a major overhaul.[42] All in all, it seemed there was hardly time to draw breath around the Dusseldorpian corporate offices, come October 1960.

It was at the height of all this activity that the economic bubble burst. As part of the boom-times that firms like Lend Lease were enjoying, share and property prices had been escalating since the late 1950s. This was all very well for a while, but when, by the end of 1960, prices were continuing to spiral, the federal government, fearful that the economy was overheating, decided it was time to slam on the fiscal brakes.[43] It raised interest rates, increased taxes, and tightened credit in a package of economic measures introduced in November 1960, thus creating a credit squeeze that would last the best part of eighteen months. The squeeze not only achieved what the government set out to do— rein in prices—it also sent the economy cratering into a recession, with the booming building industry particularly hard hit. Because most of the capital used to finance new homes, factories, and offices is borrowed, the rising cost and diminishing availability of credit is always grim news for firms in the building sector: when credit dries up, so too does demand for their services. Any such slump is hard to weather, but the 1960–61 credit squeeze would prove particularly severe, with many small builders going bankrupt, and same larger concerns following their lead.

Dusseldorp was determined that Lend Lease would not be amongst them. While some in the industry dithered and a couple tried to bluster their way through, Dusseldorp wasted no time in putting his new company into crisis mode. Work was stopped or slowed on all self-sponsored development projects under construction where the final purchasers were not yet tied in, thus freeing resources to complete those projects which, having already been sold, were to be leased back by the corporation to provide an income stream. Amongst the more speculative projects, plans for development of two new home unit blocks were abandoned (resulting in substantial cost write-offs),[44] one of the residential subdivisions was brought to market (although conditions for sellers were far from ideal), and a number of other assets were sold.[45] Borrowings were substantially increased—mainly in the form of debenture stock, unsecured notes, and mortgages[46]—and a large amount of capital was raised from new and existing shareholders. But having started it early, Dusseldorp could afford to be selective in his corporate belt-tightening: there was no way he would ditch plans for future development projects that he was sure would turn a profit once economic conditions improved. And so, although they were incurring holding costs with no immediate prospects of returning an income, the two commercial sites he had just bought at auction in Canberra were retained on the company's books, as was the agreement to buy the land for the site that would become Australia Square. Both would prove wise, and very profitable, decisions.

The capital-raising program, cost-control measures and asset sales enabled Dusseldorp not only to tide Lend Lease over, but to more than double net profits in 1960–61 and again in 1961–62 (and hence to maintain the 10 per cent dividend payment in both years).[47] Many of the corporation's competitors did not fare so well. When the credit squeeze first hit in November 1960, Dusseldorp had joined a four-man delegation of property developers and retailers to Canberra to implore the federal government to loosen its fiscal settings. Of the four businessmen on that mission, Dusseldorp was the only one to survive the ensuing recession.[48] A few other developers just limped through, hardly any of whom could match his feat of keeping the company's accounts in the black. But despite this positive outcome, Dusseldorp emerged from the experience anything but complacent. And although his new ship had proved itself seaworthy, by the time the economic skies began to clear he had determined a number of fundamental changes that he would be making to the vessel.

A recent survey of how top companies survive slumps found that more businesses failed *after* a downturn than during one.[49] Having got through the worst of it, rather than taking the opportunity to 'completely retool', many 'try to spend their way out of their misery' as conditions start to improve, in the process making themselves even more vulnerable when the next downturn hits.[50] Perhaps Dusseldorp somehow intuited this, for his top priority, having come through his corporation's first real test in the form of the 1960–61 credit squeeze, was to steady the ship and ease off on the throttle. Taking the opportunity to rethink corporate goals, he put in place a 'defensive planning strategy'[51] that would ready Lend Lease to face the next such crisis, which he knew must inevitably come. It did. In 1974 the bottom once again fell out of the Australian property market and five major developers and/or financiers fell through the gaping hole; before the decade was out, a dozen more would follow them. Once again, Lend Lease was one of the few to survive, thanks in large part to the lessons Dusseldorp had learned, and the changes in strategy he had put in place in response to the downturn of the early 1960s.

There were four key elements of his plan.

First, aware that the rapid pace at which Lend Lease's profits and earnings had taken off in its first four years was not sustainable in the longer term, Dusseldorp restructured the corporation to grow, as his successor Stuart Hornery put it, 'surely but steadily—a distance runner rather than a sprinter'.[52] This meant reorienting the corporation's activities away from a reliance on one-off development profits (which, depending on the timing of project completions, could fluctuate wildly from year to year), towards the steadier, less spectacular, but more secure returns that property investment offered. The underlying principle enshrined in Lend Lease's 'corporate bible' from this time on was to derive two-thirds of the corporation's earnings from 'income streams' or annuities. The actual source of these annuities changed over time—'initially ... [they were] achieved through management agreements over individual properties', Hornery remembers, 'then funds like GPT, then MLC'[53] (both discussed further below). But the principle stood fast. The annuities would act as a safety net for the corporation—more than covering the annual dividend payment—thus allowing the riskier and inherently more uneven profits of Lend Lease's 'entrepreneurial endeavours'[54] to be the icing on the corporate cake.

This did not mean, however, that such 'entrepreneurial endeavours' would be played down—indeed, the scale of individual property developments would grow enormously over the next three decades—for Dusseldorp knew that 'if you don't take risks, you never make money'.[55] But henceforth, and this was the second element of his defensive strategy, each such project would require at least one backstop, or contingency, plan.

So, for example, when it came to firming the arrangements for the multi-million-dollar Australia Square development—a project so huge that finance for it was coordinated by Cazenove's in London, there being no institutional funds of the required size available in Australia at the time[56]—Dusseldorp had a number of contingency plans. If planning approval for the integrated block redevelopment project was not forthcoming, he would cover the considerable expenses involved in putting together the 'largest single parcel of urban land in Sydney'[57] by re-parcelling the titles and selling them off at a profit. That was Plan 1. Plan 2 was put in place to cover the myriad risks—such as a major downturn in the commercial office rental market—that could arise during the five-year construction phase. 'The key to that was to stagger construction,' Dusseldorp's right-hand man Jack Klompe remembers. 'Australia Square was to be built in stages: first the Plaza building, and then the Tower, with the latter itself divided in three stages—low-rise, mid-rise, and high-rise—so it was able to be cut off at any stage, to be stopped if it had to be. So there again is the back-stop plan.'[58] As it happened, Dusseldorp did not need to deploy either of these contingency plans, but their very existence was pivotal in getting the board, financial, and other go-aheads that he needed to get Lend Lease's most success-ful individual project of the decade literally off the ground.

Third, with his 'natural aversion to borrowing'[59]—which many attribute to the collapse of his father's business during the Great Depression (see Introduc-tion)—high priority was given to retiring the debt that had been raised to see the corporation through the 1960–61 downturn. And once this goal was achieved, Dusseldorp went further down the same path. From the mid-1960s on, Lend Lease's reliance on borrowings dropped substantially, and before long the corporation had earned a reputation as one of the most prudentially geared in its class. 'He always made sure that we had money in the bank, and that we were always lightly mortgaged,' Jack Klompe remembers.[60] 'He was very definite about borrowing rules,' long-term Lend Lease executive David Thorne concurs. 'You didn't borrow more than a particular percentage, and you certainly didn't commit yourself to a major project until you had a major tenant. He always kept to those rules, through both the booms and busts, and that was a key to the company's success.'[61] Indeed, the corporation's low gearing stood it in good stead in the 1974 property crisis. In that year Lend Lease's borrowings amount to only 19 per cent of total assets[62]—a figure which would drop even further in years to come[63]—while gearing ratios in the high 70s and above were characteristic of many of the property developers that collapsed.[64]

The fourth key aspect of Dusseldorp's defensive strategy was to keep a watchful look-out for the first signs of an approaching storm. Rated by a respected market commentator as 'probably the shrewdest operator the Australian property market has ever seen',[65] Dusseldorp sought to institutionalise in Lend Lease something of his own capacity in this area through an emphasis on strategic planning,[66] and in his choice of Hornery—a man who shared his ability to 'see over the horizon'[67]—as his successor as Chairman of the corporation.

In combination with the other elements of his 'defensive strategy', this early-warning system proved crucial to the corporation's weathering of the property collapses of the 1970s (and beyond). Just as others were rushing into what would soon become a massively oversupplied office market in the central business district, in October 1971 Dusseldorp, predicting that some of those 'others' would 'undoubtedly ... go broke',[68] announced that Lend Lease was 'switching out of office blocks to concentrate on shopping centres and other property development'.[69] 'It took a little time for his prediction to come true', says Trevor Sykes, author of a history of corporate disasters in Australia (in which the property industry features prominently), but Dusseldorp was proved 'perfectly correct'.[70] When, in late 1973 the federal government started tightening credit to curb mounting property speculation, it was the highly geared developers holding floors of unwanted office space (and quite a few of their financiers) that collapsed.[71] At the same time these companies were meeting their nemeses, Lend Lease announced an $8.5 million net profit for 1974–75. Although this was some $2 million down on the previous year's result—the first such drop in net profits for eleven years—the colour of the ink was reassuringly black. It was also the last time that Dusseldorp would have to announce such a dip, for from then until his retirement in 1988, the net profits of Lend Lease resumed their more normal trend of annual growth.

Storm clouds on the horizon were not the only things that Dusseldorp's early-warning systems were designed to detect. He was equally quick to spot new business *opportunities*—opportunities which the team he built around him was capable of swiftly translating into ongoing revenue streams. Heading this team from 1965 until his retirement in 1977 was Lend Lease Managing Director Bill Leavey—a man whose organisational and people skills richly complemented the vision and entrepreneurial talents of the corporation's Chairman. 'Duss was an ideas man,' says David Thorne. 'He had this vision of where we were going, he was a real enthusiast and all that sort of thing. But to make it all happen on a day-to-day basis … he chose Bill Leavey as our first Managing Director—and they worked very well together, they complemented each other.'[72] 'They were an excellent combination of particular skills,' agrees long-term Lend Lease executive Ken McGrath.

> Duss would say, 'we are going to do this and we are going to do that', and then Leavey would implement it all—Bill and the people behind him, that is. Bill had terrific people skills—he was an excellent judge of character, a great picker of people and he could motivate them too—and so it worked remarkably well … Duss and he were a great partnership over those years.[73]

The key to identifying new business opportunities, Dusseldorp firmly believed, was to keep close tabs on the market. 'On the business side, I suppose what has made [the Lend Lease group] different (and very successful)', he told an interviewer in the early 1980s, 'is that our approach has always been to seek out what the marketplace wants. Most companies tend to be product-oriented. We are not like this. We seek the marketplace needs and then design a product to suit this need.'[74] This approach was much in evidence in the marketing and delivery of Civil & Civic's integrated Design & Construct package deal, as David Thorne recounts.

> One of the philosophies that Dusseldorp pioneered in the company was to recognise and respond to a customer's needs: to analyse their needs in a very definite way. And so instead of just taking the client's stated requirement for a building at face value, we got into the practice of questioning with them those instructions.[75]

Working with the client to get to the heart of their needs could sometimes result in quite significant changes to the original brief. 'The client may say, "We want to build a warehouse here"', Thorne remembers, 'but we'd say "Why? You'd be better off to sell that particular block of land, and with the profits from the sale acquire a more suitable piece of land in this other area, and put your warehouse there." '[76] In another case, a commission to design and construct extensions to a factory was turned on its head when the Civil & Civic-led project team assigned to the task came up with an alternative plan. By internally reconfiguring the existing premises, the project team discovered, the client's needs could be satisfied in a more cost-effective way. Although Civil & Civic lost a bigger job in the short term, the pay-off came in the form of a rich stream of continuing business with that client.[77]

Sometimes it worked the other way, with a small initial brief expanding out to something much more substantial. The principal of an asset-rich but cash-strapped girls' school certainly found that to be the case when, in early 1959, she called in Civil & Civic to pull down a fence and construct a temporary doorway to enable entry to the neighbouring tenement house, where the school had acquired emergency accommodation to house its burgeoning enrolments. With that small job complete, within a year the Sisters at Loreto Convent, Kirribilli, guided by Dusseldorp and his team, had come up with an integrated business plan for the school's complete rebuilding and expansion—supported by the first structured finance plan in the Catholic education sector[78]—the first stage of which, a new $100,000 Junior School building, was already built and fully operational. Not long after this first building was finished, Loreto's Mother Superior received a cheque for some $6500 in the mail from Civil & Civic— her school's share of the savings on the original quote—the receipt of which she would describe as a 'unique event in the history of our Order'.[79]

On the back of this mutually beneficial experience, Civil & Civic put in place a comprehensive marketing plan targeting the private education sector. Such plans may seem commonplace now, but for the Australian building and construction industry at the time, this concept was revolutionary. Supported by the good word from satisfied customers like Loreto, this led to some forty more commissions over the next ten years for the design and construction of schools right across the country.[80] A similar approach was applied in marketing the company's Design & Construct building service in the industrial, health, office, retail, and leisure fields. With the benefits that it offered in terms of cost, time, and quality, Civil & Civic soon found that satisfied clients provided the best advertisement for the service. As testament to this, by the 1970s Design & Construct was accounting for over 70 per cent of Civil & Civic's total turnover, some 70 per cent of which was in the form of repeat business.[81]

Dusseldorp's ability to spot new business opportunities also proved well-honed when it came to property development. Although he admits that luck played a role in some of Lend Lease's most successful development projects, careful research and planning, astute risk assessment, and the ability to see 'beyond the immediately visible'[82] were the talents that he brought to bear on the task. Echoing Dusseldorp's 'common interest' theme again, a number of these ventures shared another characteristic: they not only proved profitable for his firm, they also yielded a return to the broader community. In combination with the occasional piece of good fortune, these skills enabled Dusseldorp to spot and capitalise on opportunities which others had missed, dismissed, or simply not even thought of. A classic illustration of these attributes in action is the story of Lend Lease's involvement in the development of Australia's national capital.

'Canberra was really what put Dusseldorp and Lend Lease on the map,' says Colin Moore, long-time head of Lend Lease's development and investment divisions.

It was a small town and a small branch to start with. None of the other development companies was much interested in it, and we very nearly pulled out ourselves ... In the event, of course, we *did* stay in Canberra—it was a remarkable stroke of luck—because it was really where it all happened for Lend Lease. The *dominance* of the company in the property development field was very much associated with Canberra. We had an *extremely* successful ten years there.[83]

Dusseldorp's construction firm, Civil & Civic, had been operating in Canberra's conventional tender market since the early 1950s, but by the end of the decade the Dutchman was thinking of shutting up shop in the town. 'It was about the time that he was forming the public company, Lend Lease [in 1958],' Moore remembers. 'Dusseldorp had decided that being just a builder was dumb, because of the margins, and he'd decided that the way to go was to buy land, develop a building on the land, sell it to the institutions, and then lease it back.'[84] And while the opportunities to do this sort of development work were burgeoning in Sydney and Melbourne, it was a completely different story in Canberra.

Canberra had been created as a compromise 'new town' when, in the aftermath of Federation in 1901, the states of New South Wales and Victoria had been unable to agree which of their capital cities should be the new country's seat of political power. Although Canberra's foundation stone had been laid in 1913, and some work started on architect Walter Burley Griffin's plan for the new city in the ensuing years, the Depression and World War II had brought further development to a halt. With other priorities for postwar reconstruction uppermost in the federal government's mind, not much had changed by the 1950s, at which time Australia's national capital, home to only 34,000 people, was still little more than 'two villages divided by a floodplain'.[85] But when, in 1958, with the imprimatur of Prime Minister Robert Menzies, responsibility for Canberra's planning and development was centralised in a new and powerful National Capital Development Commission (NCDC), it seemed the would-be city's fortunes had changed.

'We were about to pull out of Canberra,' Dusseldorp remembers, 'when it started to look like it might come good. This new guy ... had been appointed to run the NCDC, and we thought we'd hang on for another year or so and wait and see what he could do.'[86] This 'new guy' was Sir John Overall, and as head of the NCDC it was his job to breathe life into Canberra, to make the place, in the words of the then Prime Minister, 'a worthy capital; something that the Australian people would come to admire and respect ... a focal point for national pride and sentiment'.[87] But although the vision was grand, the budget that Overall commanded to achieve it was not. 'The money he got from the government was hardly enough to pay for the roads and sewers,' Dusseldorp remembers.[88] 'The only way he could hope to make an impact was if he could create a climate for private enterprise to pour its money into the place.'[89] But with most private developers put off Canberra by its leasehold system of land tenure and its strict land use and planning controls,[90] the prospects for doing that looked bleak. 'When I first came to Canberra,' Overall recalls, 'it was purely a government town. Any private builders seemed to go broke, and business didn't know what was happening, because they didn't know what the disposition of land was.'[91]

Faced with an organisational budget rapidly going into the red, Overall was nonetheless determined to do what he could to attract private development capital. In 1960 he announced the NCDC's intention to put to public auction the first commercial parcels of land in the centre of Canberra. The first to go under the hammer, on 6 September that year, would be a substantial site to be developed as a shopping mall (today known as Monaro Mall); the second, some two days later, would be a contiguous parcel of land at Hobart Place comprising eight office block sites (the integrated development of which was to be in accordance with an NCDC plan). Bringing the first of these sites, in particular, to market was a gamble for Overall, although the thinking behind his move was sound. With Canberra lacking even a single department store, the town was currently losing valuable retail dollars to other cities; Overall figured that developing a full-scale shopping mall would not only plug this leak, but might even *attract* shoppers from the surrounding regions to Canberra, thus giving the nascent capital a much-needed economic boost.[92] But with the existing—and politically well-connected—small shopkeepers in town vehemently opposed to Overall's plan, and with no major retailer showing any interest in the site, going to auction was risky. 'It was a bold step,' remembers Dusseldorp.[93] 'He was playing very high stakes there': if it came off, the boost to commercial confidence in the town was potentially huge, but if he lost, 'then he would have been set back for five years'.[94]

As the September auction days drew closer, and with seemingly no bids for the mall site in the offing, an increasingly nervous Overall decided to discuss his dilemma with Dusseldorp. 'He had all but given it away,' Dusseldorp remembers.[95]

There were already plans drawn up for that Monaro [shopping mall] site to [instead] be covered in 20 foot frontages... And when he [told me] that I said 'For God's sake, you're not going to back down now. I'll suggest two things to you. Firstly, you do not need to fear that you're not going to get any bid—I guarantee a bid. I can't say how much, of course, but a bid will be forthcoming. [Secondly,] to get the shopkeepers off your back, why don't you, on the same day, auction a bunch of 20 foot frontages on that block opposite, which is already ruined anyway?'[96]

A few days later, the auction of the Monaro Mall site—as an undivided lot—went ahead. The opening bid, from an interstate company, was derisory; then a local consortium chipped in. Dusseldorp, who attended the auction personally, easily trumped both with a bid of $170,000: then the highest price ever paid for a block of land in Canberra.[97] The record would not stand for long. Two days later Dusseldorp was back in the auction rooms bidding for the office block sites at Hobart Place. Although he faced stiffer competition this time, for a shade over $630,000 Dusseldorp acquired five of the eight blocks on offer;[98] one of them, costing $214,000, broke the record for the highest price paid for land in Canberra that Dusseldorp had set just two days earlier.[99]

The next day the local newspapers were full of stories about the enigmatic Dutchman and his 'mammoth outlay' at the auctions in Canberra. 'Investments like these have made Mr Dusseldorp one of Australia's biggest and most successful investors and developers', *The Territorial* proclaimed, going on to predict that he'd be 'the man to change our city landscape'.[100] This indeed proved correct: Hobart Place and Monaro Mall were just the beginning of Lend Lease's development activities in the national capital; the corporation would undertake a huge number of office and retail projects there over the next ten years and beyond.[101] And for his part, NCDC Commissioner Sir John Overall was delighted: the auction results proved just the vote of confidence—and boost to private investment in the national capital—that he and his organisation needed. As he had hoped, the $5 million shopping complex that Lend Lease developed on the Monaro Mall site—with its two department stores and fifty specialty shops—became a magnet not just for those Canberrans who had previously shopped out-of-town, but for consumers in the surrounding regions. 'This gave impetus to further development', Overall says, 'and changed the way Canberra was viewed outside the capital.'[102]

Overall and his team at the NCDC were not the only ones smiling. Dusseldorp had done his homework, and while the amount he had paid for the Canberra sites might have been top dollar in the public's eyes, to his mind he had got them 'dirt cheap'.[103] So sure was he of their potential that, when the credit squeeze hit some two months after the auctions, Dusseldorp was adamant that these newly acquired blocks should not be let go. Conditions would improve eventually, he knew, and when they did, he was sure the Canberra developments would prove winners for the firm. Circumstances proved him right. The 1960s would turn out to be the decade in which both the population of Canberra and the shopping mall boom took off in Australia, and Monaro Mall would provide Lend Lease with an entrée into both highly profitable markets. The corporation would later develop two more major shopping complexes in Canberra and all up, during Dusseldorp's time at the helm, it would build and operate more than thirty such malls in Australia and beyond.

Meanwhile, the Corporation's office development projects in Canberra turned out to be, in Jack Klompe's words, 'a virtual licence to print money'.[104]

We built virtually the whole of that office area in Hobart Place. Then we sold the
buildings to all the big insurance companies—MLC, National Mutual, AMP,
and T&G—and then we took a lease-back, or a management agreement, on the
buildings. That was a relatively low risk thing to do, as getting tenants was almost
automatic: you filled them all with government public servants. We were the first
ones to really cotton on to that.[105]

Under a sale and leaseback arrangement, Lend Lease as the developer would sell the building to an investor (usually a financial institution), lease it back, for a period of time (usually forty years), and then sub-lease it to tenants. The owner of the building would get a guaranteed minimum annual income (called the head-lease rent), while the lessee (Lend Lease) would 'be paid for the risk taken [in guaranteeing this income] and the annual sum under-written'.[106] Under a variant called a surplus-sharing agreement, the investor and lessee would also share (usually fifty-fifty) any surplus income paid to the lessee (Lend Lease) by its sub-lessees over and above the amount of the fixed head-lease rent. The idea of the management agreement, which Dusseldorp came up with in Canberra, and which the corporation increasingly favoured from the mid-1960s on, was, according to Jack Klompe, 'ahead of its time'.

'The problem with traditional leaseback agreements', says Klompe, 'was that the manager had to give a guaranteed rent return to the owner, but he might not always have the building full of tenants.'[107] But such risks were lowered under a management agreement (in lieu of a lease), as the manager of the building (Lend Lease) did not *guarantee* a head-rent to the building owner (nor was it paid a management fee); instead, the manager's remuneration came from sharing with the owner an agreed proportion of the 'surplus income' from the building's tenants.[108]

Such agreements—and others like them entered into right around the country—enabled Lend Lease to build up its property investment portfolio, *not* in the form of physical assets—and the liabilities that go with them—but by means of an income-sharing arrangement with the financial institutions.[109] As Stuart Hornery noted above, such management agreements over individual properties provided the first form of 'annuity', or safety net income stream, for the Lend Lease Corporation.

Although others would later 'cotton onto' the opportunities that Canberra presented, by the time they did, Jack Klompe says, 'it was just too late'. 'We always outbid them because we had so much experience: we knew exactly how to sharpen the pencils and make it work.'[110] 'We mopped up all the [Canberra] auctions after that first one,' Dusseldorp agrees. 'There was more compe- tition—from the financial institutions and so forth—so we paid a bit more, but we *always* won.'[111] Win was the operative word, according to John Morschel, later chief executive of Lend Lease.

> What Dusseldorp did in Canberra was just absolutely mind-boggling. He *made* Canberra. It was *him*. He used to go there, attend an auction, buy a block of land. He'd already have a sketch design of what he was going to build on it, and knew what the building would cost. And then, before the people had left the room— the institutions who were there bidding against him, that he'd just beaten at the auction—he'd be saying to them, 'I'll sell you the building and everything on it'. And he *would* sell it to them—either that day or the day after—and we did *really* well out of it, I mean it was a fantastic approach. That was Dick when he was in his operating mode![112]

Just as 'Dick in his operating mode' had attracted a swag of emulators when he launched Lend Lease in 1958, a similar thing started to happen some ten years later.

> In the latter part of the 1960s, [Dusseldorp remembers] we started to see that
> [financial] institutions had noticed that we were successful, and that we were
> making profits, and that it was out of deals we made with them! So then,
> inevitably, people start looking into your pockets—instead of being focussed on
> their own—and they started to go into our field of business, as was, of course,
> their right.[113]

It was little wonder that the institutions had designs on Dusseldorp's patch. With the successful completion of projects such as Australia Square, the numerous Canberra ventures, and a host of others, by the end of the 1960s Lend Lease had established itself as Australia's leading property developer.[114] As the new decade dawned, the group's annual revenues topped $100 million for the first time, shareholder funds stood at $21 million, and net profits, which had grown at an average rate of 26 per cent per annum over the past decade, hit $3.8 million in 1971. Representing a return of 42.5 per cent on capital employed, these profits provided ample scope for a generous dividend payment, the rate of which had by now risen to 16 per cent.[115] With figures such as these, it is doubtful whether the institutions would have stopped to consider whether or not it was their 'right' to encroach into Dusseldorp's field: they were coming, whether he liked it or not.

If the financial institutions were coming his way, Dusseldorp figured, why not 'meet them head on and encroach on *their* territory'.[116] There were some compelling reasons for doing so. With the nature of its development business, and its preferred mode of operating, Lend Lease Corporation was already starting to bump against capital constraints to growth—at least on the scale that its Chairman had in mind. 'Buildings have a long life cycle', Dusseldorp later said in explanation of the thinking behind his next strategic move.

> They are not like tomatoes that go bad over the weekend. Every year turnover has
> to be financed. Back in the 1970s we were faced with the prospect of having to
> increase the capital of the company year by year and that meant borrowing to the
> hilt to be able to do the next year's development work.[117]

But such a course was anathema to Dusseldorp. Aside from his 'natural aversion to borrowing', going down a track that increased his dependence on the
financial institutions, just when they were becoming his competitors in the
development field, hardly seemed a wise thing to do. But if an increase in
borrowing was out, what was the alternative: how else could he get his hands
on the large (and increasing) amounts of capital the corporation now required?

It was a dilemma he had faced before (prompting the formation of Lend
Lease) and 'once again', he says, 'we started looking for unusual solutions'.[118]
The 'unusual solution' he came up with this time would not only solve these
dilemmas (and in doing so provide Lend Lease Corporation with a new,
improved source of its safety net income stream or 'annuity'), it would also lay
the foundations for a later strategic move that would transform the Lend Lease
group into a financial services giant. The solution was the creation of
Australia's first listed property trust: the General Property Trust.

Floated on the Australian Stock Exchanges in early 1971, the General Property
Trust (GPT) represented as ground-breaking a concept as had its predecessor
and sponsor, Lend Lease, on its own debut some thirteen years before. Typically, Dusseldorp also saw it as constituting a common interest, or win-win,
solution for both the corporation and the investing public. Set up in accordance
with 'ancient UK Trust laws', the assets of GPT—a selection of prime income-
earning development projects completed by Lend Lease—would be held by an
independent trustee and managed by a Lend Lease subsidiary, both jointly
responsible to the regulatory authorities for the fund's administration.[119] Potential conflicts of interest between Lend Lease and GPT would be handled by
strict and transparent rules as to which properties the latter should purchase,
and a performance-related system of setting management fees.[120] From the perspective of the corporation, GPT would not only solve the problem of finding
the 'ownership money' for (a selection of) its flagship developments, *without*
resorting to massive borrowings; it would simultaneously constitute a new way
of securing its safety-net income stream or annuity—through the fees received
for managing those properties on behalf of the Trustee.

The idea behind GPT was also a boon to the small investor, as Bill Webster,
later Investment Director of Lend Lease, sees it:

What Dusseldorp was on about [in GPT] was actually looking after, or giving an opportunity to, people who didn't have much money who thought that they might want to invest in property ... They can't go and buy an Australia Square on their own—but if it was securitised, then they can buy a small sliver of it, and trade it in the Stock Exchange: then they can get access to something that they could not possibly get access to otherwise.[121]

Although other mechanisms predated GPT in enabling small investors to buy into property tax-effectively—such as small-scale property syndicates and unlisted property trusts[122]—these shared at least one major pitfall, as GPT's first Managing Director, Ken McGrath, explains.

The problem was: if you wanted to sell your interest, how the hell did you do it? There was no market for it. [Investors in unlisted trusts, for example, could only redeem their units at the price set by the manager]. The only place there *was* an open market was, of course, on the Stock Exchange. And that got Duss thinking that you could create and list a property trust—a *general* property trust—and that would solve *everybody's* problems.[123]

Listing GPT on the Stock Exchange might have *looked* like a straight-forward solution to 'everybody's problems', but, never having been done before, Dusseldorp faced a battle getting the float away.[124] 'We had to get it passed by the state government and also by the Stock Exchange,' says Ken McGrath. 'And that was very difficult because it had never been done before: it was all new concepts. It wasn't that they were being obstructive—I don't think they understood it, basically.'[125] 'The concept behind GPT was miles ahead of what anybody else was thinking at the time,' agrees Geoff McWilliam—now head of a rival property investment and management outfit, but one time General Manager of GPT—which perhaps explains the lukewarm reception it received in the market.[126] Despite an active campaign to build support for the listing amongst the broking community, Dusseldorp and McGrath were unable to find anyone willing to underwrite the float. 'We just couldn't generate enthu-siasm', McGrath remembers; 'it was too new.'[127] Nor was the institutional investment community showing signs of keenness. 'At first all the institutions totally shunned GPT,' McWilliam remembers. 'They thought [Dusseldorp] was mad, and told him it would never get off the ground.'[128]

Convinced as he was of the concept's merit, however, Dusseldorp was neither fazed nor deterred by such resistance: he'd just find a way around it. 'Duss was very clever like that,' says McWilliam. 'He was very clever at having a clear vision of where he wanted to get to—and it didn't matter if it was over the rainbow, over the hill—he would go after it.'[129] If the broking community wasn't interested, Lend Lease would sponsor the float of GPT itself.[130] And if the institutions weren't interested in taking up units in GPT, he would rely on the public to do so—just as he had with Lend Lease. With this course of action determined, and with the approvals of the relevant authorities (eventually) obtained, Dusseldorp pressed ahead with the float. A series of two full-page advertisements were placed in the press, offering a minimum number of 500,000 units at $1 each; when the offer closed at the end of March 1971, it was oversubscribed to the tune of $6 million.[131] 'The general professional consensus was that [GPT] would never get off the ground,' Dusseldorp would later recall as he reflected on this result. 'You can imagine our surprise when we found that we had assessed the mood of the much neglected, small investor correctly!'[132]

Although at first small investors took up the great majority of GPT units, when the institutions saw the sorts of returns the fund was generating, many of them quickly joined the party. As it had been with Lend Lease, MLC was again the first institution to buck the trend and invest in GPT—quickly becoming its largest shareholder—although later it would be joined by many more institutional investors.[133] It is easy to see why. Not only was the Trust able to beat the collapse of the property boom in 1974 (with its assets then almost fully employed in shopping centres, rather than the crashing office market, unit-holders in GPT that year received a 76.9 per cent increase in income),[134] by the end of the decade GPT's total assets had passed the $200 million mark, and it could boast an unbroken record of annual increases in distributions to unitholders.[135] In the 1980s GPT expanded its portfolio to include, along with its eight major shopping centres, a number of 'superprime' commercial properties in central city locations—including Australia Square, Brisbane's Riverside Centre, and a stake in Sydney's MLC Centre—giving it 'a strategic spread of properties across the two distinct commercial and retail market segments', which in turn ensured the twin aims of long-term income and capital growth to investors.[136]

The strategy seems to have worked. By 1988, the year that Dusseldorp retired as the Chairman of GPT's management company, the fund's total assets had grown from $6 million in 1971 to $1.3 billion; its investment growth had consistently surpassed market indicators; and its record of annual increases in distributions remained unbroken.[137] And while it had attracted more than its fair share of emulators—'a stampede of listed and unlisted companies ensued, [with] one company even restructuring its operations into a trust', Dusseldorp remembers[138]—GPT was still Australia's biggest property trust[139] and one of its most successful. As well as providing substantial benefits to its unitholders, GPT had more than proved its worth to Lend Lease, having given the corporation an in-house buyer for some of its landmark developments and a steady stream of fees from the management of these properties; the latter prompted the press to describe the GPT as 'Mr G. J. Dusseldorp's remarkable money machine'.[140] Just as importantly, at least in retrospect, GPT also provided Lend Lease with an entrée to the funds management business: something that would prove particularly valuable, as we'll see in Chapter 5, when Dusseldorp took Lend Lease even further down this path with the acquisition of insurance company MLC.

What Dusseldorp looked to do [says Lend Lease Group Executive, Eric Goodwin, as he reflects on the way his company's founder built up the corporate enterprise] was to add value and maximise profit for shareholders in everything that we did. So we started off as a contractor, but he realised we couldn't add value by *just* being a contractor, so we did Design & Construction. [Then he] realised that if we wanted to add more value and make more profits, we had to become a project manager—and that means determining clients' needs. Then if you want to go to the next step, he realised, you become a [property] developer—and that was the beginning of Lend Lease. Then beyond a developer is to become a funds management organisation. (So rather than just build an Australia Square and say, 'Well, I did a successful job, I got a successful profit', say, 'Well, if I do a successful development, and if it's successful for a number of years, why don't I extract a profit out of it each year by managing it?' That's where things like the GPT ... came in. [So] at each one of those steps a new element of the business was added which both gave us a competitive advantage and gave us the opportunity to add value—which helps justify the extra profit that you get. And that was important to Dusseldorp, because his attitude was that, as an organisation, you not only look to maximise profit for shareholders on the one hand, but on the other, you look to ensure that your reputation is enhanced by being a member of the community within which you live—by being able to stand up and be counted.[141]

CHAPTER 4

Ethical Business Practice and Corporate Governance

The gentle clatter of cutlery and wafts of conversation rose against a backdrop of piped music as Dusseldorp walked into Sydney's Le Chalet Restaurant that lunchtime in August 1963. The Chalet was a favourite haunt of stockbrokers from the surrounding financial district, so it was across many tables of pinstripe-suited diners that the tall, well-dressed Dutchman glanced as he looked for the party he was meeting. His eyes came to rest on a small table by the far-side window. 'I'm with those gentlemen over there,' he told the hostess as she greeted him in the restaurant's reception area. 'Yes, Mr Dusseldorp,' she replied. 'Your friends are up to coffee, but would you care to look at the menu? We have our special Scaloppine Bohemienne on today.' 'No, I'll just have a coffee, thank you,' he told her. 'I'm afraid I'm not planning on staying long.'

Weaving his way through tables of diners, all happily dissecting the latest movements in the markets as they tucked into the Chalet's continental fare, Dusseldorp headed for a table overlooking the narrow lane running down toward Circular Quay. One of the two men seated there rose slightly as the Lend Lease Chairman approached. 'Dick, this is Mr Fitzgerald,' he said, pulling out a chair for the late arrival. 'He has been talking to me about the Bankstown Square project.'

'I see,' said Dusseldorp as he took his seat, 'and what exactly did you have to say, Mr … Fitzgerald, is it?'

'That's right,' the second man replied. 'I've just given your Mr McLeod here the phone numbers of some aldermen on the local council. I understand you're having trouble getting that shopping centre proposal of yours through the hoops, but I'm sure—for a consideration—you could persuade these particular aldermen to see things your way.'

'They're prepared to vote in favour of the project?' Dusseldorp asked.

'As long as their conditions are met,' Fitzgerald replied.

Glancing at the names on the pieces of paper before him, Dusseldorp rubbed his chin. 'There are only five names here,' he said, 'but there are eighteen people on that council, aren't there?'

'That's right,' Fitzgerald replied. 'But these five can deliver fifteen votes.'

'Who is the leader of the group?' Dusseldorp asked, taking a sip of his coffee.

'I don't know,' Fitzgerald replied, 'I don't know exactly how they work these things.'

'Then how can I be sure they'll play ball?' Dusseldorp asked. 'Have you done this sort of thing with them before, Mr Fitzgerald?'

'Yes I have,' the man replied, 'and they've always stuck to their deal in the past.'

'I see,' said the Lend Lease Chairman. 'Then that leaves the matter of the amount. How much do you think they'll want?'

'I'll leave that to you,' Fitzgerald said. 'A man in your position would know about such things,' he added with a smile.

'Talk to the aldermen and come back with a figure,' Dusseldorp said as he rose from the table. 'I'll see you back at the office, Alex,' he said as he took a last mouthful of coffee, nodded curtly at Fitzgerald, then made his way to the door.

Detective-Sergeant Walton checked his watch at his observation post at Circular Quay as he saw Dusseldorp descend the stairs of the Chalet, take a right turn into Pitt Street, and make his way along the curving harbourside walkway to nearby Lend Lease House. It was 2 pm—the Dutchman had only been in the restaurant for thirty minutes—he certainly wasn't wasting any time. As Dusseldorp walked away, Walton and his colleague, Detective-Constable Cox, resumed their watch of the Chalet's entranceway. Before long they saw the other two men emerge. After shaking hands they parted ways: McLeod following in Dusseldorp's footsteps while Fitzgerald climbed into a car to go uptown. 'We'd better follow him,' Walton said to Cox, indicating Fitzgerald as he reached for the handle of their unmarked police car. 'We can catch up with Dusseldorp and McLeod later.'

As they pulled out into the line of traffic, the two detectives watched the car a couple of blocks ahead of them begin the gentle climb up Pitt Street towards Martin Place. Heading into the city's main commercial and retail district, it soon became enmeshed in a throng of vehicles from which parcel-laden shoppers seemed to constantly pour in and out. Traffic lights changed, horns honked, cars emerged from every side street to join the busy Pitt Street snarl. Perhaps the Christmas rush was starting early this year, for there seemed to be hundreds more people about than was usual for a weekday afternoon. Whatever the reason for all the activity, it played to Fitzgerald's advantage. For by the time the detectives had made it through the city crush, their quarry was nowhere to be seen.

Some five days later, Alex McLeod had another appointment to keep. This time the venue was the Canterbury Race Course, the former home turf of the ex-bookmaker-turned-real-estate agent and local government alderman he had arranged to meet there. McLeod had little trouble picking out Alderman Little as the latter approached their designated rendezvous. He'd seen him in action the night before at the Bankstown Council Chambers, where, no money having changed hands, consideration of Lend Lease's development application had been deferred for the second time in a month.

'I've just backed a winner,' Little said, waving a bookie's ticket and smiling broadly as he walked towards McLeod.

'Let's get down to business,' was the latter's somewhat terse reply, 'because *we* seem to have backed the wrong horse.' As the two men walked towards the hill to watch the next race, the conversation turned to the events of the evening before. 'You saw what happened last night,' Little said. 'That was intended to show what can be done.' It had certainly had the desired effect.

'We *must* have the votes necessary for this,' McLeod said determinedly.

'I can get them,' Little replied. 'There's a group of us and we always work together on these things. I haven't discussed the details with Fitzgerald,' he added. 'What exactly were the terms?'

'The sum of $10,000 was mentioned,' said McLeod. '$5000 before and $5000 after?' asked Little. 'Because that would be okay with me.'

'I will have to discuss it with Mr Dusseldorp,' said McLeod, 'and then I'll let you know.'

A week later the police had resumed their surveillance activities, and once again Lend Lease Project Manager Alex McLeod was in their sights. Parking a little way downwind of a real estate agency in the Sydney suburb of Padstow, this time with a third detective in tow, Cox and Walton watched as McLeod's car drew up outside the agency. Checking the rear-vision mirror and adjusting his jacket as he opened the car door, McLeod made his way into the shop, under a sign which proclaimed it to be the premises of C. H. Little Pty Ltd. Indeed, the police contingent could see, the said proprietor—who also held an elected position on the local Bankstown Council—was standing just inside the doorway. After a few words with Little, McLeod walked back to his car, retrieved a paper-wrapped parcel from the glovebox and then returned to the building with it under his arm. As he did so, he touched the back of his neck, which was enough to prompt the constabulary to swing into action. 'Let's get him,' said Cox, as he and Special Constable Martin left their observation post and ran towards the estate agency, Detective-Sergeant Walton following close behind.

—

'Can you tell the Court what happened then, Constable Martin?' the Crown Prosecutor asked the policewoman in Sydney's Central Court of Petty Sessions some ten months later in June 1964. Before Senior Magistrate Ward were arraigned Little and four other former aldermen of Bankstown Council, along with another man going by the name of Fitzgerald, all charged with unlawful conspiracy to demand and receive payment 'in consideration of doing acts pertaining to their [aldermanic] office'.[1] It was the twelfth day of proceedings, and the police witnesses were giving their evidence on the stand. 'Detective-Sergeant Walton said to Mr Little that he'd seen a package delivered by a man a few moments ago, and asked him where it was,' Constable Martin said. 'And what was the alderman's response?' the Prosecutor asked. He had denied any knowledge of it at first, she said. But when Detective Cox had located the still-wrapped money hidden under a toilet at the back of Little's premises, the latter had realised that the game was up. And how had the police known that there was money in the parcel? They had taken down the serial numbers of the bank notes earlier in the day, the constable replied. They'd done so in Mr McLeod's office at Lend Lease House, while the latter was being wired up to tape the meeting with the alderman. 'So McLeod and Lend Lease were in on the police plan, were they?' 'They'd been in on it from the very start.'[2]

—

When Dusseldorp and his team at Lend Lease had first drawn up plans to develop a $16 million shopping mall in the mid-western Sydney suburb of Bankstown, they had no inkling that it would land them in a cloak-and-dagger subterfuge to trap a bunch of crooks. Bankstown was the fastest-growing municipality in the Sydney area in the early 1960s, its population having almost doubled over the past ten years. But, despite having been identified by the state government's postwar planners as a regional centre for retailing and employment, up till then Bankstown's commercial development had failed to keep pace with its rapidly growing population. As a result, most of the municipality's retailing dollar was escaping to the city and other suburban areas, a flow which Dusseldorp had in mind to stem. Lend Lease drew up plans to develop a regional shopping mall in early 1962, and received in-principle approval from Bankstown Council in March that year. The company then began the process of site acquisition—involving the purchase of more than 100 separate properties —while more detailed planning for the project proceeded. With further research suggesting that the area could support a more substantial shopping complex than originally envisaged, the company submitted revised plans for a larger mall to Bankstown Council in June 1963. And it was as this revised proposal started wending its way through the Council's approval procedures that the shenanigans had begun.

On 6 August 1963, the day Council was set to consider a report on the revised proposal from its Town Planning Department, Lend Lease's Project Manager for the Bankstown shopping mall, engineer Alex McLeod, received a mysterious phone call. It was from a public relations consultant, who said he was ringing on behalf of a man called Fitzgerald. The latter wanted to arrange an interview with the property development firm as he believed, given his familiarity with a number of Bankstown Council aldermen, that he could help fast-track approval for the project. Something about the call from the PR man aroused McLeod's suspicions, and he immediately told Dusseldorp about it. The Lend Lease Chairman agreed it sounded suspect and put in a call to the police. At the Council meeting that night, two plain-clothes detectives silently watched proceedings as consideration of the Lend Lease proposal was deferred. The following day McLeod received another call from the PR consultant and a meeting with Fitzgerald was arranged. Taking place in Lend Lease's headquarters at Circular Quay, that meeting removed any possibility that Fitzgerald's offer to 'fast-track' the proposal might conceivably be above board. For a monetary consideration, the man suggested, he could guarantee approval of the shopping centre at the next meeting of Council. He would leave the proposition with McLeod to think about, he said, and the two of them could discuss it in more detail over lunch in a couple of days' time. Little did Fitzgerald know that that luncheon, and the various events that followed it, would be very closely observed.

'I had twice before been confronted by somebody putting the touch on me for a bribe,' Dusseldorp says as he relates the story of the Bankstown Council corruption scandal almost forty years later.

> In both [those] instances, I went to the [political] party concerned, made them
> aware of the situation, and asked them what they were going to do about it.
> We also went to the police, but they said that they'd have to mount a stake-out
> so as to trap [the conspirators], and that I *hadn't* been prepared to do.

Word of these actions presumably got back to the parties in question, however, for when Dusseldorp refused to make the requested payments, on both occasions the problem had 'faded away'.[3] These two experiences having thus been left behind, if not resolved, when the initial signs of a third case emerged, Dusseldorp was determined to put a stop to it once and for all. Within three hours of his Bankstown Square Project Manager receiving the first suspicious phone call, Dusseldorp had contacted not only the police but also the state minister responsible for local government. This time, he told them, he was prepared to lay a trap. After McLeod's initial meeting with Fitzgerald confirmed the developer's suspicions that a bribe was being sought, plans to collect material evidence of the corruption plot were laid. The first step would be to determine who this man Fitzgerald was acting for, and to that end Dusseldorp and McLeod would pump him for more information. The police would observe this meeting and follow the identified suspect, then they would see where to take it from there. With a lunchtime appointment between McLeod and Fitzgerald already scheduled, what better place to start the stake-out than at Sydney's quayside restaurant, Le Chalet?

Bankstown Council was sacked by the Minister for Local Government in November 1963, sufficient evidence having by then been obtained to charge five of its former aldermen, and the man known as Fitzgerald, with conspiracy.

All six were committed for trial, which took place in 1965. Evidence from McLeod, Dusseldorp, and the police witnesses dominated the two weeks of the criminal proceedings, with details of secretly taped conversations, clandestine racetrack meetings, and the package of marked banknotes hidden in the backyard convenience of a local real estate agency all making sensational headlines in the Sydney press. When the trial came to an end in June 1965, three of the six men, including Alderman Little and the go-between, 'Fitzgerald', were sentenced to a year's imprisonment for their role in the crime.[4]

As for Lend Lease's plans for the Bankstown Square shopping mall, they received approval from the authorities, and construction started early in 1964. Completed in 1966, what was then Australia's largest shopping centre initially faced some tough competition from rival Westfield's nearby Roselands mall (which had opened the year before), but with innovative and aggressive marketing over time Bankstown Square became a commercial success. Indeed, for many years the mall would be Lend Lease's retailing flagship, and although it is now but one of some eighteen shopping centres in the company's Asia–Pacific retail portfolio, it still enjoys a special status in the fold. (As well as providing the backdrop to the dramatic events described above, Bankstown Square was the project on which a young Site Engineer called Stuart Hornery started to make his mark on the company that he would subsequently lead.) But the events at Bankstown Square left their imprint on Lend Lease in another respect as well. 'The funny thing was,' says Dusseldorp, 'that after that episode, I *never, ever* had anybody approach me seeking a bribe. Word had obviously gone around in the right circles: "Don't mess with that guy." '[5]

Dusseldorp's handling of the Bankstown bribery scandal sent a strong message to the outside world, but it was one already well-known in the corridors of Lend Lease. Although operating in an industry whose history of dubious tendering practices, widespread corner-cutting, and episodes of graft and corruption had earned it an unsavoury reputation, no one associated with Dusseldorp's company could be in any doubt as to how its Chairman expected his employees to behave. He set the tone, and he expected others to echo it. 'Duss was a man of integrity,' says Ern Mac Donald, former Chairman of the corporation's construction arm, Civil & Civic.

You just knew that he didn't take short cuts, he didn't dud people. He was a hard businessman—he'd drive a hard bargain—but there's two parties to a bargain ... If we did something for him—a private job, something for his house, then if you didn't have an account on his table the next day, you'd get a phone call ... He was utterly—completely—ethical. I remember one time, in the early days, when we'd done everything we could think of to try and win this job to build the new Trades Hall building in Sydney. In the end, [another company] got the contract, and I went in to report the bad news to Duss. We were talking it over and I made some passing comment to him, like 'Well, maybe we should have played it a different way', but he cut me straight off.[6]

Anything with even a hint of less-than-total-straightforwardness was ruled right out.

Of course, ethical business practice involves much more than just a commitment to playing by the rules, as important as that undoubtedly is. A broader definition of the term encompasses behaviour going well beyond the minimum standards required by law. Some firms encourage this by drawing up codes of conduct for dealing with customers, suppliers, and other parties, defining standards for these transactions which they expect all their staff to observe. But a still broader definition of what constitutes ethical business practice goes further than the matters commonly covered by such codes. It goes to issues at the heart of how, and to what ends, a corporation is run: to what it sees as its over-riding purpose, the integrity and inclusiveness of the systems and structures through which it is governed, the set of values it espouses, the way it conducts itself in relation to each of its key stakeholders, the type of goals it sets for itself and how it measures its success. In sum, it goes to the whole panoply of issues that can be grouped under the rubric of corporate governance.

Such an all-encompassing definition of ethical business practice would not be accepted by everyone. Thirty years ago, Milton Friedman said that 'There is only one social responsibility of business—to use its resources and engage in activities designed to increase its profits.'[7] A more modern tweak on this unitary purpose idea is espoused by advocates of the principle of shareholder value. 'The primary and over-riding obligation of Boards and the executive leadership and management [of a corporation]', says the Australian Chamber of Commerce and Industry, for example, 'are [sic] to pursue, within the rule of law, objectives which are in the longer term best interests of shareholders; in short, to maximise shareholder value.' Any other interests, according to the Chamber, presumably including those of employees, customers, the community, and the environment 'are subordinate to this obligation'.[8] Dusseldorp had a different view.

'It was Duss's fundamental belief that a healthy organisation had a balance between shareholder return, employee return, and customer return,' says Geoff McWilliam, former Chief Executive of Australia's first listed property trust, GPT. 'They were the three main elements that made up a healthy organisation, and if ever you got the balance out of whack, he used to say, it would catch up with you—you'd stop being a healthy group.' This sentiment was more than the expression of noble-sounding words, as an example recounted by McWilliam illustrates. 'There were four times in the period when I was at the General Property Trust that we actually voluntarily lowered the management fee,' he says, 'because it was Duss's view that the manager was getting too much at the expense of the investors.' (As discussed in Chapter 3, Dusseldorp had established GPT in the early 1970s to provide a vehicle for the public to invest in prime development projects completed by Lend Lease. The Trust paid a management fee to a Lend Lease subsidiary which managed the properties on its behalf, and it was this fee that Dusseldorp insisted be lowered.) 'Now that was *unheard* of sort of stuff,' says McWilliam. 'But he had the vision to say, "It will catch up with us one day."'[9]

John Morschel, former Chief Executive of Lend Lease, agrees that this focus on meeting stakeholder—not just shareholder—needs was the cornerstone of Dusseldorp's approach. 'It was Duss who introduced me to the stakeholder concept,' he says. 'He believed that shareholders, staff, *and* customers must all win if an enterprise is to survive and prosper.' Giving these three groups equal billing in Lend Lease's *raison d'être* was not based on some altruistic notion of Dusseldorp's. He firmly believed that following such an approach optimised rewards for *all* of the corporation's stakeholders, as Morschel goes on to explain.

> For customers, his philosophy of always structuring a proposal focused on value not cost more often than not put his customers in a winning position. This had the added advantage of developing repeat client business. For shareholders he strove to provide growth in earnings with 'no nasty surprises'. GPT is a great example of

9, 10 Caltex House (*above*), Sydney's first concrete-framed skyscraper, was completed by Civil & Civic in 1957. Its construction was virtually uninterrupted by industrial action—a notable achievement at a time when Sydney's building industry unions and bosses were in almost constant dispute. The productivity agreement struck between Civil & Civic and the NSW building trade unions in 1958 (and renewed annually thereafter) formalised the unique industrial partnership between Dusseldorp's firm, its employees and their unions. *Below*, Pat Clancy, Secretary of the Building Workers' Industrial Union (NSW Branch) (left), and Jack Mundey, his counterpart in the Builders Labourers' Federation (right), share a drink with Dusseldorp after an all-employee meeting in November 1972 which marked the extension of the agreement to Lend Lease workers Australia-wide.

11, 12 Dusseldorp on a site visit (*above*) and giving his bi-annual 'State of the Nation' address to all employees in 1984 (*below*): two of the ways he kept open the communication lines with the Lend Lease workforce.

13, 14 Building Canberra's copper-domed Academy of Science (1959, *above*) raised the profile of Civil & Civic in Australia's national capital. Scores of other buildings followed, including, in the early 1960s, an integrated office development in the city's Hobart Place (*below*).

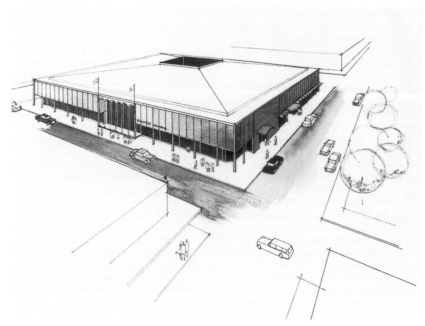

15, 16 Lend Lease developed a number of Canberra's shopping centres, including the city's first, Monaro Mall (*above*) in the early 1960s. Some ten years later the Australian Prime Minister, William McMahon (pictured *below* with Dusseldorp), opened another Lend Lease shopping mall at Canberra's Woden Plaza.

his success. Duss developed what was, at the time, a unique structure [in] GPT which has enabled it to survive the wild roller-coaster ride of several boom and bust property cycles, whilst meeting the needs of unit-holders. Today we take listed property trusts like GPT for granted, but in the early 1970s when Duss first floated the GPT concept, he was, as usual, way ahead of the times.

As for employees, Morschel continues, Dusseldorp's 'uncanny ability to understand the real needs of others' found expression in the range of workforce benefits he introduced—benefits which provided employees with both financial security and an opportunity 'to share in the results to which they contributed'. As well as providing generous superannuation benefits for all his employees at a time when such practices were unheard of, 'Duss also initiated, with shareholder approval, an egalitarian profit-sharing scheme and a range of share ownership plans. Once again, these benefits broke new ground.'[10]

To Dusseldorp, such initiatives, and in particular the idea that underlay them, were fundamental to his business success. 'I keep going back to this thing,' he says, 'to this idea of a community of interest. I see it as *the* most important aspect,' he adds. 'Because without it, I would never have had a hope in hell to do the other things I did. So if you ask me, where does my heart lie in what I've done, what do I see as my primary contribution, then it's there.'[11]

Right from day one we were convinced that a worthwhile and profitable contribution to society could only be *satisfactorily* achieved by developing a true partnership between investors and employees. The profit growth per share over thirty years attests to the economic validity of this proposition.[12]

The idea of finding or creating a community of interests pervades Dusseldorp's working life, but there is no more central expression of it than in the partnership he forged between the investors and employees of Lend Lease. Indeed, for Dusseldorp, this relationship is at the heart of corporate governance: 'how to bring shareholders, management and workers [together] in a team—that is what *I* mean by corporate governance,' he says. 'It just seemed odd to me,' he continues, 'that if people are assembled in a common enterprise—one is a shareholder, another is a manager, yet another is a worker—how *could* they go against each other, instead of working together for their *mutual* benefit?' None of these parties is powerless to press their legitimate claims to a share of the enterprise's profits—'managers want to get a good whack themselves,' he says, 'the returns to shareholders are in the public eye so they're okay, and the unions are there to protect the workers'—so it just seems counterproductive for any one of these groups to try to boost *their* share at the expense of that of the others. 'Because if instead they cooperate,' Dusseldorp says, 'then there is *more* coming out [of the enterprise]. And if there's more coming out, that means there is more to be shared. Then that in turn makes it easier to cooperate, and so it keeps on going—it's just as simple as that.'[13]

As self-evident as it seemed to Dusseldorp, such a philosophy, and the methods by which he implemented it, were little short of revolutionary in the Australian postwar business environment. (Many would argue that they still are today.) The introduction of two schemes in particular—those for profit-sharing and employee share ownership—caused something of a stir. Dusseldorp had experimented with variants of both employee participation programs in the 1950s and 1960s, but it was the company's first national industrial agreement, forged in the early 1970s with Bob Hawke—then head of the Australian Council of Trade Unions—that heralded the extension of such schemes to *all* employees of Lend Lease. The 1972 agreement introduced a flat-rate profit sharing scheme in that year, while the all-employee share ownership scheme followed the year after. The new measures did not go down well in some quarters. 'I encountered tremendous resistance,' Dusseldorp says—some of it, at the start, from within his own organisation—but the most concerted objections came from his industry peers. 'I was very unpopular in the employers' organisations,' he says, 'in fact, they hated my guts. The Master Builders [Association] were furious when I negotiated the agreement with Hawke—they really thought that was the pits.'[14]

The MBA's attitude, if extreme, was not atypical, for Australian companies have historically shown little interest in broad-based employee equity or profit-sharing schemes. And with the bulk of the country's workers and their unions prepared to let the issue lie, it is no surprise that Australia then had, indeed continues to have, one of the lowest rates of participation in such programs amongst the countries of the Organisation for Economic Cooperation and Development.[15] It was only in the 1990s that the considerable advantages to be had from such schemes became more widely appreciated, and as a result, their number is at last starting to grow. 'In the olden days—maybe five years ago— a limited number of executives and even fewer employees would participate in any type of share plan,' Edward Wright, an adviser on such plans, told workplace communications consultant Fran Simons in 2000. 'Now, all of the top 150 listed companies would have a plan of one sort or another.'[16] 'It's all over the place now,' agrees Dusseldorp. 'It was maybe a year or two ago that I read that the last big bank in the American banking system had also got into the issue of shares, the *significant* issue of shares, to its employees. That was only recently,' he says. 'So … I think I hit onto something when I introduced it here [in Australia] way back then.'[17]

There are many reasons why employee share ownership schemes are currently proving attractive. 'There is increasing growth in the use of these things to reward and retain staff, to encourage loyalty, and indeed to attract staff in the first place where you have a start-up company,' says Wright.[18] All are vital considerations for firms anxious to win 'the war for talent' and to become 'employers of choice'. But, as we have seen, Dusseldorp's motivation for the introduction of one of Australia's first such schemes (and still one of its most financially significant) went to an issue more fundamental than these—that of fostering the common interest between employees and investors in the firm. If employees were sharing in the rewards of their endeavours, he reasoned, then they would have an in-built incentive to work smarter so that the company's performance might improve. And as it did improve, so too would the returns to both them and other shareholders—making for a classic positive-sum game.

While many companies cite such an alignment of employee and business interests as a major motive for the use of such schemes in remunerating their executive and managerial staff,[19] Dusseldorp could not see why such a policy should stop at the office door. 'Why *should* that [performance motivation] be any different,' he asks, 'just because you, as a worker, have one hat and I, as a manager, have another?'[20] In his view it was essential that the Lend Lease schemes be available to *all* employees of the enterprise, be they members of the on-site construction workforce or property investment executives on the top floor of Australia Square. Likewise, the schemes had to be meaningful—not only in dollar terms for the employee, but also in terms of the amount of the company's share capital that they involved. Both parameters were adhered to, as Ern Mac Donald explains.

There was a whole range of share schemes that we introduced over the years. Initially we did it through the super scheme, then through an Employee Investment Trust, and later on through an Employee Share Acquisition Plan.[21] And every so often Duss used to give out a hundred [shares] to everyone on top of that ... We were given 800 all told—and then there was a 2-for-1 issue, so all up you'd have 1600—which, if you'd hung on to them all, would be worth a few bob today (not to mention all the earnings over time) ... Those extra hundreds—they were really treasured, you know. Because so many employees were shareholders.[22]

Still today over 90 per cent of Lend Lease's employees worldwide, and 100 per cent of its Australian workforce, have some level of equity participation in the company.[23] Mac Donald continues:

We got up to 26 per cent [employee share ownership] of the company at one stage, although it's come back from that now to about 14 per cent ... But even at the lower figure, employees are still, collectively, one of the largest shareholders in Lend Lease.[24] The profit share was good too. It was distributed to all employees equally as a flat amount. Some people say it was peanuts, but not if you're a clerical employee—a junior clerk or something—then it's not peanuts, it's a big percentage of your salary. And the idea of it is right—getting an equal share.[25]

As for the impact of the employee–investor partnership on the company's bottom line, Dusseldorp sees the evidence as unequivocal. 'I think this sums it up,' he says, pointing to the quotation which opens Lend Lease's 1988 annual report, the year in which he retired as Chairman of the group. The quotation reads: 'Right from day one we were convinced that a worthwhile and profitable contribution to society could only be *satisfactorily* achieved by developing a true partnership between investors and employees. The profit growth per share over thirty years attests to the economic validity of this proposition.'[26] 'And if you take a look at the figures,' the author of those words continues, 'you'll find out what I mean.'[27] $100 invested in the company's shares on debut in 1958, he points out, was by 1988 worth over $100,000. Over that period Lend Lease— and hence its employees and shareholders—enjoyed a virtually uninterrupted run of annual profit growth, a record that compares more than favourably with most its peers. While it is impossible to determine how much of that profit growth was *directly* attributable to the presence of the partnership initiatives, the near-unanimous approval of resolutions to implement them by both the company's shareholders and its employees indicate the value that both sides of the equation placed on them.

Over time the demonstrated returns from the investor–employee partnership convinced Lend Lease shareholders that they were on to a good thing, but what made them willing to go along with this strategy in the first place? Why did shareholders vote in favour of employee participation schemes which a good proportion of the building and construction industry evidently saw as over-generous? The answer to these questions is multi-faceted. Firstly, the profit-sharing measures that Lend Lease shareholders endorsed at annual general meetings in the early 1970s (and beyond) did not come out of the blue. Dusseldorp had always been up-front in his commitment to rewarding employees generously for their contribution to the company; in that sense, the new schemes were simply another step along that path. The measures would 'contribute to achieving economic justice', the Lend Lease Chairman told a packed shareholders' meeting at Bankstown Square shopping mall in 1973, and although their cost was substantial, he was confident that it would be absorbed from the resulting increase in productivity.[28] Judging from the applause his address received, shareholders shared his faith.

Secondly, Dusseldorp's generosity was not one-sided. 'Dusseldorp was always very much the person looking to the balance of both sides,' says Richard Longes, long-time adviser to, then director of, Lend Lease, and now the company's Deputy Chairman. 'He used to be quite hurt if people stereotyped him as a rapacious property developer, as someone ripping off the shareholders. But that was never his style. Quite the opposite.'[29] 'We used to make calculations', says long-time Lend Lease executive David Thorne, 'of the amount of money that was distributed between shareholders and employees. And basically the shareholders and employees were treated as equal people: because if you didn't have shareholders, then you didn't have money, but if you didn't have employees, you didn't have a company.'[30] The logical consequence of one of these groups being treated generously, therefore, was that the other would benefit too. In 1973, for example, the year the employee share ownership scheme was introduced, Lend Lease shareholders received their third bonus issue—one-for-two—in as many years, and the dividend payment was lifted from 10 to 12.5 cents per unit.[31]

'Duss *rattled* the whole shareholding activity,' continues David Thorne. 'In the early days, a lot of companies would pay out 10 or 20 or 30 per cent of their profits to shareholders in dividends. Dusseldorp always said—from Day One— that was ridiculous, that you should pay out a bigger proportion. And he always calculated 50, 60, 70 per cent of profits would go to shareholders.'[32] 'He was a very generous man,' agrees Richard Longes.

> He would be quite disparaging of people who looked to financially engineer things
> … He would always be generous in what he gave to shareholders, even if the
> [company's bottom line] numbers then subsequently didn't look quite so good. I
> think I, and Stuart [Hornery], learnt quite a lot from him. Rather than try and issue
> shares at a discount of 5 per cent, he'd just come straight out and say, 'It's going to
> be 10 per cent, to make sure they *really* like it'. Now, these days these things are
> the subject of very minute financial [calculations], and that's not regarded as good
> financial play, but that was his approach.

'He wouldn't have felt comfortable with a lot of what goes on *generally* these days,' Longes adds, 'because he was a much more straightforward thinker.'[33]

While demonstrated results, a proven track record, and shared rewards were key factors explaining the trust of Lend Lease shareholders in their Chairman —in his investor–employee partnership idea and more generally—a further key ingredient was his commitment to regular and effective communications. The cornerstone of Dusseldorp's shareholder relations strategy was undoubtedly the company's annual general meetings. These were large-scale events—hosted in flagship or prestige venues, with food and entertainment laid on[34]—and individual shareholders flocked to them. Although a good roll-up at such meetings may not be so uncommon these days—especially if shareholders want to let their directors know that they're unhappy with the company's performance—it was much more unusual a few decades ago. 'Lend Lease's annual general meetings are one of the few well-attended functions on the corporate calendar,' *The Australian* reported in 1983. These meetings were one of the ways, the newspaper observed, that 'shareholders … [are] made to feel they share in the company and are a vital part of its operations'.[35]

As well as the conventional fare of reporting on the company's results and prospects, Dusseldorp would use his Chairman's Address at the annual general meetings—a speech which he would write himself—to deal with meaty themes on the broader corporate and social agenda.[36] He would also take every opportunity to stress the link between the company's returns and its high level of employee involvement. 'He virtually sold the idea, at the annual meetings,' says David Thorne, 'of contributing to the benefits for the employees, because without them, he told shareholders, they wouldn't have all these profits.'[37] 'He built up this incredible trust with the audience', says Sharon Goldie, Lend Lease's Corporate Projects Director,

> because [his speeches were] user-friendly and he *delivered* on what he was
> talking about ... He would always have Question and Answer sessions [she adds],
> because he understood that if you give shareholders the opportunity of asking
> questions, they will trust you more. He understood the power of communication,
> the power of that sort of availability and interactivity ... He would keep Q and A
> sessions going for as long as people had questions, and that, in itself, is a
> signal—to investors and potential investors—that this is an open sort of
> company.[38]

Over time Lend Lease annual general meetings evolved into major productions, with the latest technology used to enable shareholders in cities across the country to participate in them. In a first for corporate Australia, Lend Lease's first nationally networked annual general meeting was held in 1983, with land-line and microwave link-ups joining venues in Sydney, Melbourne, and Brisbane. A year or two later satellite technology became available, bringing improvements to the extent and quality of national coverage, and Lend Lease was amongst the first Australian corporates to deploy the new technology in this way. The strategy did not go unnoticed by Dusseldorp's peers. 'He was a very progressive-minded Chairman about shareholder activities and investor relations and marketing,' says Frank Lowy, Chairman of rival property group Westfield Holdings. 'He was very, very innovative and very forward-looking. Some of his shareholder meetings were beamed across Australia and all this type of thing—they were big events.' But for Lowy there was a much more important measure of Dusseldorp's chairmanship. 'But basically, I mean, that sort of thing is a bit of a side-line ... Basically, fundamentally, he had a very good company, he *built* a very good company.'[39]

It is all very well to maintain good communications with shareholders when a company's performance and prospects look rosy, but what about when the news is not so good, or the outlook is more uncertain? Few would disagree that transparency and disclosure are critical components of good corporate govern-ance at *any* time, but they come to the fore in adverse, or potentially adverse, circumstances. As noted above, more often than not the results reported to Lend Lease shareholders at their annual general meetings were good ones. But the fact that some of the company's ventures had not come off as profitably as expected was no reason to stem the information flow. 'Duss's view was that if you communicated with your investors through good times and in bad,' says Geoff McWilliam, 'then they would stand by you through good times and in bad.'[40] This included a commitment to proactively protect shareholder interests if the corporation was about to embark on unusual or particularly risky ventures. The story of the float of Lend Lease Petroleum, which John Morschel relates, illustrates both characteristics.

'In the early 1980s,' says Morschel, 'we had an opportunity, in conjunc-tion with a multinational oil company, to drill some holes in [Australia's most productive oil region] Bass Strait.' It was the era of the much-vaunted resources boom in Australia—vaunted being the operative word—and a number of companies, from a range of industries, were keen to get a piece of the action.

> The seismic data looked, as it always does—fantastic, [Morschel remembers] and Dick said, 'Well, okay, if we're going to get into this we should float it as a separate organisation, because petroleum exploration—drilling for oil—really doesn't belong *within* Lend Lease.' And if you look at what happened to various other companies at the time, the ones that brought resources into a manufacturing company or a sugar company—you can see what trouble *they* got into. But Dick said, 'We'll go to the shareholders, and give them an opportunity to participate, but we shouldn't just take them in there without their informed approval.'[41]

But he also realised that if he *suggested* that they should invest in oil—he wouldn't tell them to, but if he suggested it—they would invest regardless, because they used to [be willing to] follow him over a cliff. So he said, 'We can't let that happen: they *must* be told that it's high-risk.' So on the front of this prospectus [for a separately constituted company called Lend Lease Petroleum] we put, in great big letters, in plain English, that it was a high-risk investment. Now, today's regulations might ensure that this is common practice, but unless you worked with Duss, it wasn't always the case a generation ago. Well, despite the warning, a lot of them still invested their money, and of course they, and Lend Lease, and a lot of the staff who invested in it, lost out.[42]

All four wells dug in Bass Strait by the joint-venture partners turned out to be dry. By 1984 it was clear that the project had been a fizzer and, after a full report on the damage at Lend Lease's AGM that year, Dusseldorp told shareholders, with candour, 'We gambled and we lost.'[43]

'Sometimes people forget that there were things that Dick tried that didn't work,' says Morschel—and petroleum exploration was certainly one of them—'but that didn't stop him trying new things. Nor did it alter the principles under which he operated ... With new ideas, he'd always restrict the amount of money he'd put at risk in relation to the thing, so it didn't become a calamity for the organisation.'[44] Lend Lease's write-off for its share in the petroleum exploration venture, for example, did not stop the corporation declaring a record $41.5 million profit in 1984—up 35 per cent from the previous year.[45] Morschel continues:

And he just *insisted*, that on important decisions like that, that [shareholders] should have a say ... It wasn't so much that he warned them, 'This is high-risk', it was that he said, 'We're *not* going to just take our shareholders into it by using Lend Lease's money. We're going to tell them what we think we should do, who the partners are, what the prospects are, etcetera, and if they *then* want to put their money in, that's fine, they've had an opportunity to make a decision.' And it wasn't as if the regulatory environment was constraining him. It was just that Dick had this fantastic respect for the shareholders. He didn't feel that he had this God-given right to just waltz off and take them in any direction he wanted to ... He would always talk to shareholders at meetings about the philosophy of, and the reasons for, what he was doing: he was a *lot* more open than most.[46]

Profits are not the only yardstick by which to judge performance: in fact, profit is rapidly losing its dominant position in this judgement. Society is tending to adopt the philosophy that it is better to do work that makes a better life, than to make a better living ... The time is not far off when companies will have to justify their worth to society, as indeed increasingly major public and private investments have to do now, with greater emphasis being placed on environmental and social impact than straight economics.[47]

The notion that corporations have a responsibility to the communities in which they operate, broader than that of increasing their profits (*à la* Milton Friedman), is one that, if by no means universally accepted, at least enjoys some currency today. It was a much less common view, however, for a corporate heavyweight to espouse in Australia some three decades ago. A major theme of Dusseldorp's address to shareholders at Lend Lease's 1973 annual general meeting was that the record profit he had just announced, while important, was not, and should not be, the only measure of the corporation's value. Society was starting to judge business on much broader grounds, he said, and it would undoubtedly continue to do so in the future. 'The time is not far off,' he predicted, 'when companies will have to justify their worth to society, as indeed increasingly major public and private investments have to do now, with greater emphasis being placed on environmental and social impact than straight economics.'[48]

In essence Dusseldorp's 1973 Chairman's Address prefigured the concept of 'triple bottom line' accounting—a way of focusing corporations, according to the coiner of the phrase, 'not just on the economic value they add, but also on the environmental and social value they add—and destroy.'[49] Pursuing such an approach has increasing appeal today amongst companies looking for new ways to bolster brand value and to enhance their reputation,[50] but neither consideration seems to have been a primary motivator for Dusseldorp, as Richard Longes observes.

The recognition of a community of interest between stakeholders is something that Dick had from a time when that [concept] was less well-known. He had a basic principle that the company was *part* of the community: that it had to push everything that it did to the limits. He didn't see it so much in terms of reputation—he saw it as the need to create something beautiful, something that wasn't 'just good enough' … When it came to property development, for example, it certainly wasn't 'just good enough' to take something and make money out of it. It had to be something *different* … There was a constant pressing, a constant energy to drive something to a new level.[51]

As well as this drive for excellence—his dissatisfaction with 'just good enough' solutions—a further expression of Dusseldorp's desire to do 'work that makes a better life' was the long term perspective he brought to his field. 'He often told me,' says Dick's son Tjerk, 'that what set him apart from his business contemporaries was his preparedness to take the long view. A favourite saying of his was that it takes at least seven years to develop a significant project, and at least three years to turn something around.'[52] Harry Seidler—the distinguished architect who collaborated with Dusseldorp on numerous major building projects—makes a similar point, using one such long-term project— the development of Sydney's Australia Square—as indicative of his approach.

'One could sense the fundamental decency that the man exuded in worrying that he was doing the right thing—', Seidler observes, 'that he gave something to society in what he built.'[53] A classic example of this, says Seidler, was Dusseldorp's commitment to incorporating a public plaza in the Australia Square development. As discussed in Chapter 1, this dedication of urban open space to the public was one of the features that so distinguished Australia Square from its contemporaries. While the latter buildings 'demonstrate little concern for their neighbours or life on the street', writes architectural historian Jennifer Taylor, Australia Square—'a handsome building that was successful financially and at the same time gave the city a sunny, sheltered, public square; the kind of space it was tending to lose rather than gain'—'must rank as one of Australia's most important works of the post-war period'.[54] Covering every square centimetre of the central city site with rentable office space may have yielded more profit to the developer in the short term, but to Dusseldorp the longer-term value generated by a more responsible approach to development counted for more.

This longer-term perspective was evident in many other aspects of the design and construction of Australia Square. While many other property developers were 'steeped in only spending the minimum', says Seidler, 'Dusseldorp's policy was to "build and keep". And that is a much more moral way to go about development,' he adds. Such a policy encouraged, for example, an up-front concern with the long-term costs of the building's maintenance and upkeep—factors which did not always figure in the calculations of those who 'just put something up and then hawk it'.[55] 'There were two instances,' says the architect. 'First of all he sent me to Rome,' to work with the Italian leader in concrete construction, Professor Pier Luigi Nervi, 'and I learnt how to build … [Australia Square's circular Tower building], not only *out* of concrete, but to make concrete in such a way that it will last. And look at it after forty years,' he adds, 'it *still* looks new.' A similar approach was evident in the choice of other key building materials.

> Everyone was chiselling away at the cost of the thing, [says Seidler] but then, I remember, it came to deciding what sort of glass would be used … In those days [the 1960s], glass was comparatively primitive—they didn't have float glass—and so I said to [Dusseldorp], 'The normal glass is X, but to really make this thing better—so that you don't get inaccuracies in the glass—plate glass is the thing to use. It will cost a lot more … but if you can afford it, plate glass would be the thing for that building.' He did not quibble for one minute. He said, 'You can have plate glass.' And I thought, 'My God, this is going to cost X amount more,' but he could see that if you really want to have a product that will last the distance, you should put the proper thing in [from the start].[56]

The principles that Harry Seidler describes as manifest in Dusseldorp's approach to the design and construction of Australia Square were also evident when the latter turned his attention to property development on a much larger areal scale, for example in the development of Campbelltown in Sydney's south-west. (This, and other community-level building projects, are discussed in Chapter 7.) What is most apparent from these, and other, instances is that Dusseldorp did not see 'doing something for the community' as an optional extra for Lend Lease, but as an integral part of the way the enterprise went about its business. 'The company's activities have to be socially relevant …', he told his staff in the early 1980s. 'Whilst we are busy making profits for our benefit, this should always benefit others as well, never [be] at their expense. In short,' he added, using a by-now-familiar phrase, 'the pursuit of a community of interests.'[57] Such an approach is a far cry from one which frames corporate social engagement as a matter of philanthropy, as Lend Lease's Eric Goodwin remarks.

> In the US, a lot of the people who give money back to the community usually do so after they've made a fortune. But that wasn't Duss' approach at all. His approach was ... I think his words were, 'You can either extract the most profit out of a situation, or you can leave something behind so that everybody's happy.' And that was very much his ideal: leaving something behind for the team that helped create the wealth, and something for the next generation, and for the community.[58]

A venture masterminded by Stuart Hornery in the early 1980s, with the backing of his Chairman, provides a further example of how this philosophy was given substantive shape.

The year was 1981 and Australia, like a number of countries across the industrialised world, was on the brink of recession. Inflation and unemployment, already high, were continuing to climb as the country's economic engine began to sputter and falter. Young people bore the brunt of the ensuing downturn as cash-strapped industries began to lay off their workers. It was a grim situation and the building and construction industry was not immune. 'That recession impacted in a horrible way on the apprentices,' remembers Dusseldorp.

> For the first time in memory, there were wholesale lay-offs of apprentices in the industry. That had never happened before, and it was so grotesque—it was not just a little bit, it was massive. It was such a major problem for the future. I kept on telling these people [his colleagues in the industry] that they were behaving like farmers who were eating the seed for the next harvest. They might be happy in the short term because of the savings they had made, but in the long term ...
> Well, that is all very well said, but what do you do about it?[59]

Stuart Hornery, then Managing Director of Lend Lease, had an idea. He had, for some time, been thinking about another problem besetting the training opportunities for young people who aspired to the building trade—a problem which the onset of recession would only exacerbate. Increasing specialisation and sub-contracting were already making it hard for small employers in the industry to provide apprentices with a sufficiently broad experience of their trade. With many of those businesses now going under, and with larger employers simultaneously laying off their trainees, a skills crisis was looming. Hornery was not alone in his concerns. The building trade unions were worried too, and when the Managing Director of Lend Lease suggested that they do something together to address the problem, the unions were willing to try it. As part of the 1981 renegotiation of the company's national productivity agreement with the ACTU, Lend Lease pledged $1 million over four years to create a jointly managed foundation, the charter of which would be to encourage young people to acquire skills and to encourage employers to train them.[60] A scheme to do that was drawn up at the first meeting of the ACTU–Lend Lease Foundation, and it is still in operation today.

'An initiative had been taken some years before by the Master Builders' Association,' says Dusseldorp, recounting the thinking behind the Foundation's successful first program, 'and even though we weren't a member of the Association at the time, we did notice it and thought it was a very good one. They had taken on some young people and placed them amongst their membership, thus forming Australia's first group apprenticeship scheme.' Apprentices were rotated through placements with various host employers, giving them exposure to a much broader range of skills than any one small firm could provide. 'The only problem was that [the scheme] was rather token,' says Dusseldorp, 'the idea hadn't really caught on. So when the big recession hit, we thought it would be good to pick up that idea and run a project along those lines through the [ACTU–Lend Lease] Foundation on a much wider scale.'[61] David Thorne, the Foundation's inaugural Executive Director, was given the task of putting the expanded program in place, and before the first year was out he had four group apprenticeship schemes operating in communities across New South Wales.

To make an even greater impact, however, the Foundation could do with some extra help. 'So I proposed a deal with the government,' says Dusseldorp, 'that the ACTU–Lend Lease Foundation fund the set-up of these group training companies right across Australia as a private initiative, and that they [the government] chip in by meeting the cost of the staff to run them.'[62] These staff would negotiate placements for the apprentices in local firms and coordinate their off-the-job training. Although this proposal initially met a mixed reception—while many of the states were keen, the federal government was somewhat wary—an agreement was nonetheless reached whereby the two levels of government would together match private funding for the schemes' administrative costs on a dollar-for-dollar basis. Lend Lease also looked to its own construction firm's sub-contractors for a contribution to the program. 'We encouraged the subbies to become involved with the group schemes,' says David Thorne, 'and told them that their use of apprentices and trainees would be recognised in gaining contracts from Lend Lease.' That form of persuasion had the desired effect, Thorne reports. 'A lot of them made considerable use of the group schemes set up by the Foundation. In fact at one stage the Australia Square Training Company was the largest employer of trainees in Sydney.'[63]

> So that was how the scheme kicked off, [says Dusseldorp] and it soon took on a
> life of its own. It started in New South Wales, but really spread like wildfire. In
> fact, group training has now become almost the backbone of apprenticeships. The
> traditional arrangements never really recovered from the recession. The old system
> had clearly outlived its usefulness, and now a new system has taken its place.[64]

Today group training schemes are the largest employer of apprentices and trainees in Australia—employing over 36,000 people in more than 200 locations across the country.[65] And while they are still very important in the construction industry, they extend well beyond its borders as well. 'It just goes to show', Dusseldorp told a 1994 conference charged with drawing up tomorrow's urban agenda, 'the impact that *one* initiative can have on a stubborn problem.'[66] It also goes to show, as the author of a history of the ACTU–Lend Lease Foundation remarks, what can happen when a company decides to '[use its] corporate power to make a practical difference to the lives of thousands of young people and hundreds of communities'.[67]

Dusseldorp's approach to corporate governance—his fundamental belief in the community of interest between investors and employees; his practice of sharing rewards with both these groups and with clients; and his engagement of the enterprise in the broader community—encompass a much broader definition of ethical business practice than those often encountered in the corporate world.

What is more, he saw each of these three tenets as perfectly compatible with—in fact, as essential to—running a profitable organisation. 'Lend Lease *has to* be profitable,' Dusseldorp told his employees. 'If profits stop, everything else stops with it.' But, he said in the same breath, profits were not the be-all and end-all. 'Pursuit of profits for its own sake is a sterile activity. Profits must serve a purpose.'[68] It was a philosophy that he followed, not only in building a multimillion-dollar enterprise from scratch but, as we will see in the next chapter, in turning around an even larger one.

CHAPTER 5

Organisational Overhaul: The Acquisition and Transformation of the MLC

The phone on the Lend Lease Chairman's desk rang with an urgency that reverberated around his office. When Dusseldorp picked it up, he found he voice on the end of the line more than matched its tone. 'Dick, it's Milton,' the voice said. 'We're in trouble. Brierley's buying our shares.' The year was 1981, and at that point in Australian corporate history there could be no doubt in anyone's mind about the identity of the 'Brierley' spoken of by Milton Allen, long-time friend and business associate of Dusseldorp, and Deputy Chairman of life insurer MLC. Ron Brierley (later Sir Ron) was head of Industrial Equity Ltd (IEL), a company renowned as 'one of the most active raiders, traders and greenmailers on the bourse'.[1] This was some achievement at the dawn of an era in which, as financial journalist Trevor Sykes puts it, the 'corporate cowboys rode our financial landscape as none had done before'.[2] Brierley's *modus operandi*—acquiring a strategic stake in a vulnerable, undervalued, asset-rich company and then launching a hostile takeover bid—was, by then, well known in the marketplace. So when Milton Allen got his regular briefing on movements in the MLC's share register, and saw that IEL's stake in the life office had risen to 15 per cent, it sent shivers up his spine.

Allen's sense of foreboding might not have been as great were it not for a document that a 'friendly broker' had slipped him some time earlier. He recalls:

> I had been given, *very* confidentially, a document which was surreptitiously circulating in financial, *some* financial circles, which showed what could be done if MLC was taken over, the whole of its field staff sacked, the whole of its office staff dealing with new business sacked, and the business run down as a closed fund, so that all the old fat reserves could gradually be drained off to the predator.[3]

With the MLC Ltd's main operating subsidiary, the Mutual Life & Citizens' Assurance Company Ltd, then sitting on some $1.9 billion of policyholders' assets, the 'old fat reserves' promised rich drippings indeed. 'That document had not been prepared *by* a predator,' Allen says, 'it was *seeking* a predator. It had *clearly* been prepared by a very competent actuary who had a thorough understanding of the MLC and how it operated ... It was rather disturbing news, to say the least, that anyone should contemplate going about it in that way.'[4]

To make matters worse, as Allen was well aware, the MLC was a sitting duck for such a predator. 'We had a very *small* shareholding,' he says, 'and a limited number of shareholders. And we'd been conscious of our vulnerability to takeover for years.' Indeed, Allen himself had had to act quickly, and at the highest political levels, to foil one such unwelcome attempt, by a British insurer, in 1968.[5] That experience vivid in his mind, Allen had subsequently scrutinised movements in the MLC's share registry with all the vigilance of a palace guard. 'And then when this circular got around—well, got to me,' he says, 'that meant it was moving around in circles where there was money. And it was about this time, or shortly after, that Brierley started buying.'[6]

There was no doubt in Allen's mind that the situation had all the makings of a disaster. There was the MLC, sitting on a very unstable share register, while a determined and experienced corporate raider, with access to a chilling asset-stripping plan, was buying up its shares. As the alarm bells started ringing in the MLC's headquarters in North Sydney, its Deputy Chairman reached for the phone. If his company was in trouble, there was someone else who needed to know about it.

'By that time,' says Allen, 'we were the largest shareholder in Lend Lease by a *long* way.' Having invested in Dusseldorp's corporation almost since its inception, by 1981 the MLC held some 15.9 per cent of Lend Lease's stock. 'And the two companies had so many other contracts between us, what with shopping centres and buildings and the like.'[7] MLC had written the bulk of the insurance policies for Lend Lease since the latter's inception. Meanwhile Civil & Civic had built all the major MLC office buildings in Australia and New Zealand since the 1960s, starting with extensions to its Canberra offices in 1963, and culminating in the $100 million MLC Centre in Sydney, completed in 1978. When the MLC had started to become a more active property investor in the 1970s, it had bought units in the GPT rather than following the AMP in setting up its own property trust.[8] The insurer's direct property investment portfolio also included a number of Lend Lease development projects, often purchased by the MLC prior to construction. In sum, as Lend Lease's Stuart Hornery puts it, 'They were our best customer.'[9]

Given the strength and length of their bonds, a hostile takeover of one organisation could have far-reaching ramifications for the other: a conclusion it took Dusseldorp, at the other end of the line, all of two seconds to reach. Before Allen could utter another sentence, the Dutchman zeroed in on what, for him, were the larger implications of Brierley's move. 'Milton, if they take you over,' he said with mounting tension, 'they could control Lend Lease!'

It was not *only* the possibility of Brierley acquiring, via the MLC, a strategic stake in his own corporation that worried Dusseldorp—after all, the 'close and mutually beneficial' association between Lend Lease and the life insurer was longstanding[10]—but that possibility certainly gave his subsequent strategic musings a certain edge. Quickly assembling his trusted advisers around him, Dusseldorp began to mull over the options. 'Milton [Allen] had come to us and said they'd got a problem,' remembers Stuart Hornery, then Managing Director of Lend Lease, and later Dusseldorp's successor as Chairman of the corporation. 'So Dick said to me, "What do you think about us going in as a white knight?"[11] Acquiring a strategic stake in the MLC would give the insurer some breathing space, it would give Brierley something to think about, and it would also give Lend Lease some time to consider its next move. 'I said to Dick, "Well, it's really your call," ' remembers Hornery, ' "but it sounds good to me." So we decided to take 20 per cent.'[12] The figure of 20 per cent—the cut-off point in corporations law beyond which a company had to launch an official takeover bid—was selected as the target level of ownership because it would achieve Dusseldorp's initial objectives without putting too severe a strain on Lend Lease's finances. 'That was typical of Dick's approach,' says Hornery. 'He always did things in a way that didn't break the bank. So even when we drilled some dry holes down in Bass Strait, it was never going to sink Lend Lease— and MLC was the same: we'd take 20 per cent, then look over the fence.'[13]

The plan was quickly put into action. Fortuitously, a parcel of MLC shares of approximately the right size had recently become available. A troubled banking concern, whose finance subsidiary had been ravaged in the property crisis of the mid-1970s, had indicated to MLC that it needed to sell down its stake in the insurer. When the MLC asked Dusseldorp if Lend Lease was interested in taking the shares, the answer was a decided yes. 'MLC facilitated that first acquisition,' remembers Hornery, 'and we got them for \$2.31 per share.'[14] After that purchase, and further buying on- and off-market, by June 1981 Lend Lease's stake in the insurer had reached the desired level of just under 20 per cent, making it, along with the Sun Alliance Assurance Company of London, the equal largest shareholder in the MLC. Brierley's IEL sat in third place. But if Brierley was taken by surprise by the Lend Lease move, he was by no means deterred. Over the next twelve months IEL kept on buying MLC shares, increasing its stake in the company (and taking the share price up with it) to a level matching that of the MLC's two largest shareholders. By mid-1982, with all three holding a shade under 20 per cent, the situation had reached a stand-off.

While this activity was going on in the marketplace, behind the scenes Dusseldorp and his team at Lend Lease were doing their homework and planning their next move. Although the purchase of MLC shares had started out as a defensive step, it got the Lend Lease Chairman thinking. Were there any grounds, he wondered, for his corporation to take a more substantial stake in the life office? Having recently been forced to scale down his company's operations in the United States—a number of attempts to crack that huge and wealthy market over the course of the 1970s had so far failed to fire— Dusseldorp was casting around for the next strategic move.[15] The MLC— providing as it did a platform from which Lend Lease could launch into the expanding financial services sector—looked as if it might fit that bill, as Hornery explains.

> We [had] always regarded ourselves as somewhat of a fund manager, a manager with only property. The more we thought about it, the more we reckoned that we could probably cope with managing *all sorts* of assets if we applied the same kind of principles ... It [would be] another sort of notch up, having started life out as a contractor, then a developer, then a project financier, and then funded through GPT.

Acquiring a bigger stake in MLC would be, in a way, 'just another level of the same business', a form of 'vertical integration'.[16]

Convinced of the logic of such a move, they took a closer look at the health of the insurer.

> We had a study done based on the first 20 per cent [says Hornery]. We had a look over the fence that showed [the MLC] to be in great shape as an organisation and from a reserve point of view. But they were going backwards as a business. And the genesis of that was in H. G. Palmer. They had never done a single thing after that as a shareholder-owned mutual.[17]

Unusually for an Australian life office, most of which were policyholder mutuals, the (almost) century-old Mutual Life & Citizens' Assurance Company Ltd had, since 1961, been owned by its market-listed parent, MLC Ltd. The latter had got into trouble when H. G. Palmer, a large electrical retailing and hire-purchase business that it had acquired in 1963, and 'poured millions into',[18] went bust some two years later. Although MLC Ltd was not legally required to honour the debts of its bankrupt subsidiary, disgruntled small investors and creditors of Palmer's argued strenuously in the press that the insurer, whose name featured prominently on the retailer's public debt-raising prospectuses, was morally bound to do so.[19] The courts disagreed with this view, but aside from anything else, the collapse of Palmer was a public relations disaster for the MLC—then Australia's second-largest life office. Moreover, the industry regulator ruled that the insurer had to repay its policyholders for the millions lost in the fiasco, insisting that 97.5 per cent of its subsequent profits be distributed via policyholder bonuses, thus restricting the dividend payable to MLC's shareholders to 2.5 per cent (a big cut on its previous level of 6 per cent plus).[20] The upshot of the whole sorry episode was that, although its reserves were relatively unscathed, the MLC crawled back into its shell. It began '[losing ground] against some of the more dynamic performers' in the sector, says financial commentator Philip Rennie, and by the early 1980s it had dropped back to fourth on the league of Australia's life offices.[21]

The Palmer legacy was the downside of the study of the MLC, but, as Hornery recalls, there was also an upside. Although somewhat battle-scarred and 'showing the signs of age',[22] the MLC—with its more than adequate reserves—was fundamentally a solid ship. Moreover, given the conservative basis on which some of the insurer's assets were currently valued and organised, there was considerable scope for increasing its declared profits. As Hornery puts it, 'they made an assessment that *probably* there was a pot of gold there.'[23] And that was just what Dusseldorp needed to hear. With a new captain, a shift in course, and some re-engineering, there was every indication that the MLC vessel would be an excellent addition to the Lend Lease fleet. That is, if they could get their hands on it—for they were not the only ones who had identified the MLC's potential 'pot of gold'. 'Subsequently we discovered that that's what Ron Brierley had found out, with his analysis', says Hornery;[24] and that, no doubt, was why IEL had made its move on the MLC in the first place. So now it was back to the battleground—or rather, stalemate—on the insurer's share register. How could Dusseldorp and his team at Lend Lease break that?

'Dick and his boys—Dick and Stuart finally—mulled this situation over for a while,' remembers the insurer's Milton Allen, 'and then they thought up the scheme of taking a 50 per cent interest in MLC.'[25] With this plan finding favour with the MLC board, in November 1982 Lend Lease issued a formal partial takeover offer for the insurer, offering to buy some two million of its shares for $9 each. This was a substantial premium on the $7.30 price of the shares just prior to the offer, and gave a price–earnings ratio in excess of 17. Lloyd's independent assessment of the Lend Lease offer described it as 'fair and reasonable'.[26] With Lloyd's advising shareholders it was in their interests to sell, and with the directors of the MLC also recommending acceptance of the offer, it was possible that enough small shareholders would come to the party. But 'possible' was not good enough for Dusseldorp: with the MLC's share register locked up as it was, he was keen to get one of the other top three shareholders to accept the offer as well. Brierley's IEL was showing no signs of selling, but the Lend Lease Chairman thought he might have a chance with the Sun Alliance Assurance Company of London. As a foreign company, the latter was legally blocked from *increasing* its stake in the MLC beyond 20 per cent, so perhaps, Dusseldorp thought, they might like to take the opportunity to *decrease* it.

Taking the MLC's Chairman and Deputy Chairman with him, Dusseldorp flew to London to begin his task of persuasion.

> Dick did most of the talking, [Milton Allen remembers] because he was representing the company making the move. He explained that they were making an offer to all MLC shareholders … and if the Sun Alliance really didn't want to sell, he told them, well, he wasn't worried. He'd be quite happy to have them still in (knowing damn well that they wouldn't do what *Dusseldorp* wanted!)[27]

This negotiating tactic was effective, Allen reports, and the Sun Alliance subsequently decided to accept Lend Lease's offer. As did numerous others. In fact, such was the rate of take-up that, when the offer to buy the two million shares closed, acceptances in respect of almost twice that number had been received. Ron Brierley's IEL, however, was not among them. With Lend Lease then purchasing just over half of the shares of each accepting shareholder, as the new year of 1983 dawned, the corporation's holding in the MLC stood at a shade under 50 per cent.[28] Things were going according to plan.

> Some time later, [Allen continues the story] Dick and Stuart decided if, with
> 50 per cent of MLC, they had the responsibility for running it, then they had better
> take the *whole* of it, and then they'd have a free hand—and they wouldn't have to
> share the profits of their own activities in managing it. And that is what they did.[29]

In May 1985 Lend Lease launched an offer to buy the 50.6 per cent of MLC that it did not already own. By November that year the share-swap offer—four of its own shares for every one MLC share—had netted Lend Lease just on 70 per cent of the insurer. London's Sun Alliance took up the offer in respect of its remaining MLC shares, but Brierley's IEL, by that stage holding some 20 per cent of MLC's stock, again declined to sell.[30] Had he sold, Brierley would have ended up with about 10 per cent of Lend Lease's stock, a proposition that did not unduly worry Dusseldorp and his team, for by that time they had put in place a range of measures to protect the corporation against a hostile takeover.[31] As 1985 came to a close, it was clear that both players were ready to bring the game to an end. When Lend Lease made its final offer for MLC shares—this time for $28— Brierley (and the remaining small shareholders) decided to accept.

There were celebrations all round (appropriately enough, given that 1986, the year in which the takeover was officially finalised, also marked the centenary of the insurer's birth). The MLC had avoided a hostile takeover, Brierley had netted himself a very tidy profit, and Lend Lease had acquired 100 per cent control of what was becoming a prize possession. For during the three years it had taken for the takeover drama to play itself out on the share market, Dusseldorp had not been standing idly in the wings. 'The winds of change are blowing at MLC,' financial commentator Alan Kohler had observed when Dusseldorp first joined the MLC board in July 1982, 'and it's going to be a fascinating company to watch over the next few years.'[32] And indeed it had been. For by the time Dusseldorp became Chairman of the MLC in early 1984, he had already made his mark on the organisation.

> There are two ways of approaching a takeover: you can leave the basic management in place and make strategic decisions, or completely change the acquisition's culture. Lend Lease had a clear vision of what it wanted to do at MLC, and the existing life office style of bureaucratic management did not relate to those aims.[33]

That the life insurer was in for a shake-up was clear from the time Dusseldorp first set foot in the MLC's panelled boardroom in July 1982. 'The MLC was a hundred-year-old, very proud institution,' says Hornery. 'You know, the board with the red wine, that sort of stuff.'[34] 'It was a sort of a sanctorum,' agrees Ken McGrath—a senior Lend Lease executive who would play a key behind-the-scenes role in the MLC's subsequent transformation

> [It was] deathly quiet and nobody coughed. They had a lovely set-up there: the tea ladies would come around ... it was a real home-away-from-home. And over the years this whole culture had developed ... It was, by that stage, a rather moribund, conservative, results *non*-orientated body. The idea of operating a business to make profit was foreign, they just didn't think like that. They weren't results-oriented at all.[35]

Still smarting from the H. G. Palmer fiasco—and with layer upon layer of bureaucracy and red tape 'strangling innovation'[36]—there was little to differentiate the MLC's mindset and mode of operations from those of the policyholder mutuals with which it competed. 'MLC Life, like a lot of the mutual life offices, was like a fat pussycat,' Hornery would later tell journalist Peter Freeman. 'There was a lot of excess weight to be cut away.'[37]

Scalpel in hand, Dusseldorp began the radical surgery at the top. Within nine months of his arrival, three of the ten directors had retired—amongst them a former General Manager of the insurer who had clocked up more than half a century's service—and another long-standing director was packing his bags. And that was just the beginning. By the time Dusseldorp had become Chairman of the MLC in early 1984, he had, says Hornery, 'removed virtually the whole board'.[38] Milton Allen, who had by then been with the MLC for almost fifty years, was the sole survivor of the purge.[39] A new team of directors was brought in to replace those departing—amongst the new faces were Ron Brierley, Freehills' Richard Longes, and two senior men from Lend Lease;[40] board procedures were overhauled (the number and agenda of meetings pared back to deal with strategic matters only); and the relationship between the shareholder company (MLC Ltd) and the policyholder life office (Mutual Life & Citizens' Assurance Company Ltd) was revamped, separated, and clarified.[41] To head the latter, Dusseldorp brought in, as Executive Chairman, a very experienced financial services executive, Vic Martin: previously Joint Managing Director of the National Australia Bank, and head of the 1983 inquiry into deregulation of the Australian financial system.

The changes at the top were not confined to board level. Within three months of Lend Lease acquiring a controlling interest in the MLC, Dusseldorp announced to all staff—in his first combined Lend Lease–MLC 'State of the Nation' address—that the current General Manager of the life office, and the bulk of his senior executive team, were also clearing their desks.[42] In their place, Dusseldorp installed a high-level team selected from the upper echelons of Lend Lease. 'I gave Dick a team to go over there—' says Stuart Hornery, 'six of my top twelve people—to go over to MLC and sort it out.'[43] Heading that team was John Morschel—previously Managing Director of Civil & Civic— and he soon realised the 'sorting out' would be quite a job. 'MLC had been losing market share like crazy,' says Morschel.

> It had gone to sleep, from once being the size of [Australia's largest life insurer] AMP to being very significantly smaller than AMP ... The problem was, of course, that it wasn't selling enough new business, and it wasn't efficient ... They had been breeding their own senior executive team inside the organisation. It was a very comfortable life for those there at that time. Little did they know what was about to happen.[44]

> There was no doubting the MLC's assets or potential, but it needed a good shake-up.[45]

The sight of the Lend Lease team hanging an 'under new management' sign above the door of one of Australia's conservative life offices raised eyebrows in the Australian business press. 'When we first took over MLC,' Stuart Hornery remembers, 'we were roundly criticised. "What would a bunch of engineers know about running a life insurance company?" they said. The answer was, of course, "Nothing—but we *do* know how to run a business."'[46] There were few who could disagree with *that* proposition, Dusseldorp having built Lend Lease up from nothing into what was by then regarded as 'without doubt Australia's most successful property developer'.[47] It was clear that Dusseldorp himself was going to give the overhaul of the MLC his detailed personal attention. 'His principal interest within the Group was to get MLC performing,' says John Morschel. 'He just took it upon himself ... and he *drove* it.'[48] But, although Dusseldorp was confident that his road-tested approach to business would hold him in good stead as he went about 'blowing life' into the MLC,[49] he knew that he would need to garner some industry-based expertise as well. 'They went about the whole thing in a sensible, methodical way,' Vic Martin would later recall. 'They sought advice from all around the world, from the best people they could find in each of the disciplines they were looking at.'[50] 'And that was a *major* departure for MLC,' adds long-term MLC senior executive Ted Banks, 'because never before had the MLC even looked outside its own back door for help.'[51]

At the top of Dusseldorp's 'to do' list, John Morschel recalls, was to find an independent actuarial consultant who could 'have a good look at MLC and tell us what was there'.[52] 'He wanted me to go and talk to the "two best actuaries in the world"', remembers Ken McGrath, the trusted Lend Lease executive that Dusseldorp set to work on the task.

> So I asked Tom Goodyer, the chief actuary at the MLC, who he thought might fit the bill. Goodyer came up with two names, one of which was Jim Anderson of Tillinghast, and the other was chief actuary of a consulting firm in London. So Duss said, 'Why don't you go and talk with these two guys and see who you think would best fit our needs, which is really to pull the MLC's business all to pieces, and then tell us how we go about controlling it in an effective, commercial way'. Well, it was quite obvious what he meant by that, so I went to Jim Anderson and then on from there to the English fellow ... I wasn't nearly as impressed with the latter—it was Anderson who absolutely astounded me.[53]

With a gold-plated list of clients, the Atlanta-based firm of Tillinghast, Nelson and Warren enjoyed an enviable international reputation, in no small part due to the efforts of its senior partner, Jim Anderson. McGrath recalls his first meeting with the man:

> I told Anderson about Lend Lease and I told him about the MLC and also about the [life insurance regulator's] formula that was capping the amount of dividend that could be paid to the shareholders.' ... 'I see,' said Anderson. 'And what do you want from us?' 'We want an overall financial picture [McGrath replied] but done in a way that is simple to understand, getting rid of all the gobble-de-gook.' He offered to make a submission—right then and there, and for the next three-quarters of an hour he just sat there—stood there, actually—and dictated it. And he *obviously* knew *exactly* what we were looking for. He could put it all in a codified form and it ended up being about ten pages long. At the end he just said, 'Is that what you're after?' And I thought, 'Well, if you're that good, and if Goodyer thinks you are one of the two best in the world, yes.'

With Dusseldorp giving Anderson the tick—'I showed Duss his submission,' remembers McGrath, 'and he said "Pretty good, isn't he? I think I'll ring him up and appoint him"—the firm of Tillinghast, Nelson and Warren was engaged.[54] It was the firm's first Australian commission, McGrath remembers, and, according to one of the principal consultants assigned to the job, it would end up being one of their most rewarding.[55]

'The first thing Tillinghast did for us was a detailed assessment of the MLC,' says John Morschel, 'and lo and behold'—confirming what the earlier study commissioned by Lend Lease had suspected—'they found there was a nice pot of gold there.'[56] However, the actuaries concluded, the insurer would have to undergo some pretty major changes if that pot of gold was to be 'unleashed'.[57] 'The biggest problem that we had,' says Ken McGrath, 'was this dividend policy of the MLC. The agreement with the Life Insurance Commissioner entered into in the mid-1960s constrained dividend payments to 2.5 per cent of profits as a result of the H. G. Palmer incident.'[58] Even though the policyholder losses incurred as a result of the 'Palmer incident' had effectively been paid back by the shareholders—'about twenty-fold', says John Morschel[59] —the original agreement had been struck 'in perpetuity'. That 'unrealistic agreement', according to Tillinghast, was problematic on a number of counts.

Not only were shareholders failing to get sufficient return on their investment, but the 'profit stop' was also creating a structure of performance *dis*incentive in the organisation. 'Due perhaps to the absence of a strong shareholder voice,' the Tillinghast actuaries said, 'the company [has been] managed more like a mutual life company with the profit objective secondary to sales.' Unless those conditions changed, the report warned, 'the viability of the insurer's products and systems were suspect' and 'neither may survive in the long term'.[60]

It was not the sort of finding that Dusseldorp was going to let lie. Ken McGrath remembers,

> So, for my sins, Duss gave me the task of negotiating with the MLC board, and the then Life Insurance Commissioner, to see if ... we could get a more profit- or results-oriented policy. To cut a long story short, I spent about six months going back and forth, trying to come up with a better formula, but there were just too many variables ... So I told Duss that I didn't think I was going to get there with that sort of approach—that there had to be some new way of tackling the problem—and he said 'Let me have a go, to see if we can come up with something nice and simple'.[61]

The key to tackling the problem, Dusseldorp knew, was to find a mutually beneficial solution that met everybody's needs and concerns: a way forward that would protect the interests of the MLC's policyholders (and thus satisfy the Life Insurance Commissioner) while simultaneously boosting shareholder returns. It did not take him long—'Duss met with the Commissioner a few times, but not a lot', McGrath remembers[62]—before he hit on just such a 'common interest' answer. 'What he came up with,' explains John Morschel, 'was that the stop on the percentage share of profits able to be distributed to shareholders would be gradually removed. But it would be removed in such a way that there were increased benefits for policyholders *as well as* shareholders.'[63] The 1982 profit pool, Dusseldorp proposed, 97.5 per cent of which was distributed to policyholders in the form of bonuses, would be used as a benchmark. If surpluses in subsequent years exceeded the amount of that benchmark, the proportion which shareholders were entitled to would also increase proportionally: initially up to a new limit of 10 per cent.

It was a classic win-win solution. Not only did shareholders get a boost to their earnings—while policyholders were simultaneously guaranteed, at the very least, no lesser amount of bonus—but *both* groups stood to gain if the insurer could lift its game. It was enough to satisfy the Life Insurance Commissioner: he gave Dusseldorp's proposal his blessing and the revised surplus-sharing agreement came into effect in 1984. 'By that one simple step,' says Ken McGrath, 'Dusseldorp multiplied the value of [Lend Lease's] investment in MLC by four. Now that's quite a thing.'[64] And, true to Dusseldorp's word, the benefits also flowed through to the policyholders: 'we increased bonuses—substantially—time after time,' says John Morschel.[65] In fact, such was the success of the new agreement that a few years later the regulator lifted the MLC-specific restrictions on dividend limits altogether. 'You know,' McGrath reflects, 'if I had to pick two events that, in my personal view, were most responsible for Dusseldorp and Lend Lease being so successful, it would be Australia Square, and that particular negotiation at the MLC.'[66] But negotiating a more performance-oriented incentive environment for the organisation, while critical to the MLC's overhaul, was by no means the only thing Dusseldorp had on his agenda. For if the true potential of the new profit-sharing arrangement was to be realised, there would need to be some major changes *inside* the organisation as well.

—

And we then proceeded to sort out the company. And that was a pretty challenging but interesting time.[67]

It was a total, all across the spectrum, re-direction. It was a change of culture, it was a change of pace ... There was a *fundamental* shift in how the whole MLC business ran, every aspect was addressed. It must have been a huge shock to the system.[68]

Coming as they did from a lean, flat-structured, and results-driven organisation, Dusseldorp and his team had only to walk through the doors of the century-old insurer to set off the sound of clashing corporate cultures and styles along the corridors of the MLC. One of the most striking dimensions of difference was the way the two organisations were staffed. Whereas Lend Lease, with its total project orientation, had at most five layers between the Managing Director and the 'workface', the level upon level of bureaucracy embedded in its process-oriented structure put the MLC at the other extreme. 'They found a company that was inefficient,' says Peter Vinson, successor to Tom Goodyer as Chief Actuary of the MLC when the latter retired in 1987. 'It had a huge number of staff and a huge number of agents—a lot of whom weren't performing to standards that Lend Lease were used to.'[69] There was little chance things were going to stay like that. 'It wasn't a wholesale slaughter,' says Stuart Hornery, 'but there was a lot of excess weight to be cut away.'[70]

The man wielding the knife was MLC's new Chief Executive, John Morschel.

> It was extremely difficult, [says Morschel] but as usual, Dick directed the first thing we should do was to look at employee benefits within MLC, and improve them before we started to retrench people. So, for instance, their superannuation scheme—which didn't vest until you'd been there for God knows how long—was changed to give similar sort of vesting to the Lend Lease scheme. Benefits were improved within the super fund at the same time—because it was sitting on huge reserves and it didn't have anything to do with the money, so why not give it to the people who'd earned it? So that was changed and then we proceeded to significantly reduce the staff numbers.[71]

With the cuts focused on excising redundant levels of management to produce 'a flatter and more effective structure', employment at the life office was reduced by one half over a period of some three years.[72]

The MLC's network of insurance agents was also in for a shake-up.

> They had a sales force that was dictating how the business was run [says Morschel]. But we told the agents that if they didn't perform at certain levels, measured on a quarterly basis, they'd get one quarter of counselling; and if they didn't lift their game, then two quarters—you're out. The agents couldn't understand it, because they said that they were paid on commission and not on salary—and therefore even if they produced one dollar of business the company was better off. But when you looked at the support costs—the office space, telephones, supervision, loans, all the other sorts of benefits, etcetera—it was a *huge* cost. So we worked out the minimum level of production that we could make money out of, set that as a standard and then told them, 'get up to it or get out'.[73]

The basis on which agents were paid commission was also revamped to reflect the degree of difficulty of the various product sales. 'That caused almost a riot within the organisation,' says John Morschel. 'But they eventually saw that we were serious, and when they looked around, the rest of the industry was doing that sort of thing anyway.'[74]

For those who remained within its ranks, life at the MLC was also set to change. 'At one time the [MLC] Life Company was No. 2 in the nation', Dusseldorp reminded his audience at the first combined Lend Lease–MLC 'State of the Nation' address in February 1983. 'But [it] has slipped from that place during the last decade. Nothing short of a total rethink and refocus will enable the Mutual Life & Citizens company to return to its previous eminence.'[75] Restoring the insurer to its former position—or even going one better—was, however, the goal. For the MLC's new owner did not share the asset-stripping intentions of the predatory analysis doing the rounds in financial circles prior to the takeover battle. To that end, Dusseldorp told his employees, Lend Lease would be using its controlling interest in the MLC 'to gently coax the old girl to critically examine herself ... to stop looking at the AMP, to retarget its markets, to restructure its organisation to fit the new targets, [and] to regain its confidence and come back fighting with all flags flying'.[76]

With those directions spelt out, the overhaul began—and on a massive scale. 'It was a total, all across the spectrum, re-direction,' says Bill Webster, the man who would become the MLC's new Investment Director. 'It was a change of culture, it was a change of pace ... There was a *fundamental* shift in how the whole MLC business ran, every aspect was addressed. It must have been a huge shock to the system,' he adds.[77] Nothing was taken for granted, nothing was regarded as sacrosanct: every product, process and practice was prodded, poked, and tested, and if it did not fill the measure, it was unceremoniously dispensed with. The measure itself was a characteristically Dusseldorpian one. '[Lend Lease] brought with them these business principles,' Ted Banks recalls, 'which were commonly referred to as the stakeholder principles. If it was good for the customer, if it was good for the organisation, and if it was good for the shareholder who put up the capital—then you did it. But if it didn't meet *all* of those criteria, then you didn't do it at all.'[78]

One of the first things to come under scrutiny was the insurer's existing product range. First, the criteria it would have to meet were carefully specified: 'be sensitive to the integrity of the two groups', Lend Lease and MLC; draw on their existing products and skills; cater for a basic human need; be socially acceptable and desirable; be currently undersupplied; be low capital-intensive; and offer a large, national, and long-term potential market.[79] Then the next step in the overhaul was to define an over-arching vision for the MLC's future product range. That vision, Dusseldorp announced to all staff, was for the insurer to become 'the first company in Australia to insure life cycle financial security from cradle through retirement for the Australian worker of middle income'.[80] 'Our vision for the future begins and ends with your needs –', the Chairman would later tell policyholders at the MLC's centenary celebrations in 1986, 'your *total* needs, for all the seasons of your life.'[81] And once this integrating goal was defined, the nuts-and-bolts of reviewing each existing product to measure its fit, dispensing with those that didn't, and researching and developing new products to fill the gaps, then got under way.

As well as using extensive consumer research to tailor these products to the market and keep them up-to-date, a new forum was introduced to enable policyholders and the company to get to know each other better.

There weren't any policyholder meetings prior to the Lend Lease takeover [says John Morschel]. There was no way in which [policyholders] had a real forum ... So we started an annual investor meeting—a sales-plus-information type meeting—and we'd tour that to each capital city. Those meetings cost a lot of money and they used to take a lot of time, but it was building this family of mums and dads investors ... And that, like most of those [MLC] initiatives, was driven by policies or ideas that Dick had.[82]

Immediately following the overhaul of the product range came a redesign and simplification of the processes underlying service delivery. Out went the door-to-door collection of premiums, and in came a dedicated customer-service call centre. The latter move may seem old-hat now, but at the time the resulting upgrade in the level and accessibility of information afforded to its customers put MLC ahead of the pack. Meanwhile, work teams across the organisation began redesigning core processes—both to increase customer satisfaction and eliminate waste—and *that* yielded benefits all round. 'Ninety-nine per cent of people come to work to do a good job,' observes the MLC's Peter Scott. 'So when all the things that *stop* them from doing it—such as dumb processes, inadequate training and skilling, or inadequate systems and technology—are

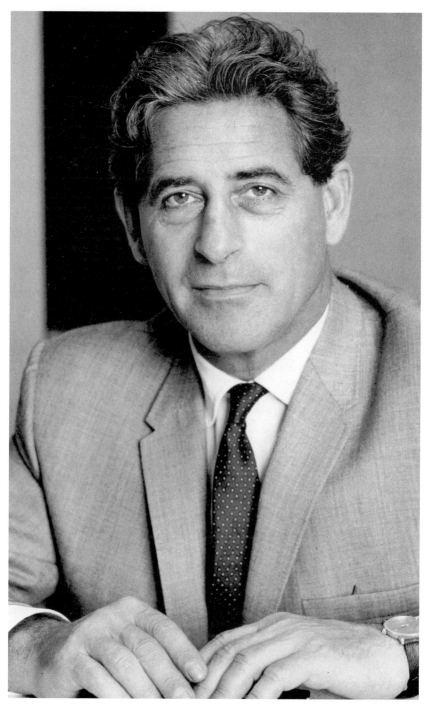

17 G. J. (Dick) Dusseldorp in his Australia Square office, c.1968.

18 Dusseldorp's collaboration with architect Harry Seidler spanned some thirty years and well over a dozen projects. Here three products of their association—Blues Point Tower, the MLC Centre, and Australia Square—shape the Sydney skyline. This photograph was taken from the north shore, looking toward the city's centre.

19 Australia Square also reshaped the city's streetscape, its public plaza returning valuable open space to the people of Sydney. Offering sun and shelter to shoppers and office workers, it quickly became a popular spot for lunch. The photo *above* was taken soon after the plaza opened in 1967.

20 As Chairman of Lend Lease, the General Property Trust, and later MLC, Dusseldorp built a strong rapport with the shareholders, unitholders and policyholders of those companies. Here he chairs the 1984 annual general meeting of GPT.

21 Dusseldorp signs in for a site visit to Lend Lease Petroleum's Bass Strait oil rig. The company's short-lived investment in petroleum exploration, via a separately constituted company, failed to yield a return.

22 The 1984 annual general meeting of MLC Ltd was held during an apparent lull in the share market battle for control of the insurance giant (see Chapter 5). At the Board of Directors' table are MLC Ltd and Lend Lease Chairman Dick Dusseldorp (far left) and the other main contender for the reins of the insurer, Ron Brierley, Chairman of Industrial Equity Limited (far right). Between them sit MLC Ltd's company secretary Ken Finley and director Alex Morokoff.

changed, when they feel the environment is actually being created for them to do extraordinary things—it's a snowball that you just can't stop.'[83] Increased job satisfaction was not the only benefit accruing to employees from this and other aspects of the process overhaul. They also gained a direct financial stake in the improvements when Lend Lease's profit-share and employee share ownership schemes were extended to cover all MLC staff and agents.[84]

The process of prodding and poking the MLC's business did not end there: not even the actuarial department was immune from the sweep of the Lend Lease broom. Some of the changes wrought there were structural—such as separating the organisation's accounting function from the actuarial function—but others went to the professionally contested question of what constituted sufficient reserves.

> When we had the consultant actuaries come in, [says John Morschel] they found contingencies everywhere. And from a business point of view you've got to ask, 'who really owns this money and how should it be distributed over a reasonable period of time?' It took quite a bit of persuasion to convince the [in-house] actuaries to release some of the pots of money, but with Tillinghast arguing the logic of what we wanted to do, and supporting it, we *were* able to distribute some of those reserves.[85]

Perhaps the most stark of the changes in the actuarial area were behavioural, with actuaries 'encouraged' to gain a broader experience of the MLC's business by working in other areas of the organisation, such as its marketing department. 'And that caused a blast of cold air ... in the actuarial profession,' says Bill Webster, 'because no one ever expected to be anything other than an actuary.'[86] 'They were really tested', says Webster, reflecting on the whole change process at the MLC almost twenty years down the track, 'and probably it was quite offensive to people who had come up in that traditional life insurance way. But it's *not* a life insurance company any more', he adds. 'It's a totally different organisation.'[87]

Along with the lifting of the profit-stop, the excision of the layers of bureaucracy, and the overhaul of the insurer's products and processes, a further main component of the massive organisational change engineered by Lend Lease was the transformation of the MLC's approach to investment management. 'No one's solely responsible for everything,' says Richard Longes, 'but it was a lot of Dick's thinking that was behind the MLC being taken, in part, from a traditional life company to becoming a funds manager … He saw that was the way to go … and that's where the real value at MLC was created, by being the early change agents in funds management.'[88]

It is hard to imagine now, but in the early 1980s, despite the fact that they were sitting on piles of policyholders' money, most Australian life insurance companies were relatively unsophisticated in the way they went about marketing and managing those funds. 'The industry in Australia was some considerable way behind where it needed to go,' says Richard Longes. 'And frankly,' he adds, 'so was the life insurance industry around the world—it wasn't that Australia was that far behind the life insurance industry elsewhere.'[89] With investments managed exclusively in-house, insurers needed to have people on staff with expertise in every conceivable portfolio—from domestic equities to fixed interest, international shares to property, bonds to cash—if they were going to fully cover the field. Of course the chances of any one life office assembling the *best* investment advisers in each asset class were virtually nil, but just as problematic was the bureaucratic mode of organisation within which these investment managers had to operate—irrespective of their level of individual expertise. And the MLC was no exception in either regard.

'It was just ludicrous', says John Morschel.

> Prior to Lend Lease's involvement in MLC, the fortnightly board meetings used to review *every* investment made in shares by the company. So you would see these great reams of paper—six or seven inches high—of computer printouts going to the board meeting where they would discuss *each share* that they were going to buy or sell.[90]

The whole process was inordinately lengthy and inefficient, with many good investment opportunities undoubtedly missed because of the in-built delays. 'The Board would *eventually* get to all these recommendations', says Bill Webster, the man who would later take over the investment reins at the MLC,

> but they didn't understand the issues. And yet they were expected to go through all the buys and all the sells. And what it did was that it slowed down the whole

process—so while BHP might have been a good buy when it was first identified by the investment manager, five months later it was a *totally* different environment.[91]

The team from Tillinghast took one look at the MLC's investment strategy and procedures, says Morschel, and they found plenty of scope to lift the insurer's game. 'They suggested to us that we needed to dramatically change and strengthen the MLC's investment strategy ... and so that was what we did.'[92]

When he had wanted an independent actuary to provide a bird's-eye view of the financial workings of the MLC, Dusseldorp had sought out the best in the world. So when it came to getting advice on overhauling the insurer's investment regime, Ken McGrath was not surprised to hear that the Chairman would be content with nothing less. Heading a small team, including the MLC's then chief investment officer, McGrath was despatched on a global search to track down that adviser.

> We teed up appointments to meet with the gurus in each of the merchant banks in the USA and the UK, [McGrath remembers] and we had this hectic month going in and out of their offices, asking what could they do for us, and on what basis they would do it ... And when we came back, I said to Duss, 'To be quite honest, they all say the same thing: they're all the best in the world, they all have asset allocations and all this sort of stuff—it was almost like a pig in a poke.' 'Well, Ken, [replied Dusseldorp] while you've been doing all that, I've been talking to a few people myself.' He'd been in touch with a number of the big companies in the USA, such as Coca-Cola and IBM, to find out who *they* lean to when they want to find out where *their* huge pension fund monies and the like should be placed. And we are talking *huge* amounts of funds. By Australian standards, it's like the entire national economy. Well, one name had kept coming up in those discussions, and that name was Frank Russell.[93]

Based in Tacoma, Washington, the Frank Russell company had, by the mid-1980s, established itself as one of the world's leading investment management and asset consulting firms (a reputation it still enjoys). With 'a select group of international clients' on its books—amongst them some of the world's largest corporations and governments—the mainstay of the 50-year-old group's business was to provide retirement-fund investing advice on the basis of in-depth evaluations of the performance of various fund management operations across the globe.[94] 'They knew all the top funds managers world-wide,' says McGrath, 'and knew, not just the best companies, but knew who were the best *people* in those companies. It was just amazing.'[95] 'Once Dick found out that [Frank Russell] were the best in the world,' says property investment analyst and ex-head of GPT Geoff McWilliam, 'he rang them up and said, "I want you to become *our* adviser." And George Russell, the Chairman of the company, said to him, "But we only have forty clients world-wide—and by the way, where's Sydney?" So Dusseldorp flew to Tacoma and said, "Come with me and I'll show you, because I'm your forty-first." '[96] It was an invitation not to be declined.

The first thing that the Frank Russell group did for their new client was to conduct a total review of the MLC's investment function. And on the basis of that review, Dusseldorp and his team made further changes to the way the insurer went about its business. The investment division was taken out of the MLC life office—leaving the latter to get on with the job, as Morschel puts it, of 'producing product, selling product, and administering the product'. The investment management function was then split, with management of the property portfolio moving to Lend Lease, and 'all the rest'—shares, fixed interest, and cash—going to the life company's parent, MLC Ltd. 'It's the principle of focus,' says Morschel. 'Don't let people get distracted by things outside their core responsibility.'[97] But arguably the most radical change resulting from the Frank Russell review—one that 'shocked many in the [Australian] finance community' of the mid-1980s[98]—was that the MLC Ltd in turn contracted out the great bulk of its investment decision-making to external specialist advisers.[99]

Bill Webster, the high-level executive who left J. P. Morgan to direct the MLC's revamped investment function, explains the thinking behind this approach.

> We basically didn't believe that we could be the best at everything. How could we reasonably claim, for example, to be the best local share manager, and also the best overseas share manager, and best fixed interest manager? So what we [did was to] appoint a number of external investment specialists within each market … to help us to achieve our objectives [essentially 'providing above-average returns with below-average risk'][100] so that we got a good performance out of every spectrum we invested in and we didn't run the risk of having a bad experience.[101]

John Morschel concurs:

> The underlying philosophy was that you can't be all things to all people—so you should go out and employ the best people in each area of investment that you possibly can. And what *your* job was—as the company—was to decide how much of the asset pool you'd give to each of these specialist advisers, and what performance benchmarks you'd measure them against ... and if they didn't perform, you'd sack them and get somebody else. And whilst [that approach] slightly increased the cost of the investment management, it *dramatically* improved the performance.[102]

Dusseldorp had built Lend Lease, and Civil & Civic before it, on a similar principle of 'never doing anything ourselves that someone else could do better',[103] so externalising the investment management function appealed to his logic. Thus, in a move greeted with a sharp collective intake of breath by the Australian finance community, the MLC became, in 1985, the first Australian life office to adopt the 'manage the managers approach'. That, along with the simultaneous decision to establish a $750 million index-linked fund—both 'ideas ahead of their time in Australia'—were, financial journalist Malcolm Maiden observed in April 2000, 'key factors in the growth of [MLC's] funds under management from about $3 billion in the mid-1980s to today's $33.8 billion'.[104] 'I think that probably was *the* key change' in the transformation of the insurer says Ian Crow, John Morschel's successor as Managing Director of MLC, 'the whole investment management approach. It gave MLC a different perception in the marketplace, and we've been able to deliver on those results.'[105]

> The business is about being in the right place at the right time sometimes. I'm sure Dick would admit, if he was here today, that, as far as the acquisition of the MLC was concerned, yes, there was a strategic intent, but there was also a little bit of luck.[106]
>
> It was probably the most successful takeover of the decade.[107]

In May 1986, some 23,000 MLC policyholders across Australia joined the insurer's staff to celebrate the birthday of the life company whose foundation stone had been laid 100 years before. With the festivities centred on the Sydney Opera House—the concrete foundations of which, the Lend Lease Chairman reflected as he addressed the assembled throng, had been mixed with his own tears—the latest satellite technology beamed proceedings to twenty-seven locations across the country in one of the first national telecasts. 'We used virtually every satellite dish available in the country,' says John Morschel, 'in big towns, small towns, all around Australia. There was a party *everywhere*. I think that it was one of the biggest centenary bashes ever.'[108] American crooner Neil Sedaka was flown in for the night, and while he, the Sydney Youth Orchestra, and a thirty-piece band warmed up the audience, the skies across Australia were lit by a nationally coordinated fireworks display marking the official beginning of the MLC's Centenary Celebrations. 'Don't worry,' Dusseldorp told an anxious-looking policyholder who was counting off the pyrotechnics in thousand-dollar lots. 'The shareholder is footing the bill for all this.'[109]

There was ample reason for such a historic celebration, the Chairman told his audience. Over its 100-year history the MLC had provided policyholders with financial security, often through economically troubled times, and that, going as it did to the heart of the MLC's role in the Australian community, was a noble achievement indeed. And now, Dusseldorp continued, the insurer was well down the track in preparing for its next 100 years of service, 'the success of which will depend on meeting all your needs as you progress through the seasons of your life'.[110] The insurer was in good shape to meet those future needs, Dusseldorp continued, as evidenced by the considerable increase in the value added to participating policies over time. Between 1981 and 1985, MLC Life's annual surpluses had increased from $87 million to $188 million, of which the amount distributed to policyholders in the form of bonuses had more than doubled to some $170 million. 'We are *all* sharing a much larger cake,' he said, 'and I'm particularly pleased to announce that we have been able to bake a record cake again this year. But, because this is our centenary year, we will add some icing, in the form of a special centenary bonus,' which brought the total distribution to policyholders that year to $190 million.[111]

It was not only the policyholders who had cause to celebrate. Having started as a strategic move to help a friend and valued customer in distress (and defend Lend Lease itself against a potentially hostile threat), the acquisition of the MLC had, by the insurer's centenary year, turned into a financial bonanza for the corporation. Financial commentator Robert Gottliebsen later described it as 'probably the most successful takeover of the decade'.[112] Since 1982, when Lend Lease first acquired a controlling in the MLC, the insurer had made an initially small, but increasingly significant, contribution to group profits.

> It took a while, [says John Morschel] but over a period of two to three years it started to turn around. In the beginning, the people in the Lend Lease Property Group used to make jokes about the MLC, and what we were doing in there, but it was only two or three years before MLC was contributing as much to group profits as was Civil & Civic. And then it became that MLC was contributing *more* than the Property Group total, and then MLC went on from strength to strength from there.[113]

By the early 1990s the MLC had become Lend Lease's *biggest* earner, contributing over half the group's total profits.

Although the transition process had been undeniably painful, the employees and agents of the MLC also had reason to smile. (Their smiles were even broader if they considered the implications of the likely alternative scenario— the insurer's acquisition by Ron Brierley's IEL. 'Remember,' Milton Allen says, 'subsequently Brierley sold out to Adelaide Steam!'[114] Adelaide Steamship, once Australia's largest industrial group, and one of the most aggressive corporate raiders of the 1980s, would collapse in the recession of the early 1990s.) Some of the benefits for staff were pecuniary—participation in profit-share, upgrading of the staff superannuation scheme, the introduction of employee share ownership—but there were less tangible rewards as well. 'Today the people at the MLC are probably almost the *leading* exponents of Lend Lease culture,' says Stuart Hornery. 'While life insurance can be a pretty boring sort of business, the team over there worked out ways of making it exciting, which is quite brilliant.'[115] Such was the change, says Bill Webster, that when the MLC itself took over another financial institution in 1990, the prospect of transforming the *acquisition's* culture filled the MLC's people with glee. 'Because then the MLC people said,' Webster reports, ' "We're part of Lend Lease. We do it the Lend Lease way. And it's so much better than how it used to be. Boy, are you guys in for a surprise." '[116]

In 2000, the year in which both Dick Dusseldorp and Milton Allen died, the organisations they had led also parted ways. In April that year Lend Lease announced the sale of the MLC to one of Australia's largest banks. With Lend Lease wanting to focus more exclusively on developing its global real estate business into a leadership position, and the MLC needing a greater domestic scale of operations if it, too, was to become a truly global player, the Lend Lease board decided to dispose of the insurer for a 'very attractive sale price'.[117] At $4.6 billion, the amount paid for the MLC by its new owner, the National Australia Bank, not only dwarfed the original cost to Lend Lease of the insurer, financial journalist Malcolm Maiden pointed out, but also the present value of MLC in Lend Lease's books ($1.85 billion).[118]

The sale was a watershed, Stuart Hornery told Lend Lease shareholders in the Corporation's 2000 annual report, marking an end of the group's push into financial services, a sector out of which they had done 'hugely well'. The relationship between the MLC and Lend Lease, and indeed of Dick and Milton, went back to the late 1950s, Hornery reflected, with the MLC a major shareholder and customer of the group almost from the start. 'We would not be where we are today without the support from MLC over the last forty-two years of our history,' he said. 'Milton called me shortly before he died,' Hornery continued, 'to tell me that, while he was delighted with the value that had been added to MLC under Lend Lease's leadership, he nevertheless was also delighted that MLC was going to have what he called a genuine home.'[119] Some twenty-two years had passed since he had made that initial call of alarm to Dusseldorp; and it was a decidedly more relaxed Milton Allen who had rung off from the Chairman of Lend Lease Corporation this time around.

CHAPTER 6

Creative Negotiation: Green Bans, Sewers, and Strata Title

The crowd milling around the entrance to Sydney's Lower Town Hall that evening in mid-May 1972 was a mixed one. University students in tie-dyed T-shirts and bearing placards mingled with the pearl-and-twinset-attired women from the city's wealthy North Shore. Dark-suited businessmen chatted in groups while more colourfully apparelled members of the city's artistic community thrust stridently lettered pamphlets into every available hand. And bevies of brawny, suntanned labourers arrived in waves to join the throng as a collection of elderly couples began filing into the hall. As the Town Hall clock chimed the quarter-hour, the observers of this strange mob—ensconced, beers in hand, at the pub across the road—traded theories as to what event could attract such a large and disparate crowd.

'There must be six or seven hundred of them,' one patron ventured, 'it must be some kind of demo.'

'Double that number for my money,' another replied. 'And those blokes handing out pamphlets look like actors to me: it's probably just a show.'

'Well, how do you explain that official-looking one with the hammer?' asked a third. 'Can't be a show—I reckon it's an auction.'

'There's only one way to clear this up,' said the first. 'I'm going to stick my head in and find out.'

'You'd better take this then, mate,' his friend replied, tossing him a rolled-up copy of the evening paper. 'You might want to make a bid!'

Inside the Lower Town Hall the seats had filled up quickly and the late-comers were starting to line the walls. More than a thousand people had gathered and the collective hum of their pre-meeting musings set the place a-buzz. Up on the stage a small group of men finished their conversation, assumed their seats, and surveyed the restive crowd before them. One of those on stage was Jack Mundey, head of the NSW Builders Labourers' Federation, whose union, by placing a series of 'Green Bans' on selected demolition and construction jobs across Sydney, was fast becoming the champion, if unofficial, protector of the city's natural and cultural heritage. Also there was architect Ross Thorne, a strong advocate of preserving the social history embodied in Australia's old theatre buildings. In the chair that night was Justice Martin Hardie of the state's Land and Valuation Court, himself enjoying a reputation as a man with a keen interest in conservation and heritage issues. Making up the foursome was the Chairman of property development company Lend Lease, Dick Dusseldorp. It was his company's plans that had sparked this event—and while many in the crowd would acknowledge that having the Top Dog show up in person was a rare occurrence, there was still little doubt in their minds. With Dusseldorp's colleagues in the property development industry seemingly bent on stripping Sydney of everything Mundey and his colleagues sought to preserve, there was no mistaking who it was that a good proportion of the audience viewed as the villain of the piece.

Looking out across the packed hall, at 7.30 pm Justice Hardie loudly tapped his gavel. 'Ladies and gentlemen,' he started, 'we are here this evening to consider the future of the Theatre Royal.' A simple enough statement it seemed, but one sufficient to elicit both loud cheers and hooting from what Mundey would later describe as the '*very* rowdy' crowd.[1] It was only 7.31 pm and the meeting was already verging on disarray. As the Chairman tried to bring it back to order, Dusseldorp looked up to see a slightly unsteady figure leave his place by the wall and start to make his way towards the stage. 'He had a rolled-up newspaper in his hand,' Dusseldorp remembers, 'and he just marched straight down the aisle, up onto the stage, and hit the judge on the head with it!' There was a moment's stunned silence as the audience took in the scene, quickly followed by total uproar. 'Of course the whole hall laughed their heads off,' remembers Dusseldorp, 'because Aussies like that, when authority gets belted.'[2] The newspaper-wielding patron returned to the pub across the road and the raucous laughter began to die down. Justice Hardie, his air of judicial dignity ever-so-slightly diminished, started again. With a few firm taps of his gavel, the meeting—to discuss whether to retain the Green Ban on the demolition of the city's Theatre Royal—finally got under way.

The gathering at Sydney's Lower Town Hall that night was but one of many held across the city in the early years of the 1970s. Public and private property developers had enjoyed free rein during the building boom of the 1960s, but as the new decade dawned the citizens of Sydney seemed to collectively lose their patience with the endless roll-out of concrete and glass. From the leafy northern suburbs to the inner city streets, local residents' action groups joined forces with environmentalists and other concerned citizens to protest the bulldozing of bushland and the destruction of the city's social and cultural fabric. Did Sydney *really* need yet another high-rise tower and carpark? they asked. How were the people whose low-cost housing was being razed to make way for the new structures going to afford a new place to live? Wouldn't it be a good idea to preserve just a *few* vestiges of Sydney's architectural past? And how was the city going to breathe when its remaining open spaces were all being paved? It was time for the jackhammers to stop, the protesters argued at a series of meetings held across the city, before Sydney became just another soulless concrete jungle ringed by an endless suburban sprawl.

Much to the initial surprise of the protesters, the operators of those jack-hammers nodded their heads in agreement. Joining the residents' groups and likeminded citizens in their opposition to 'insensitive development'[3] was a seemingly unlikely ally: the NSW Branch of the left-wing Builders Labourers' Federation (BLF). 'There were some exciting things happening amongst the [builders labourers] in the early 1970s,' says Jack Mundey, State Secretary of the union at the time.

> We were opening up this whole debate about the role of unions … and saying that, in a modern society, while of course we should be concerned about wages and conditions, increasingly we should have a look at the full gambit. That it's not *just* the hours at work that the union should be concerned about, but the *totality* of where we live, what we do, what our residences are like, what pollution we're subjected to—anything that affects the worker during the *168* hours of the week … Because what's the good of winning higher wages and better conditions, if we live in cities devoid of parks and denuded of trees?[4]

With building workers starting to ask such questions—and striking a chord with similar concerns in the broader community—the Sydney stage of the early 1970s was set for some unconventional alliances and new forms of protest. The most famous of these was the imposition of the now-legendary Green Bans.

The world's first Green Ban—where building workers refused to work on a project which they, and the majority of a publicly convened meeting, judged 'environmentally injurious'[5]—had been applied in June 1971. Within nine months four more such bans had followed, bringing work on well over $500 million-worth of development projects across Sydney to a halt.[6] A blanket ban having also been imposed on the demolition of a further 1700 historic buildings that the National Trust classified as worthy of preservation, by early 1972 Sydney's reputation as a developer's paradise was starting to wear thin. (It would be in tatters within three years, by which time some $5 billion of the city's development work had been halted by BLF actions.)[7] Against this background, property development giant Lend Lease had announced in April 1972 that, as part of its long-planned commercial redevelopment of a 0.8 hectare site in central Sydney, the contents of the 117-year-old Theatre Royal—which it had purchased a few years earlier—would be put up for auction prior to the theatre's demolition in mid-May. Within days of the Lend Lease announcement a public meeting had been convened, members of the theatrical workers' union had promised to 'lie down in front of the bulldozers to prevent [the] carnage',[8] and the BLF's (and the world's) sixth Green Ban had been imposed.

Sydney's Theatre Royal, which had been built in the 1850s and remodelled extensively in the 1920s, was, although somewhat 'dilapidated',[9] the last of the clutch of Victorian theatres that had once adorned the city's streets. With its three-tiered accommodation bringing the audience unusually close to the stage, the atmosphere and acoustics of the Royal had been heralded by some, including actor Gladys Moncrieff, as 'unbelievable' and 'near perfect'.[10] The Royal was an 'inseparable and romantic part of the city's history' for Sydney's *Daily Mirror*;[11] the impending closure was 'a tragedy' according to the city's Lord Mayor.[12] For others, however, the Theatre Royal did not hold the same allure. 'It's about as romantic as a Water Board pumping station,' wrote one critic, 'and as charming', he added. 'As long as I've known it the Royal has been grubby, uncomfortable, fetid and, I suspect, verminous. I've always left it feeling the need to scratch.'[13] But while its architectural merit (and compliance with public safety regulations) were matters of some contention, there was no debating that the Theatre Royal was one of the city's few remaining large venues for live theatre.[14] Its demolition would mean the loss of a valuable performance space, and that—combined with a more general lament that this was yet another case of 'jackhammer madness'[15]—rallied its defenders to the cause.

It was at a 'teary, after-show party' on the night of the last performance at the theatre, Jack Mundey would later recall, that 'some of the actors and their friends decided to make a stand'.[16] The Save Sydney's Theatre Royal Committee was born that Saturday night, and a call put in to Trades Hall the following Monday morning. 'Some of these theatre people were members of the militant Actors' Equity union,' writes Mundey, 'and had no hesitation in coming to us [the BLF].'[17] A public meeting was called for that evening—1 May—which Justice Hardie of the state's Land and Valuation Court agreed to chair, and the head of the BLF promised to attend.

'A good crowd came along to that first meeting,' Mundey remembers. 'It was held down at the AMP Theatrette at Circular Quay, and they had all these speakers basically saying we should keep the Theatre.' The Chairman, Justice Hardie, was one of these, bemoaning, with 'becoming partiality' according to one reporter,[18] the loss of 'all the lovely things we liked ... because Governments did not have the courage to resume them'.[19] 'Then John Tasker [Chairman of the Save Sydney's Theatre Royal Committee] got up,' remembers Mundey, 'and asked me to impose a [Green] Ban.'[20] If the actors' and theatrical workers' unions wanted it, Mundey replied, and if the citizens of Sydney—or at least the 300 or so of them gathered in the hall that evening—wished it too, the BLF was happy to accede to their request. His statement was greeted with loud cheers all round. It was then that a late entrant to proceedings raised his hand and asked if he might take the microphone. 'And who would you be?' asked Hardie from the chair. 'I'm the developer,' said Dusseldorp, 'and I'd like to make a counterpoint to some of the comments that have been made.'[21]

Having completed Australia Square in 1967—a landmark development drawing wide praise both for its bold form and the valuable city space it returned to the public through its open-air plaza—within the year Dusseldorp and his team at Lend Lease had begun planning another such project on an even grander scale.

Slowly, patiently, over a period of some four years, the company had bought up twenty-two separate properties on a block fronting Sydney's central civic square, Martin Place. There it planned to develop, in conjunction with life insurer MLC, a combined office and retail complex with open space areas— covering a good three-quarters of the site—spilling out onto Martin Place. Architect Harry Seidler had once again received the commission for the project, and over a dozen alternative schemes had been investigated. By April 1972, the most suitable of these having been selected and negotiated with no less than twenty-one public authorities, plans for Sydney's new MLC Centre were well advanced. The grand nineteenth-century Hotel Australia, which had stood on one corner of the site, had been purchased and was being demolished; the Theatre Royal, acquired two and a half years earlier, was about to meet a similar fate; and a number of smaller buildings, including those fronting Sydney's quirky, bohemian Rowe Street, were slated for the wrecker's jack picks in the coming months.

   With none of this activity having so far aroused any real sign of protest, Dusseldorp was taken aback when, returning from an overseas trip, he had touched down to the news that there was opposition brewing to his plans for the MLC Centre site.

> When we went to demolish the Theatre Royal, we had no notion that there would be problems … But when I arrived back in Sydney, the guy who met me at the airport said, 'There's trouble over the theatre.' They were having a protest meeting that night, he said, in the little AMP hall down at the Quay, and so I said, 'Let's go straight there.'[22]

Arriving at the meeting a little late, Dusseldorp at first stayed up the back to get a feeling for its mood. 'It was very greenie,' he recalls. 'So I sat there for a while, sizing things up … and in the end I put my hand up.' Announcing who he was and his desire to speak, Dusseldorp made his way to the stage. 'I started explaining the vision of the [MLC Centre] scheme and how it would fit with the city,' he recalls, 'but that didn't go down too well.' 'Mr Dusseldorp was heckled loudly when he began to speak,' the *Sydney Morning Herald* reported the next day.[23] 'And then I said that we were sorry to see the theatre go, given its long history, but that the health department had basically condemned the place'—the air conditioning and ventilation systems had 'packed up', the seats and carpets were in bad condition, and the backstage facilities obsolete[24]—'and with the cost of renovating the building prohibitive, it wouldn't be all that long before the whole thing would be unable to be used for public purposes anyway.'[25]

'So that put a bit of a dampener on the meeting,' Dusseldorp recalls. 'And then I said, "So what I suggest as a constructive proposal—as I have sympathy with your viewpoint—is this."' Dusseldorp was willing to consider including a 'fresh, modern, beautiful theatre in the new complex', he said. To that end he would ask MLC Centre architect Harry Seidler—in conjunction with two architectural firms that the Save Sydney's Theatre Royal Committee could appoint (at Dusseldorp's expense)—to 'assess the possibilities and come to a conclusion'. 'But we are not going to use that just as a way of delaying the thing,' he warned, 'so let's say that we give the architects two weeks, and ask them to present whatever they have come up with after that to a public meeting.' Promising to defer the auction of the contents of the Theatre Royal until after that date, this time Dusseldorp got a warmer reception. 'Mr Dusseldorp ... was cheered at the end of the meeting,' the *Sydney Morning Herald* reported;[26] 'he ended up being something of a crowd pleaser,' *The Review* agreed.[27] The meeting disbanded, the architects were engaged, the talks held, plans drafted and redrafted, and an announcement made that another public meeting—to hear the architects' report—would be held in Sydney's Lower Town Hall on Monday, 15 May.

In 1972, many of the environmental, heritage, and planning laws that we now take for granted were still years away from being enacted (at least in New South Wales). The avenues for resolving conflicts between developers and their critics were few. Dusseldorp would have been well within his rights to press ahead with his existing redevelopment plans for the MLC Centre site—he had jumped through the necessary planning hoops, he had obtained the 'all clear' from the relevant public authorities, and with no heritage order protecting any of the properties he planned to demolish, there was no *legal* reason why the Theatre Royal and its neighbours should not come tumbling down. But the lack of legal restrictions on his actions was by no means the only factor that Dusseldorp considered in deciding how to proceed. Sections of the community were clearly dismayed by the wave of demolitions across the city, and their opposition had been given teeth through the actions of the BLF. Dusseldorp was himself willing to defend the union's use of Green Bans: 'People are not being given adequate chance to discuss developments with local government and property developers,' he told the *Sun Herald* in 1974. 'Jack Mundey, by his actions,' he said approvingly, 'has given people time to mount their protests and opposition to projects.'[28]

In the circumstances, Dusseldorp felt, it would be unwise to push ahead with his MLC Centre redevelopment plans in their current form. (Many other developers would take the opposite course, only to find their planned projects tied up by bans for years.) But nor would he just back down and let the protesters have their way. As Chairman of Lend Lease, he had the interests of his client and his company's shareholders to consider, and keeping an unprofitable and run-down Theatre Royal on the books was hardly going to satisfy them. Characteristically, Dusseldorp looked for an alternative solution to the impasse. By getting the various architects together to come up with plans for a new theatre for the Royal site, Lend Lease was 'bending over backwards', according to *The Review*.[29] But if that was what it took to find a mutually beneficial solution, Dusseldorp was only too willing to engage in the exercise. Whether or not it would pay off, well, he would find that out in two weeks' time.

The public protests over the imminent demise of the Theatre Royal had resounded throughout the city, and with Dusseldorp's offer to find an alternative solution lacking precedent, people were understandably sceptical that a last-minute compromise could be found. As the day of the second public meeting approached, the editorials of the major Sydney newspapers all had something to say about the issue.

> The jackhammer has this city at its mercy [the *Sun* lamented]. The developers have made out a good case for bulldozing the Royal. No doubt they could make out a good case for filling in Rose Bay. Or replacing the Harbour Bridge with something modern ... A city needs character and life as well as concrete monuments to files and phones.[30]

Though not as ardent a supporter of this particular case, the editor of the *Sydney Morning Herald* agreed with the *Sun*'s general point:

If this [public] outcry, extending far beyond theatre buffs, means anything, it is the existence of a ground-swell of dismay at the steady eradication of landmarks and human amenities in the heart of the city in the name of development. It is an outcry against the dehumanisation of the inner city.[31]

The *Daily Telegraph* was not so sure.

The attempts to save the Theatre Royal are belated and unconvincing. It is an inadequate, musty, old structure, not worthy of preservation on any grounds except that we have few theatres left ... It would be inexcusable to try to stop redevelopment of the Theatre Royal site merely because of some eleventh-hour fervour by enthusiasts—who have known for a long time that the theatre was doomed.[32]

The Australian by and large concurred, and sought to draw a lesson.

It may well be that the best Sydney can do now is to accept the company's offer to erect a new theatre ... with some of the historic Theatre Royal furnishings. And the moral is that if we are really interested in preserving Australiana, we should in future act in reasonable time.[33]

It was, in part, because of this media attention that such a large crowd started to assemble outside the Lower Town Hall on the evening of 15 May. In part, but not entirely. For Dusseldorp had 'reminded' about ten of his senior Lend Lease executives that they were citizens of Sydney too—as were their spouses, colleagues, friends, and extended families—and if they had an opinion on the future of the Theatre Royal, then the city needed to hear it as well.[34]

Jack Mundey describes the scene he encountered at the Town Hall that night. 'It was a very memorable meeting, that second one,' he says. 'The MLC workers and the Lend Lease and Civil & Civic workers had been persuaded to stay back—and they'd probably been shouted a couple of drinks because by the time the meeting started ...', he says, raising his eyebrows and giving a hearty laugh as he leaves the sentence hanging. He goes on.

We used to have trouble with the builders labourers like that. We used to say that we should hold our meetings earlier, because the blokes would knock off around

4 [pm], and the grog was speaking by the time the meeting started at 8 o'clock! Well, the same thing happened that night with Lend Lease. It was a *very* rowdy meeting. When I got up to speak they all booed—it was the most hostile reception I've ever received ... and I've had a few *within* the union![35]

'Of course Jack Mundey had been doing the same thing', says Dusseldorp in defence of his invitation to his Lend Lease supporters to attend.

He'd gone along to the schools, and got a lot of students from there, plus his own cronies ... And so there was standing room only in the hall. So when Mundey leaned over to me and said, 'You bastard, you've stacked the meeting!', I just turned to him and said, 'Hey Jack, since when do you think you had a monopoly on that?'[36]

With the staunchest of its advocates and detractors there in full force, it was little wonder that the meeting to consider the future of the Theatre Royal would be described in the press the next day as 'turbulent'.[37] But despite that turbulence—'the meeting was often fiery and noisy with interjections', the *Daily Telegraph* reported, with one heckler even climbing onto the stage to take the Chairman to task[38]—considerable progress was made. The team of architects had agreed a plan incorporating a new Theatre Royal in the MLC Centre complex, the parameters of which had been drawn up to the satisfaction of both 'sides'. The new theatre would provide seating for 1000 people (against the old theatre's 800), parking for 300 cars, and a tunnel link to Sydney's underground railway. The configuration of the stage and the auditorium of the new Theatre Royal would recreate the intimacy of the old, while doing away with some of the latter's less desirable features.[39] On that basis, and considering all the evidence, Ross Thorne, architect, historian, and adviser to the Save Sydney's Theatre Royal Committee, reported that there seemed to be few rational arguments for retaining the existing Royal, and that the Committee therefore supported acceptance of what he described as 'the compromise' solution.[40] With Dusseldorp tabling a written undertaking to make good the plans to build the new theatre as agreed, Mundey and he then jointly moved a motion to lift the Green Ban on the demolition of the existing theatre. The motion was duly passed—although a 'large minority' of the audience wanted to continue the fight[41]—and a much relieved Justice Hardie brought the meeting to a close.

'It was an important victory,' Mundey would later write in his book, *Green Bans and Beyond*, 'because the committee was able to get its objective ... The Theatre Royal was to be preserved as a theatre—not as an existing structure—in accordance with the wishes of its supporters.'[42] As such, the solution negotiated between Lend Lease and the Committee, and accepted by the majority of the Town Hall audience, represented, for Mundey, 'a principled compromise'.[43] As for Dusseldorp, Lend Lease, and the MLC, they, too, were more than happy with the outcome. Although the inclusion of the new theatre would add some $4 million to the cost of the $100 million MLC Centre development,[44] those costs would be offset by the Sydney City Council's decision to allow Lend Lease to build additional rentable office space in the complex as a reward for its 'good behaviour'.[45]

With demolition of the old theatre starting on 22 May 1972—a little over three weeks since the first protest had been signalled—the way was clear for the massive redevelopment of the site to proceed. Over the next six years, many other companies' city development plans languished—hit by the combined forces of the collapse of the property boom, the onset of global recession, and escalating industrial action including, not infrequently, the imposition of lengthy Green Bans. In contrast, the MLC Centre, and its new Theatre Royal, took shape according to plan. 'A striking tribute to the negotiating skills, and honesty, of both sides in the boss/worker relationship', writes Ian Bevan, author of *The Story of the Theatre Royal*, 'is that, after the initial dispute about demolishing the theatre, only five days were lost through stoppages on the site, and the building project was finished five months ahead of schedule.'[46] When the curtain rose in the new Theatre Royal on 23 January 1976, the opening performance was *A Night to Remember*. Dusseldorp, Mundey, and the rest of Sydney's theatre-going public certainly had grounds to agree, for, through a willingness to work together to find a mutually beneficial solution, what had looked like an intractable problem had been solved to the satisfaction of all.

At the very core of creative negotiation is the idea that it is possible for everyone to get more of what they need by working together.[47]

You can get your own way if you can show how that way is also in everyone else's interest.[48]

There are four traditional ways of resolving a conflict or approaching a negotiation, according to University of California academic Gregorio Encina.[49] Of these approaches, the two most typical are to yield or compete. Both options were open to Dusseldorp and the Save Sydney's Theatre Royal Committee during various stages of the dispute, but it soon became clear that neither side was prepared to yield. Nor did either wish to withdraw, the third of the traditional approaches to negotiation.[50] At that point the situation was in danger of turning into a competitive negotiation, with neither party acknowledging the legitimate claims of the other, but instead pushing for a win for their side at all costs. This is dangerous because, as Encina points out, while one side gets its way in a competitive negotiation—or seems to at first—'in the long run both parties often end up losing'.[51] If, for example, the 'loser' is so badly done by that they are not willing to deliver on their side of the 'bargain', or to engage in future transactions with the erstwhile 'winner', then it's not just they that experience the loss. On top of that, Encina adds, resentful losers 'often hold grudges, and find ways of getting even'.[52]

Yielding, withdrawing, and competing as negotiating strategies all frame disputes as short-term episodes to be won or lost. Instead, Dusseldorp recognised that the conflict over the Theatre Royal was no one-off blip or inconvenience, and looked for a way of resolving it that was sustainable in the long term —a way of dealing with the case in point that also provided a sound basis for managing an ongoing relationship with the BLF and the broader Sydney community. And that is where the fourth of the traditional approaches to negotiation—seeking compromise—comes into its own. Requiring, as it does, a greater degree of trust and goodwill than the other approaches, a compromise strategy lends itself to being deployed in 'repeat transaction' situations. Driving the other party into the ground today makes little sense if they'll get a chance to return the favour tomorrow. But compromise can also have its downside. Sinking to the lowest common denominator that both parties 'can live with' hardly fills either with long-term satisfaction—and if it fails to address the underlying problem, compromise built on mutual concession may not be a solution at all.[53]

The drawbacks of all four strategies—yielding, competing, withdrawal and compromise—have led some to advocate a different way of managing conflict, one based on *integrative* negotiation. While sharing much with the compromise strategy—recognising that short-term, win-lose solutions have little to commend them when the players are in ongoing relationship with each other—

it goes one step further in looking for a *creative* solution to a conflict that makes *all* parties better off. 'Integrative negotiation is built upon the principle of meeting the needs of all the individuals or "stakeholders" ', writes Encina. 'This frequently calls for creative thinking that goes beyond the poorly thought out compromise.'[54] Integrative negotiation means looking for ways to 'expand the pie', rather than assuming its size is fixed and that one person's slice must be cut at the direct expense of another's. That is the approach that Dusseldorp adopted, not just in the Theatre Royal dispute, but whenever he encountered conflict, obstacles, or seemingly intractable problems in any area of his business life. He would seek 'bigger pie' solutions: ones that enabled people with different, sometimes conflicting needs, to strive together toward a common goal for their mutual benefit. The key was to find or create an over-riding common interest between them, and the two incidents discussed below show some of the ways in which he was able to do just that.

———

The Sydney that, in the early 1970s, Jack Mundey and his colleagues were dedicated to protecting had been hurtling outwards as well as upwards since the end of World War II. Suburban development had ground to a halt during the war, with tight restrictions on civilian building in place throughout much of the period of hostilities.[55] Coming as this did on top of a pre-existing deficit in the housing stock, when Sydneysiders emerged from the conflict, a good many of them were desperately searching for a new place to live.[56] With the situation soon exacerbated by rapid population growth, as the postwar baby boom and a massive immigration program began to take off, the result was a residential accommodation shortage of almost unprecedented severity. Owner-builders, government housing departments, small contractors and private developers all rushed to satisfy the demand, and by the 1950s Sydney was experiencing a building explosion, the likes of which had not been seen for some thirty years. Some 140,000 new homes were built in the ten years to 1957—an increase of nearly one-third on the 1947 housing stock[57]—and with the great bulk of these new dwellings built as detached bungalows in new subdivisions on the outer suburban fringe, the city had started to sprawl.

    The New South Wales government had not intended it to be that way. Mindful of the wasteful impacts of an unregulated subdivision boom in the

1920s, the government had set up a regional planning body—the Cumberland County Council—to draw up a blueprint for 'the orderly development' of Sydney's postwar suburbs.[58] The product of the Council's deliberations, the County of Cumberland Plan, was released in 1948 and made law some three years later. Development would be kept under control, the plan envisaged, through phased suburbanisation of people and jobs to 'self-contained urban districts'; meanwhile, city residents' access to open space would be preserved by declaring a Green Belt of 330 square kilometres around the existing built-up area. The Green Belt would act as 'a permanent barrier to suburban sprawl', with a series of satellite cities located beyond it to soak up any excess population growth.[59]

It was a fine vision but, with the Cumberland County Council lacking sufficient clout to implement it, and as Sydney's population growth began to spiral at a rate twice that projected in the plan, politicians and semi-autonomous public infrastructure authorities blithely disregarded its tenets. Responsibility for the plan's implementation initially rested jointly with the Cumberland County Council (the State Planning Authority from 1963) and local councils, but neither had power over the decision-making of key public infrastructure bodies such as the Metropolitan Water, Sewerage and Drainage Board, the Department of Main Roads, the state Housing Commission, or the regional electricity authorities. These bodies had a high degree of independence and pursued their own agendas in a way that best suited the needs of their own sub-sytems, not necessarily the integrated needs of local communities.[60] Mean-while, with population pressures mounting, and with 'no shortage of critics' of the plan's envisaged Green Belt, politicians unilaterally excised vast chunks of the latter to make room for urban development.[61] Within ten years of its appearance in the statute books, the County of Cumberland plan had effectively been shelved. More than half its reserved Green Belt had been opened up for development, and although the population of the inner suburbs was actually declining, building on Sydney's outer suburban fringe was out of control.

The problems associated with the resulting 'uncoordinated and *leap-frogging* of development', as urban studies academic Pat Troy describes it, were manifold, not least of which was that it made the efficient provision of urban services 'extremely difficult'.[62] With 'pockets of urban development in which housing was separated from shopping, community facilities (where provided at all) and employment and interspersed with rural uses and vacant land withdrawn from productive use',[63] it was well-nigh impossible to provide infrastructure services to all these new homes in a timely, efficient fashion. That did not bother many land speculators and property developers. Although the latter had recently been required by local councils to construct roads on their new subdivisions (and set aside a proportion of land as open space),[64] they were in no way obliged to ensure that water, sewerage, or electricity were available to the new blocks they were opening up on the suburban fringe. The (mainly government) bodies responsible for supply of these utilities—all of which were flat out trying to keep up with the surge and spread in demand—would get there one day, prospective land and home buyers were assured, but if that day was a long time coming, well, that was not the *developer's* problem.

It was in this environment that, in 1954, Dusseldorp's company undertook its first suburban residential development in Sydney—not on the outskirts of the city, but on a rocky and as yet undeveloped peninsula on the northern shore of the harbour. In doing so he came face to face with one of the problems—the massive backlog in the provision of sewerage services—that arguably *should* have been constraining the city's outward suburban sprawl, but at that stage patently was not. The way he went about addressing that constraint would not only solve his own immediate problem—getting the sewer pipes laid as the development occurred—but would provide the basis for the adoption of a public policy that would have profound implications for the way urban infra-structure provision was funded in the future, not just in Sydney but eventually Australia-wide.

Life is a road that makes a straight line from where you start to where you want to go ... If you find a rock slide blocking the road, try to go around it to the right, or to the left, or even try climbing over it. If all that doesn't work, *start digging*![65]

In the early 1950s Sugarloaf Peninsula, the smallest of four peninsulas jutting into the western arm of Sydney's Middle Harbour, was a rugged, heavily wooded headland which, while only some seven kilometres from the central business district, looked much the same as it had done for the past ten thousand years.[66] With its tree-lined sandstone cliffs dropping precipitously into the deep blue waters of Sugarloaf Bay, the features that gave it its beauty also accounted for its pristine state. The area had been bypassed for residential development due to the expense and difficulty of blasting through the bedrock to make road and house building possible. But with its wonderful views, foreshore location, and proximity to the city centre, the engineering challenge did not deter a certain Dutch-born developer who was looking for a spot to build his family's new home. And not just *his* family's home, Dusseldorp told his fellow directors of construction firm Civil & Civic. To him the Sugarloaf Peninsula looked like the perfect place to undertake the company's first full-scale residential estate development in Sydney, didn't they agree?

Keith Fleming and John Rothery, the two Australian directors of Civil & Civic, then still a subsidiary of the large Dutch construction firm Bredero's, were not sure. The firm had only been operating in the country for three years, and although it had successfully fulfilled a contract to build some 200 houses in Cooma for the Snowy Mountains Authority, this proposal of Dusseldorp's was in a quite different league. It would be the company's first large-scale job in Sydney—it had built some individual houses and a few small commercial premises for clients in the state capital, little more—and what Dusseldorp was proposing was by nature a speculative venture. That in itself did not worry them, with demand for housing particularly strong, but was the location that Dusseldorp had in mind the right one? 'For all its beauty,' company historian Mary Murphy writes, 'the land did not conform to the average home-buyer's current ideal.'[67] The costs of subdivision of such a rocky, wooded area would be large, necessitating relatively high sale prices if the company was to turn a profit. 'Would people be prepared to pay the prices for the higher, more rugged blocks,' the directors wondered, 'when building would be easier and cheaper on level land elsewhere?'[68]

With Dusseldorp confident that they would—blocks in the upmarket suburb of Castlecrag on the neighbouring peninsula were by then commanding premium prices—his fellow directors were willing to take the plunge. 'I was prepared to back *the man*,' says Keith Fleming of the decision to proceed, 'because by then I saw, and I'm sure John Rothery did, that he was one in a number: very energetic and very entrepreneurial.'[69] In all, the Sugarloaf Peninsula comprised some 56 hectares. Dusseldorp proposed to acquire this, then sell some 36 hectares of it for a notional sum ($2) to the state government to dedicate as a public reserve—a *contribution* to the Green Belt—provided he got the go-ahead to subdivide the remaining 20 hectares as a residential estate.[70]

The latter would be developed as a joint venture with the current owners of the land, the Greater Sydney Development Association (a consortium of developers formed by architect Walter Burley Griffin in the 1920s to purchase vast tracts of land in Middle Harbour), with Civil & Civic taking charge, but with the costs and profits shared between the two groups. These arrangements got the tick, the deal was executed, and with plans drawn up and submitted to Council, the development was soon under way.

David Thorne, a civil engineer and resident of the municipality, was one of those given the task of assessing those plans on behalf of the local community.[71] 'I was the representative of the local [residents'] Progress Associations of Willoughby Council,' Thorne says, 'and when Civil & Civic put up a proposal to subdivide the headland at Middle Cove [the name given to the new suburb], I was delegated to look at the requirements from the community's point of view.' Civil & Civic's plans got the go-ahead, Thorne recounts, because they not only kept the foreshore in public hands—a key requirement of the Progress Associations—but, in contrast to many other proposed subdivisions at the time, they also provided for a high standard of *integrated* development of the area.

> In those days most developers doing subdivisions would just carve up a whole lot
> of blocks of land and put a dirt road in between them. That's all subdivisions were
> back then: a dirt road—no kerb and gutter and no sewerage. But Dusseldorp
> thought that was absolutely ridiculous. He wanted to produce a first-class road,
> kerbs and gutters, footpaths, and sewerage. Now that was the first time that that
> had been done, and a lot of developers were very unhappy at doing that. But he
> reckoned that customers would pay the extra money to get the better quality
> environment.[72]

There was one stumbling block, however, to Dusseldorp's plans, and it was a big one. With the backlog in the Metropolitan Water, Sewerage and Drainage Board's roll-out program, the authority informed him, the sewerage system would not be able to be installed in Middle Cove for some twenty years. 'Even then,' Mary Murphy writes, 'it would be difficult and costly, because of the topography, to provide the service to this particular estate.'[73] With the prospect of septic tanks or nightsoil collectors—the only alternatives to sewerage—hardly fitting Dusseldorp's vision of a high-standard development, the developer was not inclined to let the matter rest there.

So I went to see the President of the [Metropolitan Water, Sewerage & Drainage] Board [Dusseldorp recounts] and put a proposition to him. 'What if I *loan* you the money to put in the sewer, and you can start to pay it back in, say, twenty years? That way I won't be a burden to you and I won't be affecting the Board's plans to extend sewerage to the rapidly growing outskirts of Sydney.'

The President put this idea to his Board, Dusseldorp says, but they weren't too impressed with it. 'They said that the backlog might in fact expand out to twenty-five years, and then I'd be getting a five-year advantage over the other poor suckers out there.'[74] The President was sorry, he told Dusseldorp as he relayed the Board's decision to him, but it looked like Civil & Civic's Middle Cove development would just have to take its place at the end of the (very long) queue.

To Dusseldorp, this just didn't make sense. It would surely be less costly for the Board if the sewer pipes were laid while excavations for the roads, water pipes, and other services were taking place—*before* any houses were built— rather than ripping the place up again some twenty, or twenty-five, years down the track. And it was certainly in the developer's interests for this to happen: the value of the houses and serviced blocks on the subdivision would increase substantially if they were fully sewered at the time of their initial sale. As Dusseldorp saw it, there was a community of interest between the Board and his company in laying the sewerage pipes up-front. He knew there were other imperatives competing for the Board's resources, but surely a mutually beneficial solution to the problem could be found? 'So then I put to the President,' Dusseldorp says, 'my Plan B.'[75]

Plan B took a somewhat different tack, and it held some very considerable advantages for the Board. 'What if you design the sewerage system for Middle Cove and let me build it,' Dusseldorp proposed to the President. 'Then I'll hand it back to you for the grand sum of $2?' The President was interested in this new line of thinking, and asked for some time to consider it. A few days later he came back with a counter-proposal: the Board's answer was still no, he said, unless Civil & Civic *also* paid for the cost of water reticulation to the area. With developers, at that stage, not required to make any contribution to the capital costs of installing either water or sewerage services, this was, according to Dusseldorp, a fairly cheeky response. 'They obviously thought,' he says, ' "This guy is nuts, so let's screw him for all he's worth!" ' While Dusseldorp was keen to look for a solution to the problem that met each party's needs, he refused to be played for a mug.

> So I asked the President if he would like to wake up to a *Sydney Morning Herald* headline the next day advising the citizens of Sydney that the Board had just rejected a $70,000 gift, because the donor didn't want to increase it to $90,000? 'That wouldn't read too well, would it?' laughed the President. 'Let us have another think about it.'[76]

The Board reconsidered, and in late 1956 agreement was reached. The Board's engineering experts would design, survey, and supervise the sewerage installation for the Middle Cove estate, and Civil & Civic would build it to the Board's specifications—all at the developer's own cost. On completion, the Board would buy back the system at a nominal price. Meanwhile, the capital costs of water reticulation to the subdivision would be met entirely by the Board, as was standard practice at the time. The report in the *Sydney Morning Herald* in November 1959 was no doubt more to the President's liking than the one Dusseldorp had foreshadowed. 'A privately built suburban sewerage system which cost [$70,000] will be handed over to the Metropolitan Water, Sewerage & Drainage Board this week', the newspaper reported, for the princely sum of $2.[77] It was a win-win solution all round. Although it cost Civil & Civic extra to install the sewerage pipes up-front, the increase in property values that were reaped from the fully serviced blocks upon sale certainly exceeded that expense.[78] 'It was a classic case of value creation—by spending more money', says Dusseldorp.[79] So Civil & Civic and its development partner were winners from the arrangement—and their customers were the happy beneficiaries of it.

So too was the Board. Not only were its capital costs for sewerage provision in the area reduced to almost nothing, but it also gained in the long term. 'We then suggested to [the Board],' says Dusseldorp, 'that they shouldn't treat this as a [one-off] incident, but that they should do it as a matter of course, because it is a true cost of developing land that the infrastructure be paid for. That appealed to them no end', he recalls, 'and they *did* do it.'[80] From that time forward, the Metropolitan Water, Sewerage and Drainage Board started to extend the practice of charging developers for the installation of sewerage 'in certain cases'.[81] Then in 1961 it became formal board policy to require all 'land developers to meet the cost of additional water and sewerage services required for their subdivisions ... as an essential cost of development'.[82] While similar policies were in place elsewhere in the world, this was one of the first applications of the principle of developer contributions to funding infrastructure in Australia. It made sense in a number of dimensions—not only substantially augmenting the funds available for urban service provision, but also providing better signals for efficient resource allocation and of the environmental effects of urban development—and the policy soon spread to other Australian cities and to a wider range of such services and facilities. In that sense, the residents of Middle Cove, Civil & Civic, and the Metropolitan Water, Sewerage and Drainage Board were not the only beneficiaries of Dusseldorp's win-win solution: so too was the broader community.

The community also benefited that same year (1961) when another 'common interest' solution crafted by Dusseldorp came into effect. This time it was through the creation of a new form of property title—strata title—which not only put ownership of 'home units' within reach of a much greater proportion of the population (and thus gave the construction of multi-storey apartment buildings a kick-start), but in so doing helped make possible and affordable (though far from inevitable) a pattern of urban development alternative to the endless suburban sprawl.

Most people, when they get a problem think, 'Oh No!' But not Dick. He'd think, 'Great, because this is blocking other people, so if we can solve it, we'll be ahead. What an opportunity!' It was a great kind of approach.[83]

Dusseldorp never avoided a problem. He always sought the profitable and sensible solution.[84]

'Sydney today is a city under pressure,' Dusseldorp told members of the city's Legacy Club who had gathered that evening in July 1961 to hear the property developer speak on *The Responsibility of Private Enterprise in the Rebuilding of Australian Cities*.[85] With the 'tremendous influx' of people that had seen Sydney's population increase by 22 per cent over the past decade, the joint demands of trying to house, transport, and supply these people with essential services was stretching its resources to the limit. The influx itself was not the problem. Rather, he argued, it was that the city was failing to respond to these demands creatively. Housing systems better suited to semi-rural Australia—not a huge metropolitan centre such as Sydney—were being inappropriately applied. Low-density, scattered development on the urban fringe was proceeding apace at the same time the population of the inner suburbs was declining. As a result, the costs of properly serving the city's dispersed population were rising to 'almost unbelievable' levels.[86]

If the current 'scatteration' of development continued, Dusseldorp warned, within ten years people would be travelling 70 to 80 kilometres to work in the CBD: this 'forward and backward movement of people over long distances' would choke the city into 'near immobility'. (The increased financial costs of all this travel would choke it in other respects as well.) The cost of providing urban infrastructure and services—drainage, water, sewerage, electricity and gas, etc.—to a population spread far and wide across 'partially developed areas' was huge. Many people were having to put up with 'sub-standard amenities' or 'alternatively have full standards supplied to them ... heavily subsidised by the community at large': both undesirable outcomes on equity and efficiency grounds. 'These are some of the costs of scatteration,' Dusseldorp said. 'There are other costs in terms of human values.' The time to adopt a new approach had arrived. 'It is no longer enough to just add at random to what is already here,' Dusseldorp argued; 'we must devise a creative ideal for the city of the future.' And one of the greatest opportunities for doing just that, he suggested, was to 'rebuild the inner city' through collectively planned projects for urban renewal.[87]

It was a grand vision for 'urban renewal' that Dusseldorp went on to lay out that night. Ideally such renewal projects would be done on an areal basis—'the days of individual buildings, whether large or small, unrelated to one another and their general environment, are numbered,' he predicted—and as a collaborative effort between the public and private sectors. Governments simply lacked the financial resources to redevelop urban areas on their own, he argued, and while they obviously had a contribution to make, 'private investment and private enterprise ... must ultimately carry the burden of the improvement'. What was needed if urban renewal was to succeed, Dusseldorp maintained, was a *partnership* between business and government—one based on mutual respect —which he had reason to believe was increasingly possible. 'There are signs of recognition by Government administrators that business is concerned with more far-reaching objectives than immediate profits,' he said, 'and recognition by businessmen that their contemporaries in Governmental posts have a respect for the ideals of public benefit.'[88] It was a heart-felt sentiment he expressed, and for good reason. For over the past two and a half years he had led a quite extraordinary process, enjoining the efforts of both public and private sectors to find a solution to a problem that was stalling a crucial part of the 'urban renewal' program. That problem was based in the existing system of land title.

'There are probably two fundamental kinds of land title in [Anglo-Saxon] law,' says Lend Lease's Dick Morath, 'and they're both invented in Australia ... Torrens title—which was invented in South Australia—and strata title which was invented here in New South Wales.' Torrens is a system of government-certified registration of land title, and strata is a form of title that subdivides airspace to enable private ownership of individual lots in a multi-level building.

> They're both basically *concepts* and they've gone all around the world. Not everywhere, of course, but if you look at all the different systems of land title, these two have got it over all the others. Now, Dusseldorp didn't have anything to do with Torrens [it was invented a good fifty years before he was born] but he sure had something to do with Strata.[89]

What sparked Dusseldorp's interest in the issue, says Morath, was the difficulties that most people had in financing the purchase of what Australians call 'home units' (flats or apartments to the rest of the English-speaking world).

> Dick was interested in building home units [says Morath] as a better means of accommodation for the 'average guy'—who wanted to live close to the city, or on a transport line, but who couldn't afford [or didn't want to look after] a house on the proverbial quarter-acre block. But he had this problem in that ... the only way you could do that [prior to 1961] was through company title, and the banks wouldn't lend on that. So financing it was a problem. But there's nothing Dick loved more [Morath smiles] than a problem. Most people, when they get a

problem think 'Oh no!' But not Dick. He'd think, 'Great, because this is blocking other people, so if we can solve it, we'll be ahead. What an opportunity!' It was a great kind of approach.[90]

Although multi-occupancy buildings—usually in the form of two- to three-storey blocks of flats[91]—had been built in certain parts of Sydney and its suburbs in the 1920s and 1930s, their rate of construction, having petered out during the war, had failed to increase at anywhere near that of detached houses during the postwar building boom. It was not through lack of demand. The idea of apartment living—with its ease of access to the city, without the cost or main-tenance demands of a block of land—was growing in popularity, right across the socio-economic spectrum.[92] It was on the supply side that the blockage lay. Part of the explanation for the stalling in construction growth was the continuation of wartime rent controls. Most blocks of flats were owned by investors who would rent out the individual units.[93] Rent controls limited the investment return and thus provided a financial disincentive to new construction.[94] But when these restrictions were lifted in 1954, another, seemingly more intractable, problem came to light. That problem was the form of title in which individual flats or units could be held, the most common of which was then company title.

Company title provides for what Mary Murphy describes as 'cooperative', rather than 'divided', ownership of a multi-occupancy property.[95] Freehold is vested in a company, with shareholders in that company acquiring the right to occupy a designated space in the building. A board of directors manages the building, and has the right to refuse transfer of ownership, or change in occupa-tion, of a designated space according to their own house rules. The problem with company title was that banks and other preferred financial institutions were loath to lend money to individual shareholders under this arrangement, because there was no real security for their loans. If an institution foreclosed on a loan and repossessed the defaulter's shareholding, they still could not sell the 'right to occupy space' to a would-be buyer without that buyer receiving the unanimous 'approval' of the company's board. With banks unwilling to lend, it was only the most wealthy—those who did not need to borrow—who could afford to buy home units, either to live in themselves, or to put on the rental market. And that put a dampener on the construction of new apartment build-ings in the 1950s, particularly anything rising above the traditional two or three floors, *despite* the increasing (but latent) demand.

This was the situation that confronted Dusseldorp when Civil & Civic entered Sydney's high-rise apartment market in the 1950s. By late 1958, having built a couple of blocks of home units under the company title system, and with plans on the drawing board for several more, the Managing Director of the firm had a good idea of the system's limitations. Convinced that something could surely be done to achieve a 'cleaner' form of title for home unit owners and buyers—one which would make financial institutions more willing to lend money to them, and in turn stimulate demand for his company's services—Dusseldorp turned to his fellow director and lawyer, John Rothery, for advice. Rothery told him that plans for law reform in this area had been mooted for some time, but so far to no avail. A 'Special Reporter' for the *Daily Telegraph* put it more bluntly: 'The [State] Government has been promising for some years to do something to clarify home unit titles. *The Government has done nothing except circulate considerable memoranda between the wirebaskets of the departments concerned.*'[96]

While not entirely true, it must have seemed that way to the *Telegraph*'s readers. Although many smart legal minds, from both the public and private sectors, had sought to overcome the deficiencies of the existing system of multi-occupancy title, they had encountered obstacles at every turn. What the lawyers proposed, the banks would not touch; and what the banks liked, the lawyers poked numerous holes through. Looking overseas had not helped: even though forms of common title had been around in some countries since Roman times, it seemed none provided a satisfactory model for dealing with the problems faced by would-be unit-owners in Sydney in the late 1950s. 'In no country in the world', said one NSW parliamentarian, 'have the best lawyers, conveyancers or authorities on the law of real property been able to evolve a satisfactory system of title for [multi-occupancy] buildings.'[97] And so, despite toing and froing around the halls of government, at the end of 1958 there seemed little prospect that a workable solution was suddenly about to appear in the chambers of Parliament House. Dusseldorp felt that it was time to expedite the law reform process.

I went to the Attorney-General of the day, [he recounts] and said to him, 'If we draft for you some strata title reform legislation, and get for you the support of the financial institutions and whomever else you nominate, then will you be willing to push it through Parliament?' The Attorney replied, 'Mr Dusseldorp, that would be

23 In 1965 architect and critic Robin Boyd designed a collection of six model houses for an estate Lend Lease was developing in the eastern suburbs of Melbourne. The houses on Appletree Hill were planned to harmonise with each other and the environment. Surrounded by native trees, and with no overhead power lines or front fences, Appletree Hill was a far cry from the suburbia Boyd had derided in his book, *The Australian Ugliness*.

24 Dusseldorp and then Federal Treasurer Harold Holt at the opening of the second stage of the Coach House Inn (now called the Thredbo Alpine Hotel) in 1963. Dusseldorp dreamed of turning Thredbo into a year-round alpine resort, the future development of the village and the mountain guided by a long-term, integrated Master Plan.

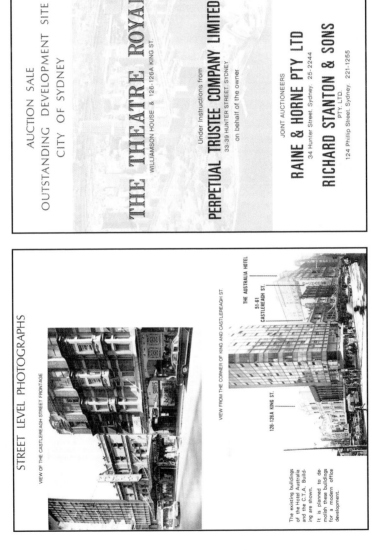

25 Excerpts from the booklet announcing the sale of Sydney's Theatre Royal in 1969. A couple of years after its purchase, Dusseldorp's redevelopment plans for the site brought him into conflict with theatre-goers and heritage activists who wanted the old building preserved. Jack Mundey's BLF imposed a Green Ban on the Royal's destruction, but a creative compromise was reached when Dusseldorp offered to include a new theatre in the MLC Centre which now occupies the site and its surrounds.

26 The MLC Centre in central Sydney, viewed from the ground level of its podium of public plazas. Designed by Harry Seidler and built by Civil & Civic, the MLC Centre comprises a 65-storey office tower, shopping arcade, open space plazas, and the new Theatre Royal.

27, 28 Apprentices competing in the Sydney regional WorkSkill Australia competition in 1984 (*above*). Regional competitions like this are held across the country to enable selection of the Australian team to participate in the international WorldSkills Competition (previously known as the Youth Skill Olympics) held every two years. *Below*, the founding Executive Director of WorkSkill Australia, Dick's son Tjerk Dusseldorp (second from right), inspects a competitor's handiwork.

the easiest piece of legislation ever achieved! But what do you want from me?'
'Only one thing,' [Dusseldorp said.] 'Come to a lunch with me and the heads of all
those institutions that you think are critical to the Bill's passage, and tell them
what you have just told me.'⁹⁸

In anticipation of a favourable response from the Attorney-General, Dusseldorp
had, some months earlier, engaged counsel—John Baalman, whom he refers to
as a 'madcap English lawyer'⁹⁹—who had studied the titles issue in depth, and
had begun to prepare just such a draft bill. With the Attorney-General agreeing
to Dusseldorp's proposal, Baalman was told to redouble his efforts. As he, in
conjunction with 'the best legal minds' from Rothery's firm and the government's Land Titles office, set to work drafting, Dusseldorp went about organising his lunch and the series of meetings which would follow.

'I got together all the heads of the finance institutions, building societies,
insurance companies, and savings banks,' Dusseldorp says. To this list was
added all the various branches of government whose bailiwick touched on the
title issue; the professional organisations of architects, surveyors, and engineers; various building industry associations; and the private and public utilities
(the Metropolitan Water, Sewerage and Drainage Board, Electricity Commission, Australian Gas Light Company, and the Postmaster-General)—any body
with any conceivable interest in resolution of the imbroglio. 'I gave them three
months notice [of the meeting] so they couldn't cop out,' says Dusseldorp,
'[and] I said, "No lawyers, no deputies; Chairmen and Managing Directors
only." '¹⁰⁰ In the end there was a 90 per cent turn-out at the lunch, which was
held in one of the top city hotels in March 1959. The Attorney-General attended
in person, and performed his part of the bargain: guaranteeing his support for
law reform, if he, in turn, could be sure of the institutions' support for it. 'He
did his bit,' says Dusseldorp, 'and he was true to form. Then I did my pleading
and said, "Look, gentlemen, Mr Torrens of South Australia one hundred years
ago reformed the whole of the title structure of the country of Australia. Isn't it
bloody well time that we today followed suit?" '¹⁰¹

'What I want you to do,' Dusseldorp continued, 'is just one thing. Shortly
our committee of lawyers will send to *your* lawyers a draft of a proposed bill.
Get all of your lawyers to attend a meeting to discuss the draft on the following
basis: anything they don't like in the draft, they provide an alternative form of
words for.' This simple condition, Dusseldorp calculates, would later knock out

about 90 per cent of potential complaints about the proposed legislation.[102] With his audience willing to take up his challenge, the reform bandwagon had started to roll. Then it was over to the lawyers. Early the next month, legal representatives of all the various institutions represented at the lunch convened with Rothery's legal team to consider the draft Strata Title Bill prepared by Baalman. This was the first of a series of intensive meetings and negotiations that took take place over the next eighteen months. Drafts and redrafts were made as lawyers representing all the different stakeholders sought to have their interests met. Dusseldorp's riding instructions to *his* legal team were twofold: 'satisfy all those people', but 'keep it simple'.[103] Meanwhile, John Rothery recalls, Dusseldorp continued his discussions with 'absolutely everyone connected to the issue':[104] making sure the heads of the relevant institutions— including the government and parliamentary opposition—were kept up-to-date with exactly what was going on.

The consultation process was no closed-shop affair. In November 1959 an in-principle draft of the proposed Strata Title Bill was tabled in the NSW Parliament, then allowed to lie there for over twelve months to enable all and sundry—both 'commercial people and the community'[105]—to comment on it. This in itself was an innovative process, which some members of the Opposition thought all such 'experimental' bills would benefit from going through.[106] As the feedback flowed in, problems and suggestions were raised, then assessed, addressed, or dismissed. New sections were inserted in the bill and old ones deleted, clauses were drafted and redrafted, phrases checked and rechecked, and words defined and refined. As the consultation process drew to a close—almost two years since that first lunch had been held—the lawyers announced they were ready to call it a day.

'The final crunch came', Dusseldorp remembers, 'when the lawyers said, "Well, we've got as far as we can go."' In line with his instructions, they had sought to keep the provisions of the Strata Title Bill identical, as far as possible, with the current procedure for subdividing land. The bill which they were now presenting to Dusseldorp, they told him, contained only six basic changes from the existing procedure. While the lawyers smiled triumphantly at their achievement, Dusseldorp was less than impressed.

> We argued the whole day, and they were down to three at the end of the day. And I said, 'Gentlemen, I can't express my gratitude. I'll now take it all away because,

obviously, this is the end of the road as far as you are concerned. I'll now give it
to the new set of lawyers who will take care of the remaining three.' Three weeks
later, they came to me with all problems out of it. And that is how [strata title]
came about.[107]

The revised bill for the introduction of strata title gained bipartisan support,
and was passed by both houses of the NSW Parliament in March 1961.[108] It was
'ground-breaking legislation', which 'eventually led to similar laws being introduced in other Australian states and territories and overseas'.[109] Other countries
that introduced it include New Zealand, Singapore, Canada, South Africa, and
some US states,[110] 'although not, as yet, ... England' Dusseldorp says.[111] The
new law quickly achieved what Dusseldorp had wanted it to. Financial institutions proved 'much more ready to lend on strata titles than on company titles',
says Sydney's urban chronicler, Peter Spearritt, and on that basis home unit
building boomed[112]—with Lend Lease and its building arm, Civil & Civic, both
contributing to and benefiting from it. The strata title concept was also extended
beyond residential multi-occupancy buildings to apply to commercial, retail,
and industrial premises in Australia. By the year 2000, some 50,000 strata
schemes were operating in New South Wales—well over 80 per cent of which
were residential—with an average of five new ones being registered each day.[113]
    The process of achieving the new form of property title was another
example of Dusseldorp's ability to find a win-win solution to a problem that
others had found intractable. Rather than sit back and let others do (or more
likely *not* do) it, Dusseldorp had grasped the nettle himself. Characteristically,
the key to his success had been to identify—and get others to recognise—a
common interest between them: one sufficient to enable diverse, sometimes
conflicting, stakeholders to work together for their mutual benefit. But, just as
typically, while Dusseldorp himself acknowledged that the introduction of
strata title was 'good for meeting individual demands', it was only one part of
achieving his 'urban renewal' agenda. 'It didn't take care of the planning
issue,'[114] he says. As we'll see in the next chapter, he soon turned his energies
to seeing what could be done about that.

CHAPTER 7

Building Communities: From Suburbia to the Snowfields and Back

In 1960 Melbourne architect and writer Robin Boyd cast his critical eye over Australia's built environment and pronounced his acerbic judgement on it in a book called *The Australian Ugliness*. With its nihilistic denial and destruction of the natural environment in which it nestled, its chaos of dysfunctional and uncoordinated built forms, and its straggle of overhead wires, poles, and 'a hundred other necessary public appliances',[1] Sydney's rapidly enlarging suburban 'smudge'[2] seemed to encapsulate Boyd's central theme.

> The recent growth of Sydney is mainly confined to three zones [he wrote]. Out west, the wooden villa, or Villawood Zone—to use the name of one of its central districts—… is a fairly typical Australian working-class development, repeating the dreary, ill-considered housing growth on the outskirts of every Australian town: the same cold comfort conservatism of villa design with the regular sprinkling of primary-tinted features.[3]

This was the zone, Boyd continued, in which the government housing department, speculative builders and private owners all 'compete with one another to reduce the bush to a desert of terra-cotta roofs relieved only by electric wires and wooden poles'. But the ugliness was not confined to Sydney's predominantly working-class west.

> The same approach extends south into the Tom Ugly Zone, to use the name of a landmark near its centre: Tom Ugly's Point … Here the familiar suburban techniques are more destructive because the houses are slightly more pretentious and the country which they strangle was obviously more beautiful before man arrived. The fibro frontier is pushed right to the water's edge.[4]

Boyd's most fervent denunciation, however, was reserved for Sydney's 'North Shore Executive Zone'. 'Here some of the most dramatically beautiful country available to suburban commuters anywhere in the world,' he wrote, 'seems to draw out a delinquent streak in nearly everyone who builds.' Although 'three or four of the most notable modern houses in Australia' were located here—including some designed by architect Harry Seidler—they were 'all but lost in a wild scramble of outrageous Featurism clearly planned for the express purpose of extracting a gasp of envy from each passing sportscar'. It was this latter characteristic—Australia's seeming obsession with Featurism, defined by Boyd as a visual style that accentuated selected separate features to the subordination of the whole[5]—that drew most of the critic's ire. And if the 'devastation' wrought by the Australian Ugliness 'seems worst in Sydney', he wrote, 'this is only because nature provided so much more to start with and the loss is so much more apparent';[6] but the disease which first took hold in that city, he continued, now 'oozes out evenly, flatly to the furthest places where Australians live'.[7]

Publication of *The Australian Ugliness* in 1960 caused something of a stir. Boyd had for some time been a regular contributor to the pages of Melbourne's broadsheet, *The Age*, and to his profession's quarterly journal *Architecture*, so his views—and biting wit—were not unknown; but the book reached a much broader audience—at least by repute if not direct readership—to judge by its uproarious reception. 'Few Australian books, before or since, have roused such tumult and shouting,' says Boyd's biographer, Geoffrey Serle. Everyone had something to say about it, with reaction running the gamut from 'wild indignation' to 'lavish praise'.[8] Some of his friends warned Boyd 'that he was doing himself harm', says Serle—a view which the latter believes 'may have held some truth with regard to future commissions'.[9] For Boyd's contemporaneous detractors, *The Australian Ugliness* was nothing more than the carping ravings of an 'angry young man'; the view that the book is 'essentially negative',[10] superficial and offering little in the way of a constructive alternative, persists amongst some writers today. Urban historian Peter Spearritt, for example, labels Boyd's critique of Sydney suburbia 'largely aesthetic', claiming that he had 'no feasible proposals for how else the urban population might be housed'.[11] Spearritt argues, *contra* Boyd and other 'left-wing intellectuals' who were equally disdainful of the 'suburban blight', that the *real* problem with it, certainly in Sydney's case, 'was not to be found in the individual homes or backyards but in the fact that so much of it was so far removed from shops, jobs, hospitals, beaches and parks'.[12]

But not everyone thought Boyd was wrong. Not long after the book's release, architect and environmentalist Milo Dunphy wrote that *The Australian Ugliness* 'was possibly the best book yet on the Australian environment'. Artist and writer Elizabeth Durack called it a 'brilliant work', while social commentator Geoffrey Hutton hailed it as 'the most important book of its era'.[13] It was even credited with inspiring Patrick White's portrait of Barranugli in his 1960 novel, *Riders in the Chariot*.[14] The book also caught the eye of a certain Sydney-based property developer whose own views on the desirability of integrated, area-based, environmentally sensitive developments were starting to be seen and heard across the city. Finding many of these views mirrored in Boyd's work, Dusseldorp decided to present the critic with a challenge. 'He had written his book,' Dusseldorp later told Lend Lease historian Mary Murphy, 'and I thought, "This guy ... is so perceptive and can see everything that is wrong ... why not give him a chance to do it right?" '[15] And so in 1965 Dusseldorp commissioned Boyd to design half a dozen houses which would form a 'demonstration village' for a subdivision that Lend Lease was undertaking in Melbourne's outer eastern suburb of Glen Waverley. If that went well, there would be more to come: 400 houses in Melbourne, to be exact, and a similar number for an estate the company was planning in Sydney's north-west. Boyd was enthusiastic—'he grabbed that [opportunity] with both hands', Dusseldorp remembers[16]—and the architect set to work on his plans for Melbourne's new Appletree Hill Estate.

———

As was the case in Sydney, Melbourne's low-density housing development had been spreading tentacle-like away from the city centre for some time. With demand for dwellings at an all-time high in the postwar years, and with the detached dwelling on the quarter-acre block most Australians' conception of the ideal home, the 1950s and 1960s saw the southern metropolis begin to develop a sprawl that, in the eyes of at least one critic, could match that of Los Angeles.[17] Subdividers first raced eastward from Melbourne's central core 'into the once beautiful green belt'[18]—usually getting there well ahead of urban services such as public transport and sewerage. Down would come the 'untidy' native trees, the remnant buildings from earlier 'pioneering' periods, and anything else that stood in the way of their bulldozers. Having thus '[cleared] the decks for action', Robin Boyd observed, up would go the 'rows of cottages and raw paling fences'—and in would go the lawns of 'clipped artificiality' and the beds of thirsty English annuals—all of which would then be decked by the 'spiders' webs of overhead wires' which '[formed] a ubiquitous veil across the civic scene'.[19] It was a less-than-inspiring picture of suburbia that Boyd painted, but now, courtesy of Dusseldorp, he had the chance to draw his own.

The Appletree Hill Estate project was not the first time that the two men had worked together. They had met in Canberra in the late 1950s, where the architectural partnership Grounds, Romberg & Boyd had designed, and Dusseldorp's Civil & Civic had built, a number of innovative civic and residential structures, most famously the domed Academy of Science, designed by Roy Grounds. Following that, when Dusseldorp's development company Lend Lease had started building high-rise apartment blocks in Melbourne, he had given Gromboyd (as the architectural principals called their partnership)[20] the first such commission. The Domain Park flats in South Yarra, overlooking the city's Botanic Gardens to the north and Port Phillip Bay to the south, were principally designed by Boyd—his first major building—and built by Civil & Civic in 1960–62 (a relatively lengthy construction period, interrupted as it was by the credit squeeze). And now the two men had plans to take on the Melbourne suburbs together.

In their sights was a once-rural area in the city's outer east, where Lend Lease had acquired a substantial parcel of land for subdivision in the early 1960s. Dusseldorp wanted to establish a 'demonstration village' there—a concept he had tested in Sydney in 1961 with the opening of the first such exhibition village at Carlingford. The idea was to put on display a range of architect-designed 'project houses' which would-be homebuyers could then have built on their own (or the surrounding) land.[21] These project homes 'were directed to the middle-class buyer who wanted something distinct and hopefully better than that generally available,' writes architectural historian Jennifer Taylor, 'but who did not want to enter into the cost and the involved process of an individually designed house.'[22] For the architect, well-designed project homes offered a way of '[educating] the public about new design ideas', says urban historian Anne Gartner, thus helping to reduce the estimated twenty-year lag in public acceptance of design features favoured by the profession.[23] For the developer, project homes were a good marketing tool—differentiating them from the purely speculative builders by offering a better-quality product—and providing some opportunity to reduce costs by standardising residential construction techniques. But, as Dusseldorp would find out, the concept was by no means risk-free.

Opened in 1965, Dusseldorp and Boyd's Appletree Hill Estate in Glen Waverley was different from just about everything that had preceded it (and a lot of what would follow it). There were no telegraph poles, no light poles, no overhead wires, and no front fences. All the power lines were laid underground —a first for the state of Victoria—a measure which added a small sum to the cost of each house, but which paid back many times over in terms of safety, aesthetics, reliability of service, and enhanced property values.[24] The six houses designed by Boyd for the demonstration village were built amongst—not at the expense of—the existing native trees, and they were positioned on the blocks in a way that enabled them, as the architect put it, 'to make the most of the views to the hills'.[25] All the houses were brick-veneer, with a range of designs offered —'half with flat roofs, half with tiles: half in red brick, half in white'[26]—none of them sporting any of the extraneous 'features' which Boyd so detested, and all designed to harmonise with their neighbours and the surrounding environment.

'It was charming—really lovely,' says Dusseldorp of the village, but in commercial terms the houses proved a flop. 'We had a lot of advance publicity,' he says, 'and we have never had more people through any demonstration village over a period of six weeks.'[27] About 150,000 people inspected it, Dusseldorp remembers, the critics having 'waxed lyrical' about the whole concept.[28]

> *There was not one single, solitary sale.* Everybody thought it was fascinating, but not for them. They were all concerned about the resale value ... it was too far ahead ... So, finally, we had to give up. We pulled the rug out. We did well out of the estate, but we had to let those houses go below cost to get them off our hands.[29]

Although the concept had excited the public imagination, the failure of the project houses at Appletree Hill Estate to sell at a price commensurate with their value was a disappointment for all concerned. Boyd himself believed that 'the scheme was withdrawn before it had a fair chance',[30] but Dusseldorp was both more hard-nosed—and philosophical—about it. In the housing market, he said, a company cannot afford to be *too* far ahead of its time. 'It can test, and then withdraw, and test again,' he told the ABC's *Monday Conference* program, 'and that is where one gets variety and the best wins out.' Competition and the experimentation it fostered were crucial to providing a variety of housing options for the consumer, he said, but in the end 'the market place is ... the one that determines the one that survives and the one that doesn't'.[31] And with Lend Lease having to off-load the Boyd-designed houses at 30 per cent below cost, it was pretty clear which way the market was rating this one.

Making a wrong call, however, did not dent Dusseldorp's desire to experiment with new ideas. 'If you don't make mistakes from time to time,' he would say, 'you're not trying. If you try new things, you *will* make mistakes—that's part and parcel of the game.'[32] And while the Boyd-designed houses at Appletree Hill did not catch on, other aspects of the development of the Glen Waverley estate had certainly demonstrated public appeal. The emphasis on improving the amenity and aesthetics of the subdivision—by burying the power cables, eliminating the light and telegraph poles, and keeping the existing native trees—*had* proved popular and, as a result, commercially rewarding.

At the same time that the Appletree Hill experiment was being conducted, Dusseldorp's Lend Lease was in the midst of a much bigger venture in Sydney, where it was developing the 'first privately sponsored Comprehensive Neighbourhood' in the new satellite city of Campbelltown.[33] Although the house designs for the Campbelltown development were more conventional than those created by Boyd, in scope and scale this experiment was more far-reaching than that at Appletree Hill. It continued the theme of developing the land and houses in relationship with each other and with their natural environment, but it was more explicit in its commitment to integrating them with the *social* environment as well. The intention at Campbelltown was to build a community, and in that sense the development there recognised that a cure for the 'Australian Ugliness' required measures that went further than just skin-deep.

The company's activities have to be socially relevant—for the simple reason that most concerned people only want to spend their life on such efforts.[34]

His company having undertaken its first residential estate development in Sydney's Middle Cove in the mid-1950s—followed by the construction of a couple of serviced subdivisions elsewhere in the metropolis and in neighbouring city Newcastle—by the end of the decade Dusseldorp was on the look-out for ways to extend Lend Lease's operations in the residential field. 'I had to grow the business', he says, 'so I was looking at all opportunities.'[35] With Sydney's growing population, its rapidly rising rates of home ownership, and its acute demand for housing, an enhanced form of the company's estate development activities seemed to fit that bill. Lend Lease's first subdivisions had been located in infill areas of Sydney's suburban belt, but for the scale of undertaking that its Managing Director now had in mind, much larger tracts of land would be required. That confined the choices to the outer suburban fringe (or beyond it), and that in turn meant trying to pick the direction in which the Sydney of the future would grow.

> Since the war, [Dusseldorp says] the city had expanded at a rapid rate, and I wanted to know where it would go next. And so I hired an economist—which was rare for the industry at the time—and I asked this guy, could he study and let me know, on the basis of his analysis of past trends, where he thought it would expand to—and by how much—over the next twenty years.[36]

The task of analysis and forecasting task was huge, as a member of the Lend Lease research team remembers. 'We looked at the population and the growth factors, at roads, transport, sewerage, and services generally ... and came up with this vast report,' says David Thorne.[37] The report identified a number of possible areas for future residential growth, but the one that caught Dusseldorp's attention was the then country town of Campbelltown, some 50 kilometres south-west of central Sydney.

Campbelltown was one of four settlements that the 1948 County of Cumberland Plan had proposed as future satellite cities[38]—self-contained centres of housing, work, and community services to be developed beyond Sydney's Green Belt—and in view of its locational advantages, it looked to Dusseldorp the area most likely to take off. One factor in particular was key.

> The research team had learnt that Sydney's water supply was estimated to run out in about twenty years, [Dusseldorp recalls] and that it would take about that long

to tap other water resources, if there was not to be a disaster. And I picked up on that, because, if it takes them twenty years to go from A to B ... then when they finished the new dam, the water from it will go first to the nearest population ... So I looked at the map and saw that in terms of accessibility to the water supply, then Campbelltown would clearly be that first cab off the rank.[39]

In 1958, Dusseldorp started to take a closer look at the land available for purchase around the Campbelltown area. He immediately liked what he saw. 'I looked at the contours, the natural environment, the rainfall, etcetera,' he says, 'and the land turned out to be naturally drained, so that was all okay.' A large proportion of the area had for many years been used for dairy farming, 'and as a result lots of the trees had gone', but, Dusseldorp reasoned, that was a problem that could easily be redressed. On the transport front, even though Campbelltown was 'a long way from Sydney',[40] the main north–south railway line went through the area—although the nearest station was some distance away from the particular piece of land he had his eye on—and the Hume Highway, linking Sydney to Melbourne, was 'reasonably close' by.[41] His talks with the local municipal council indicated that that body was keen for Campbelltown to develop further—so that also augured well for his plans. 'And when you put all that together,' says Dusseldorp, 'I decided that that was quite an opportunity, because the land there was dirt cheap.'[42]

Convinced in his own mind that Campbelltown was the place to be, and with a sizeable tract of land in the area up for sale, Dusseldorp took a proposal to buy it to the Lend Lease Corporation's board.

> It was the only time that I spent an hour in the board meeting arguing with my directors. They thought it was too far out. The valuer had said the land was worth $200 an acre, but the vendor wanted $205, and that they couldn't stomach. And so [the argument] went on. In the end I said to them, 'Gentlemen, I am proposing this. I am not one who does something without Lend Lease having the first offer. You have the first offer. If you decline it, I now give notice that I will do it myself privately.' And lo and behold that was enough to make them change their minds.[43]

In 1959 Lend Lease acquired its first parcel of land in Campbelltown, some 80 hectares (200 acres) already zoned residential,[44] a portion of which the company then sold as a serviced subdivision called the Macquarie Heights

Estate. Over the next couple of years a large parcel of adjacent rural land was acquired, and it was here that stage one of Dusseldorp's grand plans for the area began to take shape.

———

For the most part, and for good reason, many of the new residential developments on Sydney's outer suburban fringe had, by the 1960s, earned themselves a name as less than ideal places to live. What Boyd had termed the Villawood Zone was continuing to ooze westward—engulfing huge chunks of the rapidly diminishing Green Belt—as thousands upon thousands of houses were constructed to meet the massive demand. But in the rush to erect the much-needed shelter, it was not only the natural environment and urban aesthetics that were suffering. All too often the infrastructure and services required to make the new areas liveable lagged the suburban frontier by years, leaving the 'pioneering' homeowners to make do in whatever way they could. In 1968 a long-term resident—and future Prime Minister of Australia—spoke of what it was like to raise his family in Sydney's outer suburban sprawl:

> I have lived in those areas for twenty-one years. I have raised four children [there] ... We have never been connected to the sewer. In this respect we are in common with three-quarters of a million men, women and children in Sydney ...
> Furthermore, when we have gone to those places, there was no high school within 12 miles ... When [our children] were swimming, and two of them have been very good swimmers, at first they had to go 12 miles to a swimming pool ... There were no municipal libraries. There were no paved roads within a mile of where we were. There are still no paved footpaths. For telephones you would wait four years ... The only community facilities when the children were young were baby health centres. There was nothing else at all.[45]

It simply wasn't good enough, according to Dusseldorp. 'The existence of sub-standard housing in Australia reflects on the whole community,' he told the Housing Industry Association that same year.

> The greatest challenge confronting us now is to cope with the compounding effect of increased population and increased urbanization, as well as increased standards

of living. It means coming to grips with the last of the basic needs of all people. It means elevating proper housing for all from a privilege to a right … It will be the nation's ultimate test of social integrity. It is the job of the housing industry in its broadest sense to accomplish the task. The task is not only to provide more and better housing, but to relate the products of the industry more closely to the needs and desires of the people. The industry as a whole knows little about the desires of the people and cares less. No improvement, on the scale that is needed, can be expected until these desires are understood and form the goal to be aimed at.[46]

Dusseldorp was determined that Lend Lease's new development at Campbelltown would raise the bar. Soon after the company acquired its first tracts of land there, he engaged a firm of architects and town planners to come up with a master plan for the area—not just a plan for the streets and houses, but one incorporating all the community and commercial facilities needed to service the new residents—which he would use as a basis for discussions with the local and regional planning authorities. With this task under way, the first on-the-ground work on the newly acquired land began: the planting of thousands of native trees. This was done 'not to a particular plan', says Dusseldorp, 'because we didn't *know* the shape of the final plan at that stage, but we figured it would be easy to cut some of them out later if need be, and in the meantime, at least there'd be trees everywhere'.[47]

Meanwhile, Dusseldorp turned his attention to the issue of public transport —another service which many residents of Sydney's outer suburbs regularly went without.

> There was a railway line running through the area [the main Sydney to Melbourne line], and so we met with the Railway Department and said, if we were to pay for a station [near the planned development], would they put it in? 'Sure', they said, 'but why would you want to put a station there?' 'Because we are thinking of making it into a city centre,' was our reply. 'Right, so you think that there might be some more business locating there?' the Railway Department asked. 'Yes, we do.' 'Well if that's the case, and if you pay for it, then you can have your railway station.'[48]

With this commitment gained, and with the other groundwork laid, it was time to start detailed discussions with the planning departments of the Campbelltown and Cumberland County Councils.

'That was not all that easy,' Dusseldorp remembers, 'because we'd marched straight into those planners' bailiwick, and they weren't too keen on that. They were very socially oriented, and they were afraid that, as developers, we'd be trying to rip them off.'[49] The planners' wariness is understandable, given that 'premature subdivisions and scattered development' in Sydney's outer areas were, as one of their number explained, not only draining local government's 'totally inadequate resources' but also resulting in unsatisfactory and 'depressing' living environments for residents.[50]

> Our first job was to calm them down [says Dusseldorp]. And so we said to them, 'Here is the land, here is the railway station. If you take those as the *only* things given, then we are prepared to follow your design for whatever hangs off that station. And what's more we'll *give* you the land around it, and we'll take a ninety-nine year lease on it, and let's see where we can go from there.'

It was an offer too good to refuse. 'Well,' recalls Dusseldorp, 'the planners were very excited about that prospect, and from then on relations with them were good';[51] so began a 'planning partnership'[52] between the two councils, their successor bodies, and Lend Lease that would continue for the next forty years.[53]

Dusseldorp's prediction about the development potential of the Campbelltown area was confirmed in 1960 when the town was designated Sydney's first satellite city by the Cumberland County Council. Using the existing town of Campbelltown as its nucleus—located on a 'pleasantly hilly and undulating' site, and 'surrounded by some of the most attractive countryside around Sydney'[54]—the planners envisaged this satellite beyond the Green Belt growing from its current population of 8000 to accommodate some 200,000 people by 1985. Their vision for Campbelltown was a grand one: it was to be a self-contained city 'not so big that it ceases to be homogenous, one so well built that it has none of the unpleasant characteristics of outer metropolitan growth, one close enough to Sydney for its people to enjoy most of the advantages of life in a really big city'.[55] Key to its controlled development would be the creation of a series of comprehensive Neighbourhood Units, each served by a primary school and neighbourhood centre, clusters of which would in turn be serviced by District Centres providing enhanced commercial, educational and recreational facilities.[56] These centres would be built both by the government housing department and by private developers, and that is where Dusseldorp's firm came in.

The first comprehensive neighbourhood to be developed in the new satellite city would be Lend Lease's Sherwood Hills Estate which, it was hoped, would set a benchmark for all that followed. To that end, the company established building covenants for the development, both to set standards for building quality, and to give the area 'a feeling of continuity' despite 'substantial differences' in individual house design.[57] In accordance with these covenants, all the homes on the estate were to be sewered, built of brick and tile, and set amongst landscaped gardens dominated by native trees. Large tracts of land in the area would be given over to parkland, through which the Fisher's Ghost Creek would flow. As on the Appletree Hill Estate in Melbourne, there would be no front fences, no street light stanchions (pavement light boxes would be used instead), and no overhead power lines. Dusseldorp had tried to bury the power lines at Middle Cove, the first residential estate he had developed in Sydney in the mid-1950s, but even though he had offered to cover the extra costs involved, the local electricity authority had been unwilling. This time, however, the local authority proved more supportive. Encouraged by this success, the Campbelltown Council subsequently introduced a policy to underground power lines on all new developments in the area.

Phase One of Lend Lease's Sherwood Hills development got under way in 1964, with the first hundred of the planned 1500 homes built and occupied by the end of following year. Working in conjunction with the local Council, the company put in place a range of measures to entice new residents to the area. Young couples just starting their families were attracted by the prospect of buying a good-quality dwelling on comparatively cheap land, but finding enough money for the deposit on a loan was proving a stumbling block for many. Lend Lease prepared a marketing assault on the financial institutions, and before long Dusseldorp had managed to convince a number of them to provide loans with a 'comfortable repayment schedule' to prospective homeowners in the area on the basis of very low deposits.[58] Next on the agenda was the provision of a local shopping centre. Such a centre had been scheduled for development several years down the track—when the population reached a level making it economically feasible to provide—and in the interim the Council had encouraged

Campbelltown businesses to provide a free home delivery service to the estate. But in 1968 Dusseldorp decided to fast-track his company's long-term plans. 'We'd built the houses,' he says, 'but without the shops, people don't want them. So we built some local shops and *paid* shopkeepers to keep shop there.' The subsidy provided by Lend Lease ran down over time, Dusseldorp says, so as new residents moved into the area and began to frequent their local retailers, 'those shopkeepers eventually began to pay *us* rent'.[59]

Other services and facilities followed. By the time Phase Two of the Sherwood Hills estate was launched in 1968, a primary school had opened; a bus service was running; the Council and local service organisations were sponsoring a program to introduce new residents to each other and the broader community; and Lend Lease had employed a lifelong resident of Campbelltown to help new residents of the estate 'settle in'.[60] The previous year, 1967, had seen the completion of an Olympic swimming pool, built by the council on land provided by Lend Lease within the neighbourhood area;[61] this was later joined by a complex of playing ovals and basketball courts built by the company on the adjacent land. Phase Three of the estate development, begun in 1971, involved the construction of medical suites, a community health centre (the latter a prototype for other such centres right across Australia), kindergarten, churches, sporting facilities and a tavern alongside the local shops to form an integrated Neighbourhood Centre. This development phase also saw the beginning of medium-density housing in the neighbourhood via the construction of clusters of townhouses offered under strata and Torrens title. 'At the time people said I was out of my mind to build townhouses out there', remembers Dusseldorp—medium-density developments being then confined to the inner city suburbs—'but they sold like hot scones.'[62] So successful was the medium-density concept that in 1974 this phase of the Campbelltown development was judged the state's best housing development since 1960, receiving the 'Estate of Tomorrow' Award.[63]

By 1975, over 6000 people were living in Campbelltown's first comprehensive neighbourhood—whose name had been changed from Sherwood Hills to Bradbury—and Lend Lease was working on its next major development in the area: the staged construction of the adjoining suburb of Ambarvale which, the company estimated, would eventually house a further 25,000 people.[64] By that time the State Planning Authority—successor to the Cumberland County Council—was also well advanced in its planning of a new city centre for

Campbelltown, with which Dusseldorp's firm was once again involved. This was part of a joint federal–state government plan to further expand the satellite, along with its neighbouring towns of Camden and Appin, into a tri-city complex called the Macarthur Growth Centre.[65] The new Campbelltown city centre—encompassing civic, commercial, community, health, and educational facilities—would be developed on a site owned by Lend Lease which adjoined the local golf course. To give effect to these plans, the Authority acquired the company's parcel of land in the proposed city centre—part of which Lend Lease then leased back for its development of a large regional shopping mall (Macarthur Square) adjacent to the new railway station—in exchange for other tracts of land in the area, which were then rezoned for residential use. As part of the arrangement, Lend Lease also undertook to design and construct a championship golf course in its new development at Ambarvale.[66] While ownership of this facility was transferred to the council on completion, the company also benefited from it, as the scenic backdrop of the course enabled the prestige properties located on its edge to command premium prices.

By 1988, the year in which Dusseldorp retired as Chairman of Lend Lease, Campbelltown had established itself as one of the country's fastest-growing cities, its population having increased more than sixfold since 1960.[67] Although by then many other private developers were also active in the area, Lend Lease was still one of the most significant.[68] While Lend Lease was big in Campbelltown, the reverse was also the case. By 1988 the company had undertaken many other area-based residential developments—in Australia, South-East Asia, and the United States—but none of them could match the scale of its investment in this, Sydney's first planned satellite community: 'Campbelltown was *enormous* by comparison [with the other developments]', says Dusseldorp. Ten years after his retirement, he would visit another Lend Lease development, the scale of which, he says, gets close to that of the company's involvement in Campbelltown, of which more later in this chapter. 'We were still earning an annual income from Campbelltown when I retired,' he says. 'It was a fluke to have cottoned on to it.'[69]

The benefits of the company's activities in the area extended beyond its own bottom line. Not everything the planners envisaged for the satellite city was achieved—the generation of enough jobs locally to make the area self-sufficient, rather than a dormitory suburb of Sydney and Liverpool, proceeded at a much slower pace than hoped, and as a result unemployment levels for the region have been high. Nonetheless, the Campbelltown 'experiment' passes muster when judged against comparable residential developments. Sydney's 'West Sector', for example, is an area which has experienced similar rates and types of population growth since the 1960s, but its development proceeded in a less coordinated fashion through 'normal land release procedures'. A study by Meyer found that Campbelltown performed better than the West Sector on most measures of economic and social development.[70] A key reason for its compara-tive success, according to Meyer, lies in the better coordinated and planned nature of the development of Campbelltown. The consolidated land holdings, compared to the fragmented ownership which prevailed elsewhere, facilitated the early provision of services and infrastructure to the city's new residential estates.[71]

At the same time the new residential communities at Appletree Hill and Campbelltown were beginning in the mid-1960s, Dusseldorp's firm was engaged in another, quite different experiment in integrated development on an area basis. Far removed from the suburban plains of Melbourne and Sydney— in fact almost midway between the two metropolises—the Snowy Mountains rise to form the highest peaks in Australia. It was there, nestled amongst the mountains, that Lend Lease was in the process of developing the village of Thredbo—its buildings and facilities integrated with each other and the natural environment—not just as Australia's premier skiing destination, but as the country's first year-round alpine resort.

Dusseldorp's involvement with Thredbo had started in 1961 when Eric Nicholls, the architect who had designed the firm's first Sydney skyscraper, Caltex House, approached him with a proposition. Nicholls was on the board of a small company called Kosciusko–Thredbo Ltd that in 1957 had acquired an option on a long-term lease from the government to develop a ski resort capitalising on the ideal skiing conditions in the Crackenback Valley.[72] The terms of the lease required the company to provide power, water, garbage disposal, and sewerage services to the then tiny village of Thredbo, to build and maintain its internal roads, and to construct commercial hotel accommodation and a chairlift within five years.[73] Essentially a group of keen skiers, the principals of the company had started enthusiastically—building Australia's longest alpine chairlift[74] and some basic accommodation for skiers—but they had soon run into problems. Lacking sufficient capital and development skills, Kosciusko–Thredbo Ltd was in danger of forfeiting its option on the lease, as there was no way it would be able to build the 100-bed hotel, as required, by 1962. Having seen first-hand, at Caltex House, his ability to organise finance and manage a project to completion against the odds,[75] Nicholls knew that what Kosciusko–Thredbo lacked, Dusseldorp and his company could provide. Would Lend Lease be interested in becoming involved with the project, Nicholls inquired, by way of a friendly takeover?

The more Dusseldorp looked into it, the more attracted to the idea he became. Skiing in Australia dated back to the 1860s,[76] but it was only now—in the postwar era—that the sport was starting to appeal to more than a few die-hard enthusiasts. Although not a keen skier himself, Dusseldorp was convinced that the sport had a huge future in the country.[77] And yet the facilities currently on offer to this growing market left much to be desired. The NSW ski areas of Perisher Valley, Smiggin Holes, and Guthega were already in operation by this time—joining the ski areas opened up earlier in the century around the chalet at Charlotte's Pass and the old Kosciusko Hotel[78]—but facilities across the region were still relatively primitive. On the slopes, 'rope tows and T-bars were the norm, while the occasional chairlift was a rare treat indeed';[79] the standard of accommodation was patchy; and the assortment of restaurants, shops, enter-tainment, and more basic amenities that skiers today take for granted, were then rare. There was clearly great potential to develop Thredbo as a top ski resort—one that would attract skiers from both the domestic and international markets during the southern hemisphere winter—especially if it could be differentiated from its competitors in terms of the quality of facilities on offer. But not only that. With the local dignitaries talking about upgrading the existing Alpine Way to make it the main tourist road linking Sydney and Melbourne, the *year-round* traffic through the area was potentially enormous.[80] Given the limited snow season in Australia, and if the road-improving plans came to fruition, Dusseldorp believed that the summer potential of Thredbo might well exceed that of the winter.[81]

The factor that clinched it for Dusseldorp, however, was the unique structure and long-term nature of the lease. 'The lease that had been negotiated with the government was a very favourable one,' he remembers, 'so there were benefits there for the developer, if it was done in a properly managed way.'[82] To this day, in most other Australian ski resort villages, the various sub-lessees—from the operator of the mountain and lifts, through to the proprietors of the individual hotels, lodges, shops and related businesses—enter into separate and direct leasing arrangements with the government for a relatively short term (such as twenty years). The existence of multiple property rights and the limited period of the leases have tended to foster haphazard development, resulting in a hotchpotch of unrelated buildings and facilities in the absence of an integrated plan. But the situation in the Crackenback Valley was, and remains, different. Kosciusko–Thredbo Ltd as the resort operator was in a position to enter into a single, long-term, head-lease with the government. It could then, in turn, enter into sub-leases with the various concerns comprising the resort, giving the company, as de facto landlord, much greater and integrated control over the way the mountain and village developed. As Lend Lease historian Mary Murphy has observed, Thredbo thus presented Dusseldorp with 'an irresistible opportunity for a small essay in town planning–area development'.[83] Eric Nicholls didn't have to wait long for a response to his proposition: Lend Lease was coming on board.

In typical Dusseldorp fashion, once the Lend Lease acquisition of Kosciusko–Thredbo Ltd was executed in October 1961, little time was wasted in getting the project under way. There were three key priorities for the new owners. First up was to bring in a new team to tighten up the management of the resort. Second was to fulfil the outstanding requirements of the lease so as to secure it on a long-term basis; and third was to prepare a master plan for the resort's future development. While the latter two priorities were widely applauded, some of the actions to achieve the first did little to endear Dusseldorp to the locals, as his wife Anne remembers.

> Some of them disliked him because he changed the rules. There had been a fair bit of cheating on the chairlift, and people wanted their staff to continue skiing for nothing … And of course when Lend Lease took over, they put an end to that sort of behaviour. At the time a number of people were saying, 'I hope Dick Dusseldorp falls off his skis!'[84]

Dusseldorp soon obliged, breaking a leg during a private lesson with Thredbo ski instructor Leonhard Erharter:[85] an event which no doubt elicited much mirth and not a great deal of sympathy.

Meanwhile, work began on a major construction program in the resort to fulfil the requirements of the option on which the long-term lease depended. Stage 1 of the Coach House Inn (now called the Thredbo Alpine Hotel) was completed by Civil & Civic in the summer months of 1961–62, with Stage 2 finished in time for the winter of 1963.[86] A new sewage treatment works was built to serve the village, electric power brought in over the mountains, the water supply system upgraded, and a number of access roads and car parks constructed.[87] The Crackenback chairlift was redesigned, extended and strengthened, and new top and bottom stations were installed. A new T-bar was erected on the middle slopes,[88] and all the ski trails on the mountain were cleared to provide better and safer runs.[89] By 1963, a second chairlift and a new T-bar were also in operation, with more to follow in the years to come. With Lend Lease's substantial capital injection into Thredbo more than enough to satisfy the terms of the lease option, a long-term head lease with the Kosciusko State Park Trust—for 49 years with a 50-year option[90]—was signed and sealed in 1962.

Next on Dusseldorp's 'to do' list was the drawing up of a master plan— 'a conceptual town planning document'[91]—that would guide the future development of the resort. The scope of the plan would be broad, covering 'the whole village, including the mountain, ski facilities, public amenities, resort amenities, roadways, ponds, golf courses, pathways and the like'.[92] Establishing such a 'coordinated plan' up-front, Dusseldorp suggested to the Kosciusko State Park Trust, would give both his company and the lessor greater certainty as to how development of the resort would proceed in the longer term.[93] With the Trust receptive to the idea, the task of developing the master plan soon got under way. Dusseldorp himself was intimately involved. Having seen other companies' ventures fail because plans conceived in head office had neglected to come to terms with the special logistics of operating in an alpine environment, Dusseldorp was determined not to make the same mistake.[94] 'We knew we could be buying into a lot of trouble,' he remembers. 'If we didn't get the master plan right, it could mean financial disaster.'[95] As a result, the Lend Lease Chairman spent every weekend for the next two years clambering over the

Crackenback slopes, with then Resident Engineer Albert Van der Lee, as part of the planning process.[96] 'The mountain was always Duss's first port-of-call on those weekend trips,' Van der Lee remembers, 'because that was the thing that he believed should control and drive the development.'[97] Dusseldorp concurs: 'I got to know *every rock* on that mountain.'[98]

Approved by the Kosciusko State Park Trust in December 1964,[99] the master plan gave expression to Dusseldorp's vision of what Thredbo should become: a first-class winter and summer resort, differentiated from the rest of the pack both by the quality of its snowfields and leisure facilities, and by the integrated, boutique-like nature of its development. 'That Master Plan was definitely the thing that distinguished the building of Thredbo from the other resorts,' says Van der Lee, who went on to become manager of the resort. 'That and the long-term head lease. We wanted to be—and we were—very, very unique ... Small but not too small, big but not too big, and, with our control over the whole resort, able to avoid the nightmares for organisation and infra-structure that the other ski areas experienced.'[100] In consultation with the Trust, the company then put together its own building code for Thredbo, providing guidelines for sub-lessees to follow so their developments would conform to the principles of the master plan.[101] While any proposed developments still had to go through the Trust's formal approval channels, the company's building code facilitated that process;[102] it was a proactive way to ensure that the master plan did not gather dust. When Dusseldorp visited Thredbo in 1995, by which time the resort was under new ownership, he found that, far from being shelved, the original master plan was 'still providing the basic framework for manage-ment of the village today'. 'And that makes it', he remarked, 'one of the very few such plans that has actually survived thirty years or more.'[103]

Dusseldorp remained at the helm of Kosciusko–Thredbo Ltd, both officially as its Chairman and unofficially as its effective Development Manager, for the best part of a decade.[104] In successive stages, the range of accommodation options in the village expanded, and facilities on the mountain were extended and improved.[105] 'Duss ruthlessly followed his principles in developing Thredbo,' says Albert Van der Lee, 'and he made sure that we continued to do so.'[106] In line with the agreed master plan, the area was not to be 'over-developed':[107] 'if it gets too big,' Dusseldorp cautioned, 'it loses its added value.'[108] Over time Thredbo acquired a reputation as an upmarket resort, distinguished from its rivals by its village atmosphere and the breadth of its facilities, and by its claim to the longest vertical run in Australia.[109] Though perhaps that run was not long enough, at least by international standards. On one post-construction inspection, Dusseldorp is said to have remarked that there was 'only one thing wrong with this place—the mountain needs to be a thousand feet higher'. Word of his off-hand remark got straight back to Sydney, where the company's engineers—knowing Dusseldorp to be a demanding taskmaster—are said to have scratched their heads, desperately wondering how they were going to achieve that goal, before they were reassured the comment was only one of his jokes.[110]

Some of Dusseldorp's (more realistic) dreams for Thredbo took a long time to achieve. He was convinced of the resort's summer potential, development of which would enable the company to get a return from its investment over as much of the year as possible. 'Backing that principle,' Dusseldorp says, 'we decided early in the piece to run the chairlift from dawn to dusk every day—even if no-one was on it—on the off-chance that a bus load of tourists would turn up and go on it.'[111] This strategy started to pay off, especially when it was bolstered by significant investment in summer leisure facilities, such as a golf course, bowling green, tennis courts, heated swimming pool and spa. Despite these strategies, for many years the company's annual report would note that, although summer traffic at Thredbo was increasing, costs continued to exceed revenues. The much-anticipated upgrade of the Alpine Way never eventuated, and as a result, the year-round tourist traffic through the area never reached the levels that Dusseldorp had initially anticipated. It was not until the resort became popular as a corporate conference venue that the financial tables were turned. In 1984—after some twenty years—Lend Lease proudly reported that it had finally made its first profit on summer operations at Thredbo.[112]

Kosciusko–Thredbo Ltd remained in Lend Lease hands for just over twenty-five years. Although it was never a great money-spinner for the corporation—Dusseldorp is said to have told a group of Lend Lease managers that 'if anybody else but me had been responsible for the acquisition of Thredbo, they wouldn't have a job today'[113]—it clearly had a special place in his heart. He continued to visit the area once or twice a year,[114] long after he ceased to be the resort's Chairman. 'He never let go his interest in it,' recalls

Colin Moore, who later assumed that mantle.[115] In 1986 Lend Lease announced its intention to 'systematically withdraw from segments of the Australian residential, tourist and hospitality markets',[116] and as part of this process, the head-lease at Thredbo was sold in early 1987.[117] Although he was committed to the sale, Dusseldorp was sorry to see it go. As one-time Chief Executive of Lend Lease John Morschel relates:

> Shortly after the Board's decision to sell Thredbo … Duss said to me: 'John, you know I believe that in most successful corporations you will find at least one business activity which provides a sense of fun and great personal satisfaction. It may also be profitable, but that is not the point.' He went on to say that Thredbo had provided this for him.[118]

But within ten years the place that had provided such joy would be the site of incredible grief.

Late on the night of 30 July 1997, a terrible rumbling and screeching sound wakened Thredbo village.[119] Some of the residents had heard similar noises the night before, but nothing had come of them.[120] This night, however, would be different. The sounds were coming from within the earth; they signalled the beginning of a landslide. Just before midnight, the saturated fill embankment of the Alpine Way collapsed, sending a mass of earth hurtling down the hill into a ski club lodge called Carinya, that night home to a sole occupant. The force of the slide sheared Carinya from its foundations, bundling up its superstructure with the mass of mud and soil, and then thrusting it further down the slope into another lodge called Bimbadeen, where eighteen people were sleeping. Of the nineteen people in the two lodges in the slide's trajectory, only one survived: Stuart Diver was miraculously pulled from the rubble some two and a half days later. With eighteen lives lost, the 1997 Thredbo landslide was Australia's worst 'natural' disaster.[121]

The coronial inquest into the tragedy took nearly three years to complete. After 158 sitting days, hearing evidence from over 100 witnesses,[122] Dusseldorp among them, the Coroner described the causes of the tragic deaths that occurred as a result of the landslide as 'complex'.[123] He concluded that the landslide itself was triggered when water from a leaking water main saturated a corner of the fill embankment of the Alpine Way, the road running above Thredbo village.[124] The embankment of this road had been 'in a marginally stable state and extremely vulnerable to collapse if saturated by water', ever since its construction by the Snowy Mountains Authority in the mid-1950s.[125] Other landslides had occurred along the road leading up to Thredbo and adjacent to the village over the next forty years and yet, the Coroner found, the government authorities responsible for 'the care, control and management of the Kosciusko National Park and the maintenance of the Alpine Way' had failed 'to take any steps throughout that period to ensure that the Village was rendered safe from exposure to that marginally stable embankment'.[126]

Highly critical of the responsible government authorities, the Coroner recommended that the National Parks and Wildlife Service (successor to the Kosciusko State Park Trust) be the subject of an independent investigation, to assess its ability to function simultaneously as an environmental, urban planning, and road maintenance authority.[127] As a result of the subsequent inquiry, the National Parks and Wildlife Service was relieved of responsibility for the Alpine Way and also of its powers to approve major and specified developments, although it retains some responsibility for planning the ski resort villages in the National Park, under a comprehensive and detailed Regional Environmental Plan.[128] The Coroner also highlighted his 'grave concern' that the Department of Main Roads 'never expressly advised the National Parks and Wildlife Service of the need to reconstruct the road adjacent to the village to avoid the risk of death or injury due to landslide', suggesting that the department's successor, the Roads and Traffic Authority '[examine] its system of assessment of slope stability in the light of the lessons I would hope it has learned from this landslide'.[129] Since the landslide, the Authority has spent $50 million upgrading the Alpine Way.[130]

When the Coroner's report was handed down, the Chief Executive of Lend Lease, David Higgins, welcomed the government's acceptance of these recommendations. Acknowledging the company's past but long-term association with Thredbo, he said that 'Lend Lease feels that it shares in the responsibility to assist the families of the victims to now move on from this tragedy', part of which involved the payment of 'just compensation'. 'While the Coroner did not determine liability,' Higgins continued, 'Lend Lease will contribute to payment of compensation to the families of the victims. We expect the other parties who

have been involved will want to do the same.'[131] Although the company dis-
puted that the trigger for the landslide was the water main, which the Coroner
found had leaked, the pipes had been laid by Kosciusko–Thredbo Pty Ltd in
1984 when it was still under Lend Lease control. The NSW government
expressed a similar desire to settle claims for compensation out of court,[132] and
all claims lodged by relatives of the victims and rescue workers had been settled
by the end of 2001.[133]

Deeply shocked by the Thredbo tragedy, Dusseldorp flew to Australia to give
evidence to the coronial inquiry in late 1998. Although barely able to talk or
think of anything else during his stay in the country,[134] he did take time to make
a brief visit to the site of a development that Lend Lease, as a joint-venture
partner, then had underway. The following year Dusseldorp made a return visit
to that site, and it was only then that the scope of the development really
impressed itself on his mind. In concert with home building specialist Mirvac,
by 1999 Lend Lease was well-advanced in creating a completely new suburb on
90 hectares of land in the demographic centre of Sydney. 'It's a huge site,'
says Dusseldorp. 'It reminded me—in terms of scale—of the development of
Campbelltown.'[135] Called Newington, the medium-density residential and
commercial development would eventually be home to some 5000 people.[136]
But it would start out, at the beginning of the twenty-first century, in a unique
way. Located next to Homebush Bay, the first (fleeting) residents of Newington
would be the 15,300 athletes and officials participating in the Sydney 2000
Olympic Games.

The design brief for Newington was a fascinating one, as the Lend Lease
managers touring their company's founding Chairman around the development
were keen to explain. 'They were very excited to meet the old guy,' says
Dusseldorp, 'and they wanted to show me a big model of the Village and talk
to me about the design and layout of the houses.' But there was something else
that Dusseldorp needed to know first. 'I want to know', he told them, 'how on
earth you guys got to be able to do what you are doing here? It is clearly at
variance with every Australian house building regulation that *I* am aware of.
How did you *ever* get to build at such a high density?' 'It was two-and-a-quarter
times the ordinary ratio', he adds. And having had to wage battles in the past to

receive approval from Australian government authorities for residential densities even moderately greater than 'normal', Dusseldorp could not understand how this could have been achieved. 'How did you persuade the government to let you do that?' Dusseldorp asked the Lend Lease team. 'And to my greatest surprise,' he says, 'they replied: "It was not us who persuaded the government—we were somewhat reluctant—it was the government that persuaded us!" '[137]

'Faced with the need to have an Olympic Village to house the thousands and thousands of competitors and their hangers-on for two months,' Dusseldorp explains, 'the [NSW] government felt that it would have been a gross waste of money if the Village didn't have some further use.' So, in calling selected tenders for the project, the government had opted to make the development a dual-purpose one. In the short term the village would have to meet the needs of the Olympians and Paralympians whom it would temporarily accommodate in September–October 2000; but it should also be designed to meet the requirements of would-be residents of the area in the long term. To achieve both goals within the available space, Newington logically *had* to have higher densities than was the norm. That was one part of the puzzle solved, thought Dusseldorp, but he was just as curious to know how such a development was being received in the marketplace. With the suburban ideal of the detached bungalow on the quarter-acre block so deeply rooted in the Australian psyche, the former Lend Lease Chairman could well understand the developer's initial reluctance to build at the government's required densities. 'So I asked the guys who they thought was going to buy into the thing, and they told me that ... the Great Australian Dream thing had changed. People don't want to mow the lawns any more,' the team told Dusseldorp. 'And they must be right', he says, 'because when they put the first stage [of the Newington development] up for sale ... they all sold out over the weekend.'[138]

Dusseldorp was in for another surprise at Newington. 'And then, to boot,' he relates, 'they told me that this village has "community title". "What the hell is that?" I asked. "Ah," they said, "it is derived from—(guess what?)—*strata title.*" ' Just as strata title had been devised to allow for the individual ownership of 'lots' of 'air space' in a multi-storey tower—with the communal aspects of the building and its grounds managed collectively—so community title adapts this concept to the ownership and management of communal space in a (multi-building) 'planned community'. Described as 'the third generation of land law'—following Torrens and strata—the concept of community title was established in legislation passed by the NSW Parliament in 1990.[139] It was a concept that impressed Dusseldorp no end. Having been the prime mover in the introduction of strata title in Australia almost forty years before (see Chapter 6), he regarded community title as a 'closing of the circle'. Although it applies only to a limited number of planned community developments to date, Dusseldorp predicts that the concept will go 'like a flash through the nation'. 'It has potentially major implications for a totally different form of urban development,' he says. 'People can take [collective] control of their own environment, and that can only be for the better.'[140]

As Dusseldorp was guided around the Newington development, many of the things he saw resonated with ideas he had pursued decades earlier. All the powerlines run underground; the housing styles, while diverse in range, are 'united by materials and colours' to give a sense of overall cohesion to the development;[141] retail and community facilities are provided in a comprehensive neighbourhood centre; and the landscaping of communal areas is dominated by drought-resistant native species. But with advances in technology and an increase in environmental awareness since the heyday of Dusseldorp's residential development schemes, the Newington development also includes features that he could only have imagined. Drinking water and waste-water in the village are separately reticulated to enable maximum recycling of the latter; dwellings are designed and oriented on their sites to minimise energy consumption and maximise 'solar penetration'; the building materials used in their construction conform with strict principles of environmental sustainability; and the use of solar power is so extensive as to make it 'the world's largest solar-powered suburb'.[142]

'It's a very substantial, very attractive, new style residential development,' Dusseldorp says as he recounts Newington's innovative features the day after his visit to the site. 'They have built communal facilities there that are so good that the capital value of the development can only increase.' It is logical for the 80-year-old entrepreneur to now consider how the concept might be improved upon to take it that 'next step' along the road.[143] One thing immediately springs to his mind, as we will see in the next chapter.

CHAPTER 8

Building for the Future: Leaving Something Behind

There are two things in life. You can be out for the maximum amount of profit you can possibly squeeze from your efforts, or you can aim at a reasonable profit and have the feeling when you retire that you leave something behind.[1]

As October 1988 approached—the date, just shy of his seventieth birthday, that Dusseldorp had set for his retirement—the corridors of Lend Lease buzzed with a single topic of conversation. What would be the right farewell present to give the company's founding Chairman? Ideas went back and forth, with every suggestion mulled over, developed further, put on the possibles list, or unceremoniously discarded. Perhaps it shouldn't be a gift at all, some thought— perhaps it should be some kind of gesture. Everyone was agreed, however, that whatever 'it' was, it had to be both substan*tial* and substan*tive*. Ideally it would say something about the man himself: reflect the values around which he had built Lend Lease from the start. But it couldn't be *too* backward-looking— Dusseldorp had never been one for trophy-gathering or nostalgia. What could the corporation give him that was useful, that was forward-looking, that would represent a beginning, and not just an end? In typical Lend Lease fashion, a Project Control Group (PCG) was formed to consider all the options. Once a list was compiled, it was time to run the ideas past the Chairman himself.

Dusseldorp, who had got wind of all the discussions, was more than ready to put in his two cents' worth. As the PCG had anticipated, he was clear on what he *didn't* want. 'If you're thinking of a gold watch,' he told them, 'then forget it. Likewise, I don't want some hospital bed named after me.' This was hardly news to the group—but, they wondered, did he have some positive suggestions to make? As a matter of fact, he did. 'The only thing I *would* be interested in,' he told them, 'would be something that I could work on. Something that has a clear benefit for youth, particularly in the area of skills development.'[2] From the start-up of construction firm Civil & Civic, Dusseldorp had long demonstrated a commitment to encouraging skills formation in his workforce, in particular amongst the young. The firm was consistently one of the industry's largest employers of apprentices. The benefits of that commitment to youth training had been spread more widely with the establishment, in 1980, of the ACTU–Lend Lease Foundation and its group apprenticeship schemes (see Chapter 4). And while the latter had been the baby of Stuart Hornery and David Thorne, Dusseldorp himself, with his son Tjerk, had been intimately involved in nurturing another national youth skills initiative that had recently born fruit.

> In February of the year my father retired, [says Tjerk Dusseldorp] the WorkSkill Australia Foundation had hosted the Youth Skill Olympics at Darling Harbour. This event brings together the top young tradespeople from around the world to compete and celebrate in the skills of their particular trades. Six years earlier I'd involved my father, along with other corporate, trade union and government leaders, in launching this Foundation as a project initiative of [the Labor-leaning think-tank] the Evatt Foundation [of which Tjerk was then Executive Director].[3]

Dick Dusseldorp remembers that experience well.

> Tjerk picked up on this idea of the Youth Skill Olympics, and although the international competition had been running for years, no one else in Australia had ever heard of it. Well, Tjerk liked the idea, and he set his shoulders to it. So he went door-knocking and he got four businessmen to each put up $50,000, and then he came to me. He needed five people to contribute, but he wouldn't come to me first—he wanted to show me that he could get the other four on board on his own. Well, he did, and so I put my bit in.[4]

Tjerk had used this seeding capital to establish the WorkSkill Australia Foundation, and he became its inaugural Executive Director in 1982.

Drawing in players from industry, trade unions, the public vocational education provider (TAFE), and the community, WorkSkill Australia then set about organising the regional and national competitions that would enable the selection of the first team of Australians to compete at the next international Youth Skill Olympics, to be hosted by Austria in 1983. Held biennially, the international competition attracts hundreds of young skilled entrants from dozens of different countries and forty separate trades. For each skill category —fitting and machining, cooking, plumbing, or anything in between—the competitors are given identical materials and equipment and they each have to complete a set project task over a four-day period. A panel of judges then assesses their work and awards medals to the best performers, from which national tallies of comparative skill achievement can be made. Unfortunately, the official results of that first international foray were not good: Australia came home without any medals and some wounded pride.[4] But the experience had by no means been in vain, Dick Dusseldorp remembers, for although they had won no accolades, the team had learnt some valuable lessons along the way.

The TAFE teachers who had accompanied the Australian team as judges and chaperones had seen the kids perform and they said the primary problem was that the Aussies didn't plan. When they were handed the task, the Aussies thought, 'We'd better get cracking, because we've got a lot to do', and they'd just launch into the task straight away. Naturally enough, they would encounter problems along the way and then they'd have to start all over again, or live with the mistakes. Meanwhile, the Asian and European competitors spent a very large amount of time planning the whole task out—doing little sketches and what-not— and once *they* got going, they never stopped. Needless to say, it was these competitors who collected all the prizes.[5]

It was a revelation, as Dusseldorp recalls. 'It was good, because it was such a shock,' he says, 'and it helped revolutionise Australian approaches to skills development from then on.'[6] By focusing their eyes on achieving excellence on the world stage, the WorkSkill Australia Foundation began to engage young people, their teachers, trainers, and employers in the task of improving the standards and status of vocational training and job skills across the nation.[7] When Australia hosted the Youth Skill Olympics at Sydney's Darling Harbour in early 1988, the host team performance had significantly improved, winning twelve medals and placing third overall.[8] 'And now,' Dusseldorp says, 'the country is regularly placed in the top ten of the participating thirty-six nations.'[9]

This whole process inspired Dusseldorp, says his son, as he contemplated his post-retirement life.

My father had seen the development of WorkSkill from its inception as an idea to its emergence as a robust national skills recognition and promotion people movement involving many hundreds of volunteers—particularly TAFE teachers—throughout the nation. He believed its success could be pinned down to the fact that it was a stakeholder organisation—a real partnership or alliance between industry, TAFE, governments, trade unions, and communities with a clear compelling goal and a practical means to achieving it. Yet he also recognised that WorkSkill was essentially limited to mirroring the best of the skill development practices within the existing industrial and educational framework and structures. What would be possible, he wondered, if one had the independent means to pioneer new ways for young people to acquire a broader range of skills to better prepare them for the future?[10]

There was a personal imperative playing on Dusseldorp's mind. He knew from his own experience how difficult it could be to get set on the pathway leading to a fulfilling working life. Two years after he ran away to sea at age fourteen, his dreams of being a merchant sailor had been dashed by the discovery he was colour-blind. Had it not been for the efforts and encouragement of a particular teacher—who had tutored him out-of-hours so he could sit his Intermediate Certificate, which in turn enabled him to study engineering—there was no telling where he might have ended up. Yet all around him he could see that, with the arrival of the information technology revolution, the decline of traditional industries, and the collapse of the junior labour market which supported them, many kids today were doing it just as tough as he had then. 'My father always believed', says Tjerk, 'that a fundamental indicator of a society's level of "well-being" is the degree to which its young people are both encouraged and able to develop into productive, independent adulthood.'[11] For Dusseldorp both the need and the critical point for intervention were clear. 'I wanted to do something', he says, 'that tries to break down that sharp barrier between school and work':[12] to create some mechanism which would work 'towards the ideal of having no youth step straight from school into a dead end job or, worse, onto the dole'.[13]

Here was an idea that the PCG could work on: to create just such a mechanism. But before they went too far, there was one more stipulation that the retiring Chairman had in mind. 'I don't want it to be some token gesture,' he told the group. 'It must either be worthwhile, or not at all. So it must be put to the shareholders—and if they are opposed, then that is the end of it.'[14]

With these instructions clearly spelt out, the PCG went back to the drawing board. The product of the deliberations was inspired. At the 1988 annual general meeting of Lend Lease Corporation, Dusseldorp was presented with a unique retirement gift. The company's shareholders voted to establish the Dusseldorp Skills Forum: an independent, non-profit organisation with a charter to stimulate and promote continuing investment in Australia's work-force, with a particular focus on developing the skills and personal effective-ness of young people. The Forum would be funded by way of an allotment of Lend Lease shares totalling 1 per cent of the issued capital of the company: shareholders voted to meet half of this cost, Lend Lease employees voted to meet the other half.[15] Dusseldorp would be the Forum's inaugural Chairman, which, said Stuart Hornery, would 'allow his capacity for lateral thinking and vision to be put to wider use in Australian society'.[16] The benefactors knew that the new ship was in the best possible hands. 'How can we say goodbye to such a person?' long-time Civil & Civic employee Ron Bolzon said in tribute to Dusseldorp that night. 'We want him to stay a little longer to look after the Dusseldorp Skills Forum, to look after the young people—the young people coming up—and give them as great as we had when we first started in the company.'[17]

In every respect—in its originality, its purpose, its method of establishment, and its mode of funding—the gift of the Dusseldorp Skills Forum epitomised the philosophy on which Dusseldorp had built Lend Lease: bringing together labour, capital, and other stakeholders, challenging their hide-bound ways of doing things, and orienting them to a practical goal which would yield mutual benefits. Just as this philosophy had guided his working life at Lend Lease, so it would guide his retirement.

True to his wishes, one of the first ventures of the Skills Forum was a project 'to try and break down that sharp barrier between school and work'.[18] After considerable debate as to how best to address the issue, the Trustees of the Forum concluded that, as Dusseldorp puts it,

> since schools regard young people as students, and employers see them as workers,
> a third party was needed, independent of both, to see young people as young
> people and to create a bridge between education and work for them. We called the

bridge 'TRAC', and building commenced in the Hunter region [of New South Wales] in July 1989.[19]

The program started life as Training for Retail and Commerce, the sectors in which it was piloted, hence the acronym.[20]

There was a compelling need for such a program, Dusseldorp told a group of business leaders in 1991. Compared to international practice, Australia's education and training systems were wanting on a number of counts. Amongst other inadequacies, they lacked emphasis on vocational preparation of youth, and failed to provide high-quality alternatives to universities. The private sector was allocating a pittance to on-the-job training, and links between educational institutions and employers were too few. 'Australian managers', he lamented, 'seem only too happy to let governments make most of the running and foot most of the bill—an arrangement I suspect that suits the education and training establishment just fine. From a national view it is clearly courting disaster.'[21] Whereas near 80 per cent of all young people in Germany enter structured combinations of general education, training, and work prior to becoming adult workers, the opportunities for Australian kids to engage in similar structured activities were almost non-existent. That was where TRAC came in.

The idea behind TRAC, as Dusseldorp describes it, was to 'create a work-based learning phase in students' lives'[22] with a 'primary focus on employ-ability'.[23] It aimed to integrate the acquisition of core academic skills, social skills, and work skills for kids who *didn't* thrive in the regular school system, those who *weren't* destined for higher education or apprenticeship.[24] Dusseldorp explains how the program worked. 'What we did was to have youth in their last year or two at high school placed for one day a week in jobs with willing employers, who would then make available to them a mentor on a one-to-one basis.'[25] TRAC participants rotated through three or four such work placements in a year, where they followed a competency-based curriculum collectively designed by the employers. The learning they acquired both on-the-job and through study in an off-site TRAC Learning Centre was recognised as part of their formal program of secondary study. The whole thing was overseen on a local basis by an independent steering board made up of educators, employers, community leaders, and the manager of the Learning Centre.

As the benefits to all stakeholders in the scheme became clear, the TRAC program took off. By 1994 there were some twenty-six projects right across

New South Wales,[26] and although other localities were keen to participate in it, the resources of the Dusseldorp Skills Forum simply could not permit any further expansion. 'I had put one stipulation on the operation of the Skills Forum,' Dusseldorp says. 'And that was that we were not allowed to touch the capital that the donors had provided. The activities could only be financed by investment income from the assets, or by other funding that we managed to obtain.' With resources stretched to the limit, it was make-or-break time for TRAC. 'That one rule of mine', says Dusseldorp, 'forced us to either abandon it or find some other way to foster it.' Tjerk Dusseldorp, who by this time had succeeded his father as Chairman of the Skills Forum (while Dick remained its Patron), was intent on the latter course.

'Tjerk approached the Federal Labor Government to see if they were interested in taking the program national,' his father recalls. 'Well, they were interested, and that led to the formation of the Australian Student Traineeship Foundation (ASTF).'[27] After six years of operation as a federally sponsored initiative, by 2000 ASTF had spread right across Australia and included training in most sectors of the economy.[28] On an annual basis, around 50,000 students, 30,000 businesses and some 1800 schools were participating in the program, which operated in over 250 local communities across the country.[29] 'It's a good example of a public–private sector partnership,' says Dick Dusseldorp. 'It's very decentralised, and that's one of the reasons it works. It even survived the change of government—in fact, the new government was so impressed that they doubled the funding for it.'[30]

The TRAC program, and its evolution into ASTF, is a microcosm of how the Dusseldorp Skills Forum continues to work. With TRAC and like projects, the Skills Forum acts as the independent initiator, engages the relevant stake-holders, demonstrates a smarter way of tackling a problem on-the-ground, then seeks to convince the institutional players to mainstream the proven innovations.[31] This in turn allows the Forum to withdraw its own resources and redirect them to a new challenge, and so the cycle can begin again. 'We believe that *demonstrating* improved practice is a key to changing people's ideas,' says Tjerk Dusseldorp. 'We're committed to doing that by working *with* others: bringing people together to solve problems of mutual concern. But that doesn't mean we're policy speculators. Our work is informed by extensive research, a lot of which is also undertaken collaboratively.'[32] 'We are about building light-houses,' his father adds. 'Establishing a beacon that people can see, then if they want to use it to steer by, well and good, if they don't that's too bad.'[33] While those lighthouses were initially confined to Australian shores, before long they were appearing in other parts of the world as well.

———

Following his departure from Lend Lease in October 1988, Dusseldorp retired for a grand total of two weeks. 'I didn't enjoy retirement,' he says, 'so I had to go back to work.'[34] For the next twelve years, Dusseldorp maintained an active working life, not only as inaugural Chairman, then Patron, of the Dusseldorp Skills Forum, but also as Chairman of his own group of property management and investment companies in the United States and the United Kingdom, the Dusco Group. The latter did not operate, however, in Australia. 'When I left I didn't want to be underfoot of Lend Lease', he explains; 'there's nothing more awkward.'[35] Often Dusseldorp was able to combine both 'post-retirement' roles, using his foreign business ventures as fields in which initiatives inspired by the Skills Forum could be planted, tested, and spread. One of the first of these was launched at a shopping mall in Savannah, Georgia, acquired by his US-based property company in the early 1990s.

'As we were getting to know the community,' Dusseldorp says of the Savannah mall venture, 'we heard that the local school system was in a bit of a state. They had so many kids that had dropped out, or that just didn't turn up for classes at all.' Georgia consistently ranks at or near the bottom of the fifty US states in high school completion rates, with the public schools in low-income inner-city counties—such as Savannah–Chatham—more than representative of the lack-lustre performance of the state as a whole.[36] 'So I arranged with the school system to make a space [available] in the shopping centre. We fitted that space out as a full-time branch of the regular school, so that they could use it as a sort of "intensive care" unit for the kids who didn't attend, or who'd dropped out.'[37] With the retail industry providing a large number of entry-level jobs for young workers, and the shopping centre located, as Dusseldorp says, 'where the people are',[38] it was the ideal spot to start the first US version of the TRAC program.

Called the Savannah Corporate Academy, the off-campus school branch caters for approximately sixty students in their last three years of school considered to be at 'high risk' because of truancy and/or antisocial behaviour at their home school.[39]

The local education department appointed a real live-wire guy to run it [Dusseldorp says]. Whenever they took the roll, if anyone hadn't turned up he'd phone them at home to see where they were. If he couldn't get a reply there, he'd ring the parents at work. The parents *hated* that but it was very effective—an ordinary school couldn't or wouldn't do that—but this guy did. You know, the rate of attendance at that school jumped from 40 per cent to 98 per cent in about a month.

As well as sitting for the high school diploma, the students at Savannah Corporate Academy participate in a competency-tested program for developing work skills, including on-the-job training in the mall itself. The latter 'was a great pull on these kids', says Dusseldorp, 'to actually be doing something totally different for a certain number of hours per week'.[40] 'Before long the waiting list [for the Academy] had spontaneously grown to over 100 students,' he reports, 'and that provided teachers with leverage over behaviour both at the home schools and the [mall] branch.'[41]

But there was a potential downside of the Academy's location in the mall for the surrounding businesses. 'We had to make sure', as Dusseldorp puts it, 'to protect the customers from any wrong-doing.' The Academy was located on the right-hand side at the entrance to the mall, a spot which Dusseldorp describes as 'dead space' in most shopping centres.

Next to it there was a community space, used for literacy and other voluntary programs and then there was a vacant corner space. We offered that space to the Police Department—free of rent—and we also gave the police a special parking area, so there were always patrol cars coming and going. Then we arranged with two coffee shops, one on either side of the main hall, to give the police a discounted price on their coffees ... So these guys would drive up to the centre in their patrol cars, and then walk right into the centre for their cheap coffees.[42]

The impression of a hefty police presence thus created, the mall, Dusseldorp reports, did not suffer any increase in the crime-rate.

Today the Savannah Corporate Academy enjoys a better than 96 per cent graduation rate.[43] Meanwhile Dusseldorp's US-based property company has gone on to open similar schools in the Park City Shopping Mall in Lancaster County, Pennsylvania,[44] and in the Landmark Mall near Arlington, Virginia.[45] Within months of the Savannah project starting, the company was also asked to assist with the start-up of three more TRAC-like programs in other industries in the United States.[46] And when the US National Retail Federation decided to pick up and promote the TRAC/USA program, the nation's fourth mall-based high school opened in The Galleria at Crystal Run in Middletown, New York.[47] Dusseldorp also introduced the TRAC concept to the other side of the Atlantic. The first UK project was run at a large shopping mall in Nottingham—the Victoria Centre—that his company bought as its entrée into the UK retail market in 1992.[48] The UK version of the TRAC program has now been taken up within the mainstream education sector, while an associated retail skills testing program—developed by the Dusseldorp Skills Forum in Australia—has taken off in shopping centres throughout the United Kingdom.

Dusseldorp's post-retirement activities were not only concerned with the youthful end of the age spectrum, however. For many years he had been intrigued by the question of how Western societies could best cope with their ageing populations and now, he figured, he might have time to translate some of his thoughts on the matter into practice. 'Governments are wringing their hands about this problem of the demographic time bomb,' he says, 'because the demands on their budgets are increasing at the same time as their taxation revenues are decreasing.' The combined result of falling birth rates and rising life expectancy in developed nations is that, by the mid-twenty-first century, between one-quarter and one-third of their populations will be eligible for the old-age pension. With proportionately fewer people of working age contributing to the tax base, the financial implications for health and social welfare systems are potentially huge.

> And that is what I have been addressing in my head. The question of what can the *entrepreneur* bring to the table in order to alleviate that problem: not as a charity, but as a business, because something that is a business has a better chance of being sustained ... And that is what my last project—my English scheme—is all about.[49]

Dusseldorp's 'English scheme', the vision for which he actively pursued for the last few years of his life, was aimed at creating a financial vehicle to release cash out of residential property for the elderly. Centred in his long-held belief that property equity *should* be able to be securitised, the proposed scheme— which he describes as conceptually 'very simple, but one that has never been done before'—would, characteristically, yield benefits for all its participants. It would be particularly attractive, he believed, to middle-income, post-retirement home-owners.

> The only investment that many elderly people have—at least those in the middle [of the socio-economic spectrum]—is their house [he says]. They've spent their whole lives paying off the mortgage from the building society or whatever. But then they find their income stream has virtually finished, just at the time when they need more—not for living it up, but just for staying alive.[50]

Dusseldorp's scheme would enable these homeowners to sell a portion of the equity in their house—while keeping the right to occupy it (thus enabling them to stay in their own local community)—in return for which they would receive units in a Stock Exchange-listed Property Trust. Their investment in the Trust would not only provide them with a much-needed income stream, but, by diversifying their wealth across the property sector, the scheme would also protect them from fluctuations in the residential property market. Meanwhile the Trust, while not receiving a cash flow on its piece of equity until the house was sold (which would only happen when the elderly occupier ceased to need it), would reap its share of the asset—and any capital appreciation on it—at that point.[51]

'It wouldn't be a product that appealed to everyone,' Dusseldorp says. 'It doesn't apply to the rich, and it doesn't apply to those in subsidised housing— it's more a product that "the middle" might like to choose.'[52] But given the growing dimensions of the age bracket at which the product would be targeted —soon to include that 'financially significant'[53] and 'consumption-orientated'[54] segment of the population, the baby-boomer retirees—the potential market for it was huge indeed. And to the extent that it *was* taken up by 'the middle', at least some of the pressure could be taken off future governments' purse-strings. Seeking to inspire support for the residential securitisation concept amongst the Investment Property Forum, an influential industry lobby group in the United Kingdom, Dusseldorp drew on the predictions of a well-known management adviser to make his case. 'Peter Drucker has postulated that the most needed innovation for the [twenty-first] century is going to be investment products to finance the next generation's survival into old age,' Dusseldorp told his audience in late 1996.

> The rising awareness of the bankruptcy of national benefit schemes, particularly for old age pensions, [is] generating social upheaval everywhere with increasing intensity. Young professionals recently—for the first time—were the major subscribers to the mutual funds in the USA. They have now seen that there won't be a free lunch for them when their turn comes. Then there is the shock of post-recession Britain which left many home-owners reeling from the effect of negative equity. It turned an Englishman's castle … into his prison. My instinct tells me that there is a deep correlation between these phenomena and that property securitisation will be found at the centre of a solution. It stands to reason that of the £1,000 billion worth of owner-occupied residences [in the UK], most of the properties will survive their occupant several times over. They should not only provide shelter for the owners, but also their financial survival into old age in the absence of the State being able to undertake that task.[55]

Dusseldorp concluded his speech with a 'clarion call' to the Forum, to join with him in embracing 'a vision powerful enough to inspire the integration of financial and social engineering, covering all sectors of property—no matter how they are traditionally owned—for the benefit of all our tomorrows'.[56] There was a reason for his zeal, for if his 'English scheme' was to reach fruition, he could do with their help in assembling the various building blocks—and overcoming the remaining structural hurdles—necessary to make it work.

He had already had some initial success, having convinced the London Stock Exchange to change its rules to allow the listing of property trusts, the vehicle through which he hoped the scheme would operate. For Dusseldorp, who had waged a similar battle to list the GPT in Australia some twenty years before (see Chapter 3), this had been a *déjà vu* experience. The United Kindom had never before listed such trusts—'British authorities have been lagging behind the rest of the world in this area', he told the business press[57]—and there was a great degree of scepticism about the concept at first—'even a number of my colleagues thought I was mad', he says.[58] His three-year battle paid off when the London Stock Exchange finally gave the go-ahead for authorised property unit trusts to list in 1996.

Dusseldorp then set about finalising preparations for what he hoped would be the launch of Britain's first such vehicle—a joint venture between his firm, Dusco, and Hermes Pension Management Ltd, one of Britain's largest fund managers—when another hurdle was erected. 'We were ten days off the launch date of the property trust,' he says, when a change to the tax laws 'went right slap in our face.' The tax changes in July 1997 had the effect of imposing a new 20 per cent tax on income distributed by the trust to pension funds.[59] As such funds were expected to be a very significant segment of the trust's initial market—at least until Dusseldorp could put in place the other elements of the residential securitisation scheme that would make it directly attractive to elderly homeowners—the joint-venture partners judged it impossible to proceed with the launch at that time.[60]

'So I then had the choice of either giving it away, or switching tactics,' Dusseldorp says.[61] Characteristically, he chose the latter—starting work, as he approached his eightieth birthday, on designing a revamped, tax-transparent vehicle through which to offer his residential securitisation scheme to the aged. That was not the only task on his drawing board. If the scheme was to be available to the broadest possible market—including people living in 'planned communities' along the lines of the one he had seen at the Sydney Olympic Village at Newington—then it might be worth suggesting to the British legislators that they take a look at Australia's new system of community title, with a view to introducing a similar system. Having personally led the coalition to introduce a new form of property title (strata title) in Australia almost forty years earlier, he knew that such reforms were won neither quickly nor easily. So he'd better get cracking ...

Hanging up his hat in retirement was clearly not Dusseldorp's style. 'He was always interested—he was interested at every stage—in learning,' says Dick Morath, part of the Lend Lease team who showed their founding Chairman around Sydney's Olympic Village in 1999. 'He was *fascinated* with the community land tenure thing that he saw in place at Newington, because that had a bearing on what he was looking at in terms of the securitisation of residential real estate in the UK.' And as far as the latter project was concerned, says Morath, that in itself indicated something of the uniqueness of the man.

He was a special sort of person—always going with the challenging idea, right to the end. It could take twenty years of hard work to bring that [residential securitisation] thing off. No one could ever criticise Dick Dusseldorp for having small visions—that is the biggest vision left—how do you securitise this huge block of assets worldwide?

Despite the dimensions of the task—and the obstacles to be surmounted in achieving it—Dusseldorp was 'never one for giving up', says Morath.[62] And although his mind never *did* give up, his body finally called it a day. Dusseldorp died in April 2000, before his 'English scheme'—his 'last project'—could be brought to fruition.

When Dusseldorp retired from Lend Lease in 1988, Stuart Hornery recalled the words of the company's founding Chairman uttered some thirty years before.

> 'There are [Dusseldorp had said] two things in life. You can be out for the maximum amount of profit you can possibly squeeze from your efforts, or you can aim at a reasonable profit and have the feeling when you retire that you leave something behind.' [Hornery continued:] There is no doubt that Dick succeeded in making a reasonable profit [in 1957], and, in fact, in every year that followed. When you consider the spirit, the teamwork, the dedication that unites all people who comprise Lend Lease you realise that Dick is leaving something behind that is more than just valuable. It is quite literally priceless.[63]

With the Dusseldorp Skills Forum and Dusco also part of his legacy, there is little doubt that Dusseldorp achieved his goal of leaving something behind.

> One of Dick's major principles in running his companies was that there are three groups of people that must be *equally* cared for: clients, employees, and shareholders. Not one, not the other, but all three. This was pertinent to everything he did.[64]

> [Dusseldorp] gave people a sense of what might be possible … He always saw the big picture. He introduced a new dubiousness about what we were seeing in things

that we were inclined to accept. Having been convinced that there was a potential better way, we were encouraged to move on to find it.[65]

What enduring lessons can be learned from Dusseldorp's working life? Can features of his experience be distilled that still demand our attention today? Or has the world changed so much—with the globalisation of capital, labour, information, and product markets—that his long-term, stakeholder-driven approach is no longer relevant? The premise of this book is that there is much to learn from the working life of this quite remarkable man. The story of how he created one of Australia's most successful corporations is not just of historical interest. The global business environment may well be changing shape, but the questions of how to create and manage a successful business, how to foster a culture of innovation, how to engage clients, shareholders and employees in the pursuit of common goals, and how to do all of that in a socially responsible way—are still at the top of the contemporary corporate agenda.

What factors, then, did Dusseldorp himself see as critical to his success? Which aspects of his distinctive approach to business did he think would stand the test of time? What issues did he see as critical for the corporation of the future to grapple with, and how did he think they should deal with them? The founding Chairman of Lend Lease addressed many of these questions in a speech he gave to his employees on the occasion of the property development company's twenty-fifth birthday.[66] The year was 1983, and having recently acquired a controlling stake in the life insurer MLC, Lend Lease was about to embark on a new stage in its development. The world of finance beckoned, Dusseldorp told the assembled audience, and how the company fared in it would be largely determined by the next generation rather than by old hands such as he. With the organisation poised at a significant threshold, what advice would he give to the 'second generation', the people who would have to steer the corporation through the changing waters when he was no longer at the wheel?

Dusseldorp asked them to consider 'the most basic issue', which, as he saw it, came down to one question: 'For whose benefit does the enterprise exist?' 'Having carefully observed people's behaviour over a long period', the Lend Lease Chairman continued, it seemed that, in general terms, most organisations 'exist primarily for the benefit of [their] dominant members'.

The *first principle* that has guided Lend Lease from the start, has one qualification to this general rule, namely, it exists for the benefit of all its members, not just the officers, but the entire crew. I would venture to pass this word of advice to the next generation … should Lend Lease depart from this first principle it would do so at its peril.

Pursuit of profits for its own sake is a sterile activity. Profits must serve a purpose; at the same time, without profits there simply is no organisation … not for long anyway. This is the *second principle*: Lend Lease has to be profitable. If profits stop, everything else stops with it.

Whilst making profits for the benefit of all its members, the *third over-riding principle* that emerges from the past can be stated. The company's activities have to be socially relevant—for the simple reason that most concerned people only want to spend their life on such efforts. And without concerned people, the direction of the enterprise will be lost.

In other words, whilst we are busy making profits for our benefit, this should always benefit others as well, never [be] at their expense. In short, the pursuit of a community of interests.[67]

It was this philosophy—the pursuit of a community of interests—pioneered in the rough and tumble of the Australian building and construction industry of the 1950s and 1960s, which Dusseldorp believed should continue to guide the organisation into the future. It was a philosophy that embodied a big-picture view of what made an organisation work, and a long-term view of what it was there for. The focus was *not* on maximising short-term shareholder returns; and while creating long-term shareholder value was a primary long-term goal, it was by no means the only one. As Milton Allen, long-time director of Lend Lease and MLC, would remark some twenty years later: 'One of Dick's major principles in running his companies was that there are three groups of people that must be *equally* cared for: clients, employees, and shareholders. Not one, not the other, but all three. This was pertinent to everything he did.'[68]

Dusseldorp's approach to stakeholder relations—his fundamental belief in the community of interests—enabled him to build Lend Lease into one of Australia's most successful, and admired, corporations. It put him decades ahead of industry practice at the time, but does such an approach still have resonance today? The current Chairman of Lend Lease, Jill Ker Conway, seems to think so. When Dusseldorp's successor Stuart Hornery retired as Chairman in 2000, the corporation once again found itself at a turning point. By then Lend Lease operated in forty different countries, employed over 10,000 people globally, and its shareholder funds exceeded $5 billion.[69] Describing itself as 'a fully integrated global real estate group',[70] the business had shed some elements since Dusseldorp's day—most notably the MLC—but added others. In his last Chairman's Report, Hornery reiterated Dusseldorp's deep commitment to the 'community of interest' philosophy, calling it 'a fundamental plank of our existence', one that defined 'the Lend Lease Way'.[71] Incoming Chairman Jill Ker Conway, stressed its continuing relevance to the 'electronically networked global enterprise' which Lend Lease had by now become.

> It's a tall order to move from the face-to-face community in which our founder,
> Dick Dusseldorp, developed his beliefs about the relationship between employees,
> clients, shareholders and the communities in which we work—beliefs that have
> been key to the entrepreneurial spirit, because they have linked the growth of
> employee knowledge of the business and share ownership to the provision of
> superior services to clients. But that is exactly what we must do to continue the
> company's long record of building shareholder wealth while delivering first class
> services to all stakeholders.[72]

What of the world beyond Lend Lease? Does Dusseldorp's stakeholder philosophy have any continuing bearing there? There are good reasons to suggest it does. Management academic Dexter Dunphy says there are two intertwined issues consuming the minds of corporate leaders in the United States and United Kingdom today—how to create a sustainable business, and the role of business in society.[73] There are strong *commercial* grounds for their concerns, according to Australian business spokeswoman Katie Lahey.

> With the growing consumer backlash becoming more evident every day, it is
> time for businesses of all sizes to embrace the principles of corporate social
> responsibility ... While companies are required to meet certain financial demands,
> they are often seen to be slipping in meeting their social obligations in the wider
> community. And yet, the results show that being socially and environmentally
> responsible can markedly affect a consumer's decisions.[74]

Lord Holme of Cheltenham beats a similar drum.

> Any company which is seriously misaligned with the hopes and fears of its fellow citizens in society is likely to pay a price in lost reputation or sales for getting out of step. This has become all the more true with the globalisation of media which has already created 'one world', in respect of instant news and comment at least. No international company can afford double standards if it wants to escape the scourge of publicised criticism for its hypocrisy.[75]

While the potential impact of loss of reputation on the bottom line is pushing companies to examine their social and environmental behaviour, so too are they being pulled in this direction by a host of positive factors. Responsible engagement with society gives companies 'a greater chance of a stable and harmonious atmosphere in which to do business', Lord Holme argues. It puts them more in touch with their markets, and it provides 'greater satisfaction in a job well done for managers and employees'.[76] It is these positive, internal drivers, he says, that have the potential to make an enduring impact on a corporation's 'rules of engagement' with society, rather than changes wrought as a short-term response to criticism. If corporate social responsibility is to become 'intrinsic, systematic and embedded' in a company, he argues, it must be 'both part of the core value system of the manager and a key objective of the corporation which employs him or her'.[77] Dusseldorp's leadership of Lend Lease provides a demonstration of how it can be done.

There was a phase in the late 1980s when numerous tripartite missions left Australia to scour the world for ideas about how Australian industry could lift its game and aspire to the global stage. They brought back ideas on better ways of working, smarter modes of investment, new roles for government, and a commitment to best practice and international competitiveness—the scope and vision for change was broad indeed. Despite their best intentions, it seemed that all too often the specific practices the missionaries sought to implant in Australia did not flourish in the quite different institutional environment of their home patch. While a number of good ideas bore early fruit, without a wholesale package of reforms, most were left to wither on the vine. Realising this, one such group embarked on no less a task than seeing *Australia Reconstructed*.[78] But as the authors of this report later found, turning around whole systems was hard—too hard for an individual, or a company, even a whole industry or labour movement to achieve.

One of the most empowering lessons from Dusseldorp's working life is his demonstration of the *possibility* of doing things differently, of achieving change on a small, but real—and growing—scale. Indeed, Dusseldorp provides a full working model of a better way of doing business—a showcase which others can surely learn from. Dusseldorp 'gave people a sense of what might be possible', says Chris Rumsey, chief executive of Dusseldorp's UK-based property investment company Dusco.

> He always saw the big picture. He introduced a new dubiousness about what we were seeing in things that we were inclined to accept. Having been convinced that there was a potential better way, we were encouraged to move on to find it …
> [He] lived his life giving to many people the same message and example: that if we only listen to the world around us and question it a little, then, with application and a sense of social responsibility, we are capable of achieving anything.[79]

Epilogue

In 1998, the year in which Lend Lease Corporation marked its fortieth anniversary, Dick Dusseldorp flew back into Sydney from his home in Tahiti with a video under his arm. He had decided that in addition to addressing the celebratory annual general meeting, which he was attending as a special guest, he would play this video, which had just been completed by his granddaughter Teya Dusseldorp. The video told the story of a project that brought together two gold-medal-winning national champions. One was Kip Keino, Kenya's legendary Olympic athlete, and the other Glenn Brasen, Australia's first gold-medallist—in bricklaying—at the 1985 WorldSkills Competition (previously known as the Youth Skill Olympics) held in Osaka, Japan.[1]

Keino's youth foundation had been building a home for orphaned children in Makwe, a small village in Southern Zimbabwe, when they discovered that the local primary school was in a desperate state. Limited classroom space and a lack of furniture left many of the children squatting on concrete floors or out in the open, resulting in poor school attendance and related health problems. The WorldSkills organisation saw this as an opportunity to draw on the many skilled young champions who had competed in WorldSkills Competitions to share their skills with young people in developing countries lacking such opportunities. In March 1998, with support from the Keino Foundation, a multinational, multi-skilled team of five WorldSkills volunteers led by Glenn Brasen arrived in Makwe. There they joined forces with seven young locals, and work began on rebuilding the school. The whole community joined in the effort, with all the materials, the hand-made bricks, and the water being carted onto the site by hand. One of the local women working on the project was heard to quip that it was the first time in her whole life that she had seen white men working!

Six months later the project was complete. Makwe school now boasted a new classroom, a new amenities block, and for the first time ever, an entire primary school kitted out with desks and benches. And the Makwe community also boasted seven young adult villagers with 'practical, reproducible vocational skills'.[2] By mid-2000, a further dozen school-building projects had been completed by similar multinational teams in Zimbabwe, Kenya, and Kosovo, all under the auspices of the 'Skills Across the World' program, sponsored by the WorldSkills organisation. Under the newly elected President of WorldSkills, Tjerk Dusseldorp, the program looks set for further expansion in the years ahead.

The Makwe story having been captured on video by Tjerk Dusseldorp's daughter Teya, it was a very proud grandfather who played it for the shareholders and employees of Lend Lease at their fortieth anniversary bash. 'It was a smash hit,' Dick Dusseldorp reported. 'It got a five-minute standing ovation.'[3] Symbolising so much of what Dusseldorp himself believed in, and representing the only type of philanthropy that he saw as worthwhile, the Makwe story was a fitting way for him to say a formal goodbye. For that was the last Lend Lease annual general meeting that he would attend. Some two years later, at a memorial service in St Aloysius College Chapel in Sydney in May 2000, his grandchildren placed before the hundreds of mourners assembled there four symbols of their grandfather's driving passions: a briefcase symbolising his dedication to work; a compass for his life-long love of sailing; a brick from the Tank Stream under Australia Square to represent his love of construction; and the Book of Employee Tributes presented to him on his retirement from Lend Lease as a symbol of his care for all his employees. The final tribute to him was paid by his son Tjerk.

To me, my father was always captain of the ship. As a boy he ran away to sea and dreamt of one day captaining his own vessel into all parts of the world. And although the vessel he launched turned out to be a land-based group of enterprises, he captained them with the same all-consuming around-the-clock attention and care as is demanded on the open sea.

On those rare shore leaves with us, his family, we heard his dazzling tales of high adventure. And in my mind, I conjured up images of him as part explorer, merchant mariner, and yes, occasional pirate.

My father's approach to captaining avoided the hierarchical traditions of the Navy, but rather adopted the style of the expert crews who manned the famous sailing clipper ships which had fired his youthful imagination.

Shareholders, managers, and employees were the owners, officers and crew of his ship. And he saw his role as maintaining a fair balance between their respective interests for the benefit of all.

And while he, like all sailors, enjoyed the balmy days, he particularly relished the opportunity to chart new waters and test the capacities of his officers and crew in tough conditions, in order to develop their confidence and competence to face the challenges ahead.

I, like others, initially misinterpreted his often stern demeanour which in fact was a reflection of his acute sense of responsibility for the conduct, safety and well-being of everyone on board.

My father was a born navigator, with an uncanny ability to look over the horizon and anticipate the changing conditions through which he journeyed. Invariably he adopted a conservative approach to risk, even if it meant the appearance of falling behind. As he liked to say, 'If you have your destination clearly in mind, and worth reaching, it doesn't matter whether it takes a little longer to achieve, for after all, it is only the eventual safe landing that counts'.

Both before and after he relinquished the helm of Lend Lease, over a decade ago, my father captained a number of other smaller vessels.

One was the *Benedic*, an ocean-going sailing ketch in which he realised the dream of his boyhood to sail the oceans of the world.

Another is the Dusseldorp Skills Forum, which was funded by a gift of shares from his employees and institutional shareholders to mark the occasion of his retirement. He focused the Forum's initial efforts on opening up new connections between the worlds of work and education for the benefit of future generations. And they're at work right now. My father believed that every young person deserves the opportunity of a right of passage into adulthood, similar to what was afforded him in his youth.

During the time we worked together in the Forum, I grew to understand his approach, to turning what appeared to be insurmountable obstacles into opportunities and innovative solutions. He had long mastered the art of creative thinking: the rare combination of knowledge, obsession and daring. Qualities he had in abundance, and which will continue to inspire us at the Forum.

My father spoke matter-of-factly about death. And like with everything else in his life, he began to systematically prepare for its eventuality. He died as he hoped he would: still up on deck, scanning the horizon.[4]

Notes

Introduction

1 'Sydney Police Centre Site Office: Unregistered Papers, 1968–86', CGS 4355. 12/13222–37 (Kingswood, Government Architect. State Records of New South Wales, 1968–86); Susan Wyndham, '10 Years and $63m Later, the Sydney Police Centre Will Open—God and the Unions Willing', *Canberra Times: Good Weekend*, 22–23 June 1985; 'Decision. Minister for Employment and Industrial Relations Seeking Declaration Re Australian Building Construction Employees' and Builders Labourers' Federation', *Australian Conciliation and Arbitration Commission* C No. 1852 (1985) (Melbourne).

2 The Qantas International Centre building—now known as the AAP Tower—has been described as 'one of the most protracted constructions in Sydney's history'. Graham Jahn, *Sydney Architecture* (Sydney, Watermark Press, 1997), p. 183. It took nine years to build and ended up costing some $110 million—twice the time and amount originally estimated. Oscar Gimesy, *Built from Nothing: A History of the Building Industry in Australia* (Carlton, Vic., Building Careers Resource Centre of Australia, 1992), p. 160; Key Centre of Design Computing and Cognition. Faculty of Architecture. University of Sydney, 'AAP Building (Formerly Known as the Qantas Building)', *SAM Database* <http://www.arch. usyd.edu.au/kcdc/caut/html/AAP/front.htm>.

3 Paul Coombes, 'How Lend Lease Stays Out of Trouble with the Unions', *Rydge's*, December 1981, 18.

4 Geraldine O'Brien, 'Now, a Better Box from the Butterbox', *Sydney Morning Herald*, 31 July 2000.

5 Bruce Stannard, 'Inside the BLF: Growls and True Grit', *Bulletin*, 22 April 1986.

6 Three times as many working days were lost as a result of industrial disputes in the Australian construction industry in 1983 than in the rest of Australian industry. The Australian construction industry remained consistently more troubled than its domestic and international counterparts throughout the rest of the decade. Table 7.1, Days Lost as a Result of Industrial Disputes in the Construction Industry: Australia, UK, USA, Germany and Canada, in Australia, in Industry Commission, *Construction Costs of Major Projects*, Report No. 8 (Canberra, Australian Government Publishing Service, 1991).

7   The descriptors are from Jane Richardson, 'Building Goodwill with a Profitable Pact', *Australian*, 17 August 1981.

8   'At any one time', *The Australian* observed in 1981, 'it would be safe to put a value of millions on developments being held back by strikes and black bans.' Ibid.

9   'Lend Lease's fairy-tale construction progress on Sydney's Regent Hotel', reported *Rydge's*, 'has astounded many in these days of industrial disputation on building sites.' Coombes, 'How Lend Lease Stays Out of Trouble with the Unions', p. 18. *The Australian*, likewise, reported that the Regent was 'pushing skyward at a rate of knots', contrasting progress on the Circular Quay site with 'the $100 million Qantas building—due in June 1981, finishing date now unknown'. Richardson, 'Building Goodwill with a Profitable Pact'.

10 Bill Webster, Interview with Lindie Clark (Roseville, 3 July 2000).

11 Frank Cuzzocrea, Interview with Lindie Clark (Concord, 21 July 2000).

12 Lend Lease Corporation Ltd, *26th Annual Report* (Sydney, Lend Lease Corporation Ltd, 1983), p. 20.

13 Steve Black, NSW Secretary of the Builders Labourers' Federation, in Richardson, 'Building Goodwill with a Profitable Pact'.

14 Pat Clancy, National Secretary of the Building Workers' Industrial Union, in ibid.

15 Richardson, 'Building Goodwill with a Profitable Pact'.

16 The descriptor is that used by the Hon. Robert J. L. Hawke in, 'Foreword', *Link: Commemorative Issue to Mark the Retirement of the Chairman of Lend Lease Corporation, G. J. Dusseldorp* (Sydney, Lend Lease Corporation Ltd, 1988).

17 Robert Gottliebsen, 'The Prince of Property', *Business Review Weekly*, 21 December 1990; Gordon Bradley, 'Dusseldorp's Day', *Bulletin*, 11 January 1961; Trevor Sykes, *Two Centuries of Panic: A History of Corporate Collapses in Australia* (North Sydney, Allen & Unwin, 1988); John Wasiliev, 'The Golden Rules of Investing', *Australian Investment*, April 1988.

18 Polly LaBarre, 'The Company Without Limits', *Fast Company* 27, September 1999; V. J. Carroll, former Editor-in-Chief of the *Sydney Morning Herald* and former Editor of the *Australian Financial Review*, cited in Andrew Clark, 'Building Genius Played It Tough', *Age*, 6 May 2000; 'Dick Dusseldorp Sells a Monument', *Sun Herald*, 31 March 1974; 'A Boss Who Really Cares', *Sun News-Pictorial*, 1 November 1972.

19 David Thorne, Interview with Lindie Clark (Sydney, 10 April 2000). 'If we made a lot more money on a project than was anticipated,' Thorne says in explanation of the latter, 'we would hand some of that back to the customer. That was part of the contract system that we had. But we *all* benefited from it in the end because it brought us continuing work—customers had never experienced it before.'

20 John Elkington, 'What Is the Triple Bottom Line?' in SustainAbility <http://www.sustainability.com/philosophy/triple-bottom/tbl-intro.asp>, c.2001.

21 Lord Holme of Cheltenham, 'Responsible Business Engagement with Society', *BCA Papers* 1, no. 2 (October 1999) <http://www.bca.com.au/bcapapers/v1n2/15.htm>.

22 The first such surveys began to appear in the mid-1980s, from which time Lend Lease has been consistently ranked in the top echelon of Australia's most admired companies. See, for example, Christopher Jay, 'People Management and Innovation', *Australian Financial Review*, 20 February 1985; Kevin Forde, 'Smart, Smarter, Smartest: We Pick the Top 22 Performers in Corporate Cleverness', *Rydge's*, February 1985. Gottliebsen, 'The Prince of Property', p. 34; Russell Skelton and Gerard Noonan, *Best Companies: The Good Reputation Index, 2000* (Sydney, Age/Sydney Morning Herald, 2000).

23 Eric Goodwin, Communications with Lindie Clark (Sydney, 2000–02).

24 Mary Murphy, *Challenges of Change: The Lend Lease Story* (Sydney, Lend Lease Corporation Ltd, 1984).

25 I am indebted to John Buchanan for this point.

26 G. J. Dusseldorp, 'Chairman's Address', cited in Lend Lease Corporation Ltd, *31st Annual Report* (Sydney, Lend Lease Corporation Ltd, 1988), p. 7.

27 Robert Gottliebsen, 'Comment', *Business Review Weekly*, 6–12 November 1982, 4.

28 G. J. Dusseldorp, 'Chairman's Address', cited in Lend Lease Corporation Ltd, *31st Annual Report*, p. 7.

29 Jack Mundey, Interview with Lindie Clark (Croydon Park, 10 July 2000).

30 Dusseldorp's contribution in this area was also recognised by the bestowal of one of Australia's highest honours: appointment as an Officer of the Order of Australia (Hon.).

31 The Forum was funded by way of an allotment of Lend Lease shares totalling 1 per cent of the issued capital of the company: shareholders voted to meet one-half of this cost, Lend Lease employees voted to meet the other half.

32 The Dusco Group.

33 Australia. Snowy Mountains Hydro-Electric Authority, *The Snowy Scheme* (Sydney & Melbourne, Horwitz, 1962), p. 3; Cathryn Game, *Monash Biographical Dictionary of 20th Century Australia* (Clayton, Vic., Reed Reference Publishing in association with National Centre for Australian Studies, Monash University, 1994), p. 262.

34 Michael Howard, *State, Business and Unions in the Restructuring of the Building Industry in Australia, 1938–52*, Industrial Relations Papers (Canberra, Australian National University Research School of Social Sciences, 1987).

35 Howard, *State, Business and Unions*, p. 126; G. J. Dusseldorp, Interview with Monica Penders (1995).

36 G. J. Dusseldorp, 'Holland: Dredge, Drain and Reclaim!!' (Canberra, c. September 1959); F. Broeze, 'The Settlers: Dutch', in *The Australian People*, ed. James Jupp (North Ryde, NSW, Angus & Robertson, 1988), p. 354.

37 G. J. Dusseldorp, Interviews with Lindie Clark (Sydney, 7–15 September 1999).

38 Ibid.

39 Hank Dusseldorp to Lindie Clark (Kitchener, Ontario, 8 September 2000).

40 Anne Dusseldorp, Interview with Lindie Clark (Middle Cove, 10 August 2000).

41 Ibid.

42 The Germans had promised this railway to the Danish government in return for neutrality. When the Germans nonetheless occupied Denmark in April 1940, the railroad project initially went ahead.

43 Their job was design a hangar for the company's new Junker airplane. H. Dusseldorp, Letter to Lindie Clark.

44 A. Dusseldorp, Interview with Lindie Clark.

45 Linda M. Woolf, 'Survival and Resistance: The Netherlands Under Nazi Occupation', Paper, Conference Held at the United States Holocaust Memorial Museum (Washington, DC, 6 April 1999); Louis de Jong, *The Netherlands and Nazi Germany* (Cambridge, MA, Harvard University Press, 1990).

46 Woolf, 'Survival and Resistance'.

47 Zena Stein et al., *Famine and Human Development: The Dutch Hunger Winter of 1944–1945* (New York, Oxford University Press, 1975), p. 44.

48 People literally dropped from exhaustion in the streets, fights broke out in families over what scant food could be foraged, mortality rates tripled in the cities, and over 20,000 people died of starvation in the region as a whole. Ibid.; A. Dusseldorp, Interview with Lindie Clark; de Jong, *Netherlands*, p. 47.

49 A. Dusseldorp, Interview with Lindie Clark.

50 Ibid.

51 Ibid.

52 Dick's eldest daughter Lenneke recalls her father's stories about this time: 'His sisters often had to warn him if there was someone in sight,' she says. 'And a couple of times, he told me, he just had no option but to brazen it out. He was just lucky. One time the person he met was a young German, but he [the German] had no intention of doing anything to anyone, and so Dad got away with it.' Lenneke Quinlan, Interview with Lindie Clark (Ryde, 18 August 2000).

53 'The Bredero's Story', *Link*, September 1959, 1.

54 Jan de Vries, 'Bredero's Bouwbedrijf and Its Organisation', unpublished paper (21 June 1960), p. 1.

55 A. Dusseldorp, Interview with Lindie Clark.

56 Jan L. van Zanden, *A Small Open Economy in the 'Long' Twentieth Century* (London & New York, Routledge, 1998), p. 107.

57 Dusseldorp, 'Dredge'; Stein et al., *Famine and Human Development*, p. 45.

58 Broeze, 'Dutch', p. 354.

59 Ibid.

60 de Vries, 'Bredero's Bouwbedrijf and Its Organisation'.

61 A. Dusseldorp, Interview with Lindie Clark.

62 Ibid.

63 Ibid.

64 Ibid.

1 Production Management

1 G. J. Dusseldorp, Interviews with Lindie Clark (Sydney, 7–15 September 1999).

2 Sydney Opera House, 'The Genesis of the Sydney Opera House', *Timeline* <http://www.soh.nsw.gov.au/files/timeline/timeline_genesis.html>. The quote is from the handbook produced for competition entrants, Appendix 5 of which set out mandatory requirements for the design of the building.

3 'January 30 1957. Sydney is to Have a New Opera House', in *Chronicle of Australia*, ed. John Ross (Ringwood, Vic., Viking, 2000).

4 Cited in David Messent, *Opera House Act One* (Sydney, David Messent Photography, 1997), p. 107.

5 John Yeomans, *The Other Taj Mahal: What Happened to the Sydney Opera House* (Camberwell, Vic., Longman, 1973 [1968]), p. 63.

6 Before the Opera House was complete, Utzon would resign and lodge a writ of claims against the NSW Government for unpaid fees and expenses. He was never to return to Australia. Vincent Smith, *The Sydney Opera House* (Sydney, Paul Hamlyn, 1974), p. 116. Ove Arup & Partners, the structural engineers on the job (who also fell out with Utzon), believed that they were lumbered with 'far more' responsibility for managing the job 'than could possibly be construed as falling under our duties as structural engineers'. Ove Arup, in a letter to the Minister for Works dated 26 March 1963, cited in Yeomans, *Other Taj Mahal*, p. 74. They seriously contemplated withdrawing from the project at the end of Stage 2, although in the end they saw the Opera House through to completion.

7 Civil & Civic Pty Ltd, *Dossier of Construction Projects by Civil & Civic Pty. Limited from the Company's Inception in 1951* (internal company document, c.1969); Eric Goodwin, Communications with Lindie Clark (Sydney, 2000–02).

8 Civil & Civic Pty Ltd, *Dossier*.

9 Gordon Bradley, 'Dusseldorp's Day', *Bulletin*, 11 January 1961, p. 10.

10 Ibid.

11 G. J. Dusseldorp, 'The Law of Triviality: Its Effect on the Cost of Building', *Rydge's*, 1 May 1958, p. 430.

12 G. J. Dusseldorp, 'Planning to Build', Speech given to Australian Institute of Management (28 February 1962), p. 4.

13 This characteristic is still evident today. See Australia. Productivity Commission, *Work Arrangements on Large Capital City Building Projects*, Labour Market Research Report (Canberra, AusInfo, 1999), pp. 14–15. Dissatisfied with this adversarial approach, some parties today opt instead for what the Productivity Commission refers to as 'alliance contracting'. Alliance contracting as a concept has much in common with Dusseldorp's idea of the 'building team' and 'Design & Construct package deals' discussed below.

14 G. J. Dusseldorp, Interviews with Lindie Clark.

15 Ibid.

16 Dusseldorp, 'Law of Triviality', p. 430.

17 'Newcomer Gets Contract', *Daily Telegraph*, 9 February 1959.

18 G. J. Dusseldorp, Interviews with Lindie Clark; G. J. Dusseldorp, Interview with Tjerk Dusseldorp (Middle Cove, March 1973).

19 This high-profile job resulted in a flow-on of work for the firm in Canberra. A similar strategy was employed by Dusseldorp's Civil & Civic in breaking into the Victorian market

20 Liberal MLA Robin (later Sir Robert) Askin, who would become Premier in 1965, cited in Messent, *Opera House Act One*, p. 119.

21 Yeomans, *Other Taj Mahal*, p. 56.

22 Ibid., p. 65.

23 Ibid., p. 55.

24 Civil & Civic Pty Ltd, *Dossier*.

25 Yeomans, *Other Taj Mahal*, p. 71.

26 Ibid.

27 Richard Hammond, Interview with Lindie Clark (Clontarf, 16 May 2000).

28 Yeomans, *Other Taj Mahal*, p. 71.

29 Hammond, Interview with Lindie Clark.

30 Smith, *Sydney Opera House*, p. 88.

31 Ove Arup, in a letter to the Minister for Works dated 26 March 1963, cited in Yeomans, *Other Taj Mahal*, p. 74.

32 Michael Baume, *The Sydney Opera House Affair* (Melbourne, Thomas Nelson Australia, 1967), p. 10.

33 G. J. Dusseldorp, Letter to Ove Arup & Partners, Civil & Civic Pty Ltd internal company files (Sydney, 24 March 1960).

34 Baume, *Sydney Opera House Affair*, p. 10.

35 Dusseldorp, Letter to Ove Arup & Partners.

36 Smith, *Sydney Opera House*, p. 10.

37 G. J. Dusseldorp, Interviews with Lindie Clark.

38 Ibid.

39 Yeomans, *Other Taj Mahal*, p. 71.

40 Ibid.

41 Mary Murphy, *Challenges of Change: The Lend Lease Story* (Sydney, Lend Lease Corporation Ltd, 1984), p. 77.

42 G. J. Dusseldorp, Interviews with Lindie Clark.

43 'The job started without enough detail—a known, sure ingredient for a blow-out on costs,' says Civil & Civic's Richard Hammond. 'We acted in good faith with our tender and complied with the 40-odd sketches and conditions made available. And although our work cost more than initially expected, Stage 1 ended up costing a mere 5 per cent of the total—the most significant cost overrun came later in Stage 2.' Hammond, Interview with Lindie Clark.

44 For more on the unfolding drama that characterised the Opera House project, see Baume, *Sydney Opera House Affair*; Yeomans, *Other Taj Mahal*; Smith, *Sydney Opera House*; Messent, *Opera House Act One*; Philip Drew, *The Masterpiece. Jørn Utzon: A Secret Life* (Hardie Grant Books, 1999).

45 Lend Lease Corporation Ltd, *Twenty Years: The Lend Lease Story* (Sydney, Lend Lease Corporation Ltd, 1977).

46 Gary Hamel, 'Leading the Revolution', *Australian Financial Review BOSS Magazine* 1:7 (September 2000), pp. 22, 24.

47 G. J. Dusseldorp, Interview with Tjerk Dusseldorp.
48 G. J. Dusseldorp, Interview with Monica Penders (1995).
49 G. J. Dusseldorp, Interviews with Lindie Clark.
50 Ibid.
51 Ibid.
52 Ibid.
53 The 1992 Royal Commission into Productivity in the NSW Building Industry found that successful tenderers were paying competitors 'unsuccessful tender fees' and industry associations (who were also part of the racket) 'special fees'. Australia. Productivity Commission, *Work Arrangements on Large Capital City Building Projects*, p. 31. Roger Gyles QC, the Royal Commissioner, found that collusive tendering in the NSW industry was 'not just some temporary aberration. It was widespread, systematic and covert', resulting in clients being 'undoubtedly cheated on a large scale'. Gyles, *Royal Commission into Productivity in the Building Industry in New South Wales, Volume 7: Final Report* (Sydney, Southwood Press Pty Ltd, 1992), p. 85.
54 G. J. Dusseldorp, Interviews with Lindie Clark.
55 Ibid.
56 Leslie M. Perrott Jnr, 'The Revival of a Building Revolution', unpublished paper (c.1959).
57 Oscar Gimesy, *Built from Nothing: A History of the Building Industry in Australia* (Carlton, Vic., Building Careers Resource Centre of Australia, 1992), p. 6.
58 The Australian building firm Paynter Dixon was possibly the first to introduce the concept to Australia. It had used the Design & Construct concept, particularly on its industrial projects, since 1948. Ern Mac Donald, Interviews with Lindie Clark (Sydney, 2000–02); Paynter Dixon Queensland, 'Experience', in Paynter Dixon Queensland <http://www.paynter.com.au/interest.htm.>, 22 October 1998.
59 Milton Herbert Allen, Interview with Lindie Clark (Waitara, 22 May 2000).
60 Design & Construct packages meant a 'diminution of the Architect's field of control and supervision', and architectural associations around the world were aghast at their intrusion. Perrott Jnr, 'Revival', pp. 3–4.
61 Murphy, *Challenges of Change*, p. 141.
62 Dusseldorp, 'Planning to Build'.
63 Ibid.
64 Robert Harley, 'The Culture Builders', *Australian Financial Review BOSS Magazine*, 1:7 (September 2000), p. 54.
65 'Superior–subordinate' chains of command were kept to a minimum in Civil & Civic—and in its subsequent parent firm Lend Lease—with project-based management structures preferred in their stead. Lend Lease Corporation Ltd, *Twenty Years*. The project team approach was pioneered by Dusseldorp on a residential subdivision Civil & Civic undertook in the mid-1950s (discussed in Chapter 6). Even twenty-five years later, when the Lend Lease group employed some three to four thousand people, there were still no more than five layers

between Managing Director and the workface. Stuart Hornery, *State of the Nation (August)*, Managing Director's address (Sydney, Lend Lease Corporation Ltd, internal company document, 1983).

66 Allen, Interview with Lindie Clark.

67 'Streamlining for Greater Efficiency', *Link*, September 1959; Barry Wynne, 'Design', Lend Lease Property Development Course (Sydney, Lend Lease Corporation Ltd, February 1969), p. 3.

68 Hammond, Interview with Lindie Clark.

69 G. J. Dusseldorp in G. J. Dusseldorp and Stuart Hornery, Lend Lease Video, 1980.

70 Murphy, *Challenges of Change*, p. 29. Some years earlier Civil & Civic had been the first private construction company to employ a professional engineer, and it had always been company policy to employ its own quantity surveyors. To this professional complement were then added architects; structural, electrical and mechanical engineers; draftsmen; and plumbing design specialists. Over time Civil & Civic became one of the largest single employers of many such professionals. Civil & Civic Contractors Pty Ltd, 'Organisation Manual' (internal company document, August 1958); Murphy, *Challenges of Change*, pp. 29, 72.

71 John Morschel, Interview with Lindie Clark (Greenwich, 25 July 2000).

72 Goodwin, Communications with Lindie Clark.

73 Gimesy, *Built from Nothing*, p. 5.

74 'Construction Expert to Meet Press', *Daily Telegraph*, 7 March 1959.

75 Cited in Murphy, *Challenges of Change*, p. 23.

76 Lend Lease Corporation Ltd, *Lend Lease Corporation Ltd* (M. S. Simpson & Sons Ltd, c.1962), p. 16.

77 Lend Lease Corporation Ltd, *Lend Lease Corporation Ltd*, p. 16.

78 'All About the R&D Section', *Link*, May–June 1977.

79 Civil & Civic Pty Ltd, *Innovation: The Drive to Find a Better Way* (Sydney, Civil & Civic Pty Ltd, c.1988), p. 23.

80 'Progressive Strength' won the principal award for excellence presented by the Concrete Institute of Australia in 1973. See G. J. Dusseldorp, 'Chairman's Address', Lend Lease Corporation Limited, 16th Annual General Meeting (Sydney, 12 October 1973).

81 Civil & Civic Pty Ltd, *Innovation*, p. 22. The man behind all of these inventions was methods engineer Alan Cull, whose twenty-year stint with Civil & Civic began in the firm's R&D department in 1960. Innovative thinkers like Cull were attracted to, and stayed with, the company because it provided an environment in which their talents could blossom. 'The people, the cooperation, the atmosphere, the culture—I couldn't have done what I did without all that, in some other place.' Alan Cull, Interview with Lindie Clark (Clareville, 19 June 2000).

82 Cited in Murphy, *Challenges of Change*, p. 59.

83 The Sydney contemporaries of Caltex House (1957) included the MLC's new headquarters at North Sydney (1956), Qantas House at Chifley Square (1957), and Unilever House and the ICI building on Bennelong Point.

84 Graham Jahn, *Sydney Architecture* (Sydney, Watermark Press, 1997), p. 147.

85 Jack Mundey, Interview with Lindie Clark (Croydon Park, 10 July 2000).

86 M. T. Daly, *Sydney Boom, Sydney Bust: The City and Its Property Market* (Sydney, George Allen & Unwin, 1982).

87 The *1912 Height of Buildings Act*, prompted by construction of the 170-foot (52-metre) Culwulla Chambers in the same year, would restrict city buildings to a maximum of 150 feet (46 metres) for the next four and a half decades.

88 Jahn, *Sydney Architecture*, p. 166.

89 'City Development', *The Valuer*, January 1961; Murphy, *Challenges of Change*, p. 80.

90 Murphy, *Challenges of Change*, p. 83.

91 Harry Seidler, *Australia Square* (Sydney, Horwitz Publications, 1969), p. 4.

92 Murphy, *Challenges of Change*, p. 83; G. J. Dusseldorp, 'Roof Ceremony: Australia Square', unpublished speech (Sydney, May 1967), p. 1.

93 Eric Martin, 'Australia Square', in Royal Australian Institute of Architects (RAIA) Nomination for the International Union of Architects' (UIA) World Register of Significant Twentieth Century Australian Architecture <http://www.raia.com.au/rstca/>, 18 August 2000.

94 Martin, 'Australia Square'.

95 G. J. Dusseldorp, Interview with Monica Penders.

96 Harry Seidler, cited in Alice Spigelman, *Almost Full Circle. Harry Seidler: A Biography* (Rose Bay, NSW, Brandl & Schlesinger, 2001), p. 263.

97 Patrick Bingham-Hall, *Austral Eden: 200 Years of Australian Architecture* (Sydney, Watermark Press, 1999), p. 165.

98 A number of alternative shapes for the Tower had already been considered and rejected by the project team. By late 1961 the range of alternatives for the shape of the Tower had been narrowed down to three: one circular, the second a square, and the third an 'H-shaped' building. The first of these was estimated to be the most expensive to build and develop, but because it generated more useable office space, its net annual income was estimated to be greater, which meant a greater return on capital. Lend Lease Corporation Ltd. File note comparing costs of alternative schemes, dated 17 November 1961.

99 John Stigter, 'Australia Square: A Mammoth Product of Civil & Civic's Integrated Design and Construction Service', *Building Materials* 8:3 (February–March 1967), 3.

100 Murphy, *Challenges of Change*, p. 83; Martin, 'Australia Square', p. 4.

101 John Maxwell Freeland, *Architecture in Australia: A History* (Ringwood, Vic., Penguin Books, 1972 [1968]), p. 302.

102 Martin, 'Australia Square', p. 5.

103 Harry Seidler, '50 Years of Architectural Practice in Australia', Wilkinson Lecture (University of Sydney, 6 April 2000); Spigelman, *Almost Full Circle*, pp. 179–80.

104 Harry Seidler, Interview with Lindie Clark (Milson's Point, 23 June 2000).

105 Seidler, Interview with Lindie Clark.

106 G. J. Dusseldorp, Interviews with Lindie Clark.

107 Spigelman, *Almost Full Circle*, p. 282.

108 Seidler, Interview with Lindie Clark.

109 Harry Seidler, 'Space: Dusseldorp Magic', *Australian Financial Review BOSS Magazine* 1:4 (June 2000).

110 Seidler, Interview with Lindie Clark. Australia Square was one of Dusseldorp's firm's 'self-sponsored' development projects.
111 G. J. Dusseldorp, *Urban Renewal: Implementation*, Address to Royal Victorian Institute of Architects, 24 November (1960), p. 4.
112 Seidler, 'Space: Dusseldorp Magic'.
113 Seidler, Interview with Lindie Clark. Seidler's Harvard classmate I. M. Pei had worked with the famous US property developer William Zeckendorf on a number of large-scale 'urban renewal' projects. Dusseldorp was initially keen to have Seidler and Pei jointly design the Australia Square development, but by 1961 Dusseldorp was convinced that Seidler could do it on his own. Spigelman, *Almost Full Circle*, pp. 253–61; Seidler, Interview with Lindie Clark.
114 Seidler, Interview with Lindie Clark.
115 G. J. Dusseldorp cited in Seidler, 'Space: Dusseldorp Magic'.
116 Harry Seidler and Penelope Seidler, 'Two of Us', *Sydney Morning Herald. Good Weekend*, 22 July 2000.
117 Seidler, Interview with Lindie Clark.
118 Murphy, *Challenges of Change*, p. 96.
119 Minutes of Planning Meeting, Australia Square Plaza and Tower, 13 July 1962, File 6265–213 Australia Square Tower and Plaza: Notes from Planning Meetings.
120 Robinson, Interview with Lindie Clark.
121 Cull, Interview with Lindie Clark.
122 Stigter, 'Australia Square', p. 8.
123 'Portrait of a Manager: He's Building His Own Monuments', *The Australian Manager*, December 1961, p. 24. Elevators Pty Limited (later EPL–Kone), timber company Bowman's Pty Ltd, metal window manufacturer J. Connolly Ltd, brickmaker Autobric Industries, lightweight aggregate producer Lite-Crete, and Unbehaun & Johnstone Ltd electrical suppliers all joined Dusseldorp's corporate fold between 1959 and 1962.
124 Seidler, Interview with Lindie Clark.
125 Cull, Interview with Lindie Clark. Cull believes that Civil & Civic was the first company to use multi-activity charts—sophisticated scheduling tools which explain in detail how a complex process is to be organised—in the Australian construction industry.
126 Freeland, *Architecture in Australia*, p. 302.
127 'Big Day for Sydney Giant', *Daily Telegraph*, 5 May 1967.
128 Ibid.
129 Dusseldorp, 'Roof Ceremony: Australia Square'.
130 'Sulman Medal to City Tower', *Daily Telegraph*, 14 June 1967.
131 Bingham-Hall, *Austral Eden*, p. 204.
132 John Haskell, *Sydney Architecture* (Sydney, University of New South Wales Press, 1997), p. 40.
133 With the two buildings on the site covering only 40 per cent of its area, the project returned to the people of Sydney 'a major public open space'. Haskell, *Sydney Architecture*, p. 40.
134 Ibid.
135 Martin, 'Australia Square'.

2 Labour Management

1 While in 1952 the building industry had accounted for 1.65 per cent of all industrial disputes recorded by the Australian Government Statistician that year, by 1960 the figure was 8.6 per cent, and still climbing. See Glenn Mitchell, *On Strong Foundations: The BWIU and Industrial Relations in the Australian Construction Industry* (Sydney, Harcourt Brace, 1996), pp. 152, 85, 103.

2 ' "Getting Tough" Lands Industry in Doleful Plight. The Building Trade Part 1', *Sydney Morning Herald*, 10 December 1957.

3 The ACTU is the peak national body to which most trade unions in Australia are affiliated.

4 The Victorian Trades Hall, and its counterparts in other states (often known as Trades and Labour Councils) are the state-based equivalents of the ACTU.

5 Simon Blackall, 'Albert Monk', in *The People Who Made Australia Great* (Sydney, William Collins Pty Ltd, 1988), p. 286.

6 Quoted by G. J. Dusseldorp, Interviews with Lindie Clark (Sydney, 7–15 September 1999).

7 Repeated union applications for re-entry to the system over the next couple of years—a period of rabid anti-communism in Australia—would all be denied. See Mitchell, *On Strong Foundations*.

8 The Master Builders' Association of New South Wales, for example, made two applications to deregister that state's branch of the BWIU during the 1950s. One of these was (briefly) successful in 1957, but the union was quickly readmitted to the fold when it gave 'various undertakings to the [Arbitration] Commission regarding industrial disputes'. Ibid., p. 103.

9 Amongst the rivals was the breakaway Amalgamated Society of Carpenters and Joiners of Australia (ASC&J), formed by the anti-communist, Catholic-backed 'Groupers' in opposition to the communist-led BWIU. The ASC&J was granted registration in the federal industrial arena in the early 1950s but not in New South Wales. The main labourers' union in the industry—the BLF—was another member-poacher at this time. Mitchell, *On Strong Foundations*.

10 Under the leadership of Pat Clancy, for example, the NSW branch of the BWIU pursued a strategy of 'refined militancy'. This involved united action with other unions to achieve improved wages and conditions for building workers, but with a commitment to resolve disputes within the formal conciliation and arbitration framework rather than taking direct action including illegal strikes. Roger Vincent Gyles QC, 'History of Industrial Relations in the Building Industry in New South Wales. Appendix C', in *Royal Commission Into Productivity in the Building Industry in New South Wales, Volume 7: Final Report* (Sydney, Southwood Press, 1992), p. 152.

11 Jack Mundey, *Green Bans and Beyond* (London & Sydney, Angus & Robertson, 1981), p. 24.

12 Jack Mundey, Interview with Lindie Clark (Croydon Park, 10 July 2000).

13 Prior to the 1970s the NSW Master Builders' Association (and its counterparts in other states) was the dominant voice of construction firms in industrial relations matters. Today they mainly represent smaller contractors. Research and Policy Divisions. Royal Commission into Productivity in the Building Industry in New

South Wales, *Industrial Relations in the Building Industry: Historical Overview and Avenues for Change* (Sydney, Royal Commission, 1992); Gyles, 'Report of the Hearings Part III(a): Industrial Relations', *Royal Commission into Productivity in the Building Industry in New South Wales, Volume 5* (Sydney, Southwood Press, 1992).

14 Stan Sharkey, Interview with Lindie Clark (Clovelly, 29 June 2000).

15 G. J. Dusseldorp, Interviews with Lindie Clark.

16 Strikes were relatively rare in the Netherlands from the 1920s onwards. Jan L. van Zanden, *A Small Open Economy in the 'Long' Twentieth Century* (London & New York, Routledge, 1998), p. 81. Just after World War II there was a temporary eruption of industrial conflict as more militant communist-led unions emerged to challenge the status quo. John P. Windmuller, *Labor Relations in the Netherlands* (Ithaca, NY, Cornell University Press, 1969), p. 113. Dusseldorp himself had some pretty hair-raising encounters with the communist rabble-rousers. Ern Mac Donald, Interviews with Lindie Clark (Sydney, 2000–02). But by the end of the 1940s their 'threat' had been by and large contained, and the Netherlands once again became 'a showcase of almost completely appeased labour relations'. Van Zanden, *Small Open Economy*, p. 82.

17 Windmuller, *Labor Relations in the Netherlands*, p. 85.

18 Ibid., p. 86.

19 Dani Rodrik, 'The Debate Over Globalization: How to Move Forward by Looking Backward', Paper given to a conference on The Future of the World Trading System (Washington, DC, 15 April 1998); Sheryle Bagwell, 'Going Dutch a Pointer to the Third Way', *Australian Financial Review*, 20–25 April 2000; F. Broeze, 'The Settlers: Dutch', in *The Australian People*, ed. James Jupp (North Ryde, NSW, Angus & Robertson, 1988); Anton Hemerijck and Jelle Visser, 'Change and Immobility: Three Decades of Policy Adjustment in the Netherlands and Belgium', *West European Politics* 23:2 (April 2000); 'The Netherlands', in *Encyclopaedia Britannica* <http://www.britannicca.com/bcom/eb/article/5/0,5716,115635+2+108757,00.html>, 1999.

20 G. J. Dusseldorp, 'Holland: Dredge, Drain and Reclaim!!' (Canberra, c. September 1959); G. J. Dusseldorp, Interviews with Lindie Clark; William Z. Shetter, *The Pillars of Society: Six Centuries of Civilization in the Netherlands* (The Hague, Martinus Nijhoff, 1971).

21 Quoted by G. J. Dusseldorp, Interviews with Lindie Clark.

22 G. J. Dusseldorp, Transcript of interview with Mary Murphy (Sydney, 24 August 1981), p. 2.

23 G. J. Dusseldorp cited in 'New Agreement Makes History in Building', *Management News (AIM Sydney Division)* 10:6 (December 1958).

24 G. J. Dusseldorp, Interviews with Lindie Clark.

25 Gordon Bradley, 'Dusseldorp's Day', *Bulletin*, 11 January 1961, p. 10.

26 Mary Murphy, *Challenges of Change: The Lend Lease Story* (Sydney, Lend Lease Corporation Ltd, 1984), p. 22.

27 An alternative to the more conventional steel beam and column method then used in Australia, the flat plate technique relies on a thickened floor with

columns at its edge to distribute the load—thus minimising, if not eliminating, the need for beams. Dusseldorp chose this method as it would both speed construction and yield greater floor space in the finished building. Civil & Civic Pty Ltd, *Dossier of Construction Projects by Civil & Civic Pty. Limited from the Company's Inception in 1951* (internal company document, c. 1969); 'Civil & Civic's Management Matrix', *Rydge's*, January 1977.

28 Murphy, *Challenges of Change*, p. 17.

29 Insurance companies would come to dominate the city high-rise market in future years, but in the 1950s, most of their investments were still in low-risk and low-yielding vehicles such as bonds and mortgages: property, and shares, were then anathema to their risk-averse boards. Milton Herbert Allen, Interview with Lindie Clark (Waitara, 22 May 2000); Geoffrey Blainey, *A History of the AMP, 1848–1998* (St Leonards, NSW, Allen & Unwin, 1999), pp. 262–4.

30 Murphy, *Challenges of Change*, p. 18; G. J. Dusseldorp, Interviews with Lindie Clark.

31 Dusseldorp, Transcript of interview with Mary Murphy, p. 1.

32 Mitchell, *On Strong Foundations*, p. 68.

33 Sir Charles Spry, Director-General of ASIO, 1950–69, cited in ibid., p. 119.

34 Australian Archives, Series A6119, Item 332, cited in ibid., p. 120.

35 This is the assessment of Tom McDonald, BWIU organiser, contained in an article in the Communist Party's newspaper *Tribune*, cited in Glenn Mitchell, 'The State and the Communist Party of Australia: Surveillance of Dissident Politics, 1945–55', Surveillance Conference (University of Wollongong, November 1995).

36 Conversation relayed by David Thorne, in an interview conducted by Kaye Schofield, cited in Schofield, *'You Can Make a Difference': The Story of the ACTU–Lend Lease Foundation, 1980–2000* (Sydney, Pot Still Press, 2000), p. 7.

37 'You don't talk to unions! Jeez, they're your enemies' was the attitude prevailing amongst the master builders at the time. Jack Klompe, Interviews with Lindie Clark (Sydney, 13 April 2000; 11 January 2001).

38 Albert Ricci, Interview with Lindie Clark (Concord, 21 July 2000).

39 'Man in the City: Mr. G. J. Dusseldorp, Managing Director, Civic and Civil Contractors', *Sunday Telegraph*, 3 March 1960.

40 Mac Donald, Interviews with Lindie Clark.

41 This would remain the case in much of the industry until the 1970s: it was not until 1975 that the National Building Trades Construction Award introduced one day's notice. Elizabeth A. Evatt, *Interim Report of the Inquiry Into Employment in the Building Industry* (Sydney, Australian Conciliation and Arbitration Commission, 1975), p. 21.

42 G. J. Dusseldorp, Interviews with Lindie Clark.

43 A 1999 Productivity Commission Inquiry into work arrangements on large capital-city building projects cited evidence of this. Australia. Productivity Commission, *Work Arrangements on Large Capital City Building Projects*, Labour Market Research Report (Canberra, AusInfo, 1999), p. 19.

44 This award provision dated from the 1920s and equated to 8 days per annum of lost wages. Evatt, *Interim Report of the Inquiry into Employment*, p. 21.

45 Sharkey, Interview with Lindie Clark.

46 Klompe, Interviews with Lindie Clark.

47 Mitchell, *On Strong Foundations*, p. 95.

48 Ibid.

49 Klompe, Interviews with Lindie Clark.

50 G. J. Dusseldorp, Address to the Australian Institute of Management (Sydney Division), c.1957, cited in '"Getting Tough"'.

51 Ricci, Interview with Lindie Clark.

52 Civil & Civic Pty Ltd, *Dossier*.

53 E. L. 'Banjo' Patterson, 'Caltex House: A Step Forward', *Builders Labourers' Journal: Official Organ of the ABLF, NSW Branch*, October 1957.

54 'Portrait of a Manager: He's Building His Own Monuments', *The Australian Manager*, December 1961, p. 24.

55 '"Getting Tough"'.

56 G. J. Dusseldorp cited in John Wasiliev, 'The Golden Rules of Investing', *Australian Investment*, April 1988.

57 '"Getting Tough"'.

58 G. J. Dusseldorp cited in ibid.

59 G. J. Dusseldorp, 'The Law of Triviality: Its Effect on the Cost of Building', *Rydge's*, 1 May 1958.

60 'Portrait of a Manager', p. 24.

61 'The Bredero's Story', *Link*, September 1959, p. 1.

62 Jan de Vries, 'Bredero's Bouwbedrijf and Its Organisation', unpublished paper (21 June 1960), p. 6.

63 Klompe, Interviews with Lindie Clark.

64 G. J. Dusseldorp cited in John Child (Minute secretary), 'Minutes', Industrial Relations Society Symposium on Overseas Companies in Australia: Their Impact on Industrial Relations (Stawell Hall, Sydney, 1 April 1959), p. 3.

65 Patricia Huntley, 'Interview with the Founder of the Lend Lease Corporation: Mr G. J. (Dick) Dusseldorp', *Industrial Relations & Management Letter*, 9 March 1984, 18.

66 Dusseldorp, 'Law of Triviality', p. 429.

67 G. J. Dusseldorp cited in Child, 'Minutes', p. 3.

68 Ibid., p. 4.

69 Ibid.

70 Ibid.

71 G. J. Dusseldorp, 'Industrial Relations', Notes for a speech on industrial relations, Industrial Relations Society Symposium, 'Overseas Companies in Australia: Their Impact on Industrial Relations' (Sydney, 1 April 1959).

72 G. J. Dusseldorp cited in Child, 'Minutes', p. 4.

73 Dusseldorp, 'Industrial Relations'.

74 Ibid.

75 Ibid.

76 Ibid.
77 'Building Unions in Incentive Pact with Big Company', *Sydney Morning Herald*, 17 October 1958.
78 'New Agreement Makes History in Building'.
79 Jane Richardson, 'Building Goodwill with a Profitable Pact', *Australian*, 17 August 1981.
80 Building Trades Unions (NSW) and Civil & Civic Contractors Pty Ltd, *Productivity Agreement* (1958), Preamble.
81 Mac Donald, Interviews with Lindie Clark.
82 Sharkey, Interview with Lindie Clark.
83 Building Trades Unions (NSW) and Civil & Civic Contractors Pty Ltd, *Productivity Agreement*, Clause 1.
84 Ibid., Clauses 1(g), 9. The latter clause was changed to a commitment to weekly hire in the 1960 version of the agreement. Civil & Civic Pty Ltd, 'Employees Handbook' (c. 1961), Clause 9; 'NSW Productivity Agreement Renewed', *Link* 4:4 (October 1960).
85 Building Trades Unions (NSW) and Civil & Civic Contractors Pty Ltd, *Productivity Agreement*, Clause 2(a).
86 Calculated from the State On-site Award Rates for the 'lower grade' of builders labourer as at December 1957, cited in the *Builders Labourers' Journal*, December 1957.
87 Mac Donald, Interviews with Lindie Clark. The complicated formula by which the actual 'savings' would be calculated—based on the difference between expected and actual labour costs—was spelt out in the agreement.
88 Peter Ciacciarelli, Interview with Lindie Clark (Concord, 21 July 2000).
89 G. J. Dusseldorp, 'Building Trades Group—Civil & Civic Agreement', Company circular to all employees (internal company document, c. 1959).
90 Dusseldorp, 'Industrial Relations'.
91 Mac Donald, Interviews with Lindie Clark.
92 Dusseldorp, 'Building Trades Group—Civil & Civic Agreement'.
93 Quoted in Richardson, 'Building Goodwill with a Profitable Pact'.
94 Quoted in 'Spotlight on Vince (Banjo) Patterson', *Link*, October 1959.
95 'It has already led to much better feeling between the firm and its workers,' he said. 'It has meant better wages for building workers; it has given workers a feeling of security in employment because of the three months' guarantee; it has given workers a feeling of safety because of its free insurance cover; it has given progressively minded building workers a chance to improve themselves under the free training schemes. More important still, it promises better things for the future … I wish other firms would adopt the practice.' F. McCauley, cited in *Link*, 3:7 (January–February 1960), p. 1.
96 Sharkey, Interview with Lindie Clark.
97 Ibid.
98 G. J. Dusseldorp, 'Chairman's Retirement Address', Lend Lease Corporation Limited, 31st Annual General Meeting (Sydney, 27 October 1988), p. 1. The rest of the construction industry would be 'dragged unwillingly' into an

industry-wide superannuation scheme in 1984. Gerard Noonan, 'Australia's Most Admired Corporations: The Ways of IBM and Lend Lease', *Australian Financial Review*, 18 February 1985.

99 Lend Lease—the new company Dusseldorp floated on the Australian Stock Exchange in 1958—acquired Civil & Civic from its Dutch parent firm in 1961.

100 Pat Clancy (BWIU) and Steve Black (BLF), cited in Richardson, 'Building Goodwill with a Profitable Pact'.

101 Joe Purcell, Interview with Lindie Clark (North Ryde, 14 July 2000).

102 Sharkey, Interview with Lindie Clark.

103 G. J. Dusseldorp, Interviews with Lindie Clark.

104 While safety remained the responsibility of site management, the roving safety advisers would assist them by carrying out inspections, providing advice, assisting with planning prior to a job, liaising with government and unions on safety, and conducting on-site education.

105 G. J. Dusseldorp, Interviews with Lindie Clark. When, in December 1959, Civil & Civic won its first major construction job in central Melbourne, a 26-storey office building for Consolidated Zinc Corporation that would be the city's tallest, the company's full safety armour was donned for the project. Before work started, an Executive Safety Committee (comprising senior management of both Civil & Civic and the client) planned the safety campaign. The various unions gave the program strong support, a host of hazard-reduction measures were put in place, and an on-site committee monitored conditions. When the ConZinc tower was completed in early 1962, its low accident rate won Civil & Civic a National Safety Council Award, the first of many such awards for the company. Ian McDonald, Safety Officer on the ConZinc site, cited in 'Safety on Melbourne's Tallest Building: Outstanding Record for Zinc Corporation Job', *Link*, June 1961; 'Safety Pennant Award: Big Moment for Top Vic. Safety Officer', *Link*, November 1961; Lend Lease Corporation Ltd, *5th Annual Report* (Sydney, Lend Lease Corporation Ltd, 1962), p. 11.

106 Sharkey, Interview with Lindie Clark.

107 Purcell, Interview with Lindie Clark. Purcell, who started with the company as 'an ordinary plumber', rose to Leading Hand Plumber on the company's Australia Square project in the 1960s, Foreman Plumber on the MLC Centre in the 1970s, and Site Coordinator on the Bank of New South Wales project in the 1980s.

108 Eric Goodwin, Communications with Lindie Clark (Sydney, 2000–02).

109 Cited in Crispin Wood, 'Pruned Construction Giant Strives for Sustainable Growth', *Business Review Weekly*, 17 November 1997.

110 Lend Lease Corporation Ltd, *Twenty Years: The Lend Lease Story* (Sydney, Lend Lease Corporation Ltd, 1977).

111 Ibid.

112 David Thorne, Interview with Lindie Clark (Sydney, 10 April 2000).

113 Ibid.

114 Alan Cull, Interview with Lindie Clark (Clareville, 19 June 2000).

115 Stuart Hornery, *State of the Nation (August)*, Managing Director's address (Lend Lease Corporation Ltd, internal company document, 1985).

116 Mac Donald, Interviews with Lindie Clark.

117 Hornery, *State of the Nation (August 1985)*.

118 Richardson, 'Building Goodwill with a Profitable Pact'.

119 Lend Lease Corporation Ltd, *26th Annual Report* (Sydney, Lend Lease Corporation Ltd, 1983), p. 31.

120 Mac Donald, Interviews with Lindie Clark.

121 Ibid.

122 Bradley, 'Dusseldorp's Day', p. 10.

123 Frank Cuzzocrea, Interview with Lindie Clark (Concord, 21 July 2000).

124 Klompe, Interviews with Lindie Clark.

125 Meredith Burgmann and Verity Burgmann, *Green Bans, Red Union: Environmental Activism and the NSW Builders Labourers' Federation* (Sydney, University of New South Wales Press, 1998), p. 17.

126 Ibid., emphasis added.

127 Goodwin, Communications with Lindie Clark.

128 Sharkey, Interview with Lindie Clark.

129 Dusseldorp, 'Industrial Relations'.

130 Karl Pahl, Interview with Lindie Clark (Dee Why, 4 August 2000).

131 Dusseldorp, 'Chairman's Retirement Address', pp. 1–2.

132 Ibid., p. 2.

133 Max Weber, *The Protestant Ethic and the Spirit of Capitalism*, trans. Talcott Parsons (London, Unwin University Books, 1967 [1904–05]).

134 Richard H. Tawney, 'Introduction', in *The Protestant Ethic and the Spirit of Capitalism*, ed. Max Weber (London, Unwin University Books, 1967), cited in Dusseldorp, 'Chairman's Retirement Address', p. 2.

135 Dusseldorp, 'Chairman's Retirement Address', p. 3, emphasis in original.

136 Ibid.

137 Lend Lease Corporation Ltd and Australian Council of Trade Unions, 'Memorandum of Understanding Between Company and Unions' (30 October 1972).

138 The profit-share amount started out at 2.5 per cent of profits in 1973, rose to 5 per cent by 1979, and to 7.5 per cent in 1988, the year that Dusseldorp retired.

139 G. J. Dusseldorp and Stuart Hornery, 'State of the Nation (July–August)', *Link*, July–August 1978.

140 Dusseldorp, 'Chairman's Retirement Address', p. 3, emphasis in original.

141 Ibid. For more on the form and impact of employee share ownership in Lend Lease, see Chapter 4.

142 Trevor Sykes, *Two Centuries of Panic: A History of Corporate Collapses in Australia* (North Sydney, Allen & Unwin, 1988), pp. 445–6. The 1970s would be marked by industrial disputation and confrontation on a scale and in a form not seen in the industry before. And, as more than one Royal Commission into the building industry would find, the decade was also marked by graft, corruption, blackmail, and violence on both sides of the industrial fence. J. S. Winneke QC,

Report of the Commissioner Appointed to Inquire into Activities of the Australian Building Construction Employees and Builders Labourers Federation (Canberra, Australian Government Publishing Service, 1982); Roger Vincent Gyles QC, *Royal Commission into Productivity in the Building Industry in New South Wales, Volume 7: Final Report* (Sydney, Southwood Press, 1992).

143 Alluding to this and similar reactions to his approach, Dusseldorp in his Retirement Address to Lend Lease shareholders and employees would observe: 'peer reaction to our actions was almost universally negative, for our practices involve a system of relationships between shareholders and employees that is sharply at variance with conventional wisdom. Indeed it required of us as pioneers breaking from the net that capitalism had woven, all of the originality, self-confidence and tenacity of purpose as Tawney had predicted it would.' Dusseldorp, 'Chairman's Retirement Address', p. 4.

144 When, some ten years down the track, the MBA asked Civil & Civic to rejoin the association (fee-free), the company accepted the olive branch and did so. Mac Donald, Interviews with Lindie Clark.

145 Robert J. L. Hawke, Interview with Lindie Clark (Sydney, 25 August 2000).

146 Robert J. L. Hawke, 'Foreword', in *Link: Commemorative Issue to Mark the Retirement of the Chairman of Lend Lease Corporation, G. J. Dusseldorp* (Sydney, Lend Lease Corporation Ltd, 1988).

147 Hawke, Interview with Lindie Clark.

148 Dusseldorp, 'Chairman's Retirement Address', p. 4.

149 Ibid., pp. 4–6.

150 Ibid., p. 6.

151 Ibid.

3 Business Development

1 G. J. Dusseldorp, Interview with Monica Penders (1995).

2 Ibid.

3 G. J. Dusseldorp, Interviews with Lindie Clark (Sydney, 7–15 September 1999).

4 G. J. Dusseldorp, Interview with Tjerk Dusseldorp (Middle Cove, March 1973); G. J. Dusseldorp, Interviews with Lindie Clark.

5 Although all three parties came out well from the Caltex House experience, the one on top was undoubtedly the AMP: with virtually no effort on its part, the life office secured a rental income stream from a premier class tenant that would continue, guaranteed, for at least 40 years into the future.

6 Dusseldorp, Interview with Tjerk Dusseldorp.

7 'Long-Term Aims of Civil & Civic Contractors Pty Ltd', Memorandum to directors, Civil & Civic Contractors Pty Ltd, internal company files: L-C1.1 Directorate (c.1957), p. 7.

8 G. J. Dusseldorp, Interviews with Lindie Clark; Barbara Martinez, 'Dick Dusseldorp, Lend Lease', in *ArchE+/BBZine. The Chronicle of Architecture in Competitions, Polemics, Commercials, Trivia, and Other Nonsense* <http://www.bbzine.com/archeplus/extension01/BBZext103.html>, 22 December 1999.

9　The name Lend Lease was later chosen by Dusseldorp to describe the main activities of the new organisation. Half a dozen other names he had earlier proposed had been turned down by the Australian regulator as they were too close to those of other ventures. Dusseldorp was not aware at the time that the term 'lend-lease' had been used to described the multi-billion dollar loans program through which the US provided aid to the allies during World War II. G. J. Dusseldorp, Interviews with Lindie Clark; John Montague Rothery, Interviews with Lindie Clark (Mosman, 1 and 15 June 2000; 11 January 2001).

10　Dusseldorp, Interview with Monica Penders; G. J. Dusseldorp, Transcript of interview with Mary Murphy (Sydney, 24 August 1981), p. 5.

11　Charles Herbert Locke et al., 'Lend Lease Corporation Limited. Prospectus', For initial public float (Sydney, 23 April 1958), p. 2.

12　Charles A. Ord and Minnett, 'Lend Lease Corporation Ltd (Australia)', Report. Confidential briefing for use of clients and correspondence only (Sydney, October 1961), p. 3.

13　A couple of such companies, however, had recently gone public to raise capital, including A. V. Jennings and Erwin Graf's Stocks & Holdings. Don Garden, *Builders to the Nation: The A .V. Jennings Story* (Melbourne, Melbourne University Press, 1992), p. 93; Robert Harley, 'Graf Steps Down from Stockland Helm', *Australian Financial Review*, 12 October 2000. Real estate firm L. J. Hooker had gone public in 1947, but it was not until 1958 that it established the L. J. Hooker Investment Corporation Ltd as the group's main vehicle for property development. Frank Lowy's float of Westfield came a couple of years later, in 1960.

14　Oscar Gimesy, *Built from Nothing: A History of the Building Industry in Australia* (Carlton, Vic., Building Careers Resource Centre of Australia, 1992), p. 184.

15　De Vries was also the Managing Director of Civil & Civic's Dutch parent company, Bredero's Building Company.

16　Keith Fleming, Interview with Lindie Clark (Eastwood, 26 May 2000).

17　G. J. Dusseldorp, Interviews with Lindie Clark.

18　The Mutual Life & Citizens' Assurance Company Ltd.

19　Milton Herbert Allen, Interview with Lindie Clark (Waitara, 22 May 2000). Keith Steel was the man within AMP who had persuaded the life insurance company to back Dusseldorp in the development of Caltex House. Having joined the AMP Society in 1934 as a junior clerk and typist, Steel went on to become its NSW Manager (the job he held when Dusseldorp wanted him to join the Lend Lease board), and eventually General Manager in 1966. Geoffrey Blainey, *A History of the AMP, 1848–1998* (St Leonards, NSW, Allen & Unwin, 1999).

20　It took a little while for other financial institutions to follow the MLC's lead—the AMP, for example, did not buy into Lend Lease until February 1962—but by 1964 large investors accounted for 68 per cent of the company's issued capital (up from 54 per cent in 1962). Sydney Stock Exchange Limited. Research and Statistical Bureau, 'Lend Lease Corporation Ltd', *Company Review* L43 (c.1965); G. J. Dusseldorp, 'Chairman Reviews Co. History: Solid Base for Future', *Link*, September–October 1964.

21 Robert Gottliebsen, 'The Prince of Property', *Business Review Weekly*, 21 December 1990, p. 34.

22 G. J. Dusseldorp, Interviews with Lindie Clark.

23 From Civil & Civic came Dusseldorp himself, Jan de Vries, and John Rothery. The other foundation directors of Lend Lease were: C. H. (Bert) Locke, a director of several well-established Australian public companies; R. L. (Bob) Taylor QC; and R. H. Chapman, the recently retired manager of the main Sydney city branch of the Australia & New Zealand Bank Limited. Locke, et al., 'Lend Lease Corporation Limited. Prospectus'. Bert Locke was the Chairman of Lend Lease for its first three years of operation, and he remained a director of Lend Lease until his death in 1977, but in 1961 Dusseldorp took over as Chairman. Initially Dusseldorp also retained the role of chief executive of Lend Lease, but in 1965 Bill Leavey became Managing Director of the corporation (having shared the role with David Elsworth since 1964), a position he would hold until retirement some 12 years later. Leavey was succeeded as Managing Director by Stuart Hornery in 1978; in 1988, on Dusseldorp's retirement, Hornery became Chairman of the group.

24 'Lend Lease: H.P. for Buildings. A Critical Look', *Australian Financial Review*, 1 May 1958.

25 Westpac Banking Corporation, 'Westpac: Australia's First Bank', in About Us. Our Proud History <http://www.westpac.com.au/internet/publish.nsf/Content/WIAWAU+Our+Proud+History>, 2001.

26 Sydney Stock Exchange Limited. Research Service, 'Lend Lease Corporation Ltd', *Company Review* L43 (c.1978).

27 'Lend Lease: H.P. for Buildings. A Critical Look'.

28 Headline cited in Mary Murphy, *Challenges of Change: The Lend Lease Story* (Sydney, Lend Lease Corporation Ltd, 1984), p. 32.

29 'A Critical Look: The End of an Era for Lend Lease', *Australian Financial Review*, 9 March 1964, 8.

30 'Lend Lease: H.P. for Buildings. A Critical Look'.

31 Rothery, Interviews with Lindie Clark.

32 Locke et al., 'Lend Lease Corporation Limited. Prospectus'.

33 Murphy, *Challenges of Change*, p. 31.

34 Lend Lease Corporation Ltd, 'Shareholding at 15th May 1958' (internal company document, 15 May 1958).

35 'Two Good Beginnings', *Australian Financial Review*, 22 May 1958.

36 Lend Lease Corporation Ltd, *Annual Report* (Sydney, Lend Lease Corporation Ltd, various years).

37 'Company Profile. Lend Lease Corporation', *Financial Standard* 117:2942 (18 October 1961), p. 18. Indeed, those Day One investors who had stuck with the stock, and sold sufficient rights to take up new share issues, now held, after four years, an investment worth ten times its initial cost. Deduced from Lend Lease Corporation Ltd, *31st Annual Report* (Sydney, Lend Lease Corporation Ltd, 1988).

38 'Company Profile', pp. 17–18.

39 Gottliebsen, 'The Prince of Property', p. 34.

40 Lend Lease Corporation Ltd, *4th Annual Report* (Sydney, Lend Lease
    Corporation Ltd, 1961), p. 6.
41 Murphy, *Challenges of Change*, p. 59.
42 While most of Lend Lease's new acquisitions would prove profitable in the long
    term, some required a major overhaul and experienced a few lean years before
    they started to contribute to group earnings.
43 Trevor Sykes, *Two Centuries of Panic: A History of Corporate Collapses in
    Australia* (North Sydney, Allen & Unwin, 1988), p. 310.
44 Dusseldorp, 'Chairman Reviews Co. History'.
45 Lend Lease Corporation Ltd, *4th Annual Report*, p. 4.
46 Ibid., p. 5.
47 Lend Lease Corporation Ltd, *4th Annual Report*; Lend Lease Corporation Ltd,
    5th Annual Report (Sydney, Lend Lease Corporation Ltd, 1962). Even though
    shareholder capital increased significantly in both years, the ratio of net profits
    on average paid-up capital dipped only slightly in both these years.
48 Gottliebsen, 'The Prince of Property', p. 35.
49 The survey of 377 Fortune 500 companies who had lived through industry
    slumps and economic recessions over the past decade was conducted by
    Bain & Company. Its findings are reported in Darrell Rigby, 'How to
    Survive the Bad Times', *Australian Financial Review BOSS Magazine* 2:7
    (July 2001).
50 Ibid., p. 48.
51 Lend Lease Corporation Ltd, *Twenty Years: The Lend Lease Story* (Sydney, Lend
    Lease Corporation Ltd, 1977).
52 Stuart Hornery describing Dusseldorp's business philosophy at 'Lend Lease
    Corporation Annual General Meeting' (Sydney, Transcript produced by John P.
    Nolan Professional Reporting Services, 27 October 1988), pp. 2–3.
53 Stuart Hornery, 'Message from the Chairman', in *Annual Report 1999* (Sydney,
    Lend Lease Corporation Ltd, 1999).
54 Ibid.
55 G. J. Dusseldorp, Interviews with Lindie Clark.
56 Christopher Palmer-Tomkinson, 'Tribute to Dik Dusseldorp', Eulogy, Memorial
    Service for G. J. Dusseldorp (London, 26 June 2000), p. 3.
57 Ibid.
58 Jack Klompe, Interviews with Lindie Clark (Sydney, 13 April 2000; 11 January
    2001).
59 G. J. Dusseldorp, 'Key Presentation', AIC Conference (Charter Suite, Waldorf
    Hotel, Aldwych, London, 25 September 1996), p. 3.
60 Klompe, Interviews with Lindie Clark.
61 David Thorne, Interview with Lindie Clark (Sydney, 10 April 2000).
62 G. J. Dusseldorp, *Chairman's Address*, Lend Lease Corporation Ltd, 17th Annual
    General Meeting (Sydney, 1974).
63 Between 1974 and 1988, the year Dusseldorp retired, Lend Lease's ratio of total
    borrowings to total assets averaged just under 14 per cent. Calculated from data
    in Lend Lease *Annual Reports*.
64 Sykes, *Two Centuries of Panic*, pp. 434 ff.

65 Ibid., pp. 437–8.
66 Lend Lease Corporation Ltd, *Twenty Years*.
67 G. J. Dusseldorp in G. J. Dusseldorp and Stuart Hornery, Lend Lease Video 1980.
68 G. J. Dusseldorp, cited in Sykes, *Two Centuries of Panic*, p. 437.
69 Sykes, *Two Centuries of Panic*, p. 437.
70 Ibid., p. 438.
71 In the four months between July and October 1974, five major property companies collapsed: Home Units Australia Ltd, Mainline Corporation, Cambridge Credit Corporation, Landall, and Keith Morris. A dozen more large property developers and/or financiers would follow them before the 1970s were out. Ibid., pp. 434, 467 ff.
72 Thorne, Interview with Lindie Clark.
73 Ken McGrath, Interview with Lindie Clark (Abbotsford, 29 May 2000).
74 Patricia Huntley, 'Interview with the Founder of the Lend Lease Corporation: Mr G. J. (Dick) Dusseldorp', *Industrial Relations and Management Letter*, 9 March 1984, p. 16.
75 Thorne, Interview with Lindie Clark.
76 Ibid.
77 Ern Mac Donald, Interviews with Lindie Clark (Sydney, 2000–02).
78 G. J. Dusseldorp, Interviews with Lindie Clark.
79 Helen Stevenson to Mr W. M. Leavey, General Manager, Civil & Civic Pty Ltd, internal company files (Sydney, 10 April 1961). It was Civil & Civic policy to share with clients any savings on the original estimate for a Design & Construct job: one-third to the client, two-thirds to Civil & Civic. Mac Donald, Interviews with Lindie Clark. On the Loreto job, however, all the savings were returned to the client.
80 In accordance with the Marketing Plan, the state branches of the company surveyed all private schools, asking about their future building plans and the level of proposed expenditure. Survey returns were analysed to segment and prioritise the prospective market. A tailored marketing brochure was mailed and Civil & Civic branch staff made personal approaches to likely schools. Meanwhile, Dusseldorp and his senior executives made contact with church funding bodies in the private school sector. By the mid-1960s the flow of work thus generated justified establishment of a specialist Education Building Division in Civil & Civic. An educational policy consultant was engaged to advise the company, and overseas visits ensured the company kept up to date with best practice internationally.
81 Murphy, *Challenges of Change*, p. 141; Huntley, 'Interview with G. J. (Dick) Dusseldorp', p. 17.
82 Palmer-Tomkinson, 'Tribute to Dik Dusseldorp', p. 1.
83 Colin F. Moore, Interview with Lindie Clark (St Ives, 29 June 2000).
84 Ibid.
85 John Wallace Overall, *Canberra: Yesterday, Today, and Tomorrow. A Personal Memoir* (Fyshwick ACT, Federal Capital Press of Australia, 1995), p. 54; John Wallace Overall, Interview with Lindie Clark (Canberra, 16 June 2000).

86 Dusseldorp, Interview with Tjerk Dusseldorp.
87 Sir Robert Menzies (1972) *The Measure of the Years*, p. 143, cited in Overall, *Canberra: Yesterday, Today, and Tomorrow*, p. 31.
88 Dusseldorp, Interview with Tjerk Dusseldorp.
89 Dusseldorp, Transcript of interview with Mary Murphy, p. 7.
90 Neither deterred Dusseldorp. On the contrary, he figured that such measures were in everyone's interests as they lessened the uncertainty of development. 'The bulk of the building was determined by the plans. So you knew exactly what you could do with the site. But you also knew exactly what your neighbour could do … It took the lottery element out of [the development process].' Dusseldorp, Interview with Tjerk Dusseldorp. So persuaded was he of the system's advantage that in the early 1970s Dusseldorp would push— unsuccessfully—for the leasehold system to be extended to all non-residential land in Australia.
91 Overall, Interview with Lindie Clark.
92 Overall, *Canberra: Yesterday, Today, and Tomorrow*, p. 69.
93 Dusseldorp, Interview with Tjerk Dusseldorp.
94 Dusseldorp, Transcript of interview with Mary Murphy, pp. 7–8.
95 Dusseldorp, Interview with Tjerk Dusseldorp.
96 Dusseldorp, Transcript of interview with Mary Murphy, p. 8.
97 '£5 Million Building Planned for Canberra', *Sydney Morning Herald*, 9 September 1960.
98 Murphy, *Challenges of Change*, p. 65.
99 '£5 Million Building Planned for Canberra'.
100 'The Man to Change Our City Landscape', *The Territorial*, 6 July 1961.
101 'Lend Lease or its offshoot Civil & Civic bid for all the buildings it could get its hands on in Canberra,' Sir John Overall would later record in his memoirs. 'In the early 1960s, wherever you looked in Canberra there were Civil & Civic signs plastered over building sites.' Overall, *Canberra: Yesterday, Today, and Tomorrow*, pp. 69–70.
102 Ibid., p. 69.
103 Dusseldorp, Interview with Tjerk Dusseldorp.
104 Klompe, Interviews with Lindie Clark.
105 Ibid.
106 Jack Klompe, 'Refinancing of Projects', Lend Lease Property Development Course (Sydney, Lend Lease Corporation Ltd, February 1969).
107 Klompe, Interviews with Lindie Clark.
108 G. J. Dusseldorp, *State of the Nation*, Transcript of Chairman's Address (Sydney, Lend Lease Corporation Ltd, internal company document, 1977), p. 3; Klompe, 'Refinancing of Projects'.
109 Advantages accrued to both parties to the arrangement, as Dusseldorp explains. 'The institutions picked up the capital gains and we earned cash on no investment for very long terms.' Dusseldorp, 'Key Presentation', pp. 3–4.
110 Klompe, Interviews with Lindie Clark.
111 Dusseldorp, Interview with Tjerk Dusseldorp.

112 John Morschel, Interview with Lindie Clark (Greenwich, 25 July 2000).

113 G. J. Dusseldorp in Dusseldorp and Hornery, Lend Lease Video 1980.

114 Guy R. Corrigall, 'A Report on Lend Lease Corporation Ltd', MBA thesis University of Sydney, 1982. With a market capitalisation of almost $100 million, Lend Lease was almost twice the size of its nearest competitor, L. J. Hooker ($56 million). Ibid., Table: Australian property developers—financial standing as at 30th June 1971.

115 Lend Lease Corporation Ltd, *14th Annual Report* (Sydney, Lend Lease Corporation Ltd, 1971).

116 Huntley, 'Interview with G. J. (Dick) Dusseldorp', p. 21, emphasis added.

117 Ibid., p. 21.

118 Ibid.

119 Dusseldorp, 'Key Presentation', p. 6.

120 Management fees, paid to the Lend Lease subsidiary set up to manage the GPT on behalf of the independent trustee, were only payable if the Trust earned over a set percentage (initially 8.5 per cent) for the unitholders, with returns above this amount shared between the manager and unitholders. Murphy, *Challenges of Change*, p. 138. On at least four occasions, Dusseldorp voluntarily lowered the management fee because he believed that Lend Lease was getting too much at the expense of the Trust's investors. Geoff McWilliam, Interview with Lindie Clark (Sydney, 1 August 2000). The other potential conflict of interest (that relating to the selection of properties which GPT would invest in) was guarded against by requiring an independent market appraisal of the property's value, and vesting the decision-making authority on investments and divestments with the independent Trustee. Lend Lease Management Limited, *General Property Trust. Letter of Offer 27 May 1981 to Unitholders. 16th Issue of 45,800,000 Units at $1.56 Each* (Sydney, Lend Lease Corporation Ltd, 1981), p. 7. Dusseldorp strictly enforced these provisions, often driving harder bargains on behalf of GPT unitholders in regard to the purchase of Lend Lease properties than the corporation's Property Division felt it was able to get with external organisations. Morschel, Interview with Lindie Clark.

121 Bill Webster, Interview with Lindie Clark (Roseville, 3 July 2000).

122 Property syndicates, which were first set up in Australia in the mid-1960s, were small syndicates of investors that would come together to buy a property such as a small shopping centre. Unlisted property trusts differed from property syndicates in that they were larger and more diversified in their portfolio but they still stumbled on the same hurdle. Because these securities could not be exchanged on a market, unit-holders in such trusts were exposed to what John Morschel describes as 'the disastrous situation' whereby, if the economy took a dive, 'they couldn't redeem their units at the very time they wanted to, because the property values were down'. Morschel, Interview with Lindie Clark. Meanwhile, in the absence of a market, buy-back provisions incumbent on the Trustee also put the latter in an invidious position. The Trustee was building up what Dusseldorp describes as a 'horrendous liability' which, in the event of a run on funds, 'could wipe you out overnight'. Dusseldorp and Hornery, Lend Lease Video 1980.

123 McGrath, Interview with Lindie Clark.
124 The idea of a property trust in itself was not new—a number of developers, Dusseldorp amongst them, had set up such vehicles in the past—but GPT would be different from these in a couple of key respects. First, unlike earlier trusts it would invest in a diversified *portfolio* of *prime* properties (rather than just a single, or small collection, of smallish buildings). Second, and most importantly, it would be listed on the Stock Exchange, giving unit-holders the ability to easily realise their investment if need be.
125 McGrath, Interview with Lindie Clark.
126 McWilliam, Interview with Lindie Clark.
127 McGrath, Interview with Lindie Clark.
128 McWilliam, Interview with Lindie Clark.
129 Ibid.
130 This strategy did not expose Lend Lease shareholders to any additional risk, as Ken McGrath explains. 'It wasn't a big deal for Lend Lease itself to underwrite the issue because if it failed, we owned [the two properties listed as initial property investments in the prospectus] anyhow.' McGrath, Interview with Lindie Clark.
131 Murphy, *Challenges of Change*, p. 138.
132 Dusseldorp, 'Key Presentation', p. 6.
133 This was ironic in light of the factors that prompted GPT's formation, as Geoff McWilliam recalls. 'Dusseldorp started GPT when he saw the institutions, as he put it, "starting to put their hands in my pocket". They [the institutions] totally shunned GPT at first, but then they all bought back into it, and by the time we got to the end of the 1970s, the institutions were starting to claim back *his* institution!' McWilliam, Interview with Lindie Clark.
134 'General Property Trust's Record Distribution', *Australian Financial Review*, 19 July 1974.
135 General Property Trust, *Annual Report* (Sydney, General Property Trust, 1980).
136 General Property Trust, *Annual Report* (Sydney, General Property Trust, 1987), p. 8.
137 Lend Lease Corporation Ltd, *31st Annual Report*, p. 36.
138 Dusseldorp, 'Key Presentation', p. 7.
139 Russell Lander, 'Five-Year Pattern Holding', *Bulletin*, 30 August 1988.
140 'General Property Trust: Mr Dusseldorp's Amazing Money Machine Lifts Its Sights', *National Times*, 2-7 April 1973.
141 Eric Goodwin, Communications with Lindie Clark (Sydney, 2000–02).

4 Ethical Business Practice and Corporate Governance
1 'Regina v. Martin Earle Kitchener Goode, William Thomas Delauney, Charles Henry Bohen Little, George Allardice Johnstone, Alfred Frederick McGuren, and Murt O'Brien', *Transcript of the trial, 29 March to 15 April* (1965) (Court of Quarter Sessions, Sydney).
2 The account of these events has been compiled by reference to newspaper reports of the charges and the preliminary court hearing, the transcript of the subsequent

trial, and Dusseldorp's personal recollections. Various articles in the *Sydney Morning Herald*, *The Sun*, and *Daily Telegraph*, November 1963 to April 1965; 'Regina v. Goode and Others'; G. J. Dusseldorp, Interviews with Lindie Clark (Sydney, 7–15 September 1999).

3 G. J. Dusseldorp, Interviews with Lindie Clark.

4 The other three aldermen facing charges were acquitted, the judge finding the evidence against two of them not strong enough to support a conclusion that they were parties to the conspiracy, and the jury reaching a similar conclusion in regard to the third. 'Conspiracy Charges: Two Freed' and 'Two Former Aldermen Gaoled for Conspiracy; Third Alderman Freed', *Sydney Morning Herald*, 14 and 16 April 1965. Much to Dusseldorp's dismay, however, the conclusion of the court case did not signal the end of the affair. Because threatening phone calls had been made to McLeod's household, he and his family had been placed under police protection during the course of the trial. But the danger did not end when the sentences were handed down. 'Someone threw a blood-soaked copy of the *Herald* into the front-yard of my guy [McLeod] when the case was over,' says Dusseldorp. There was only one thing for it: McLeod and his family had to be removed from the danger. 'So we sent him and his wife and kids up to ——', says Dusseldorp, 'and they started a new life there.' G. J. Dusseldorp, Interviews with Lindie Clark.

5 G. J. Dusseldorp, Interviews with Lindie Clark.

6 Ern Mac Donald, Interviews with Lindie Clark (Sydney, 2000–02).

7 Cited in Christopher Laszlo and Jeremy Nash, 'Six Facets of Ethical Leadership: An Executive's Guide to the New Ethics in Business', *Journal of Business Ethics and Organization Studies* 6:1 (May 2001).

8 Australian Chamber of Commerce and Industry, 'Corporate Governance and Responsibility', in Policy Statements <http://www.acci.asn.au/>, n.d.

9 McWilliam, Interview with Lindie Clark (Sydney, 1 August 2000).

10 John Morschel, 'Tribute', G. J. Dusseldorp Memorial Service (St Aloysius College Chapel, Sydney, 8 May 2000).

11 G. J. Dusseldorp, Interviews with Lindie Clark.

12 G. J. Dusseldorp, Chairman's Address, cited in Lend Lease Corporation Ltd, *31st Annual Report* (Sydney, Lend Lease Corporation Ltd, 1988), p. 7.

13 G. J. Dusseldorp, Interviews with Lindie Clark.

14 Ibid.

15 'Australia's ESP participation is well behind most of the other OECD countries and it could be argued, up to 30 years behind Japan', according to a submission to the recent parliamentary inquiry into employee share ownership in Australia. Australia. House of Representatives Standing Committee on Employment Education and Workplace Relations, *Shared Endeavours: Inquiry into Employee Share Ownership in Australian Enterprises*, Report (Canberra, Parliament of the Commonwealth of Australia, 2000), p. 24.

16 Cited in Fran Simons, 'A Piece of the Action', *Australian Financial Review BOSS Magazine* 1:5 (July 2000).

17 G. J. Dusseldorp, Interviews with Lindie Clark.
18 Cited in Simons, 'A Piece of the Action'.
19 The parliamentary inquiry into employee share ownership cited above found that alignment of employee and employer interests was a major motivation for many such schemes; it also found, however, that such schemes were largely confined to the managerial and executive ranks. Australia. House of Representatives Standing Committee on Employment Education and Workplace Relations, *Shared Endeavours*.
20 G. J. Dusseldorp, Interviews with Lindie Clark.
21 The latter is run as a Trust, with equal representation of employer and employee trustees. Lend Lease Corporation Ltd, 'Submission on Employee Share Ownership in Australia', House of Representatives Standing Committee on Employment, Education and Workplace Relations, Inquiry into Employee Share Ownership Plans (Parliament House, Canberra, 12 May 1999), p. 2. Although Australia's peak trade union body, the ACTU, has historically been wary of employee share ownership schemes, it has consistently praised those in place at Lend Lease. When, in the early 1990s, the ACTU issued a publication on employee financial participation schemes, it used Lend Lease's Employee Share Acquisition Plan as an example of its preferred model. Australian Council of Trade Unions and Australian Employee Share Ownership Association, *Handle with Care*, Publication on Employee Financial Participation (Melbourne, Australian Council of Trade Unions, 1993), pp. 21–2.
22 Mac Donald, Interviews with Lindie Clark.
23 Lend Lease Corporation Ltd, 'Submission on Employee Share Ownership in Australia', p. 2.
24 'One of the reasons it has run down a bit', says Mac Donald, 'is that the Federal Government, back in the 1980s, introduced a law that said a super fund couldn't hold more than 10 per cent of the *value* of the company's shares—not the *number*, which would have been fair enough, but the *value*—which was crazy because it penalises you: the more successful the company was, the less employees as shareholders could hold.' Mac Donald, Interviews with Lindie Clark.
25 Ibid.
26 G. J. Dusseldorp, Chairman's Address, cited in Lend Lease Corporation Ltd, *31st Annual Report*, p. 7.
27 G. J. Dusseldorp, Interviews with Lindie Clark.
28 G. J. Dusseldorp, 'Chairman's Address', Lend Lease Corporation Limited, 16th Annual General Meeting (Sydney, 12 October 1973); Ian Perkin, 'Reasons Outlined for Pace-Setting Industrial Pact', *Australian Financial Review*, 15 October 1973. 'Our employees' stake in the Company is growing year by year,' Dusseldorp told Lend Lease shareholders in 1974. 'We know of no better way to link the interest of shareholders and employees. In opposition, neither can succeed. Standing together, we cannot fail.' G. J. Dusseldorp, 'Chairman's Address', Lend Lease Corporation Limited, 17th Annual General Meeting (Sydney, 1974).

29 Richard Longes, Interview with Lindie Clark (Sydney, 25 August 2000).
30 David Thorne, Interview with Lindie Clark (Sydney, 10 April 2000).
31 There were seven more bonus issues during Dusseldorp's time as Chairman
    of Lend Lease, and in 1988, the year he retired, shareholders received a fully
    franked bonus dividend of 50 cents, on top of the ordinary dividend, which by
    then had risen to 50 cents. Lend Lease Corporation Ltd, *Annual Report* (Sydney,
    Lend Lease Corporation Ltd, various years).
32 Thorne, Interview with Lindie Clark.
33 Longes, Interview with Lindie Clark.
34 The 1981 annual general meeting of Lend Lease, for example, was held in the
    Concert Hall of the Sydney Opera House. More than 1500 shareholders, and
    their invited guests, were treated to a 'quite extraordinary' evening's
    entertainment of organ recitals, chamber ensembles, wandering minstrels, and
    free food and champagne. 'Last year a variety troupe played and sang for the
    members in the Manufacturers' Pavilion at the showgrounds. The year before
    they were treated to an exclusive performance of *Annie* at Her Majesty's Theatre.
    This time around Lend Lease [put] on its own show', the *Sydney Morning Herald*
    reported. And as the audience was regaled with evidence of the company's
    excellent results and prospects, stockbrokers—wearing red carnations for easy
    identification—wandered throughout the crowd, just in case anyone felt impelled
    to immediately buy more Lend Lease shares. Michael Lawrence, 'That
    Extraordinary Annual Meeting: Lend Lease Family Reunion', *Sydney Morning
    Herald*, 24 October 1981; Roger Covell, 'Mozart not the Only Music to the
    Ears', ibid.; David Wheeler, 'A Rather Extraordinary Annual Meeting: A Night
    at the Opera—but not with Dame Joan', ibid., 17 October 1981.
35 'Dick Dusseldorp', *Australian*, 31 December 1983. Dusseldorp's charismatic
    presence at these annual general meetings was one of the reasons they proved
    so popular. 'The large attendance is due to Mr Dusseldorp's chairmanship and
    rapport with the shareholders', *The Australian* reported, 'just as much as the
    show and snacks which accompany the meeting.' 'Duss had an aura about him
    that was just *so* invigorating,' agrees Lend Lease's Director of Corporate
    Projects, Sharon Goldie. 'People would walk on hot coals or across an ocean for
    him because he just instilled in you that confidence … He would write his own
    speeches for the AGM,' she adds, 'and it's always much more powerful if people
    in those positions do, because they come from the heart and they know what they
    want to say. You could hear a pin drop when he delivered them.' Sharon Goldie,
    Interview with Lindie Clark (Sydney, 7 July 2000).
36 Such themes included his call for broader measures of corporate performance
    than simply profits (1973); the frequently detrimental impact of hostile takeovers
    on employees (1981); and the changing role of women in society (1985).
37 Thorne, Interview with Lindie Clark.
38 Goldie, Interview with Lindie Clark.
39 Frank Lowy, Interview with Lindie Clark (Sydney, 4 April 2001).
40 McWilliam, Interview with Lindie Clark.
41 John Morschel, Interview with Lindie Clark (Greenwich, 25 July 2000).

42 Morschel, Interview with Lindie Clark; Morschel, 'Tribute'.
43 'Lend Lease Corporation Annual General Meeting' (Hilton International Hotel, Sydney, Transcript produced by John P. Nolan, Professional Reporting Services, 25 October 1984), p. 7.
44 Morschel, Interview with Lindie Clark.
45 Lend Lease Corporation Ltd, *27th Annual Report* (Sydney, Lend Lease Corporation Ltd, 1984).
46 Morschel, Interview with Lindie Clark.
47 Dusseldorp, 'Chairman's Address 1973'.
48 Ibid.
49 John Elkington, 'What is the Triple Bottom Line?' in SustainAbility <http://www.sustainability.com/philosophy/triple-bottom/tbl-intro.asp>, c.2001. 'At its narrowest,' Elkington continues, 'the term "triple bottom line" is used as a framework for measuring and reporting corporate performance against economic, social and environmental parameters. At its broadest, the term is used to capture the whole set of values, issues and processes that companies must address in order to minimise any harm resulting from their activities and to create economic, social and environmental value.'
50 Recent research conducted for the SustainAbility management consultancy found that 'many companies are convinced that enhanced corporate reputation and brand are among the most significant benefits of superior TBL [triple bottom line] performance'. Lynne Elvins, 'Branding and the Triple Bottom Line', *SustainAbility Radar* March 2000 <http://www.sustainability.com/news/articles/core-team-and-network/lynne-elvins-branding.asp>.
51 Longes, Interview with Lindie Clark.
52 Tjerk Dusseldorp, Communications with Lindie Clark (Sydney, 1999–2002).
53 Harry Seidler, Interview with Lindie Clark (Milson's Point, 23 June 2000).
54 Jennifer Taylor, *Australian Architecture Since 1960* (Red Hill, ACT, National Education Division, Royal Australian Institute of Architects, 1990 [1986]), p. 21.
55 Seidler, Interview with Lindie Clark.
56 Ibid.
57 G. J. Dusseldorp, *State of the Nation. August*, Chairman's Address (Sydney, Lend Lease Corporation Ltd, internal company document, 1983).
58 Eric Goodwin, Communications with Lindie Clark (Sydney, 2000–02).
59 G. J. Dusseldorp, Interviews with Lindie Clark.
60 Lend Lease Corporation Ltd and Australian Council of Trade Unions, 'Agreement Between Lend Lease Corporation and the ACTU' (19 March 1981).
61 G. J. Dusseldorp, Interviews with Lindie Clark.
62 Ibid.
63 Thorne, Interview with Lindie Clark.
64 G. J. Dusseldorp, Interviews with Lindie Clark.
65 Kaye Schofield, *'You Can Make a Difference': The Story of the ACTU–Lend Lease Foundation, 1980–2000* (Sydney, Pot Still Press, 2000), p. 22.
66 G. J. Dusseldorp, 'Integrate or Perish', Nottingham Urban Regeneration Conference (Nottingham, 25 February 1994), p. 2.

67 Schofield, *'You Can Make a Difference'*, p. 2. This publication discusses the origins of the ACTU–Lend Lease Foundation, including the set-up of the group training schemes, and also provides an overview of other employment and training-related programs subsequently developed by the Foundation.
68 Dusseldorp, *State of the Nation. August 1983*.

5 Organisational Overhaul
1 Trevor Sykes, *The Bold Riders: Behind Australia's Corporate Collapses* (St Leonards, Allen & Unwin, 1994), p. 563.
2 Ibid., p. xvii.
3 Milton Herbert Allen, Interview with Lindie Clark (Waitara, 22 May 2000).
4 Ibid.
5 When the shareholdings of a handful of separate trustee companies started to rise in the late 1960s, Allen had become suspicious. 'They were even-pegging,' he says, 'and that *never* happens unless there's a common denominator. And the trading was happening at a sufficient volume to suggest that someone with plenty of money was behind it.' It didn't take Allen long to come to the conclusion that an overseas company was mounting a front from which to launch a raid. 'So I was able then to present Fred Deer—who was General Manager of the MLC at the time—with the details, and he hopped off to Canberra and saw the then Prime Minister, and he promptly amended the Life Insurance Act to limit the proportion of shares that any overseas holding can hold to 15 per cent. So that brought the Sun Alliance Assurance Group of England out of the gloom.' Ibid.
6 Ibid.
7 Ibid.
8 Robert Gottliebsen, 'The Prince of Property', *Business Review Weekly*, 21 December 1990, p. 36.
9 Stuart Hornery, Communications with Lindie Clark (Sydney, 2000–02). The links were also personal. Milton Allen, who had represented the MLC's interests on the Lend Lease Board since 1959, had risen to become Deputy Chairman of both companies, and he and Dusseldorp were friends as well as business associates.
10 Milton Herbert Allen, 'Chairman's Address', The MLC Limited. 21st Annual General Meeting (Sydney, 20 May 1983), p. 1.
11 Hornery, Communications with Lindie Clark. 'White knight', used in this context, means 'a company … who is friendly to a company under threat from a corporate raider and is willing to purchase its shares to protect the current ownership'. *The Macquarie Concise Dictionary* (Sydney, Macquarie Library, 1998).
12 Hornery, Communications with Lindie Clark.
13 Ibid. The story of the 'dry holes in Bass Strait' is told in Chapter 4.
14 Ibid.
15 Part of the problem with the company's initial US ventures was cyclical— property markets around the world were in dire straits in the mid-1970s—but there had been strategic management errors as well. 'What [Dusseldorp] was

trying to build in the US was virtually a mimic of Lend Lease in Australia,' says John Morschel, who, as then head of construction firm Civil & Civic, was called in to review a number of the more problematic American projects. 'But there were some development problems, and some construction contracts that caused a bit of a problem—and we were probably trying to operate on too many fronts at once. I think the other thing was that we hadn't fully appreciated what the support mechanism of the total Lend Lease machine was in Australia. We had taken people out of the second or third level down within the Australian organisation and plonked them in a new country to start a business—it was the wrong thing to do. I think that now it has been realised that you've got to take people from the very top if you want to do that.' John Morschel, Interview with Lindie Clark (Greenwich, 25 July 2000). Once these problems were addressed, however, Lend Lease went on to grow dramatically in the US market. In fact, by 1999 Lend Lease was America's leading institutional real estate investor, with some $US25 billion in assets under management. Paul Armstrong, 'Dutch Courage and Australian Rules in Garden of England', *Financial Times*, 2 July 1999. It also now operates, through Bovis Lend Lease, a successful project management and design and construction business in the United States (the latter subsidiary was project manager for the clean-up of the World Trade Center site in New York City after September 11). Bovis Lend Lease, 'About Us' <http://www. bovislendlease.com/>.

16 Cited in Gottliebsen, 'The Prince of Property', p. 38, emphasis added.

17 Cited in ibid., p. 38.

18 Ibid., p. 35.

19 Financial commentator Trevor Sykes observes that the MLC 'had not guaranteed repayment in any of the prospectuses [issued by H.G. Palmer to raise capital from debentures and notes]. However, it had not prevented Palmer from using the fact that it was a wholly-owned MLC subsidiary as an enticement in prospectuses.' Trevor Sykes, *Two Centuries of Panic: A History of Corporate Collapses in Australia* (North Sydney, Allen & Unwin, 1988), p. 376.

20 Malcolm Maiden, 'Chanticleer. MLC Equities Sell-Off Leaves the Decks Clear', *Australian Financial Review*, 8 August 1984.

21 Philip Rennie, 'Dusseldorp's Highly Profitable New Order at the MLC', *Rydge's*, July 1984, p. 34; Brian Robins, 'Palmer Fiasco Condemned MLC to 2.5pc Penance', *Australian Financial Review*, 28 October 1982.

22 Rennie, 'Dusseldorp's Highly Profitable New Order', p. 34.

23 Hornery, Communications with Lindie Clark.

24 Ibid.

25 Allen, Interview with Lindie Clark.

26 Lloyds International, 'Independent Report', in *Offer to Acquire up to 2,000,000 Ordinary Shares in the Capital of the MLC Ltd for $9.00 Cash Per Share*, (Sydney, Lend Lease Corporation Ltd, 1982), p. 19.

27 Allen, Interview with Lindie Clark.

28 Going to this level was a necessary first step in Lend Lease's acquisition strategy, as John Morschel, then head of Civil & Civic, and later a big player in the

ensuing drama, explains. 'If we had gone over 50 per cent then we would have had to sell the Lend Lease stock out of MLC [as corporations' law prohibited a subsidiary company holding the stock of its parent]. We needed some time to do that—MLC held 16 per cent of Lend Lease stock, remember, and we couldn't sell it immediately—so the first step was to go to 49 per cent. And that went on market bid.' Morschel, Interview with Lindie Clark.

29 Allen, Interview with Lindie Clark.

30 The MLC had, by this time, cancelled all its shares in Lend Lease, as it was required to do by company law (because it was now a subsidiary of Lend Lease). Kevin Forde, 'Lend Lease Aims for as Much Class in Finance as Property', *Rydge's*, October 1985, p. 55.

31 'The best protection was a high share price,' says Hornery, 'only sustainable by continued out-performance. Unlike some other stocks, Lend Lease was not undervalued, so if Brierley had wanted us, we would have been an expensive buy.' Hornery, Communications with Lindie Clark. Furthermore, with employees by that stage owning some 20 per cent of Lend Lease, and with the corporation's shareholders having recently approved a 'poison pill', Brierley would have had his hands full had he decided to take the plunge.

32 Alan Kohler, 'Chanticleer', *Australian Financial Review*, 14 July 1982.

33 Gottliebsen, 'The Prince of Property', p. 38.

34 Hornery, Communications with Lindie Clark.

35 Ken McGrath, Interview with Lindie Clark (Abbotsford, 29 May 2000).

36 Robert Gottliebsen, 'Comment', *Business Review Weekly*, 6–12 November 1982.

37 Cited in Peter Freeman, 'Lend Lease Trims the Fat—and Branches Out', *Sydney Morning Herald*, 15 November 1986, p. 40.

38 Hornery, Communications with Lindie Clark.

39 Having assumed the chairmanship of MLC in July 1982, Milton Allen himself had, on medical advice, stepped down from that role in February 1984, although he remained a director of the company.

40 One of these, Alex Morokoff, was a director (later Deputy Chairman) of Lend Lease; the other, the property developer's finance director, Mark Dowling.

41 The MLC Ltd and the Mutual Life & Citizens' Assurance Company Ltd were given greater independence from each other (with separate boards, different directors, and the institution of arm's-length transactions between them), and loans of policyholder funds 'to the MLC, its shareholders, or any affiliated company of those two groups' were banned. Robins, 'Palmer Fiasco'. (These measures were designed, *inter alia*, to prevent something like the Palmer fiasco happening again.) The restructure also stripped the life office of its other businesses (such as general insurance), so that it could concentrate on its main game (life assurance).

42 G. J. Dusseldorp, *State of the Nation (February)*, Chairman's Address (Sydney, Lend Lease Corporation Ltd, internal company document, 1983), p. 4.

43 Hornery, Communications with Lindie Clark.

44 Morschel, Interview with Lindie Clark.

45 Forde, 'Lend Lease Aims', p. 55.

46 Hornery, Communications with Lindie Clark; MLC, *MLC History Parts 1 & 2* (MLC, internal company video, c. 1999).
47 Gottliebsen, 'Comment', p. 4.
48 Morschel, Interview with Lindie Clark.
49 Dusseldorp cited in Jefferson Penberthy, 'How Dick Dusseldorp Will Tap MLC', *Business Review Weekly*, 6–12 November 1982, p. 11.
50 Cited in MLC, *MLC History Parts 1 & 2*.
51 Ibid.
52 Morschel, Interview with Lindie Clark.
53 McGrath, Interview with Lindie Clark.
54 Ibid.
55 Ibid.; Morschel, Interview with Lindie Clark. Mike Toohey, one of Anderson's principal colleagues, told John Morschel why he found the work he did for Lend Lease on the MLC , 'even to today', one of the most rewarding consulting engagements the firm ever had. 'Firstly they were asked for their view,' relays Morschel. 'Secondly when they gave it, we debated it and agreed what was right and what was wrong and amended the report accordingly. Thirdly, we implemented what they said ... And apparently *that* doesn't happen very often!' Morschel, Interview with Lindie Clark.
56 Morschel, Interview with Lindie Clark.
57 Ibid.
58 McGrath, Interview with Lindie Clark.
59 Morschel, Interview with Lindie Clark.
60 Cited in Ian Muil, 'New-Look MLC Gets Better Deal', *Australian*, 2 August 1983; Malcolm Wilson, 'MLC Parent Aims for a Bigger Bite', *Sydney Morning Herald*, 24 August 1983; Brian Robins, 'Plan to Lift MLC's Share of Mutual Life Distribution', *Australian Financial Review*, 24 August 1983.
61 McGrath, Interview with Lindie Clark.
62 Ibid.
63 Morschel, Interview with Lindie Clark.
64 McGrath, Interview with Lindie Clark.
65 Morschel, Interview with Lindie Clark.
66 McGrath, Interview with Lindie Clark.
67 Morschel, Interview with Lindie Clark.
68 Bill Webster, Interview with Lindie Clark (Roseville, 3 July 2000).
69 Cited in MLC, *MLC History Parts 1 & 2*.
70 Cited in Freeman, 'Lend Lease Trims the Fat'.
71 Morschel, Interview with Lindie Clark.
72 MLC Ltd, *Annual Report 1984* (Sydney, MLC Ltd, 1984), p. 5; John Morschel in 'Lend Lease Corporation Annual General Meeting' (Concert Hall, Sydney Opera House, Transcript, 13 October 1987), p. 19.
73 Morschel, Interview with Lindie Clark.
74 Ibid. Later the MLC's network of tied agents would undergo another transformation, as their role moved away from straight-out sales towards the

provision of financial planning advice. Richard Longes, Interview with Lindie
Clark (Sydney, 25 August 2000).
75 Dusseldorp, *State of the Nation (February 1983)*, p. 3.
76 Ibid.
77 Webster, Interview with Lindie Clark.
78 Cited in MLC, *MLC History Parts 1 & 2*.
79 Dusseldorp, *State of the Nation (February 1983)*, pp. 5–6.
80 Ibid., p. 6.
81 G. J. Dusseldorp in MLC, *MLC Centenary Celebration, 1886–1986*, Video of
live telecast from the Sydney Opera House (MLC Ltd, 1986). In Australia's
'quaint' financial system, he continued, 'the financial services one needs are
scattered over different organisations like fallen leaves. Well, those leaves have
now been gathered into a compact pile which has an MLC sign on top.'
Dusseldorp in MLC, *MLC Centenary Celebration*. To that end, the MLC's new
product range ran the gamut from a residential securitisation offering for old-age
pensioners, through a range of investment funds and unit trusts for 'empty-
nesters', income protection insurance for prime-aged workers and their families,
to a savings plan for the young. Of these, the funds management products would
prove to be particularly profitable, tapping as they did into a market which
burgeoned following the Australian government's introduction of compulsory
superannuation in 1986.
82 Morschel, Interview with Lindie Clark.
83 Cited in MLC, *MLC History Parts 1 & 2*.
84 Lend Lease Corporation Ltd, *28th Annual Report* (Sydney, Lend Lease
Corporation Ltd, 1985), p. 1.
85 Morschel, Interview with Lindie Clark.
86 Webster, Interview with Lindie Clark.
87 Ibid.
88 Longes, Interview with Lindie Clark.
89 Ibid.
90 Morschel, Interview with Lindie Clark.
91 Webster, Interview with Lindie Clark.
92 Morschel, Interview with Lindie Clark.
93 McGrath, Interview with Lindie Clark.
94 'Chanticleer', *Australian Financial Review*, 1 June 1984; Monte Enbysk,
'Getting to Know Frank Russell Co', in Washington CEO <http://www.
washingtonceo.com/archive/feb96/0296-InterBusiness.html>,
February 1996.
95 McGrath, Interview with Lindie Clark. By monitoring well over 1200
money managers internationally, Frank Russell 'maintains one of the most
comprehensive and sophisticated investment-management databases on the
planet', according to *Washington CEO*. Enbysk, 'Getting to Know Frank
Russell Co'.
96 Geoff McWilliam, Interview with Lindie Clark (Sydney, 1 August 2000).

97   Morschel, Interview with Lindie Clark.
98   Jennifer Kitchener, 'What Makes Lend Lease Tick', *Australian Business* 5:22 (4 September 1985), p. 133.
99   Needless to say, the board of the MLC Ltd no longer considered every buy and sell proposition, but was instead briefed on how these external investment managers were performing against benchmarks.
100 Lend Lease Corporation Ltd, *35th Annual Report* (Sydney, Lend Lease Corporation Ltd, 1992), p. 11.
101 Bill Webster in 'Lend Lease Corporation Annual General Meeting 1987'. The built-in diversification of asset classes, regions, sectors and investment management styles embodied in this 'manage the managers' approach was one of the factors that enabled the MLC to ride out the October 1987 stock market crash. 'We came out of it, not *very* well,' says Webster 'but certainly better than the majority.' Webster, Interview with Lindie Clark.
102 Morschel, Interview with Lindie Clark.
103 Stuart Hornery, cited in Christopher Jay, 'People Management and Innovation', *Australian Financial Review*, 20 February 1985.
104 Malcolm Maiden, 'Developer is Forever Renovating Itself', *Sydney Morning Herald*, 10 April 2000.
105 Ian Crow in MLC, *MLC History Parts 1 & 2*. The MLC's Investment Management service has delivered 'consistently higher returns than the average [funds] manager' for the past 14 years. Chris Condon, 'MLC Investment Service (DFM): The Way Ahead', *Keynote. The MLC Investor Magazine* 5 (Winter 2001).
106 Morschel, Interview with Lindie Clark.
107 Gottliebsen, 'The Prince of Property', p. 37.
108 Morschel, Interview with Lindie Clark.
109 Dusseldorp in MLC, *MLC Centenary Celebration*.
110 Ibid. Never one to miss an opportunity, Dusseldorp would use his Centenary Address to outline the MLC's recently overhauled product range, and to encourage policyholders to provide immediate feedback on it to badged MLC staff deployed in venues across the nation.
111 Ibid.; Lend Lease Corporation Ltd, *30th Annual Report* (Sydney, Lend Lease Corporation Ltd, 1987), p. 9.
112 Gottliebsen, 'The Prince of Property', p. 37.
113 Morschel, Interview with Lindie Clark.
114 Allen, Interview with Lindie Clark.
115 Hornery, Communications with Lindie Clark.
116 Webster, Interview with Lindie Clark.
117 Lend Lease Corporation Ltd, *Proposal to Return Part of the Proceeds of MLC Sale to Shareholders*, Proposal to Lend Lease shareholders dated 17 July (Sydney, Lend Lease Corporation Ltd, 2000), p. 11.
118 Maiden, 'Developer is Forever Renovating'.
119 Stuart Hornery, 'Chairman's Report', in *Lend Lease Annual Report 2000* (Sydney, Lend Lease Corporation Ltd, 2000), p. 10.

6 Creative Negotiation

1 Jack Mundey, Interview with Lindie Clark (Croydon Park, 10 July 2000).
2 G. J. Dusseldorp, Interviews with Lindie Clark (Sydney, 7–15 September 1999).
3 Jack Mundey, *Green Bans and Beyond* (London and Sydney, Angus & Robertson, 1981), p. 3.
4 Mundey, Interview with Lindie Clark.
5 Meredith Burgmann and Verity Burgmann, *Green Bans, Red Union: Environmental Activism and the NSW Builders Labourers' Federation* (Sydney, University of New South Wales Press, 1998), p. 3. 'Environmentally injurious constructions' were quite broadly defined to include projects which involved the destruction of parts of the natural, social, and/or cultural fabric of the city. The term 'Green Ban' was itself first coined by Jack Mundey in February 1973, according to the authors of a major study of the BLF's environmental activism in this period, 'to distinguish [the new form of action] from the traditional union black ban imposed by workers "to push their own issues". He [Mundey] argued that the term was "more applicable as they are in defence of the environment".' Ibid., p. 8.
6 The first Green Ban had been placed in the wealthy harbourside suburb of Hunters Hill, where a group of women residents had called on the BLF to, as Mundey tells it, 'put our theory into practice' and help protect a patch of bushland set to be bulldozed to make way for a new private housing development. With that ban successfully imposed in June 1971, others had followed. Two bans were imposed in November that year: one on the Eastlakes housing estate in the inner south-eastern suburbs, where a private developer was reneging on his promise to provide bountiful open space amongst a collection of soaring high-rise towers; the other in the inner-city Rocks district, where the state government looked set to destroy historic buildings and low-cost housing with its plans for a massive high-density commercial and residential redevelopment of the area. More bans followed in the first few months of the New Year, including one on the demolition of a historic church in the heart of the CBD, and another on the construction of the 'forgotten' underground car park for the Sydney Opera House, the building of which would have destroyed some magnificent old fig trees in the Botanic Gardens. Mundey, Interview with Lindie Clark; Mundey, *Green Bans and Beyond*; Burgmann and Burgmann, *Green Bans, Red Union*.
7 The estimate of the value of development projects halted by Green Bans by 1975 is from Burgmann and Burgmann, *Green Bans, Red Union*, p. 4.
8 John McQuaid, Secretary of the Theatrical and Amusements Association, cited in 'Move to Blockade Theatre', *Daily Telegraph*, 1 May 1972.
9 *Sydney Morning Herald*, 3 May 1972, cited in *Save Theatre Royal: Vital Public Meeting*, Pamphlet prepared for the meeting held at the Lower Town Hall, Sydney, 15 May 1972 (Sydney, Save Sydney's Theatre Royal Committee, 1972).
10 Gladys Moncrieff in *Daily Mirror*, 5 May 1972, cited in *Save Theatre Royal*.
11 Editorial, 'The Final Act', *Daily Mirror*, 1 May 1972.
12 Sir Emmett McDermott, Lord Mayor of Sydney, in *Daily Telegraph*, 2 May 1972, cited in *Save Theatre Royal*.

13 Ron Saw, 'Why Save That Old Fleapit?', *Daily Telegraph*, 2 May 1972.
14 Three other large theatres had been pulled down in the past four years, and the Sydney Opera House, which would go some way to making up the deficit, had not been completed. Katharine Brisbane, 'A Royal Requiem, But the Fight Continues', *Australian*, 13 May 1972; Saw, 'Why Save That Old Fleapit'?
15 'Playing Out a Tragedy', *Sun*, 1 May 1972.
16 Mundey, *Green Bans and Beyond*, p. 96.
17 Ibid.
18 Brisbane, 'A Royal Requiem'.
19 Justice Martin Hardie, quoted in 'Meeting Seeks to Save Theatre', *Sydney Morning Herald*, 2 May 1972.
20 Mundey, Interview with Lindie Clark.
21 G. J. Dusseldorp, Interviews with Lindie Clark.
22 Ibid.
23 'Meeting Seeks to Save Theatre'.
24 Brisbane, 'A Royal Requiem'.
25 G. J. Dusseldorp, Interviews with Lindie Clark.
26 'Meeting Seeks to Save Theatre'.
27 'Let's Keep the Devil We Know! Saving Sydney's Theatre Royal', *Review*, 13–14 May 1972.
28 'Dick Dusseldorp Sells a Monument', *Sun Herald*, 31 March 1974. Reflecting on the whole Green Ban movement some years down the track, Dusseldorp would pay tribute to its contribution to protecting Sydney's heritage. 'It stopped a lot of crazy developments,' he said. 'The movement was disorganised, it was irrational at times, but it was a people's movement for a very good reason … because everything was getting trampled down.' G. J. Dusseldorp, Interviews with Lindie Clark.
29 'Let's Keep the Devil We Know!'
30 'Who Speaks for Sydney', *Sun*, 2 May 1972.
31 Editorial, 'Sentence Suspended?', *Sydney Morning Herald*, 3 May 1972.
32 'Theatres', *Daily Telegraph*, 3 May 1972.
33 'Just 3 Years Too Late', *Australian*, 3 May 1972.
34 G. J. Dusseldorp, Interviews with Lindie Clark.
35 Mundey, Interview with Lindie Clark.
36 G. J. Dusseldorp, Interviews with Lindie Clark.
37 'Fight for Royal Ends in Draw', *Sydney Morning Herald*, 16 May 1972.
38 'Approval for New Theatre', *Daily Telegraph*, 16 May 1972.
39 'Plan to Build New Theatre Royal', ibid., 6 May 1972.
40 Ross Thorne, cited in Katharine Brisbane, 'When the Public Gets up and Asserts Itself', *Australian*, 19 May 1972; 'Fight for Royal Ends in Draw'.
41 Burgmann and Burgmann, *Green Bans, Red Union*, p. 239.
42 Mundey, *Green Bans and Beyond*, pp. 97-8.
43 Mundey, Interview with Lindie Clark.
44 Ian Bevan, *The Story of the Theatre Royal* (Sydney, Currency Press, 1993), p. 192.

45 Ibid., p. 194.

46 Ibid.

47 Gregorio Billikopf Encina, 'Creative Negotiation', *Labour Management in Agriculture* <http://www.cnr.berkeley.edu/ucce50/ag-labor/7labor/17.htm>, 2001a.

48 G. J. Dusseldorp, Interviews with Lindie Clark.

49 Gregorio Billikopf Encina, 'Creative Negotiation', in *Agricultural Labor Management*. Articles <http://www.cnr.berkeley.edu/ucce50/ag-labor/7article/article02.htm>, 2001b.

50 For example, Dusseldorp could have tried to circumvent the union's ban on the theatre's demolition, or the Committee might have refused to engage in constructive talks with the developer: both strategies would constitute a 'withdrawal' from negotiation.

51 Encina, 'Creative Negotiation', 2001a, p. 3.

52 Ibid.

53 Encina illustrates this point with the story of the two siblings who argued over which of them would get an orange. They compromised by taking half each: then one ate his half and threw away the peel; the other, who was cooking, grated the peel and threw away the rest of the fruit. Ibid., p. 5.

54 Ibid., p. 2.

55 This had resulted, according to the then Premier of New South Wales, in the 'loss' of some 45,000 homes. William McKell, *Five Critical Years* (Sydney, Australian Labor Party, 1946), p. 100, cited in Peter Spearritt, *Sydney's Century: A History* (Sydney, University of New South Wales Press, 2000), p. 83.

56 The NSW Premier's 1946 estimate put the shortfall at some 90,000 dwellings. McKell, *Five Critical Years*, p. 100, cited in Spearritt, *Sydney's Century*, p. 83.

57 Cumberland County Council, *Economics of Urban Expansion*, Report. December (Sydney, Cumberland County Council, 1958), p. 1.

58 Spearritt, *Sydney's Century*, p. 91.

59 Robert Freestone, 'Sydney's Green Belt, 1945-1960', *Australian Planner* 30:2 (1992), p. 71.

60 Patrick Nicol Troy, *The Perils of Urban Consolidation: A Discussion of Australian Housing and Urban Development Policies* (Leichhardt, NSW, Federation Press, 1996), p. 5; Edward Gough Whitlam, *The Whitlam Government 1972–1975* (Ringwood, Vic., Viking, 1985), p. 379.

61 Freestone, 'Sydney's Green Belt, 1945–1960', p. 72.

62 Troy, *Perils of Urban Consolidation*, p. 1, emphasis in original.

63 Ibid., p. 1.

64 Ibid., p. 6; Max Neutze, *Funding Urban Services: Options for Physical Infrastructure* (St Leonards, NSW, Allen & Unwin, 1997), p. 117.

65 Carolus Theodorus J. Dusseldorp, G. J. (Dick) Dusseldorp's father, cited in Hank Dusseldorp to Lindie Clark (Kithener, Ontario, 8 September 2000).

66 Ten thousand years prior the sea level had risen some 65 metres with the ending of the last Ice Age, drowning the coastal plains of the Sydney basin to form headlands such as that of Sugarloaf Peninsula.

67 Mary Murphy, *Challenges of Change: The Lend Lease Story* (Sydney, Lend Lease Corporation Ltd, 1984), pp. 12–13.
68 Ibid., p. 13.
69 Keith Fleming, Interview with Lindie Clark (Eastwood, 26 May 2000).
70 G. J. Dusseldorp, Interviews with Lindie Clark.
71 A couple of years later Thorne actually joined Dusseldorp's firm as a project engineer, but at that stage—in the mid-1950s—he was employed at the Commonwealth Oil Refinery.
72 David Thorne, Interview with Lindie Clark (Sydney, 10 April 2000).
73 Murphy, *Challenges of Change*, p. 13.
74 G. J. Dusseldorp, Interviews with Lindie Clark.
75 Ibid.
76 Ibid.
77 'Board to Take Over Sewerage System', *Sydney Morning Herald*, 3 November 1959.
78 Dusseldorp's firm's share of the proceeds from the Middle Cove estate were, in fact, the first profits to be entered into the books of his new development company, Lend Lease, in May 1958. Ray Steele, Interview with Lindie Clark (Bonnells Bay, 5 June 2000).
79 G. J. Dusseldorp in G. J. Dusseldorp and Stuart Hornery, Lend Lease Video 1980.
80 Ibid.
81 Lionel G. Milsop, 'The Effect of Land Development on Water and Sewerage Facilities', *Sydney Water Board Journal*, July 1961, p. 53.
82 Ibid., p. 54.
83 Dick Morath, Interview with Lindie Clark (Sydney, 6 July 2000).
84 Milton Herbert Allen, Interview with Lindie Clark (Waitara, 22 May 2000).
85 G. J. Dusseldorp, *The Responsibility of Private Enterprise in the Rebuilding of Australian Cities*, An address to members of Sydney Legacy, July 1961 (Sydney, Lend Lease Corporation Ltd, 1961).
86 Ibid.
87 Ibid. Dusseldorp also viewed the development of planned, integrated estates in new satellite cities as an essential part of the solution to Sydney's growth problems; he was simultaneously developing such an estate at Campbelltown (see Chapter 7).
88 Ibid.
89 Morath, Interview with Lindie Clark.
90 Ibid..
91 Spearritt, *Sydney's Century*, p. 67.
92 Murphy, *Challenges of Change*, p. 48; Alex Ilkin, 'History of Strata Titles in New South Wales', in *Strata Schemes and Community Schemes Management and the Law* (Sydney, Law Book Company, 1998).
93 Spearritt, *Sydney's Century*, p. 67.
94 Murphy, *Challenges of Change*, p. 47.
95 Ibid., p. 48.

96 'Company's Move: Plan for Home Unit Title', *Daily Telegraph*, 14 February 1959, p. 7, emphasis in original.
97 Mr Connor, Member for Wollongong–Kembla, in New South Wales Legislative Assembly, *Conveyancing (Strata Titles) Bill*, Parliamentary Debates. First Reading, 1 December (Sydney, 1959).
98 G. J. Dusseldorp, Interviews with Lindie Clark.
99 Ibid.
100 G. J. Dusseldorp, Transcript of interview with Mary Murphy (Sydney, 24 August 1981).
101 Ibid.
102 G. J. Dusseldorp, Interviews with Lindie Clark.
103 Dusseldorp, Transcript of interview with Mary Murphy.
104 John Montague Rothery, Interviews with Lindie Clark (Mosman, 1 and 15 June 2000; 11 January 2001).
105 Richard Thompson, in New South Wales Legislative Council, *Conveyancing (Strata Titles) Bill*, Parliamentary Debates. Second Reading, 14 March (Sydney, 1961).
106 'I hope that we do not lose sight of this sort of approach. In the past we have not often taken this action but in the future we should seize upon the opportunity to see that people likely to be interested in legislation in a new or more or less experimental form are given similar opportunities to make suggestions and express their views upon it.' Richard Thompson, in ibid.
107 Dusseldorp, Transcript of interview with Mary Murphy.
108 The first building to be registered under the new Strata Title scheme was a Seidler-designed Lend Lease development called Blues Point Tower.
109 New South Wales Department of Fair Trading, *Review of Strata Schemes Management Act 1996*, Issues Paper (Sydney, NSW Consumer Protection Agency, 2000), p. 8.
110 Dusseldorp, Transcript of interview with Mary Murphy; Ken McGrath, Interview with Lindie Clark (Abbotsford, 29 May 2000); Morath, Interview with Lindie Clark; Murphy, *Challenges of Change*, p. 50.
111 G. J. Dusseldorp, Interviews with Lindie Clark.
112 Spearritt, *Sydney's Century*, p. 102. The number of flats and townhouses completed in Sydney in the five-year period 1961–66 (41,000) was almost double that of the previous five-year period (22,000). In 1966–71 the figure jumped again, to 70,000. Spearritt, *Sydney's Century*, Table 5.5, p. 103.
113 New South Wales Department of Fair Trading, *Review of Strata Schemes Management Act 1996*, p. 8.
114 G. J. Dusseldorp, Interview with Tjerk Dusseldorp (Middle Cove, March 1973).

7 Building Communities
1 Robin Boyd, *The Australian Ugliness* (Melbourne, Cheshire, 1960), p. 26.
2 Ibid., p. 141.
3 Ibid., pp. 80–1.
4 Ibid., p. 81.

5 Ibid., p. 9. Although not confined to Australia, Featurism was 'more apparent, all pervasive and devastating in its effect' in that country: ruling 'almost everywhere that man has made his mark on [the] continent', not just in the built environment but in seemingly every item of popular culture. Ibid., pp. 33, 9. What Boyd meant by 'featurism' is best grasped when he contrasts it with its antithesis: a holistic and functional approach to design. Ibid., p. 12.

6 Ibid., p. 33.

7 Ibid., p. 91.

8 Geoffrey Serle, *Robin Boyd: A Life* (Melbourne, Miegunyah Press, 1995), p. 213.

9 Ibid., p. 213.

10 Ibid., p. 220.

11 Peter Spearritt, *Sydney's Century: A History* (Sydney, University of New South Wales Press, 2000), p. 106.

12 Ibid., p. 107.

13 Milo Dunphy writing in *Architecture in Australia* (RAIA), March 1961, March 1962; Elizabeth Durack writing to Robin Boyd, 28 March 1961; Geoffrey Hutton writing in *The Age*, 18 October 1971, all cited in Serle, *Robin Boyd*, pp. 213–20.

14 Milo Dunphy made the initial link, and Serle agrees that White (whose *Riders in the Chariot* was published a few months after *The Australian Ugliness*) was inspired by Boyd's description of the 'Tom Ugly Zone', but that White picked it up from Boyd's earlier newspaper articles, not the book. Serle, *Robin Boyd*, p. 221.

15 Cited in Mary Murphy, *Challenges of Change: The Lend Lease Story* (Sydney, Lend Lease Corporation Ltd, 1984), p. 141.

16 Cited in ibid.

17 Philip Goad, *Melbourne Architecture* (Sydney, Watermark Press, 1999), p. 7.

18 Robin Boyd writing in the Melbourne *Herald*, 30 November 1954, cited in Serle, *Robin Boyd*, p. 151.

19 Boyd, *Australian Ugliness*, pp. 78, 21, 75, 88.

20 Serle, *Robin Boyd*, p. 141.

21 A.V. Jennings is credited as the first to build a 'display house' in Australia—at the Beauville Estate in Victoria in the 1930s—and is still one of the largest project home builders in the country. Anne Gartner, 'Death of the Project House? Reflections on the History of Merchant Builders', in *The Cream Brick Frontier: Histories of Australian Suburbia*, ed. Graeme Davison, Anthony Edward Dingle and Seamus O'Hanlon (Clayton, Vic., Monash Publications in History, 1995), p. 109; Michael Howard, *State, Business and Unions in the Restructuring of the Building Industry in Australia, 1938–52*, Industrial Relations Papers (Canberra, Australian National University Research School of Social Sciences, 1987), p. 89. Robin Boyd himself designed Melbourne's first postwar project home, the 'Peninsula House', for a company called Contemporary Homes, in 1953. Jennifer Taylor, *Australian Architecture Since 1960* (Red Hill, ACT, National Education Division, Royal Australian Institute of Architects, 1990 [1986]), p. 142. Sydney's first such house was designed by Geoffrey Lumsdaine for Sunline Homes in 1960. Taylor, *Australian Architecture Since 1960*, p. 142 fn. 2. The latter

company was subsequently acquired by Lend Lease. Ken McGrath, Interview
with Lindie Clark (Abbotsford, 29 May 2000).

22 Taylor, *Australian Architecture Since 1960*, p. 142. Especially during their heyday
in the 1960s and 1970s, Taylor adds, 'these houses made a lasting contribution
to the suburban life of the middle of the spectrum of the population. From the
Carlingford village to the solar houses [the first of which were designed in the
late 1970s] they have been progressive, passing directly to the general buying
public the advantages of improved design.' Ibid., p. 144.

23 Gartner, 'Death of the Project House?' p. 109.

24 The additional cost per house of putting the lines underground was about $300.
Serle, *Robin Boyd*, p. 291. This represented between 1.4 and 1.8 per cent of the
price of the houses in the village, which ranged from $17,000 to $21,000 at the
time. 'Project Houses Around Australia', *Architecture Today* 8:9 (July 1966),
p. 20. Underground cabling is still rare in Australia, except in the most recent outer
suburban developments, but it was estimated in 1998 that, hypothetically,
a typical suburb whose cables were laid underground would reap an increase in
property values of up to 3 per cent per site. Victoria. Valuer-General, *Valuation
Opinion: The Effect of Putting Cables Underground on Local Residential Property
Values* (Melbourne, Department of Natural Resources and Environment, 1998).

25 Boyd to J. H. Strain, 17 March 1970, letter in the Grounds, Romberg & Boyd
Archive in the La Trobe collection of the State Library of Victoria, cited in Serle,
Robin Boyd, p. 291.

26 Ibid., cited in Serle, *Robin Boyd*, p. 291.

27 Cited in Murphy, *Challenges of Change*, p. 141.

28 Australian Broadcasting Commission, 'Monday Conference—No. 61',
Transcript of interview with Mr G. J. Dusseldorp (Sydney, Australian
Broadcasting Commission, 16 October 1972). The journal *Architecture Today*
featured Appletree Hill Estate, as well as some of Lend Lease's project houses at
Carlingford demonstration village in Sydney, in a 10-page spread called 'Project
Houses Around Australia' in July 1966. Along with other innovative firms such
as Melbourne's Merchant Builders and Sydney's Pettit and Sevitt, Lend Lease
was praised for allowing architects to both 'control the design of their range of
houses' and advise on how each house should be 'correctly orientated [*sic*] to its
site', which in turn resulted in designs which 'represent the step forward in the
project building field and domestic architecture'. 'Project Houses Around
Australia', p. 15.

29 Cited in Murphy, *Challenges of Change*, p. 141, emphasis added. Ironically,
concern about resale value seems to have proved a false worry, at least for the
original buyers. 'Possibly the Boyd designs were ahead of their time', writes
urban historian Sally Wilde, with 'their popularity (and value) [taking] a while to
establish'. But by 1971, she observes, 'houses on Appletree Hill appear to have
been selling at something of a premium'. Sally Wilde, '4. The Pattern of
Subdivision', in *City of Monash: Environmental History, 1946–1995* <http://
www.monash.vic.gov.au/city/section_c4>, 1996.

30 Boyd to J. H. Strain, 17 March 1970, cited in Serle, *Robin Boyd*, p. 291.

31 Australian Broadcasting Commission, 'Monday Conference'.
32 Cited by Bill Webster, Interview with Lindie Clark (Roseville, 3 July 2000). That said, as Lend Lease director Bill Webster recalls, Dusseldorp was not one to countenance mistakes made due to sloppy work or woolly thinking. While he often told his colleagues that he accepted that mistakes were 'part and parcel' of experimenting with new ideas, he made it equally clear that he 'could not abide failure'. 'There was a very big difference in his mind,' says Webster 'and quite rightly in my view, between making mistakes while you're having a shot, and having a failure … because you haven't thought things through properly.' Webster, Interview with Lindie Clark.
33 Lend Lease Corporation Ltd, *Sherwood Hills Residential Neighbourhood at Campbelltown: Planning and Development and the Requirement for Mortgage Finance* (Sydney, Lend Lease Corporation Ltd, 1966).
34 G. J. Dusseldorp, *State of the Nation. August*, Chairman's Address (Sydney, Lend Lease Corporation Ltd, internal company document, 1983).
35 G. J. Dusseldorp, Interviews with Lindie Clark (Sydney, 7–15 September 1999).
36 Ibid.
37 David Thorne, Interview with Lindie Clark (Sydney, 10 April 2000).
38 The other three settlements were located further west or northwest of Sydney, at St Marys, Blacktown, and Riverstone. Graham Jahn, *Sydney Architecture* (Sydney, Watermark Press, 1997), p. 144. For more on the County of Cumberland Plan, see Chapter 6.
39 G. J. Dusseldorp, Interviews with Lindie Clark.
40 Ibid.
41 Cumberland County Council, *Campbelltown: A New City in the County of Cumberland* (Sydney, Cumberland County Council, 1960), p. 19.
42 G. J. Dusseldorp, Interviews with Lindie Clark.
43 Ibid. Given the subsequent success of what would become 'the largest new city project ever attempted in Australia', 'I sure now wish', Dusseldorp adds, 'that they *had* turned me down!' Lend Lease Homes Pty Ltd, *Ambarvale: Yesterday, Today & Tomorrow* (Sydney, Lend Lease Homes Pty Ltd, c. 1975), p. 1; G. J. Dusseldorp, Interviews with Lindie Clark.
44 Lend Lease Corporation Ltd, *3rd Annual Report* (Sydney, Lend Lease Corporation Ltd, 1960), p. 4.
45 Edward Gough Whitlam, *The Whitlam Government 1972–1975* (Ringwood, Vic., Viking, 1985), p. 372. Having spent his own childhood years in well-planned and well-serviced Canberra, the contrast in lifestyle for Gough Whitlam, the author of these remarks, was all the more stark. As a result of his own experience, Whitlam's 'great objective' when he became a parliamentarian was 'to dramatise the deficiencies [in the outer suburbs of Sydney] and devise practical government programs to deal with them'. Ibid. He got the chance to do so when he was elected Prime Minister in 1972.
46 G. J. Dusseldorp, 'The Challenge of Change in the Housing Industry', Address, Annual Convention of Housing Industry Association (Sydney, 2–5 April 1968), pp. 3–4.

47 G. J. Dusseldorp, Interviews with Lindie Clark. As a result of this exercise, he adds, 'the whole landscape just changed, year by year'.

48 Ibid. The rail link would enable residents to commute to jobs in nearby Liverpool and central Sydney—at least until sufficient industries could be attracted into the Campbelltown area—and in the long term, Dusseldorp hoped, it would be used to bring workers and shoppers from other areas into Campbelltown itself. This indeed is what happened when the new station, called Macarthur, was opened in the early 1980s. '$2.6m Station to Serve a Growing Population', *Sydney Morning Herald*, 30 November 1983.

49 G. J. Dusseldorp, Interviews with Lindie Clark.

50 G. Spielman, 'Economics of Various Distributions of the Increasing Population', Speech (c.1958), p. 7.

51 G. J. Dusseldorp, Interviews with Lindie Clark.

52 Lend Lease Homes Pty Ltd, *Ambarvale*, p. 3.

53 So impressed was the incoming Whitlam Labor government with Dusseldorp's demonstrated appreciation of the advantages of leasehold tenure for urban planning purposes that they appointed him to their national Commission of Inquiry into Land Tenures in May 1973.

54 Cumberland County Council, *Campbelltown*, p. 15.

55 Ibid., p. 7.

56 Objectives cited in Lend Lease Corporation Ltd, *Sherwood Hills Residential Neighbourhood at Campbelltown*.

57 Lend Lease Homes Pty Ltd, *Ambarvale*, p. 3.

58 Ibid., p. 5.

59 G. J. Dusseldorp, Interviews with Lindie Clark.

60 Lend Lease Homes Pty Ltd, *Ambarvale*, p. 7.

61 The day after the pool opened, a local historian notes, some 1152 people went through the turnstiles, thus 'proving the need' for the facility. William Alan Bayley, *History of Campbelltown, New South Wales*, revised (Campbelltown, Campbelltown Municipal Council, 1974), p. 184.

62 G. J. Dusseldorp, Interview with Tjerk Dusseldorp (Middle Cove, March 1973).

63 'Sherwood Hills: The Estate of Tomorrow', *Link*, September–October 1974; Lend Lease Homes Pty Ltd, *Ambarvale*, p. 10.

64 Lend Lease Homes Pty Ltd, *Ambarvale*, p. 11.

65 New South Wales State Planning Authority, *The New Cities of Campbelltown, Camden and Appin*, Structure Plan (Sydney, State Planning Authority of NSW, 1973); Robert Meyer, 'Macarthur: Sydney's Successful South Western Satellite?' *Australian Planner* 28:3 (1990).

66 Murphy, *Challenges of Change*, p. 155.

67 In 1961 Campbelltown's population stood at 18,700; by 1986 it had reached 121,297. Carol Liston, *Campbelltown: The Bicentennial History* (North Sydney, Allen & Unwin, 1988), p. 226.

68 The company had built a large proportion of the city's private housing stock— and that 'to a very high standard' according to the government's director of

planning and development for the region. Robert Meyer, 'An Answer to Sprawl', *Royal Australian Planning Institute Journal* 15 (November 1977), p. 119.

69 G. J. Dusseldorp, Interviews with Lindie Clark.

70 Meyer, 'Macarthur'.

71 Ibid., p. 26.

72 A Czech called Tony Sponar, in the early 1950s, had first identified the potential for the area around Thredbo as a ski resort. Sponar, at the time a hydrographer with the Snowy Mountains Authority, had worked as a ski instructor at the Austrian resort of St Anton in an earlier life. When his then employer built the Alpine Way through the mountains as part of the construction of the hydro-electric scheme, a happy by-product for Sponar was to make the Crackenback area more accessible to the skiing public. With Charles Anton, Geoffrey Hughes, and Eric Nicholls, Sponar formed a syndicate in mid-1955 to develop the resort. Businessman Andrew Thyne Reid joined the group a few months later, and when they reorganised into a public company, Reid became the first Chairman of Kosciusko–Thredbo Ltd. In 1957 this company acquired an option on a 99-year lease from the Kosciusko State Park Trust for the land that would become Thredbo village. Kosciusko–Thredbo Pty Ltd, *Thredbo Village Self-Guided Heritage Walk*, Pamphlet (Thredbo, NSW, Kosciusko–Thredbo Pty Ltd, n.d.); Siobhan McHugh, *The Snowy: The People Behind the Power*, 2nd edn (Sydney, Angus & Robertson, 1995 [1989]), p. 257; Derrick Hand, *Report of the Inquest Into the Deaths Arising from the Thredbo Landslide*, Coroner's report (Sydney, 2000), p. 61.

73 Kosciusko–Thredbo Pty Ltd, *Thredbo Village*; Murphy, *Challenges of Change*, p. 103; Freehill Hollingdale & Page, 'Submissions on Historical Issues by the Lend Lease Group of Companies', Coronial Inquest into the Deaths Arising from the Thredbo Landslide (Sydney, May 2000), paragraph 6.25.

74 Australian Skiing and Snowboarding, 'Australian Resorts in 1961', *Chill Factor* 1996 <http://www.chillfactor.com.au/features/archives/61res/>.

75 Murphy, *Challenges of Change*, p. 103.

76 Australian Skiing and Snowboarding, 'Australian Resorts in 1961', p. 1.

77 G. J. Dusseldorp, Interview with Kosciusko–Thredbo Pty Ltd (Thredbo, 1995).

78 Murphy, *Challenges of Change*, p. 102.

79 Australian Skiing and Snowboarding, 'Australian Resorts in 1961'.

80 Colin F. Moore, Interview with Lindie Clark (St Ives, 29 June 2000); Albert Van der Lee, Interview with Lindie Clark (North Sydney, 9 June 2000).

81 Dusseldorp, Interview with Kosciusko–Thredbo Pty Ltd.

82 Ibid.

83 Murphy, *Challenges of Change*, p. 103.

84 Anne Dusseldorp, Interview with Lindie Clark (Middle Cove, 10 August 2000).

85 Dusseldorp, Interview with Kosciusko–Thredbo Pty Ltd.

86 Murphy, *Challenges of Change*, p. 104.

87 Ibid.; 'The Thredbo Story', *Link*, March 1963, p. 4.

88 Murphy, *Challenges of Change*, p. 104; Kosciusko–Thredbo Pty Ltd, *Thredbo History 1957–2001*, Media release (Thredbo, NSW, Kosciusko–Thredbo Pty Ltd, 2001).

89 'The Thredbo Story', p. 4.

90 Van der Lee, Interview with Lindie Clark.

91 Freehill Hollingdale & Page, 'Submissions on Historical Issues', paragraph 6.9.

92 Ibid.

93 G. J. Dusseldorp, 'Statement', Coronial Inquest Into the Deaths Arising from the Thredbo Landslide (Sydney, 26 October 1998), p. 2.

94 Dusseldorp, Interview with Kosciusko–Thredbo Pty Ltd.

95 Ibid.

96 Architect John James was the third of the trio responsible for the plan.

97 Van der Lee, Interview with Lindie Clark.

98 Dusseldorp, Interview with Kosciusko–Thredbo Pty Ltd.

99 Freehill Hollingdale & Page, 'Submissions on Historical Issues', paragraph 4.30, fn 59.

100 Van der Lee, Interview with Lindie Clark.

101 Freehill Hollingdale & Page, 'Submissions on Historical Issues', paragraph 4.30.

102 Ibid.

103 Dusseldorp, Interview with Kosciusko–Thredbo Pty Ltd.

104 By the early 1970s, with Lend Lease's US investments consuming more of his time, Dusseldorp began to withdraw his close personal oversight of Thredbo. 'The master plan was in place, the right people were there to implement it, and he'd put enough watchdogs on the Board of the company to ensure that if something went wrong, they'd let him know.' Van der Lee, Interview with Lindie Clark.

105 Despite the somewhat fractious start, under Lend Lease management Kosciusko–Thredbo Ltd also developed a reputation for its good relationship with staff and with the local community. Ibid.

106 Ibid.

107 Tjerk Dusseldorp, Communications with Lindie Clark (Sydney, 1999–2002).

108 Dusseldorp, Interview with Kosciusko–Thredbo Pty Ltd.

109 It is hard to obtain an independent assessment of the relative merits of the different Australian ski resorts, but these characteristics are mentioned in most reviews of Thredbo.

110 Dick Morath, Interview with Lindie Clark (Sydney, 6 July 2000).

111 Dusseldorp, Interview with Kosciusko–Thredbo Pty Ltd.

112 Lend Lease Corporation Ltd, *27th Annual Report* (Sydney, Lend Lease Corporation Ltd, 1984), p. 23.

113 Andrew Clark, 'Obituaries: Dick Dusseldorp', *Sydney Morning Herald*, 11 May 2000.

114 Van der Lee, Interview with Lindie Clark.

115 Moore, Interview with Lindie Clark.

116 Lend Lease Corporation Ltd, *30th Annual Report* (Sydney, Lend Lease Corporation Ltd, 1987), p. 21.

117 Kosciusko–Thredbo Pty Ltd, *Thredbo History 1957–2001*.

118 John Morschel, 'Tribute', G. J. Dusseldorp Memorial Service (St Aloysius College Chapel, Sydney, 8 May 2000).

119 Witness evidence cited in Hand, *Report of the Inquest*, paragraph 680.

120 Ibid., paragraphs 678–80.
121 Ibid., paragraph 4.
122 'Thredbo Landslide a Disaster Waiting to Happen', *7.30 Report*, 29 June. Transcript (Australian Broadcasting Corporation, 2000).
123 Hand, *Report of the Inquest*, paragraph 5.
124 Investigating the cause of the landslide, the Coroner heard evidence from technical experts who all agreed that an increase in groundwater pressure in the material placed in the slope above Carinya lodge during the construction or upgrading of the Alpine Way had triggered the landslide. They also agreed that the increase in groundwater pressure resulted from an influx of water, but disagreed as to the source of that water. Ibid., paragraph 56. Those engaged by Lend Lease argued that it was due to increased groundwater infiltration occasioned by the construction of a retaining wall at nearby Winterhaus Corner by a contractor to the National Parks and Wildlife Service in early 1997, some four months before the landslide. Ibid., paragraphs 569, 574. The alternative theory was that the water had leaked from a water pipe installed in the fill embankment in 1984, when the resort was in Lend Lease's ownership. Ibid., paragraph 438. The Coroner was satisfied that, 'on the balance of probabilities', the leaking water main theory was correct. Ibid., paragraph 706.
125 Ibid., paragraph 4.
126 Ibid., paragraph 5.
127 Ibid., paragraph 13.
128 Bret Walker, *Inquiry into Certain Matters Including NPWS Urban Communities and Road Maintenance Responsibilities Arising from the Coroner's Report on the Thredbo Landslide*, Report (Sydney, 2000); Bob Debus, 'Government's Response to Walker Report', News release (Sydney, Minister for Environment, 20 February 2001).
129 Hand, *Report of the Inquest*, paragraph 14.
130 'Thredbo Landslide a Disaster Waiting to Happen'.
131 Lend Lease Corporation Ltd, 'Lend Lease Response to Findings of Coronial Inquest Into Thredbo Landslide', Media release (Sydney, 29 June 2000).
132 Damien Murphy, 'Debus Offers to Settle with Thredbo Families', *Sydney Morning Herald*, 1 July 2000.
133 ABC News Online, 'Most Thredbo Claims Finally Settled', in ABC News Online. Local News: Bega <http://www.abc.net.au/news/regionals/bega/monthly/regbeg-16oct2001-1.htm>, 16 October 2001; Eric Goodwin, Communications with Lindie Clark (Sydney, 2000–02).
134 Van der Lee, Interview with Lindie Clark.
135 G. J. Dusseldorp, Interviews with Lindie Clark.
136 Mirvac Lend Lease Village Consortium, *Newington: A New Suburb for a New Century* (Sydney, Mirvac Lend Lease Village Consortium, c.1999), p. 11.
137 G. J. Dusseldorp, Interviews with Lindie Clark.
138 Ibid.
139 Michael Allen and Tony Cahill, 'Community and Strata Title Conveyancing', Papers Presented for the Continuing Legal Education Department of the College

of Law, 97/13 (St Leonards, NSW, Continuing Legal Education Department, College of Law, 7 March 1997). As a legal commentator explains, the law provides 'a reliable means, through legal registerable title, to common ownership and common governance of land and facilities outside the boundaries of the individual parcels of the ownership'. The land not included in individual lots in the community 'is owned communally by all the lot owners in the scheme through a Community Association', which in turn is responsible for the care and maintenance of those lands. Peter Haler, 'Australian Field Study. Report by Chief Executive, LEASE' <http://www.lease-advice.org/ausmain.htm>, March 2001.

140 G. J. Dusseldorp, Interviews with Lindie Clark.
141 John Sandeman, 'The Village People', *Sydney Morning Herald*, 10 April 2000.
142 Mirvac Lend Lease Village Consortium, *Newington: A New Suburb*.
143 G. J. Dusseldorp, Interviews with Lindie Clark.

8 Building for the Future

1 G. J. Dusseldorp (1957) cited in 'Lend Lease Corporation Annual General Meeting' (Sydney, Transcript produced by John P. Nolan Professional Reporting Services, 27 October 1988), p. 17.
2 G. J. Dusseldorp, Interviews with Lindie Clark (Sydney, 7–15 September 1999).
3 Tjerk Dusseldorp, 'Opening Remarks', Manava II (Coogee, 3–4 November 2000).
4 G. J. Dusseldorp, Interviews with Lindie Clark.
5 Ibid.; Tjerk Dusseldorp, Communications with Lindie Clark (Sydney, 1999–2002).
6 G. J. Dusseldorp, Interviews with Lindie Clark.
7 WorldSkills Australia, 'What is WorldSkills Australia?', <http://www.workskill.org.au/about.htm>, 2001.
8 T. Dusseldorp, Communications with Lindie Clark.
9 G. J. Dusseldorp, Interviews with Lindie Clark.
10 T. Dusseldorp, 'Opening Remarks'.
11 Ibid.
12 G. J. Dusseldorp, Interviews with Lindie Clark.
13 G. J. Dusseldorp in 'Lend Lease Corporation Annual General Meeting 1988'.
14 G. J. Dusseldorp, Interviews with Lindie Clark.
15 The employees contributed by forgoing the share issue planned for them that year. Lend Lease Corporation Ltd, *31st Annual Report* (Sydney, Lend Lease Corporation Ltd, 1988), p. 43.
16 Stuart Hornery in 'Lend Lease Corporation Annual General Meeting 1988'.
17 Ron Bolzon in ibid.
18 G. J. Dusseldorp, Interviews with Lindie Clark.
19 G. J. Dusseldorp, 'Bridging the Gap Between Education and Work', Copland Memorial Address, Committee for Economic Development of Australia (Sydney, July 1991), p. 3.
20 Erica Smith, 'Following Country TRACs: A Study of a School–Work Program in Rural Towns', *Rural Society* 6:1 (1996).

21 G. J. Dusseldorp, 'Bridging the Gap Between Education and Work', p. 2.
22 Ibid., p. 4.
23 G. J. Dusseldorp, 'Address', Nottingham Development Enterprise Board (Nottingham, 25 March 1993), p. 2.
24 G. J. Dusseldorp, 'Integrate or Perish', Nottingham Urban Regeneration Conference (Nottingham, 25 February 1994), p. 2.
25 G. J. Dusseldorp, Interviews with Lindie Clark.
26 Smith, 'Following Country TRACs'.
27 G. J. Dusseldorp, Interviews with Lindie Clark.
28 Smith, 'Following Country TRACs'; 'ASTF Update', Program report on ASTF (National TRAC program) (5 September 1999); 'ECEF History', in The Enterprise & Career Education Foundation <http://www.ecef.com.au/web/AB_home.nsf/ECEF/>, 2002.
29 'ASTF Update'; John Stapleton, 'Working to Learn', Australian, 13 September 1999. In 2001 ASTF was incorporated into a broadened program, called the Enterprise & Career Education Foundation, which continues the job of 'helping young Australians move successfully from school to work'. 'About ECEF', in The Enterprise & Career Education Foundation <http://www.ecef.com.au/web/AB_home.nsf/ECEF/>, 2002.
30 G. J. Dusseldorp, Interviews with Lindie Clark.
31 T. Dusseldorp, 'Opening Remarks'.
32 T. Dusseldorp, Communications with Lindie Clark.
33 G. J. Dusseldorp, Interviews with Lindie Clark.
34 Ibid.
35 G. J. Dusseldorp, Interviews with Lindie Clark.
36 Mary Carr Mayle, 'Communities in Schools Kicks off 2001 Fund-Raiser, Looks to Spark More Success', Savannah Morning News, 6 April 2001; Editorial, 'No Excuses', ibid., 30 May 1999; United Health Foundation, 'High School Graduation', in State Health Ranking, 2001 Edition <http:\www.unitedhealthfoundation.org/rankings2001/components/lifestyle/hsgrad.html>, 2001.
37 G. J. Dusseldorp, Interviews with Lindie Clark.
38 G. J. Dusseldorp, 'Integrate or Perish', p. 2.
39 Ibid., p. 3.
40 G. J. Dusseldorp, Interviews with Lindie Clark.
41 G. J. Dusseldorp, 'Integrate or Perish', p. 3.
42 G. J. Dusseldorp, Interviews with Lindie Clark.
43 '13 Corporate Academy Students Win Scholarships', Savannah Morning News, 8 August 1999.
44 'Snapshot: Lancaster County Academy', in School-to-Work Intermediary Project <http://www.intermediarynetwork.org/pdffiles/LancasterAcademy.pdf>, 7 September 1999.
45 G. J. Dusseldorp, 'Integrate or Perish', p. 3.
46 G. J. Dusseldorp, 'Shopping Centres as 21st Century Communities', ICSC European Conference (Seville, Spain, 3 April 1993), p. 5.

47 'Commerce Learning Center Academy', in Orange/Ulster BOCES Commerce Learning Center <http://www.ouboces.org/alternative/commerce/commerce.html>, 2001.

48 Glenda Korporaal, 'Dik Puts His Trust in Property to the Test Once Again', *Sydney Morning Herald*, 19 May 1997; G. J. Dusseldorp, 'Integrate or Perish'.

49 G. J. Dusseldorp, Interviews with Lindie Clark.

50 Ibid.

51 Upon death of the occupier(s), their heirs would have the option of either buying back the share of the house that had been sold to the property trust, or of selling the balance of the home to it.

52 G. J. Dusseldorp, Interviews with Lindie Clark. As specifically conceived, the scheme would also be most financially attractive to the elderly in countries, like England, where estate duty comes into play above a certain minimum value of assets. Dusseldorp planned to structure the English scheme so that the 'residual' value of the asset, upon the occupier's death, was below that tax-attracting threshold.

53 G. Bryant, 'Life After the Flood of Money', *Business Review Weekly*, 11 May 2001, cited in Diana J. Beal, 'Home Equity Conversion in Australia: Issues, Impediments and Possible Solutions', *Economic Papers* 20:4 (December 2001), p. 59.

54 Hugh Mackay, *Generations* (Sydney, Pan Macmillan, 1997), cited in Beal, 'Home Equity Conversion in Australia', p. 63.

55 G. J. Dusseldorp, 'Keynote Address', Investment Property Forum Conference (London, 2 October 1996), pp. 6–7.

56 Ibid., p. 7.

57 Cited in Korporaal, 'Dik Puts His Trust in Property'.

58 G. J. Dusseldorp, Interviews with Lindie Clark.

59 Pension funds in Britain are not taxed on income earned from direct property investment. The Actuarial Profession, 'Report on Equity Release Mechanisms', *The Actuarial Profession. Making Sense of the Future* January 2001 <http://www.actuaries.org.uk/equity_release/rpt.pdf>. If they instead made (a portion of) their property investment through the listed property trust, they would become liable for the 20 per cent tax on any earnings received from it—a substantial disincentive for the funds to invest in the trust.

60 Alastair Ross Goobey, 'Quoted APUTs—Liquidity at Last', Speech (25 June 1997); Hermes Pensions Management Ltd and Dusco (Bda) Ltd, 'Dusco Joint-Venture Ends', Press release (London, 3 November 1997). Although the Investment Property Forum has been waging a battle with 'the Revenue' on this front, the unfavourable tax treatment of such vehicles is still a stumbling block to their listing, at least as I write this in early 2002. Alex Catalano, 'Securitisation: The Work Continues', *Forum View: Magazine of the Investment Property Forum* 5, August 2000; The Actuarial Profession, 'Report on Equity Release Mechanisms'.

61 G. J. Dusseldorp, Interviews with Lindie Clark.

62 Dick Morath, Interview with Lindie Clark (Sydney, 6 July 2000).

63 'Lend Lease Corporation Annual General Meeting 1988'.
64 Milton Herbert Allen, Interview with Lindie Clark (Waitara, 22 May 2000).
65 Chris Rumsey, 'Tribute to G. J. Dusseldorp', Eulogy, Memorial Service for G. J. Dusseldorp (London, 26 June 2000).
66 G. J. Dusseldorp, *State of the Nation. August*, Chairman's Address (Sydney, Lend Lease Corporation Ltd, internal company document, 1983).
67 Ibid.
68 Allen, Interview with Lindie Clark.
69 Lend Lease Corporation Ltd, *43rd Annual Report* (Sydney, Lend Lease Corporation Ltd, 2000).
70 Ibid., p. 4.
71 S. G. Hornery in ibid., p. 10.
72 J. K. Conway in ibid., p. 13.
73 Cited in Catherine Fox, 'Losing Our Way in a Win-Win Race', *Australian Financial Review*, 1 August 2000.
74 Katie Lahey, 'Good Business is About Stakeholders, not Just Shareholders', *Sydney Morning Herald*, 18 May 2001. Citing recent research on the issue, Lahey says that only 13 per cent of respondents thought Australian businesses were currently achieving the right balance between the pursuit of profit and corporate social responsibility. Interestingly, the research found that 'the most important factor characterising a "good" company was how it looked after its employees'. Ibid.
75 Lord Holme of Cheltenham, 'Responsible Business Engagement with Society', *BCA Papers* 1, no. 2 (October 1999) <http://www.bca.com.au/bcapapers/v1n2/15.htm>.
76 Ibid., p. 63.
77 Ibid.
78 ACTU/TDC Mission to Western Europe, *Australia Reconstructed: A Report by the Mission Members to the ACTU and the TDC* (Canberra, Australian Government Publishing Service, 1987).
79 Rumsey, 'Tribute to G. J. Dusseldorp'.

Epilogue
1 Teya Dusseldorp, *Skills Across the World* (1998).
2 Dusseldorp Skills Forum, 'Skills Across the World' <http://www.worldskills.org/saw/brochure/default.htm>, 2001.
3 G. J. Dusseldorp, Interviews with Lindie Clark (Sydney, 7–15 September 1999).
4 Tjerk Dusseldorp, 'Tribute', G. J. Dusseldorp Memorial Service (St Aloysius College Chapel, Sydney, 8 May 2000).

Index